Law and Class in America

CRITICAL AMERICA

General Editors: Richard Delgado and Jean Stefancic

For a complete list of titles in the series, please visit the New York University Press website at *www.nyupress.org*.

Law and Class in America

Trends since the Cold War

EDITED BY

Paul D. Carrington and Trina Jones

New York University Press

NEW YORK AND LONDON

New York University Press
New York and London
www.nyupress.org

Library of Congress Cataloging-in-Publication Data
Law and class in America : trends since the Cold War /
edited by Paul D. Carrington & Trina Jones.
p. cm. — (Critical America series)
Includes bibliographical references and index.
ISBN–13: 978–0–8147–1654–0 (cloth : alk. paper)
ISBN–10: 0–8147–1654–7 (cloth : alk. paper)
1. Law—Social aspects—United States. 2. Law—Economic aspects—
United States. 3. Sociological jurisprudence. I. Carrington, Paul D.,
1931– II Jones, Trina, 1966– III. Critical America.
K370.L385 2006
340'.115—dc22 2006001468

New York University Press books are printed on acid-free paper,
and their binding materials are chosen for strength and durability.

Manufactured in the United States of America

10 9 8 7 6 5 4 3 2 1

Contents

Preface

This work examines the present moment in the evolution of American law's governance of relationships of economic class. In the last half-century our law has often concerned itself with issues of race, religion, gender, age, disability, national origin, and sexuality. Issues of wealth distribution have been linked to these other issues of hierarchy. But they have a pervasive significance of their own, and that significance seems to us to have fallen into neglect.

We perceive that for at least the last quarter of a century, American law has increasingly advanced the interests of those who enjoy wealth and shown diminishing concern for the interests of those who have less, with the result that differences of economic class have steadily enlarged. To assess this perception, we have asked our essayists to observe the direction of recent changes in the law in the field each knows best. We did not ask our contributors to propose remedies for any undesirable or unjust situations they observe, but many have done so. As a general matter we leave it to the reader to form his or her own agenda of law reform from among the contributors' suggestions or other ideas that may occur. As mere editors, we do not present our own agenda but are satisfied to call attention to a national situation.

PAUL D. CARRINGTON and TRINA JONES

National tragedies sometimes reveal troubling gaps and disturbing trends in governmental policies and commitments. The suffering of citizens of limited means during the destruction of New Orleans in September 2005 evoked little concern by those responsible for their protection. Much as the Johnstown Flood of 1891 marked the beginning of an era of progressive legal reform, might the aftermath of Hurricane Katrina mark a new direction in American law? The essays contained herein invite consideration of this question. *Photograph by Eric Gay, courtesy of AP/Wide World Photos.*

Law Made in Skyboxes
An Evolution in American Law

Paul D. Carrington and Trina Jones

The founders of the American Republic viewed class conflict as a serious threat to their enterprise. And class divisions have since its beginning been a chronic challenge to the nation's stability. This chapter offers a few words of American history to put those that follow in historical perspective.

I. The Founders' Plan regarding Class Conflict

Most who gathered in Philadelphia in 1787 to write the Constitution had read Baron Charles de Secondat Montesquieu's *Spirit of Law* and had received his caution that popular self-government would endure only in an egalitarian environment.[1] Montesquieu believed such an environment was possible only in small and homogeneous tribes or nations where people enjoyed a sufficient level of mutual trust arising from their common fates.[2] Larger and more diverse societies, the Baron insisted, required a class of aristocrats (like himself) who shared sufficient wealth and power to constrain the despotism resulting from the chaos to which all failed republics had returned when ignorant peasants had rallied to the flags of promising tyrants.

The Founders resisted Montesquieu's pessimism, resting their hopes for a large republic on law and the principle of federalism. This scheme would potentially enable the people of each state to exercise substantial power over their own fates while simultaneously subjecting them to necessary constraints imposed by the federal government. A half century after the founding, Alexis de Tocqueville, another French aristocrat, proclaimed the Founders' efforts a success.[3] America's legal institutions, Tocqueville reported to his French readers, afforded most citizens a sense of participation in government under constraints enabling them to avoid the cycle of mistrust-leading-to-chaos-leading-to-despotism that Montesquieu had depicted. Within this framework, lawyers and judges performed the role Montesquieu had assigned to the aristocracy.

Few have questioned Tocqueville's conclusion that the law was the stabilizing influence in a potentially chaotic situation. As Francis Lieber[4] and Frederick Grimké,[5] two Americans of that time observed, the primary stabilizing mechanisms were the democratic courthouses found in every community of size. Everywhere in America, aggrieved citizens could have their complaints heard by a jury of their neighbors. They could do this at very little cost because (1) the legal profession of the time, at least in most states, in contrast with its English antecedent, was virtually open to all who aspired to it, and (2) the novel "American Rule," whereby each party paid its own attorney's fees regardless of outcome, prevented the taxation of substantial litigation costs against losing parties.[6] Further, to secure the independence of judicial decisions from the improper influence of those with power, many states in Tocqueville's time began to require that judges stand for election by the people they served and to whom they were expected to owe fidelity.[7] In the rural society served by the village lawyers that Tocqueville observed, this system seemed to work.

But the ability of the secular and democratic courthouse to secure the social stability required for economic stability was not guaranteed to abide. Even at the time of Tocqueville's writing, abundant stress arose from conflicts of interests between borrowers and creditors. Chronic currency deflation was a source of rage for farmers who needed to borrow money to buy land, but who were required to repay their loans with dollars more valuable than the ones they had borrowed. Although Shays' Rebellion of 1787 had forcefully called that problem to the attention of the Founders,[8] they did not resolve it. Instead, state courts became the forums in which these issues would be decided. And many state courts became scenes of struggles, causing strong political reactions that were sometimes embedded in state constitutions. Perhaps the most extreme reaction was that of the Kentucky legislature in 1834. In response to judicial decisions deemed unduly favorable to creditors, that legislature simply abolished the state's highest court.[9] While Congress was explicitly empowered to enact "uniform bankruptcy laws," its exercise of that power in the nineteenth century was intermittent and inconsequential. Indeed, the federal government in Tocqueville's time played a modest role in domestic affairs. Its most important engagements with issues of class were its ambivalence toward the institution of slavery and its relations with the remaining indigenous peoples whom it reduced to penury by taking their lands and redistributing them to settlers of European ancestry. The most important antebellum decision of the Supreme Court bearing on future class tensions was its holding that private, immortal organizations chartered by states were entitled to the same protections against state power that the Constitution afforded mortal individual citizens.[10]

Tocqueville made no mention of these recurring problems. And, only a quarter century after Tocqueville's inspection, America fell apart. The Civil War exemplified the limited willingness of most humans to share authority with others distant or different from themselves. The problem of slavery from which the War resulted was one that at all times had an obvious solution that could have been applied but for human failings on both sides of the divide. Neither those loyal to the culture of slavery nor those committed to the antislavery cause were willing to bear their share of the costs of emancipation and of providing a suitable start in a market economy for former slaves. Instead, the adversaries waged a war with a much higher cost than compensated emancipation. That war demonstrated that America is not immune from the tendency of human societies to self-destruct.[11]

II. Economic Unification: The Gilded Age

While the Civil War brought an end to slavery, it did not make America a promised land for most citizens. Following a brief period of Reconstruction, America did not embrace former slaves and their descendents. Nor did it willingly accept many in the new waves of European immigrants. Sectional mistrust remained. And the decades following the domestic war saw a closing of the frontier and a resulting loss of its democratizing effect. The relatively shallow class lines that had existed at the time of the Founding deepened.

This deepening was driven in part by the development of a national economy which produced great corporate enterprises in which prosperous Americans could invest. Indeed, the economic development of that time demonstrated the insight of Adam Smith's *Wealth of Nations* regarding the power of free markets to create wealth.[12] American law protected these new enterprises by withholding rights claimed by individuals with whom the corporations dealt. And state governments legislating within the federal system were almost powerless to protect their citizens from overreaching by corporations engaged in interstate business. Entrepreneurs could simply respond to unwelcome regulation by moving their affairs to states less prone to regulation, presenting perhaps the world's first experience with what the twenty-first century calls "outsourcing."

A consequence of the growth of the national economy was an elevation of the ambitions of traditional professions to qualify their members as scientists, or at least as highly trained technicians, to serve the growing moneyed class. And higher education became, increasingly, a prerequisite to many economic opportunities and to social status.

Importantly, the cross-country laying of rail lines spurred the nationalization of commerce. This ambitious project created its own set of class-related problems. The rail system was overbuilt, to the ruin of many diverse enterprises,[13] and many individuals were induced to risk their savings in ill-conceived and ill-managed ventures. Some privately owned railroads were even funded by gifts from the federal government or by state and local governments who paid under threat of isolation from the national economy. These "gifts" came from tax revenues paid almost entirely by persons of lesser means.

Those engaged in the dangerous work of laying rails were said to assume the risk of injury resulting from the negligence of their fellow servants.[14] Even passengers and shippers received scant concern from railroad owners and managers whose primary goals were to reduce costs and to maximize benefits for themselves. As railroads opened up the west, hopeful farmers were sold millions of acres of western land notwithstanding the grossly inadequate water resources available to them, and without regard for the foreseeably tragic environmental consequences.[15]

In addition to attesting to the power of free markets to create wealth, the burgeoning national economy affirmed another of Adam Smith's insights. Smith had warned that while many people could be expected to share concern and bear burdens for others within their view, few citizens would do more than share a moment of regret for the suffering of those seen only in the distance, even when that suffering came on a vast scale.[16] As class lines deepened across America, it became increasingly evident that those benefiting most from the national economy could not be expected to forgo significant benefits available to themselves merely to diminish burdens or risks inevitably falling on fellow citizens having less access to the wealth being created, such as the farmers and laborers who were, with their children, doing the nation's work, and who were in numerous ways distant from those with status and power.

In this setting, a growing number of Americans, like their European contemporaries, began to share Karl Marx's belief that the rich were at war against the poor.[17] This Marxist sentiment was expressed by ill-organized but outspoken American Populists, Socialists, Anarchists, and Communists.[18] These groups encountered the more numerous and equally outspoken Social Darwinists, who were sure that the poor deserved their poverty.[19] It was the Darwinists and their allies who generally had the ear of Congress and the Supreme Court. They succeeded, for example, in convincing the federal courts to issue strike-breaking injunctions impeding the efforts of workers to secure rights through collective bargaining. Federal courts issued, on average, almost a strike injunction a day for half a century, which held the American labor movement substantially in abeyance.[20]

Despite impediments to enforcement of state laws protecting the weak from the strong, the American common law of torts, which had long been subordinate to property and contract rights, began to emerge in the post-War era. State courts, most of whom were by then accountable to democratic electorates, gradually began to enlarge the rights of workers, passengers, and shippers.[21] And state legislatures began to proscribe child labor.[22] But the U.S. Supreme Court invalidated state attempts to regulate the hours and conditions of work for adults and thereby vindicated the claims of business to freedom of contract. Most states also amended their constitutions to empower local governments to exercise "home rule" to regulate predatory business practices within their communities.[23]

The commitment to freedom of contract as an element of the market economy allowed members of the deregulated legal profession to contract with clients to enforce their rights for fees contingent on their success.[24] And private enforcement of public law by contingent fee lawyers, often representing impecunious clients, became an accepted norm.

One step taken by all the states to reduce class divisions was the investment of public revenue in schools.[25] Compulsory attendance laws were enacted in an effort to prepare all children for roles in the market economy. But in the former slave states, the descendants of slaves seldom received much of even that limited form of assistance.[26]

On a national level, federal law began, even in the Gilded Age of the Social Darwinists, to play a regulatory and sometimes redistributive role.

Federal regulation of railroads was initiated in 1887, in part to protect the weak from the strong.[27] The Sherman Act of 1890 was enacted to protect small businesses from the predatory practices of larger competitors; in providing for treble damages, the Act sought to encourage private enforcement of that public policy.[28] In 1891, the intermediate federal courts were created to assure even-handed enforcement of the growing body of federal law.[29] A progressive income tax was enacted only to be invalidated by the Darwinist Supreme Court.[30]

III. The Progressive Era

In 1895, Adam Smith's observation about the absence of moral sentiment in regard to the suffering of distant folk was forced on public attention by a flood that destroyed the city of Johnstown, Pennsylvania, drowning much of its population.[31] The flood resulted from the collapse of a dam erected to provide the first families of Pittsburgh with a scenic environment for their elegant second homes. As Smith foretold, the first families expressed regret and made token contributions to disaster relief. But they successfully resisted liability because the victims were unable to prove that the families' negligence caused the disaster.

One response to the Johnstown disaster was widespread law reform imposing liability without fault on landowners with broken dams. Another response was a widespread recognition that those with wealth and power could not be expected to restrict their pursuit of self-interest merely to protect lesser fellow citizens. Because unconstrained enterprise could potentially destroy the social fabric on which such enterprise ultimately depended, unregulated capitalism was increasingly seen as a menace not only to those of lesser means, but to the stability of government and therefore to prosperous capitalists themselves. Those most apprehensive about the threat of Marxism thought reform and regulation were essential to give all members of society a stake in the whole. Roscoe Pound, no champion of redistribution, memorably proclaimed the inadequacy of freedom of contract as a basic organizing principle of law.[32]

The two decades following Johnstown were the Progressive years.[33] These years were marked by legal changes that sought to improve the general welfare of all Americans. State and local governments raised taxes to provide for diverse public programs and supplemented traditional taxes on land with taxes on retail sales, personal income, and inheritance. Hope for progressivity in taxation arose, if not its reality.

During this period, government began to provide public services such as water, public sanitation, and fire protection for all. And public utility regulation emerged to assure that services were generally available on fair terms. Public welfare was provided for those in great need who were deemed worthy of support, especially poor widows with children. Public hospitals were erected and health care began to emerge from its humanistic past to gain a rudimentary basis in science. Even with the latter change, the medical profession remained bound by the Hippocratic Oath to provide care without regard to ability to pay.[34]

Many states enacted laws to provide workers with compensation for work-related injuries, and commercial enterprises were increasingly required to respect public health and the environment. Most states enacted laws to protect from diverse forms of fraud the ill-informed citizens who were being invited to invest their savings in corporate enterprises.

Progressivism was also marked by efforts to enhance the accountability of government to the governed. Many state constitutions were amended to empower voters to enact laws by referendum.[35] On the other hand, "merit selection" of judges became a celebrated standard aimed at assuring the professionalism of the judiciary.[36]

Changes occurred at the federal level as well. Congress enacted bankruptcy legislation, in part to provide a system to discharge the debts of overburdened debtors. The Department of the Interior gained greater prominence as attention turned to protecting the nation's natural resources. The Department of Agriculture became responsible for protecting national forests from improvident but profitable harvesting.

Progressive federal income taxation was constitutionalized and reenacted.[37] The federal gift and estate tax was enacted, partly as a revenue measure and partly to inhibit the development of a permanent ruling class sustained by inherited wealth. The tax also shielded states from the consequences of tax avoidance by mobile taxpayers.

Federal legislation was enacted to provide compensation to railroad workers[38] and seamen for industrial accidents.[39] And legislation seeking to assure pure food and safe drugs was passed.[40] The use and sale of substances deemed dangerous was subjected to control.[41] Federal antitrust law was reinforced better to protect small business.[42] The Federal Trade Commission was created and empowered to assist in enforcement.[43] All these Progressive reforms were achieved not merely for humanitarian reasons but because they were seen as being in the long-term interest of all.

IV. The Era of Normalcy

The Great War brought an end to the Progressive Era. It also brought a brief period of disorder led by those who saw the War and its aftermath as a manifestation of the class war decried by Marx. In 1919, the home of the Attorney General of the United States was bombed, presumably by a Marxist subversive.[44] But in 1921, the president was able to announce a "Return to Normalcy."[45]

The ensuing decade was a giddy time of rampant self-aggrandizement. But law reforms were enacted even in that era to protect those who were seen to need protection. These reforms aimed more frequently at moral than at economic advancement. This was exemplified by the national prohibition against the sale and consumption of alcoholic beverages.[46] For the first time, a national police force emerged and federal prisons were erected. As is true today, most prisoners were not persons of means.

During this time, the automobile led Americans to reconstruct their social order. Suburbs appeared around every prosperous city, increasing the distance between those with greater resources and those with less, and reducing the possibility of mutual interest and concerns. Zoning law was devised to protect property owners from unwelcome land uses by their neighbors.[47] Elite suburban school districts emerged which gave an added advantage to the children of the elite over those in less well-funded districts.[48]

One significant federal reform during this era was legislation putting an end to the use of federal courts as a source of strike-breaking injunctions.[49] There was also ferment on other matters. Perhaps most notable was the work of Adolf Berle and Gardiner Means calling attention to the conflict of interests between corporate management and impotent shareholders.[50] The authors observed that shareholders were only marginally of more concern to corporate management than workers and consumers.

V. The New Deal

Normalcy ended with the Great Depression. In 1933, the administration of President Franklin Roosevelt undertook to end the Depression with diverse programs designed to restore the national economy to its headier days. At first the New Deal was a cooperative endeavor between government and corporate enterprises seeking to escape the desperate straits in which they were trapped. But in its later stages, Congress enacted many new laws that were redistributive in purpose and effect.

In part, the New Deal sought to create consumer buying power to which businesses might appeal. Federal legislation established minimum wages[51] and the right of workers to bargain collectively—a right that was enforced by the National Labor Relations Board.[52] Laws were passed to protect small farmers and sharecroppers from depressed prices due to overproduction. Congress established a federal welfare program and the social security system to assist the elderly and the disabled. Retirement benefits were advanced to senior retirees or disabled workers who had not participated in the savings program. Federal employment was provided for many engaged in diverse public works. And much needed public housing was erected in urban neighborhoods.

Other New Deal programs were designed to send dollars into areas in which they were most scarce, as it did, for example, in the depressed rural areas of Tennessee where the federal government undertook to provide electric power and an influx of cash by constructing hydroelectric dams. Later New Deal initiatives were directed at business practices deemed harmful to smaller enterprises. The federal government undertook a very vigorous program of antitrust enforcement for that purpose, and Congress passed a federal law against price discrimination.[53] New Deal measures also sought to protect individual investors from diverse forms of fraud practiced by management and by management's promoters on Wall Street.[54]

Not a New Deal program, but promulgated in its time were the Federal Rules of Civil Procedure.[55] The feature of the Rules most pertinent to this book was the elaborate provision for discovery of evidence.[56] Through discovery, litigants could seek to prove their claims by accessing information in the possession and control of their adversaries. Most state courts soon adopted this practice. The result gave new meaning to the concept of the private attorney general and added force to much of the legislation enacted to regulate predatory business practices. Misdeeds that previously went undetected or unchallenged were exposed to light and to challenge.

All these measures together provided only minimal relief from the hardships of the Depression, which came to an end only with the advent of World War II. Because the war was expensive, one of its consequences was a mighty increase in the rate of federal income taxation to pay for armaments. Another consequence was a period of more-than-full employment, with many women entering the workforce. War also resulted in substantial shortages of desirable consumer goods, and a system of rationing was created to assure their fair distribution. Rent controls were imposed to prevent landlords from exploiting opportunities created by the war effort. It was understood that the war required widespread sacrifice and these redistributive efforts drew few complaints. The lives lost in combat were those of individuals with families, not those of corporate enterprises. Few wealthy persons protested that they were bearing more than their fair share of the costs.

The New Deal was followed by President Truman's Fair Deal. In 1946, candidates were elected to Congress in protest against a meat shortage allegedly caused by federal regulation. But that moment of hostility to redistributive national policies was soon silenced by the new cause of anti-communism, which became, with the arrest of "atom spies," a national obsession. Those threatened by international communism generally saw the importance of governmental policies that would gain at least the acceptance, if not the approval, of those citizens who might otherwise be attracted to the Marxist program of extreme redistribution.

The 1950–54 war in Korea, although not without its critics, tended to restore the patriotic willingness of most wealthy persons to forbear enjoyment of some of their advantages, in much the same way as they had sacrificed to the effort to wage World War II. Indeed, the widely perceived need to win the global "war for men's minds" made success unlikely for those who opposed the continued efforts of the Eisenhower administration to maintain a visible manifestation of concern for the rights of those less advantaged, many of whom were being required to perform combat duty in Korea or guard duty in Germany or Japan.

The civil rights movement of the 1950s was not without connection to the Cold War. While that movement was not anticommunist in its aim, its appeal was enhanced by the looming prospect that the continued denial of equal rights to citizens of color might lend strength to the "international conspiracy" that the United States opposed. And so it was against this background of international threat that John Kennedy could tell Americans in 1961 that they should be asking what they might do for their country rather than what it might do for them.

The mid-1960s also witnessed the creation of Medicare.[57] The program was in part a response to the rising cost of health care resulting from pricey scientific advances and the rapidly increasing life spans of Americans. Because the cost of health care insurance was tax deductible to employers but not to employees, group health insurance had become widely available to workers. That benefit, however, was generally discontinued at retirement. Medicare became a safety net for those most in need.

VI. The Great Society

It was Kennedy's successor, President Johnson who proclaimed the goal of establishing a Great Society—an America in which the rights of racial minorities and the economically disadvantaged would be assured. A War on Poverty was declared.[58]

Many of the initiatives taken in that "war" reflected the president's commitment to the civil rights movement. Public housing, public transportation, and the reconstruction of blighted urban areas were three major topics of attention, all of them supplementary to the controversial and prolonged national effort to integrate racial minorities into the larger social order. Federal aid to public schools was also enlarged.

Among the more successful initiatives undertaken in the War on Poverty was creation of the Legal Services Program, which provided federal funding for law offices serving those in need. One argument favoring such a reform was that it would make the nation less vulnerable to the Marxist appeal.[59] Legal Services lawyers were commissioned to seek out targets for claims that would result in redistributive effects; in this respect the program was more ambitious than traditional legal aid. Another successful program was legislation to induce commercial lenders to finance construction in poor areas. For a time, the Supreme Court of the United States caught the spirit and focused its attention on rights for the economically disadvantaged.

Concurrent with Great Society programs was the Supreme Court's extension of First Amendment speech protections, an event that seems to have produced a counter-redistributive effect.[60] The Court's decisions virtually removed the law of defamation from politics, established a right to communicate political ideas anonymously, and substantially undermined efforts to constrain monetary expenditures on political advertising. With the emergence of television as a universal feature of American life, politics became increasingly an indoor competition waged on the tube. Those with more money were privileged to air their views with infinitely greater force than those without money to spend for that purpose. Negative advertising was almost instantaneous; the Johnson presidential campaign of 1964 used television advertising shamelessly to malign its adversary by portraying a vote for Goldwater as a vote for nuclear war.[61]

Television advertising would also later contribute substantially to the rising cost of health care as drug companies used that means to communicate directly to patients, thereby increasing the demand for goods and services. This demand would soon begin to outpace the ability or willingness of many employers to cover the cost of health care insurance.

Not a result of federal legislation, but a development compatible with the Great Society Initiatives was the 1966 amendment of the Federal Rules of Civil Procedure enlarging the availability of the class action as an instrument for private enforcement of public law.[62] Already widely used in civil rights cases, the class action became useful in a variety of regulatory settings.

The Great Society rhetoric was a casualty of the war in Vietnam. President Nixon was elected in large part because of popular dissatisfaction with that war.[63] While Nixon ended talk of a Great Society, his administration did not undo many of its programs. And it did secure enactment of major federal legislation beneficial to workers and consumers. These included the Occupational Safety and Health Act, extensions of the Fair Labor Standards Act to apply to public employment, the Truth in Lending Act, and the Clear Air and Clean Water Acts.[64] In addition, guaranteed student loan programs were extended to make higher education more available.

To replace the rhetoric of the War on Poverty, President Nixon spoke of a War on Drugs. This new "war" bore an uneasy resemblance to Prohibition. It was highly moralistic in tone and touted steadily rising punishments imposed on a steadily rising number of offenders.[65] The federal effort was superimposed on that of the states. The War on Drugs, however, differed from Prohibition in one key respect; whereas the offenders against Prohibition laws had been spread across the social spectrum, most of those against whom the War on Drugs was waged were the offspring of parents of limited means. The growing prison population consisted substantially of poor, undereducated young minority males who were employed in a drug industry serving largely middle-class users. As these low-level players were arrested and imprisoned, their jobs in the industry were taken by others and illegal trafficking continued—indeed, expanded.

The ambitions of President Carter were resonant with the programs of the Great Society, but no domestic program associated with his administration bears notice in this brief account. It can be said that at the end of his term in 1980, American law was striving in countless ways to advance the interests of those citizens who were least able to take advantage of the prospering market economy. And there were few citizens indeed who could say that they were not in some way served by the law.

VII. The Reversal of the 1980s

The election of President Reagan in 1980 marked a sharp turn in American law and politics. Persons interested in promulgating policies based on Social Darwinism came forth with a new and dominant image—that of the Welfare Queen. The Welfare Queen (generally envisioned as Black) was accused of milking public resources while maintaining a degraded lifestyle and bearing countless children who would grow up to be similarly dependent or criminals. Although few Great Society programs were repealed in the 1980s, funding became scarce for many. The American Bar Association successfully resisted an effort to abolish the Legal Services Program, but its lawyers were effectively put out of the business of crafting legal theories to advance novel means of redistribution.[66]

The major event of the 1980s was the collapse of the Soviet Union. There are surely many reasons for the collapse and it is possible that American policy was a contributing factor. Whatever its cause, the event had effects radiating across America as the unifying threat of international communism disappeared. The world rightly celebrated the diminished threat of a global nuclear holocaust. But being the world's only superpower unleashed the American ruling class from certain constraints that had arisen from its obvious dependence on the tolerance and loyalty of fellow citizens. Any last lingering shadow of a simmering proletariat to rally to the Marxist cause dissipated in the dust of the Berlin Wall.

At the same time, a new imperative to compete in world markets was provided by the external world. While American investors could profit from global markets, it was not clear that Americans who work for a living could do so. The state of the world turned President Kennedy's inaugural injunction on its head as owners and managers of great corporations were free not only to disavow their support for redistributive programs but to insist that the incomes and rights of workers be subordinated to the need to make their goods and services competitive with those produced by some of the world's most impecunious people. The reassurance was sometimes given that a rising economic sea lifts all boats.

It is the expression of that hopeful notion that gives rise to the mind-set implied in the title of this chapter. In this view, the least advantaged should, as Thomas Frank has recently suggested, riot in demand of tax cuts for the wealthy[67] and support tort reform and economic deregulation.

Much such thinking has emerged from think tanks such as the Heritage Foundation, the Cato Institute, and the Manhattan Institute. These are environments where theorists funded by business interests can unite without the distractions of students, critical colleagues, or contact with those who work for a living. Inhabitants of those institutions view the world from intellectual skyboxes resembling those remote and luxurious venues from which privileged persons watch athletic contests free from contact with the combatants or the lower classes of fans, who remain exposed to the elements. These environments nourish a faith in economic fundamentalism, which supposes the accumulation of great wealth by the few to be a benefit to all.

This ideology also comes from corporate boardrooms where executives have concentrated on short-term profits as measured by loose accounting standards, at cost and risk to employees, consumers, and investors. The boardroom is, like the think tank, a kind of skybox from which to view the realities faced by those physically engaged in competition or by other lesser observers sitting in the weather.

It is from this vantage that we have asked our essayists, through examination of laws most familiar to them, to consider whether America is entering a Second Gilded Age. We caution the reader that the responses collected here do not exhaust the subject. In recent decades, the law of intellectual property has exploded.[68] We do not address whether there are any features of that development that are protective of the public domain, the interests of individuals as consumers, or small business. Nor do we in this volume take full note of what has happened to the Fair Labor Standards Act in recent years to diminish its protection of minimum wage workers.[69] Nor have we fully examined the fate of diverse state and federal laws enacted to protect small business from big business, such as the franchise investment laws.[70] Even with these and other omissions, the essays do

"Never mind about me, God. Just bless America,
and maybe some of it will trickle down."

yield ample confirmation that American law in recent decades has become steadily less protective of the less advantaged. There are, as the *Economist* put it, missing steps in the ladder to success.[71] American workers and those who only wish they could be laboring are increasingly exposed to the wonders and risks of the world market economy and to the inspired self-aggrandizement of their more privileged countrymen. It thus appears that America is indeed receding gracelessly into a second Gilded Age.

NOTES

1. PAUL SPURLIN, MONTESQUIEU IN AMERICA, 1760–1801 (2d ed. 1969).

2. CHARLES DE SECONDAT, BARON DE MONTESQUIEU, THE SPIRIT OF LAWS, Bk. V, chs. 1–7 (T. Nugent trans., 1750) (1748).

3. ALEXIS DE TOCQUEVILLE, 1 DEMOCRACY IN AMERICA 297–307 (H. Reeves trans., undated).

4. *See generally* FRANCIS LIEBER, ON CIVIL LIBERTY AND SELF-GOVERNMENT (1854).

5. *See* FREDERICK GRIMKÉ, CONSIDERATIONS UPON THE NATURE AND TENDENCY OF FREE INSTITUTIONS (1848).

6. *See* 1 ANTON-HERMANN CHROUST, THE RISE OF THE LEGAL PROFESSION IN AMERICA 85–327 (1965).

7. For a contemporaneous account and defense of this reform, see GRIMKÉ, *supra* note 5, at 341–78; *see also* Caleb Nelson, *A Re-Evaluation of Scholarly Explanations for the Rise of the Elective Judiciary in Antebellum America*, 37 AM. J. LEGAL HIST. 190 (1993).

8. RICHARD D. BROWN, *Shays' Rebellion and the Ratification of the Federal Constitution, in Massachusetts, in* BEYOND CONFEDERATION: ORIGINS OF THE CONSTITUTION AND AMERICAN NATIONAL IDENTITY 69, 70–77 (Richard Beeman et al. eds., 1987).

9. ARNDT H. STICKLES, THE CRITICAL COURT STRUGGLE IN KENTUCKY, 1819–1829 (1929).

10. Dartmouth College v. Woodward, 4 Wheat. 518 (1819).

11. JARED DIAMOND, COLLAPSE: HOW SOCIETIES CHOOSE TO SUCCEED OR FAIL (2005).

12. ADAM SMITH, AN INQUIRY INTO THE NATURE AND CAUSES OF THE WEALTH OF NATIONS (1776).

13. Herbert Hovenkamp, *Regulatory Conflict in the Gilded Age: Federalism and the Railroad Problem*, 97 YALE L.J. 1017 (1988).

14. WILLIAM M. MCKINNEY, A TREATISE ON THE LAW OF FELLOW SERVANTS (1890).

15. *See* JONATHAN RABAN, BAD LAND: AN AMERICAN ROMANCE (1996).

16. ADAM SMITH, THE THEORY OF MORAL SENTIMENTS, Pt. III, ch. 3 (1759).

17. KARL MARX, DAS KAPITAL (1868).

18. For a review of Marxist literature in America, see JAMES F. MURPHY, THE PROLETARIAN MOVEMENT (1991).

19. *See* ALEXANDER ROSENBERG, DARWINISM, in PHILOSOPHY, SOCIAL SCIENCE, AND POLICY (2000).

20. PHILIP S. FONER, HISTORY OF THE LABOR MOVEMENT IN THE UNITED STATES: FROM COLONIAL TIMES TO THE FOUNDING OF THE AMERICAN FEDERATION OF LABOR 78–79, 154–56 (1947).

21. The first books on the subject were FRANCIS HILLIARD, THE LAW OF REMEDIES FOR TORTS (1867) and THOMAS M. COOLEY, A TREATISE ON THE LAW OF TORTS OR THE WRONGS WHICH ARE INDEPENDENT OF CONTRACTS (1879).

22. STEPHEN B. WOOD, CONSTITUTIONAL POLITICS IN THE PROGRESSIVE ERA: CHILD LABOR AND THE LAW (1968).

23. For a contemporaneous account, see HOWARD L. MCBAIN, AMERICAN CITY PROGRESS AND THE LAW (1918).

24. MAXWELL BLOOMFIELD, AMERICAN LAWYERS IN A CHANGING SOCIETY, 1776–1876, at 277 (1976).

25. HENRY J. PERKINS, THE IMPERFECT PANACEA: AMERICAN FAITH IN PUBLIC EDUCATION, 1865–1965 (1968); DIANE RAVITCH, THE GREAT SCHOOL WARS (1974).

26. GARY ORFIELD, THE RECONSTRUCTION OF SOUTHERN EDUCATION 1–46 (1969).

27. The Interstate Commerce Act, Act of Feb. 17, 1887, 24 Stat. 379.

28. Sherman Antitrust Act of 1890, 26 Stat. 209 (codified as amended at 15 U.S.C. § 1).

29. Act of March 3, 1891 (Evarts Act), ch. 517, 26 Stat. 826.

30. Pollock v. Farmers' Loan & Trust Co., 157 U.S. 479 (1985).

31. *See* DAVID G. MCCULLOUGH, THE JOHNSTOWN FLOOD (1968).

32. Roscoe Pound, *Liberty of Contract*, 18 YALE L.J. 454 (1909).

33. *See generally* RICHARD A. HOFSTADTER, THE AGE OF REFORM: FROM BRYAN TO F.D.R. (1955).

34. *See generally* PAUL STARR, THE SOCIAL TRANSFORMATION OF AMERICAN MEDICINE (1982).

35. For a critical assessment of this form of politics, see WILLIAM DEVERELL & TOM SITTON, CALIFORNIA PROGRESSIVISM REVISITED (1994).

36. Proposed by Albert Kales in 1914, it was first adopted in Missouri in 1940. Maura Ann Schoshinski, *Towards an Independent, Fair and Competent Judiciary: An Argument for Improving Judicial Elections*, 7 GEO. J. LEGAL ETHICS 839 (1994).

37. U.S. CONST. amendment XVI, ratified in 1913.

38. Federal Employers Liability Act (FELA), 35 Stat. 65 (1908) (codified as amended at 45 U.S.C. §§ 51–60).

39. Appropriation Act of June 12, 1917, 40 Stat. 157.

40. Food and Drugs Act of June 30, 1906, 34 Stat. 768.

41. Anti-Narcotics Act of Dec. 17, 1914, P.L. 63-343, 38 Stat. 785 (commonly called the Harrison Narcotics Act).

42. Clayton Act of 1914, 38 Stat. 731 (codified as amended at 15 U.S.C. § 15).

43. The Federal Trade Commission Act, 38 Stat. 717, 719 (1914) (codified as amended at 15 U.S.C. § 41).

44. The story is told in ROBERT K. MURRAY, RED SCARE: A STUDY OF NATIONAL HYSTERIA (1954).

45. *See* ROBERT K. MURRAY, THE POLITICS OF NORMALCY (1973).

46. JAMES H. TIMBERLAKE, PROHIBITION AND THE PROGRESSIVE MOVEMENT 1900–1920 (1963).

47. *See generally* RICHARD F. BABCOCK, THE ZONING GAME REVISITED (1985).

48. *See* JOHN E. COONS ET AL., PRIVATE WEALTH AND PUBLIC EDUCATION (1970).

49. *See* FELIX FRANKFURTER & NATHAN GREENE, THE LABOR INJUNCTION (1930).

50. Adolf A. Berle & Gardiner Means, The Modern Corporation and Private Property (1932).

51. Dora L. Costa, Hours of Work and the Fair Labor Standards Act (1998).

52. National Labor Relations Act of 1935, 49 Stat. 449; on its enactment, see Arthur Schlesinger, The Coming of the New Deal 397–406 (1958).

53. On the policy against price discrimination, see J. C. Palamountain, The Politics of Distribution 188–234 (1955).

54. William O. Douglas & George Bates, The Federal Securities Act of 1933, 43 Yale L.J. 171 (1933); William O. Douglas, Protecting the Investor, 23 Yale Rev. 521 (1934).

55. Act of June 19, 1934, 48 Stat. 1064; see generally Stephen B. Burbank, The Rules Enabling Act of 1934, 130 U. Pa. L. Rev. 1015 (1982).

56. Fed. R. Civ. P. 26–37.

57. See Starr, supra note 34, at 366–78.

58. For an account by the leading figure in the "War," see Joseph A. Califano, Inside: A Public and Private Life 151–87 (2004).

59. Emery Brownell, Legal Aid in the United States iv (1951).

60. See Paul D. Carrington, Our Imperial First Amendment, 34 U. Rich. L. Rev. 1167 (2000).

61. Kathleen Hall Jamieson, Dirty Politics (1992).

62. Fed. R. Civ. P. 23(b)(3).

63. Theodore Harold White, The Making of the President, 1968 (1969).

64. James T. Patterson, Grand Expectations: The United States, 1945–1974, at 719–29 (1996).

65. See generally Steven B. Duke & Albert C. Gross, America's Longest War (1993).

66. See Susan E. Lawrence, The Legal Services Program (1991).

67. Thomas Frank, What's the Matter with Kansas? (2004).

68. See Kathy Eden, Friends Hold All Things in Common (2001).

69. William P. Quigley, A Fair Day's Pay for a Fair Day's Work: Time to Raise and Index the Minimum Wage, 27 St. Mary's L.J. 513, 548 (1996); Annie Biegelsen, Actual Deductions Test for Determining Overtime Eligibility: Auer v. Robbins, 39 B.C. L. Rev. 389 (1998).

70. E.g., Cal. Corp. Code § 31000 et seq.

71. America's Sorting Out: The Missing Rungs in the Ladder, Economist 17 (July 16–22, 2005); A Survey of America, Economist 3–20 (July 16–22, 2005); see also the New York Times special series entitled Class Matters, which ran from May 15 through June 12, 2005 (available at http://www.nytimes.com/pages/national/class/).

The Regress of Courts, Legislatures, and the Bar

When (Some) Republican Justices Exhibited Concern for the Plight of the Poor
An Essay in Historical Retrieval

Sanford Levinson

The great achievement of New Deal jurisprudence was to overturn earlier cases that had suggested that a welfare state, which by definition transfers resources from haves to have-nots, was a constitutional impossibility. At the end of the 1960s, there was even a brief shining moment when it appeared thinkable that some version of a welfare state was not just a constitutional possibility, but a constitutional duty. In 1969, Frank Michelman published his magisterial *Harvard Law Review* article, *Protecting the Poor through the Fourteenth Amendment.*[1] Michelman built his argument on several cases during that decade that could be read to support the proposition that the Fourteenth Amendment *did* offer some measure of protection for the poor. Although most of these cases involved the Equal Protection Clause,[2] they attended not so much to "equality" per se as to the notion that every American citizen—indeed, perhaps every member of the American community, including resident aliens—is entitled to some basic mix of necessities. This notion was sometimes labeled a "minimum subsistence income."

Such hopes (or, for some, fears) were dashed by the replacement of "Warren Court" justices by appointees of Republican presidents, only one of whom, Lewis Powell, was even a nominal Democrat (who, in today's political world, would certainly have migrated to the Republican Party along with most other conservative Virginia Democrats). In fact, no Democratic president made an appointment to the Supreme Court between 1967, when Thurgood Marshall joined the Court, and 1993, when Bill Clinton named Ruth Bader Ginsburg to succeed Byron White.

Cass Sunstein has recently suggested that Michelman's vision might have prevailed if only Hubert Humphrey had won the 1968 election.[3] Sunstein's book, tellingly entitled *The Second Bill of Rights*, refers to President Franklin Roosevelt's 1944 call for an affirmative "social bill of rights" to complement the more classic set of "negative rights" protected by the 1789 Bill of Rights.[4] Humphrey, especially, might well have appointed old-line New Dealers like himself who would have given the cases of the 1960s their most capacious readings. We will, of course, never know.

I share Sunstein's basic view that there are indeed significant ideological differences between Democratic and Republican justices, discernable in their votes across a wide variety of issues, including the treatment of poor people. In the following pages, though, I want to look rather closely at two opinions by Republican justices that are, in fact, remarkably radical in their implications. My aim is to engage in a certain sort of historical retrieval. It is also to emphasize the extent to which the modern Republican Party—and, perhaps especially, contemporary Republicans who make it to the Supreme Court—inhabit a far different ideological world than that which existed earlier in the twentieth century. Indeed, one may well wonder if any contemporary Democratic appointee would be capable of writing opinions as radical as those written by Charles Evans Hughes or Potter Stewart, who were both Republican appointees.

I. Republican Recognition of the Plight of the Poor

A. West Coast Hotel Co. v. Parrish

The first case, *West Coast Hotel Co. v. Parrish*,[5] is a classic chestnut. In that 1937 case, the Supreme Court reversed earlier precedents and upheld the power of a state to require that private employers pay their employees a minimum wage. One way of understanding the case is simply as the Court's announcement of its willingness to defer to legislatures on what counts as wise social and economic policy. After all, in a seminal 1905 dissent in *Lochner v. New York*,[6] in which the majority of the Court rejected as unconstitutional a New York maximum hour law, Justice Holmes emphasized as dispositive "the right of a majority to embody their opinions in law."[7] This conclusion had nothing to do with Holmes's "agreement or disagreement" with the law in question. Indeed, Holmes stated that "state constitutions and state laws may regulate life in many ways which we as legislators might think as injudicious or if you like as tyrannical."[8] Reasonable persons can disagree about the status of such social regulation, some viewing it as socially beneficial, others as "tyrannical," as may have well been the case with Holmes himself, who tended to be something of a Social Darwinist in his thought. Regardless, Holmes's view was that the Court should simply uphold the rights of political majorities to have their way.

But this is not the rhetoric informing Chief Justice Hughes's opinion in *Parrish*. Hughes had been a progressive Republican Governor of New York prior to his first appointment to the Supreme Court, from which he resigned in 1916 to challenge Woodrow Wilson for the presidency in a contest that he lost by a very narrow margin. Thereafter, he served as Secretary of State under Warren Harding. He was reappointed to the Court, this time as Chief Justice, by President Hoover in 1930, following the death of William Howard Taft, a decidedly less progressive Republican.

Hughes was not a judge who simply felt a duty to submit to raw political power, as did Holmes. In *Parrish*, he emphasized that "the liberty safeguarded is liberty in a social organization which *requires* the protection of law against the evils which menace the health, safety, morals and welfare of the people."[9] "What can be closer to the public interest," he asked, no doubt believing that the question was rhetorical, admitting of only one answer, "than the health of women and *their protection from unscrupulous and overreaching employers*?" Hughes emphasized that a minimum wage law applied to "the class receiving the least pay, . . . the ready victims of those who would take advantage of their necessitous circumstances."[10] Hughes had little trouble describing the legislature as responding to "the evils of the 'sweating system,' the exploiting of workers at wages so low as to be insufficient to meet the bare cost of living."[11]

Reading these passages, one might well believe that one was reading the work of socialist Norman Thomas or even Eugene V. Debs, the leading socialist politician of the twentieth century, who had received almost a million votes in his 1912 campaign for the presidency. Hughes in effect recognized the existence of what Marx called a "reserve army of the unemployed,"[12] who were sufficiently desperate to work that they would do so for a pittance. This reserve gave employers the option of providing wages that covered only the "bare cost of living" in the most literal sense, and not one penny more.[13]

Hughes further defended the constitutional legitimacy of the Washington State law, noting:

> The exploitation of a class of workers who are in an unequal position with respect to bargaining power and are thus relatively defenseless against the denial of a living wage is not only detrimental to their health and well being but casts a direct burden for their support on the community.[14]

Why is this so? According to Hughes, the answer was that "[w]hat these workers lose in wages the taxpayers are called upon to pay. *The bare cost of living must be met.*"[15] Yet, Hughes added, "[t]he community is not bound to provide what is in effect a subsidy for unconscionable employers. The community may direct its law-making power to correct the abuse which springs from *this selfish disregard of the public interest.*"[16] This is surely for the twenty-first-century reader one of the most astonishing paragraphs in the entire *United States Reports*. It is unimaginable today, for example, that anyone affiliated with the post-Reagan Republican Party, including judges appointed by Reagan and his Republican successors, would use such language in regard to low-wage employers.

Cases are inevitably ambiguous, and one might read Hughes as offering only what might be termed a "descriptive" argument. That is, he might be saying merely that Americans are a generous people who will in fact provide what we often call "welfare" to those who cannot adequately support themselves by working. One often hears, even in contemporary American political campaigns, that the "working poor" are entitled to our sympathies (and even support), in a way, presumably, that the nonworking poor (i.e., those persons who are unable—or, even more so, unwilling—to participate in the labor market) are not. To the extent that employers do not pay their "fair share," which is defined as at least the minimum wage, then they are in fact being "subsidized" by other Americans who will feel a duty to pitch in and help through taxes or private charity.

But Hughes can also be read to suggest a far more radical possibility, that taxpayers do indeed have a legal/constitutional duty to provide at least "the bare cost of living" to those who are unable to procure such funds, perhaps because of economic downturns most dramatically manifested in the Great Depression itself. This comes quite close to the notion of the "constitutionally required welfare state" that would be articulated by Michelman some three decades later. In any event, a distinguished Republican judge found it possible to use language and suggest possibilities that are quite radical in their implications. The free market cannot in fact be trusted to provide an adequate income to every deserving person, and the state may have a duty to make up for this deficiency by redistributive programs. Indeed, Hughes's opinion was signed by another Republican, Harlan Fiske Stone, who had been Calvin Coolidge's Attorney General (and who would be successfully nominated by FDR to succeed Hughes as Chief Justice in 1941).

B. Kras v. United States

Parrish, for lawyers, is a seminal case that signaled the Court's willingness to legitimize the redistribution that is necessarily part of a welfare state, not least because the majority, as revealed in Chief Justice Hughes's powerful language, appeared to have substantially accepted the ideological underpinnings of such redistribution. The second case, *Kras v. United States*,[17] has a far different message. Decided in the early 1970s, thirty-six years after *Parrish*, *Kras* decisively rejected the Michelman vision of constitutional meaning and possibility.

Justice Blackmun, who wrote the opinion for a majority of five justices, accepted as true the following facts as alleged in Kras's affidavit:

> 1. Kras resides in a 2 1/2-room apartment with his wife, two children, ages 5 years and 8 months, his mother, and his mother's 6-year-old daughter. His younger child suffers from cystic fibrosis and is undergoing treatment in a medical center.
> 2. Kras has been unemployed since May 1969 except for odd jobs producing about $300 in 1969 and a like amount in 1970. His last steady job was as an insurance agent with Metropolitan Life Insurance Company. He was discharged by Metropolitan in 1969 when premiums he had collected were stolen from his home and he was unable to make up the amount to his employer. Metropolitan's claim against him has increased to over $1,000 and is one of the debts listed in his bankruptcy petition. He has diligently sought steady employment in New York City, but, because of unfavorable references from Metropolitan, he has been unsuccessful. Mrs. Kras was employed until March 1970, when she was forced to stop because of pregnancy. All her attention now will be devoted to caring for the younger child who is coming out of the hospital soon.

3. The Kras household subsists entirely on $210 per month public assistance received for Kras' own family and $156 per month public assistance received for his mother and her daughter. These benefits are all expended for rent and day-to-day necessities. The rent is $102 per month. Kras owns no automobile and no asset that is non-exempt under the bankruptcy law. He receives no unemployment or disability benefit. His sole assets are wearing apparel and $50 worth of essential household goods that are exempt under [New York law]. He has a couch of negligible value in storage on which a $6 payment is due monthly.

4. Because of his poverty, Kras is wholly unable to pay or promise to pay the bankruptcy fees, even in small installments. He has been unable to borrow money. The New York City Department of Social Services refuses to allot money for payment of the fees. He has no prospect of immediate employment.[18]

Like millions of other poor Americans, Kras wanted to file for bankruptcy in order to get a "fresh start" by having the state wipe out his debts. Kras, however, did not have the funds to pay the $50 filing fee.[19] As an indigent, Kras claimed that it was unconstitutional to require him to pay the fee in order to gain access to the federal bankruptcy court. He based his argument, in part, on a 1971 case, *Boddie v. Connecticut*,[20] that held that it was unconstitutional to impose a filing fee on an indigent seeking divorce. In *Boddie*, the Court reasoned that because only the state has the power to dissolve a marriage, it would be a violation of due process to deny that boon to indigents simply because they could not afford to pay the filing fee. Kras argued that bankruptcy was similar.

Justice Blackmun had been appointed to the Court by Richard Nixon after the *Boddie* opinion, and he rejected Kras's arguments on several grounds. First, Blackmun found bankruptcy relatively unimportant when compared to other interests deemed "fundamental" by the Court. "Gaining or not gaining a discharge will effect no change with respect to basic necessities. We see no fundamental interest that is gained or lost depending on the availability of a discharge in bankruptcy."[21] One hardly knows what to say, though one might well read Elizabeth Warren's contribution to this collection to get some sense of the interest that beleaguered persons might have in being able to file for bankruptcy. At the very least, what trained (and invariably elite) lawyer/judges view as "fundamental" often has precious little overlap with what ordinary people might deem "fundamental" to their own abilities to lead reasonably decent lives.

Justice Blackmun's second argument is stunningly formalistic. He denied that "the government's control over the . . . dissolution of debts [is] nearly so exclusive as Connecticut's control over the marriage relationship. In contrast with divorce, bankruptcy is not the only method available to a debtor for the adjustment of his legal relationship with his creditors."[22] Although Justice Blackmun had the grace to admit that it might be "unrealistic," he noted that it was still possible that "a debtor, in theory, and often in actuality, may adjust his debt by negotiated agreement with his creditors."[23] Finally, in a comment for which a considerably transformed Blackmun had the grace to apologize two decades later, he noted that if the indigent pays the filing fee over a six-month period, as is allowed, "the average weekly payment is lowered to $1.28. This is a sum less than the payments Kras makes on his couch of negligible value in storage, and less than the price of a movie and little more than the cost of a pack or two of cigarettes."[24] This "let them eat cake (or go to the movies)" passage drew a withering riposte in a dissent by Justice Thurgood Marshall:

> It may be easy for some people to think that weekly savings of less than $2 are no burden. But no one who has had close contact with poor people can fail to understand how close to the margin of survival many of them be. . . . A pack or two of cigarettes may be, for them, not a routine purchase but a luxury indulged in only rarely. The desperately poor almost never go to see a movie, which the majority seems to believe is an almost weekly activity. They have more important things to do with what little money they have— like attempting to provide some comforts for a gravely ill child, as Kras must do.
>
> It is perfectly proper for judges to disagree about what the Constitution requires. But it is disgraceful for an interpretation of the Constitution to be premised upon unfounded assumptions about how people live.[25]

Marshall's comments were certainly well taken and eloquently delivered.

In many ways, though, the most interesting of the three dissents—a third one-paragraph dissent was written by Justice Douglas, joined by Justice Brennan—was that written by Justice Potter Stewart (and joined by Justices Brennan, Douglas, and Marshall). A Cincinnati native and Yale graduate, Stewart was a quintessential "Ohio Republican," appointed by

President Eisenhower to the Court in 1956. Nobody confused him with another of Ike's 1956 appointments—one he would later publicly lament—William J. Brennan, who would become the intellectual leader of the liberal wing of the Court for the next thirty years. Yet Stewart wrote the principal dissent in *Kras*, which was, in its own way, at least as radical in its implications as Hughes's earlier opinion in *Parrish*.

For Stewart, there was no real difference between the named litigant in *Boddie* and Mr. Kras:

> [T]he debtor, like the married plaintiff in *Boddie*, originally entered into his contract freely and voluntarily. But it is the government nevertheless that continues to enforce that obligation, and under our "legal system" that debt is effective only because the judicial machinery is there to collect it. The bankrupt is bankrupt precisely for the reason that the State stands ready to exact all of his debts through garnishment, attachment, and the panoply of other credit remedies. [Kras] can be pursued and harassed by his creditors since they hold his legally enforceable debts.
>
> . . . Unless the government provides him access to the bankruptcy court, Kras will remain in the totally hopeless situation he now finds himself. The government has thus truly preempted the only means for the indigent bankrupt [who by definition has nothing by way of assets to bargain with his creditors] to get out from under a lifetime burden of debt . . .
>
> The Court today holds that Congress may say that some of the poor are too poor even to go bankrupt. I cannot agree.[26]

What makes Stewart's opinion so astonishing is not its sympathy for the indigent litigant, however commendable that might be. Rather, it is Stewart's analysis of what "precisely" constitutes the indigent's situation, which is that the state both defines the content of property rights and stands ready to exert its coercive power on behalf of those to whom specific property rights are allocated. Thus, Stewart adopts perhaps the most basic insight of early-twentieth-century American legal realism: Property is not a "pre-political" or "pre-legal" notion; instead, it is a creation of the state.[27]

This insight explodes the distinction, at least with regard to property, between "private" and "state" action. Because the state monopolizes the power to define and allocate "property," it is ultimately responsible for the consequences of any existing distribution of property. Without the formal legal system of property (and contract), after all, an indigent could not be said to "owe" debt; just as much to the point, the indigent could, in the absence of criminal laws safeguarding property, simply reach into an unguarded till and take the money (which would no longer be defined as "theft"). And, of course, there is nothing sacrosanct about initial definitions or allocations of property rights. Even the slightest awareness of legal history illuminates the ability of the state to redefine and reallocate what counts as property. Surely the most dramatic example in American legal history is the uncompensated emancipation of slaves, by which slaveowners found themselves totally devoid of what had been, for many of them, their most important economic assets.

I do not want to overemphasize Justice Stewart's concern, as a judge, for the plight of the poor. He had, after all, written the Court's opinion in *Dandridge v. Williams*,[28] an important 1970 case that upheld Maryland's right to cap welfare payments at what the state itself admitted would provide less than a subsistence level of income. Although he acknowledged "the dramatically real factual differences" between the circumstances presented in *Williams*, dealing with the poorest of the poor, and what might be termed the "standard-model" socioeconomic regulation case, in *Williams* he nonetheless applied the extremely deferential standard of review, termed "minimum rationality," that results in the Court upholding almost all state regulations. Indeed, the "minimum rationality" standard was one of the signature doctrinal consequences of the New Deal judicial revolution. For some it is instantiated in cases like *West Coast Hotel v. Parrish*. However, in his own opinion, Chief Justice Hughes seems to have treated the minimum wage law in question as far more than "minimally" rational.

My major point does not really concern formal legal doctrine. Rather, I believe that one sees in both Hughes's and Stewart's opinions an openness to critical reflection on the class dimensions of American life and law. They appear willing to address the desire of some exploitative employers to take advantage of vulnerable employees. I would argue that a fundamental examination of this class dimension would reveal the extent to which American law is in its entirety skewed to favor the rights of those with property, including creditors, against those without.

It is not the case, of course, that the United States does not reach out, in significant ways, to help the poor. Lyndon Johnson's Great Society and even, we can now recognize, the successor administration of Richard Nixon, did much to succor the poor through such programs as Medicare and food stamps. The point, though, is that these are now treated by the judiciary as mere matters of legislative grace, to be provided or withdrawn at the will of legislative majorities, a very different direction than that described by Michelman when he envisioned the Court moving toward recognizing a constitutional right to some degree of "affirmative protection" and minimum subsistence by the state.

II. The Triumph of Olympian Indifference

A plethora of decisions demonstrate the modern Court's understanding. Typical is *Lyng v. UAW*,[29] a 1988 case involving a 1981 law that deprived striking workers and their families of access to food stamps. This legislation followed the election of Ronald Reagan, whose public references to the poor tended to involve so-called welfare queens and other supposed leeches on the public fisc. The provision of food stamps to strikers and their families was viewed by the administration and its allies in Congress as a "subsidy" to those who chose, by striking, not to work. The Court, through Justice White, held that Congress could reasonably believe that provision of food stamps tilted the playing field too much toward strikers and against management. White seemed to express no views of his own about whether this was in fact the case, though Justice Marshall, in dissent, charged that the majority failed to "address systematically the irrationalities they identified in the striker amendment."[30] In particular, the United States had asserted the presence of three "governmental goals"[31] that justified the legislation: (1) the striker amendment reduces federal expenditures; (2) the amendment channels limited public funds to the most needy; and (3) the amendment fosters governmental neutrality in private labor disputes.[32]

The first argument clearly fails. Consider a federal law that reduced the "universality" of some federal program by providing, say, that only Republicans or whites or Christians would be allowed to benefit from a program. That could surely be said to "reduce federal expenditures," but, just as surely, it would be rejected as resting on illegitimate discrimination.

Similarly, there is no plausible argument that Congress made a systematic study of "the needy" and determined that the households of strikers were less "needy" than other claimants. "As a threshold matter," Marshall wrote, "households denied food stamps because of the presence of a striker are . . . denied food stamps *despite* the fact that they meet the financial eligibility requirements of [federal law], even after strike-fund payments are counted as household income." By definition, households include the dependents of strikers, including "the infants and children of a striking worker. Their need for nourishment is in no logical way diminished by the striker's action. The denial to these children of what is often the only buffer between them and malnourishment and disease cannot be justified as a targeting of the most needy: they are the most needy."[33]

Finally, Justice Marshall skewers the so-called "neutrality" argument.

> Even on the most superficial level, the striker amendment does not treat the parties to a labor dispute evenhandedly: forepersons and other management employees who may become temporarily unemployed when a business ceases to operate during a strike remain eligible for food stamps. Management's burden during the course of the dispute is thus lessened by the receipt of public funds, whereas labor must struggle unaided. This disparity cannot be justified by the argument that the strike is labor's "fault," because strikes are often a direct response to illegal practices by management, such as failure to abide by the terms of a collective-bargaining agreement or refusal to bargain in good faith.
>
> On a deeper level, the "neutrality" argument reflects a profoundly inaccurate view of the relationship of the modern Federal Government to the various parties to a labor dispute. Both individuals and businesses are connected to the Government by a complex web of supports and incentives. On the one hand, individuals may be eligible to receive a wide variety of health, education, and welfare-related benefits. On the other hand, businesses may be eligible to receive a myriad of tax subsidies through deductions, depreciation, and credits, or direct subsidies in the form of Government loans through the Small Business Administration (SBA). Businesses also may receive lucrative Government contracts and invoke the protections of the Bankruptcy Act against their creditors. None of these governmental subsidies to businesses is made contingent on the businesses' abstention from labor disputes, even if a labor dispute is the direct cause of the claim to a subsidy. . . . When viewed against the network of governmental support of both labor and management, the withdrawal of the single support of food stamps—a support critical to the continued life and health of an individual worker and his or her family—cannot be seen as a "neutral" act. Altering the backdrop of governmental support in this one-sided and devastating way amounts to a penalty on strikers, not neutrality.[34]

Justice Marshall seems far more persuasive than the majority when he suggests that the congressional legislation is best explained (and legally interpreted) as a blatant effort by a newly empowered conservative majority to crack down on labor. I refer to the essay in this volume by Professor Getman for additional insight on the decline of the American labor movement, part of which may reflect broad developments in American society, but some of which surely reflects the use of state power to discipline, as it were, laborers who join together in concerted action. (Consider in this context Ronald Reagan's ruthless firing of striking air traffic controllers, which, among other things, established beyond doubt that there is not a constitutional right to strike at all.)

It is often suggested that the Supreme Court follows the election returns. Sometimes this suggests that the Court in making its own decisions is sensitive to the results of recent elections and the public opinion presumably manifested therein. In a broader sense, though, the membership of the Court is a clear function of election returns because the winners of presidential elections get to mold the courts—most visibly the Supreme Court—by nominating ideological allies to serve on the bench.[35] Presidents Reagan and George H. W. Bush were certainly uninterested in any critical examination of the class structure within the United States, and their nominees reflect this fact. President George W. Bush seems actively committed to sharpening class differences by redistributing resources to the already well-off, leaving everyone else to his and her own devices. He has now been presented the opportunity to fill two vacancies on the Supreme Court, and his appointments seem in line with his general sensibility as to the plight of the poor. There is certainly no reason to believe that Chief Justice John Roberts shares the sensibilities of his Republican predecessor Charles Evans Hughes. Similarly, if Judge Samuel Alito is confirmed (as seems likely at this time, November 2005), it seems equally unlikely that he will take his fellow Republican Potter Stewart as a jurisprudential model. One assumes that these earlier justices would be redescribed by most contemporary Republicans as Democrats manqué, to be dismissed as irrelevant (if not outright evil).

Are Democrats necessarily any better? At the level of the Supreme Court at least, the evidence is both scanty and mixed. One should recall that Justice White, who upheld the cutback on food stamps for strikers in *Lyng*, was a Kennedy appointee. He was, generally speaking, reasonably sympathetic on civil rights, perhaps reflecting his service with Robert Kennedy prior to appointment to the Court, but manifested little concern during the course of his thirty years on the Court for the plight of the poor. It was, after all, Lyndon Johnson who launched a "war on poverty," not John Kennedy, and Johnson's legacy regarding the Court was cut short not only by his premature departure from the White House because of Vietnam, but also by his atypical political ineptitude with regard to the Supreme Court. To be sure, one of his appointees, Thurgood Marshall, certainly made a mark on the Court as someone who expressed special concern for the interests of the poor (a disproportionate percentage of whom, of course, were (and still are) African American). Less happily, Johnson engineered the resignation of Arthur J. Goldberg, who had been the leading labor lawyer of his generation, in order to be able to appoint to the Court Abe Fortas, a longtime friend and ally of Johnson. Fortas did not seek the appointment and continued to serve as an advisor to Johnson even after joining the Court. When Earl Warren announced his resignation early in 1968, Johnson attempted to raise Fortas to the Chief Justiceship, nominating Rep. Homer Thornberry of Texas to succeed Fortas as Associate Justice. The Republicans successfully filibustered Fortas's nomination, thereby making the nomination of Thornberry moot.[36] Moreover, Fortas would be forced to resign early in the Nixon Administration because of ethical improprieties, to be succeeded by Harry Blackmun, the author of the strikingly wooden opinion in *Kras*.

There would be no appointments to the Court by a Democratic president until Bill Clinton's nominations of Ruth Bader Ginsburg (to succeed White) and Stephen Breyer (to succeed Blackmun, who by the time of his retirement was thought to be the most liberal member of the existing Court). Both voted in *M.L.B. v. S.L.J.* in favor of an indigent mother's right to appeal an order terminating her parental rights without having to pay over $2,000 to prepare the trial record for submission to the court of appeals.[37] But it is scarcely the case that either Ginsburg or Breyer has taken up the plight of the poor as any kind of special constitutional cause. They were in fact in the majority, as Justices O'Connor, Souter, Stevens, and Kennedy agreed with the indigent mother. Rehnquist, Scalia, and Thomas predictably dissented. Indeed, Thomas, who is often reported to be, together with Scalia, George W. Bush's favorite justice,[38] suggested that earlier Warren Court decisions on which Justice Ginsburg relied in her opinion for the Court should be overruled.[39] In his view, there is no constitutional right to appeal a decision of a trial court—the demands of "due process of law" are satisfied if one gets one bite at the apple—and the opportunity to appeal adverse decisions can therefore be limited to people who can afford to pay for it.[40]

Conclusion

I should conclude by noting that I am more than a bit ambivalent about the wisdom of judges taking on the task of requiring significant redistribution. There are all sorts of institutional reasons compelling a certain modesty with regard to the judiciary's role in ordering programs that inevitably involve major decisions about taxation and the overall choice among competing social goods (e.g., education, health, individual and national security, etc.). No one can believe that resources are unlimited, and a certain amount of "rationing" will thus always be required. There may be good institutional reasons, as Lawrence Sager has notably suggested,[41] for the judiciary to "underenforce" certain constitutional norms such as those involved in determining the actual parameters of the American welfare state. However, expressing justified caution about the correct judicial role is not identical to a judgment on the merits about the meaning of the Constitution, especially if one takes seriously the promise of the Preamble that the Constitution should serve as an instrument to "establish Justice."

Even if one accepts the legitimacy of Sager's seminal insight, which counsels a certain amount of judicial caution with regard to the actual implementation of welfarist norms, it may become ever more important that judges be willing to write opinions like those authored by Hughes in *Parrish* or Stewart in *Kras*, for each keeps front and center certain realities that the American legal system seems all too willing to suppress. Even if a court (rightly) decides that judicial capacities are limited, it should nonetheless feel a duty to write opinions that, in Felix Frankfurter's memorable term, "sear [. . .] the consciences"[42] of legislators, presidents, and citizens. Given contemporary American political reality, one may believe that the American conscience—especially as reflected in those who purport to lead us—is, alas, all too effectively insulated against being seared.

Notes

1. Frank Michelman, *On Protecting the Poor through the Fourteenth Amendment*, 83 HARV. L. REV. 7 (1969); *see also* Ralph Winter's reply, *Poverty, Economic Equality, and the Equal Protection Clause*, 1972 SUP. CT. REV. 41. Symbolic (and also explana-

tory) of the fate of Michelman's arguments is that Winter (author of the second cited article and then-Yale Law Professor) was one of Ronald Reagan's first appointments to the Second Circuit Court of Appeals in December 1981, even as Professor Michelman remained at the Harvard Law School.

2. *See, e.g.*, Harper v. Va. Bd. of Elections, 383 U.S. 663 (1966) (invalidating Virginia's requirement of a $1.50 poll tax as prerequisite to voting); Douglas v. California, 372 U.S. 353 (1963) (invalidating a California law requiring an "independent investigation" of potential claims before providing court-appointed counsel for appeals by indigents); Griffin v. Illinois, 351 U.S. 12 (1956) (requiring states to provide free trial transcripts to indigent criminal defendants wishing to appeal their convictions).

3. *See* Cass R. Sunstein, The Second Bill of Rights: FDR's Unfinished Revolution and Why We Need It More Than Ever 108 (2004) ("What stopped this development? The answer lies in the 1968 election, as Richard M. Nixon narrowly defeated Hubert Humphrey. . . . President Nixon appointed four justices who promptly reversed the emerging trend, insisting that the Constitution does not include social and economic guarantees.").

4. *See id.* at 235 (reprinting as "Appendix I" FDR's State of the Union Message on January 11, 1944).

5. 300 U.S. 379 (1937).

6. 198 U.S. 45, 74 (1905).

7. *Id.* at 75.

8. *Id.*

9. 300 U.S. at 391 (emphasis added).

10. *Id.* at 398 (emphasis added).

11. *Id.* at 399.

12. Karl Marx, 1 Capital 373.

13. Hughes, of course, was no Marxist. Might it be relevant, though, that he lived during a time in which Marxism was taken seriously by many prominent intellectuals and required some response even from non-Marxists? After all, one recent interpreter of Theodore Roosevelt's embrace of a robust form of Progressive politics, which included a critique of the excesses of an unregulated capitalist marketplace, emphasizes the seriousness with which he took the anarchist ideology that was widely believed to have motivated the assassination of President William McKinley. *See* Eric Rauchway, Murdering McKinley: The Making of Theodore Roosevelt's America (2003). And, of course, Eugene V. Debs was a serious presence in the presidential election of 1912, which was surely of interest to Hughes. *See* James Chace, 1912: Wilson, Roosevelt, Taft and Debs—The Election That Changed the Country (2004).

14. 300 U.S. at 399. Hughes was building on a critique of "freedom of contract" that can be traced, within respectable American legal circles, at least as far back as Roscoe Pound's essay, *Liberty of Contract*, 18 Yale L.J. 454 (1909). *See generally*

Barbara H. Fried, The Progressive Assault on Laissez Faire: Robert Hale and the First Law and Economics Movement 29–70 (1998).

15. 300 U.S. at 399 (emphasis added).

16. *Id.* at 399–400 (emphasis added).

17. 409 U.S. 434 (1973).

18. *Id.* at 437–38.

19. The present fee, as of November 2003, is $209. It is, of course, possible that the "couch of negligible value" might have commanded $50 from some buyer, but that is only a surmise.

20. 401 U.S. 371 (1971).

21. 409 U.S. at 445.

22. *Id.*

23. *Id.*

24. *Id.* at 449.

25. *Id.* at 459–60.

26. *Id.* at 455–57.

27. *See* Fried, *supra* note 14, at 70–107.

28. 397 U.S. 471 (1970).

29. 485 U.S. 360 (1988).

30. *Id.* at 376.

31. *Id.*

32. *Id.*

33. *Id.* at 377–78.

34. *Id.* at 381–83.

35. *See generally* Jack M. Balkin & Sanford Levinson, *Understanding the Constitutional Revolution*, 87 Va. L. Rev. 1045, 1067–68 (2001) (setting out the theory of "partisan entrenchment" on the Supreme Court).

36. *See, e.g.,* Laura Kalman, Abe Fortas 327–33 (1990).

37. 519 U.S. 102 (1996).

38. *See, e.g.,* Meet the Press (NBC television broadcast, Nov. 21, 1999); Lorraine Woellert, *What the New Court Will Look Like*, Business Week Online, Nov. 22, 2004,   at http://yahoo.businessweek.com/magazine/content/04_47/b3909039_mz011.htm.

39. Ironically, they included the criminal justice cases on which Frank Michelman had relied in 1969 for his argument about the constitutional foundations of some kind of welfare state.

40. 519 U.S. at 129–30.

41. *See* Lawrence G. Sager, Justice in Plainclothes: A Theory of American Constitutional Practice 84–128 (2004) (discussing judicial "underenforcement" of constitutional guarantees); *see also* Sunstein, *supra* note 3, at 209–29.

42. Baker v. Carr, 369 U.S. 186, 270 (1962) (Frankfurter, J., dissenting).

3

Money and American Democracy

Burt Neuborne

Democracy has always been beset by an internal contradiction. The ethos of democracy calls for the equal exercise of political power by the governed, but the practice of democracy has tended to generate electorates that exclude the weak and reinforce the strong. In fact, until very recently, democracy has been as much about exclusion as it has been about empowerment.

The ancient Greeks invented democracy, but the Athenian Constitution parceled out the vote to a fraction of the potential electorate, excluding women, slaves, and aliens.[1] The Italian city-states popularized democracy, but both the Florentine and Venetian versions of democracy were government by merchant princes.[2] The British proved that democracy could work, but did not formally embrace universal suffrage until 1884, and, even then, denied the vote to women.[3] Not surprisingly, American democracy began its existence in the eighteenth century by formally denying the vote to the weakest elements of American society—blacks, women, and the poor.[4]

Efforts at democratic reform in the United States have concentrated on expanding the formal definition of the franchise. The 15th Amendment sought to end racial obstacles to the ballot. The 19th Amendment guaranteed the vote to women. The 24th Amendment banned poll taxes in federal elections.[5] The 26th Amendment extended the vote to eighteen-year-olds. A blizzard of Supreme Court opinions wiped out property qualifications for voting,[6] and rejected extended durational residence requirements.[7] Congress barred literacy tests. A combination of the Voting Rights Act and vigorous judicial enforcement finally ended the shameful de facto exclusion of racial minorities from the electorates of many states. By 2000, with the important exceptions of ex-felons in a number of states, notably Florida, and the long-standing dilemma of how to treat resident aliens, the formally defined American electorate embraced all the governed, with virtually no islands of exclusion.

And yet, the age-old contradiction between democracy's inclusionary aspiration and its exclusionary reality continues. The fact is that as we enter the twenty-first century, the rosy picture of a universal American electorate masks a political reality that looks suspiciously like the exclusionary electorates of the past. Voting in the United States remains skewed in favor of the wealthy and the better educated, and against the poor and uneducated.[8] After one hundred fifty years of success in removing formal barriers to voting, only about half the eligible electorate actually votes, with the nonvoters clustered at the low end of the economic and educational ladder.[9] In this chapter, I ask why the exclusionary voting patterns of the past have persisted into the present. I hope to identify the ways current law and practice combine to overrepresent the rich and underrepresent the poor, and to canvass the legal obstacles to reform. I conclude reluctantly that efforts to decrease the massive roles that wealth and poverty play in American political life are constrained, not by legal obstacles rooted in the constitution but by a continuing mistrust of the poor.

I. The Three Tiers

Viewed realistically, American democracy is divided into three tiers. An economically elite top tier, consisting of the wealthiest 1 to 2 percent of the population, wields enormous political power. These "super-citizens" fund the electoral process with their voluntary contributions.[10] They set the national political agenda (we talk about estate taxes, not minimum wage); select the candidates (no one can run for office without significant seed money support from super-citizens); bankroll the election (virtually all campaign contributions come from the top 2 percent of the economic ladder); and enjoy privileged access to government officials (whose telephone call does a busy Senator take?).

Membership in the top tier is not defined by law, nor is it confined to the wealthy. It is possible to become a super-citizen on the basis of talent, fame, good looks, inheritance, or sheer persistence. But money gets you in with no questions asked. Likewise, membership in the top tier is not formally confined to white men. A few women and people of color crack the ceiling. But having substantial disposable income for politics is still over-whelmingly a white male prerogative in this society.

A second tier, "ordinary citizens," is made up of the 50 percent of the eligible population that actually votes. Ordinary citizens navigate between and among the choices made available to them by super-citizens. Once super-citizens have set the table by deciding what issues are worth debating, what campaign speeches are worth funding, and what candidates are worthy of running, ordinary citizens—like jurors in a lawsuit or judges in a beauty pageant—listen to the elites (or elite wannabes) arguing with one another, and vote on the issues and candidates that have been framed for them.

Ordinary citizens still wield real power. Choosing between and among alternatives proposed by someone else can be important, as long as the alternatives pose real choices and tend to approximate the full spectrum of available options. Given the economic and social homogeneity of the top tier, however, the quality of the options offered to ordinary citizens can vary widely. Sometimes, the alternatives are stark and well defined. Often, the candidates and issues look and sound like Tweedledee and Tweedle-dum. Almost always, the alternatives are constrained by the relatively homogeneous worldview of the narrow slice of the electorate that actually formulates them.

Ordinary citizens also play an indirect but vital role in the exercise of power by super-citizens. A feedback effect causes the top tier to consider persuasion of ordinary citizens when formulating and framing the options to be presented for electoral resolution. The modern fixation with polling and focus groups allows—indeed requires—super-citizens to gauge the opinions of ordinary citizens in deciding how to package and present the available political options to them. Unfortunately, the feedback loop runs both ways, with super-citizens occasionally manipulating ordinary citizens into preferred "choices" by controlling the flow of information to them.

If ordinary citizens constituted the entire population, the interaction between super-citizens and ordinary citizens would closely resemble Joseph Schumpeter's theory of democracy, in which an entrepreneurial elite interacts with the populace to produce a form of controlled popular governance.[11] But ordinary citizens do not reflect the entire American electorate, much less the entire population. A troublesome web of value judgments has constructed a third tier of disproportionately poor nonpar-ticipants. I call them "spectator citizens," made up of the 50 percent of the eligible electorate that does not vote.

The persistence of a disproportionately poor nonparticipating third tier produces an American political reality in which a small economic elite—the first tier—interacts with a large second tier of relatively comfortable voters to produce a form of popular governance that exalts the rich and virtually excludes the very poor from effective political power. In short, we have evolved a caricature of Schumpeter's theory. A century ago, political participation by ordinary citizens was rationed by formal prohibitions denying the vote to women, the poor and relative newcomers, as well as de facto prohibitions that prevented Blacks and Latinos from voting. Today, it is rationed by the predictable operation of our system of campaign finance, voter registration, and election administration, a system that predictably overrepresents the rich and virtually excludes the bottom economic quarter of the voting population from effective political power.

Spectator citizens live—and die—with the decisions made by the interplay between super-citizens and ordinary citizens, but play almost no role in the process. The existence of a nonvoting bloc of almost half the eligible electorate—if it stood as one—could pose a serious challenge to the status quo in any democracy. Effective government in a democracy—government capable of imposing real change on established power centers—depends upon an electoral mandate. But a nonparticipation rate of almost 50 percent makes it mathematically impossible to assemble the powerful electoral mandate needed to alter the status quo. Bill Clinton won the presidency in 1992 with about 48 percent of the popular vote; but only about 50 percent of the electorate voted. So Clinton was governing with an actual electoral mandate of about 24 percent, an extremely daunting challenge for any vigorous Executive hoping to push an ambitious agenda. No wonder it was so easy to derail his health care proposals. George Bush faces the same quandary today. In 2000, he failed to win a popular majority at all, and sought to govern with a mandate of less than 24 percent. Is it any wonder he was driven to exaggerate external threats in order to build an artificial internal mandate? 2004 isn't much better. President Bush now has a popular majority, but it's a narrow majority of the 59 percent of the eligible electorate who voted, or a mandate of about 30 percent.

Even if the nonvoters were a random slice of the population, a potentially volatile pool of alienated nonparticipants constituting almost half the eligible voting population poses a constant threat to any democracy, acting as a proverbial loose cannon just waiting for demagogic exploitation. But the problem is far worse in the United States because the third tier is not a random slice of the population. Spectator citizens are more likely to be poor, badly educated and nonwhite. Thus, an electorate skewed in favor of the powerful, once imposed by law, is now produced by less formal but almost equally effective means.

The existence of a third tier containing disproportionate numbers of poor nonvoters poses an immense moral challenge to American democracy. Most obviously, the consent of the governed is a far less compelling concept when that consent is granted by an electorate that does not reflect the will of the poorest and weakest segment of the society. Less obviously, the feedback interaction between elite and ordinary citizens is robbed of much of its legitimacy when the feedback is generated by an artificially truncated slice of ordinary citizens that does not reflect the needs and concerns of the weak and the poor.

Thus, while formal mechanisms of exclusion have been dismantled, we continue to operate a democracy that significantly overrepresents the rich and underrepresents the poor and the weak. Defenders of the existing three-tier system tell us that this allocation is simply the natural result of a series of individual choices reflecting differences in preference, ability, and relative political sophistication. After all, spectator citizens *choose* not to vote; super-citizens *choose* to play an intense role in politics; and ordinary citizens *choose* who wins the election. As long as the formal rules do not compel such a result, defenders of the status quo argue that a government devoted to individual autonomy should just get out of the way and permit the interplay of individual choices to determine the outcome.

But a three-tiered democracy is neither a natural inevitability nor a constitutional given. The first and third tiers are legal constructs, the predictable consequences of a series of discretionary decisions about how to structure American democracy. The economically elite first tier exists in its current form only because we have decided to treat the necessary costs of operating a complex democracy as an off-the-books expense to be borne by rich volunteers. Once the financial burden of operating democracy is off-loaded to volunteers, it is inevitable that the volunteers will tend to be rich and will come to exercise disproportionate political power. Moreover, we have immensely complicated the problem of regulating the disproportionate political power exercised by the first tier by confusing the unlimited spending of money in political campaigns with constitutionally protected speech, forcing campaign finance reform to run the gauntlet of the First Amendment.

The nonparticipating third tier is also a legal construct, the predictable result of the adoption of an opt-in voting system burdened by a series of unnecessarily high transaction costs to register and vote. The third tier exists only because we have decided to treat voting differently from jury service, census cooperation, or draft registration, by declining to view it as a civic duty. Moreover, the disproportionately poor and uneducated makeup of the third tier is a function of decisions to: (1) radically decentralize the administration of the electoral process into many thousands of local units; (2) place responsibility for assembling the voting rolls on the individual, not the state; (3) force prospective voters to register long in advance of the election; and (4) hold elections on a workday under conditions calculated to discourage electoral participation by the poor.

In short, by choosing to: (1) delegate the financing of democracy to private volunteers; (2) treat electoral spending as though it were speech; (3) require citizens to opt-in to the voting electorate; and (4) impose significant transaction costs on the act of registering and voting, we have constructed a political system that dramatically overrepresents the strong and woefully underrepresents the weak.

Why do we continue to operate such a system? One possible answer is that we must as a matter of fidelity to the Bill of Rights and our commitment to individual autonomy. A less palatable explanation is that deep down what we want is a political system that formally embraces political equality, but that actually tilts strongly against the very poor and toward the rich and better educated.

II. Does Fidelity to the Bill of Rights Compel a Three-Tiered Democracy?

Defenders of the current system often claim that it would violate the Bill of Rights, especially the First Amendment's protection of freedom of speech, if we took effective action to eliminate either or both the first and third tiers.

A. The Constitution and the First Tier: Confusing Money and Speech

It is true, of course, that wealth has always played a role in allocating political power in the United States and elsewhere. But the growth of the mass media, especially television, and the increasingly sophisticated tools needed to run an effective modern political campaign have vastly increased the need for large sums of cash if a candidate harbors any serious hope of winning. Since the amounts currently raised and spent on electoral campaigns are far beyond the means of all but the richest Americans, the funds must come from somewhere else. That "somewhere else" is the wallets of super-citizens, leading to a vast shift in political power to those willing to pay democracy's expenses.

Defenders of the current system often argue that the disproportionate power exercised by the economically elite first tier is immune from effective reform because the First Amendment protects the right of wealthy persons to spend as much money as they want in support of a candidate, just as it protects the right of everyone to speak out as much as they want in favor of a candidate. Proponents of a laissez-faire system of financing democracy often point to a pungent metaphor in the seminal 1976 Supreme Court campaign finance case, *Buckley v. Valeo*.[12] In *Buckley*, the Court analogizes money to fuel, and a political campaign to a drive in the country, reasoning that money is the fuel that determines how far the car can go. The Court reasoned that since money fuels campaign speech, any governmental effort to limit campaign money is the functional equivalent of an effort to limit campaign speech.

The *Buckley* metaphor obscures more than it clarifies. While it is true that money fuels campaign speech, an election campaign is not a recreational drive in the country. It is a race. And a race in which one side has considerably more fuel than the other is hardly a model of competitive fairness. Moreover, the winner of a race is not usually expected to reward those who provided the fuel. Nevertheless, the flawed metaphor continues to haunt efforts to limit the disproportionate economic power of the first tier. By treating campaign spending as the legal equivalent of campaign speech, the *Buckley* Court required most, if not all, efforts at campaign finance reform to satisfy the demanding First Amendment test requiring government to demonstrate a compelling interest that cannot be advanced by less drastic means before resorting to restrictions on speech.

To make things worse, the *Buckley* Court rejected equalization of political power as a permissible interest of campaign spending reform. Equalization of political power is possible, ruled the Court, only by strengthening weak voices; not by limiting strong ones. In fact, the only government interest deemed sufficient by the Court in the context of campaign finance reform was a desire to remove the appearance or reality of corruption. Unfortunately, the *Buckley* Court failed to define what it meant by corruption, setting off a debate between those who believe that proof of a quid pro quo bordering on bribery or extortion is necessary, and those who believe that the political system is "corrupted" whenever campaign money plays an inappropriate role in allocating political influence. After a long period of indecision, a narrow majority of the modern Court appears to have adopted the broad view of "corruption," upholding reasonable limits on the size of campaign contributions in settings where no quid pro quo has been proven, but where a significant concern exists that campaign money is buying unequal access and influence.[13]

Finally, the *Buckley* Court invented two razor-thin distinctions. The first is between expending political money yourself and contributing the same political money to a candidate. First-person expenditures in support of a candidate, whether made by the candidate or by supporters acting independently, were viewed by the *Buckley* Court as virtually immune from government regulation as to size, although they were deemed subject to rules requiring public disclosure. On the other hand, contributions to candidates were viewed as amenable to regulation as to size, source, and disclosure, both because the evolution of a contribution into speech was more indirect, and because the possibility of corruption was deemed greater.

The second razor-thin distinction is between spending money to advance an idea, which is immune from government regulation, and spending money to advance a candidate, which may be regulated in different ways depending on whether the spending is an "independent expenditure" or a "contribution." Under *Buckley*, independent expenditures must be reported, but cannot be limited as to size, while contributions can be regulated as to size, source, and disclosure.

The net effect of the two distinctions is that, under *Buckley*, while no restrictions may be placed on the amounts *expended* by a campaign, political *contributions* can be regulated as to size ($2,000 per candidate per election); source (corporations and labor unions may not contribute funds from their treasuries); and public disclosure (prompt disclosure of contributions of more than $100). Independent expenditures by supporters unconnected to the campaign may not be regulated as to amount, but may be regulated as to source (corporations and labor unions may not expend funds to support a federal candidate),[14] and public disclosure (prompt disclosure of expenditures of more than $100). Finally, the funding of so-called "issue speech," designed to advance an idea—not to elect a candidate—cannot be regulated at all, whether the funding takes the form of an expenditure or a contribution of any size, and whether it comes from corporations or labor unions.

Thus, *Buckley* bans efforts to limit the amount a campaign spends, while permitting regulation of the size and source of contributions to the campaign, making it impossible to control the demand for campaign cash while permitting significant regulation of the supply. The predictable result has been a frantic scramble for loopholes.

For many years, large contributors exploited *Buckley* to create two massive loopholes that threatened to overwhelm any effort to regulate campaign financing. First, large contributors, including corporations and labor unions, avoided restrictions on the size or source of campaign contributions by earmarking their contributions to the candidate's political party, to be used for "party-building" and state and local campaigns, as opposed to federal campaign activities. While such "party-building" contributions were subject to public disclosure, they provided an end run around efforts to wall off corporate and labor treasuries from campaigns, and allowed wealthy contributors to exceed the maximum limits on individual contributions.

Second, large contributors, including corporations and labor unions, avoided all regulation by arguing that their speech was issue-related as opposed to campaign-driven. Since the funding of issue speech is not subject to any regulation, phony "issue" speech that was clearly aimed at altering the result of an election enabled massive sums to be poured into campaigns with no disclosure and no limit on source or size.

The two major loopholes were plugged by the McCain-Feingold law which treats contributions to a candidate's political party as if they were contributions to the candidate for the purpose of enforcing limits on the size or source of a contribution; and treats advertisements on electronic media that cost more than $10,000, display a candidate's face, and are broadcast within sixty days of the election, as regulated campaign ads, no matter how much they may be disguised as issue speech.

Despite dire predictions that the Supreme Court would invalidate McCain-Feingold, and that its restrictions would wreak havoc with political fund-raising, especially by the Democrats, the reform legislation survived Supreme Court review[15] and functioned successfully in the 2004 presidential election, virtually eliminating corporate and labor money from the campaign and imposing effective limits on the amounts individuals could contribute to a candidate.

Predictably, a world of unlimited demand for campaign funds and effective regulation of the size and source of campaign funds has led to intense searches for new forms of campaign funding. One new device, the solicitation of relatively small contributions on the Internet from large numbers of contributors, provides the potential for increasing the size of the first tier by making it possible for large numbers of otherwise ordinary citizens to play a role in funding democracy. But, while reliance on an Internet-driven technique for raising private campaign funds may expand membership in the first tier from the richest 1 or 2 percent of the population to the comfortable top 10 percent of the population, it hardly brings the poor into the process. An expanded top tier is a significant step forward, but vesting disproportionate political power in the top 10 percent, as opposed to the top 2 percent, will not materially change the narrow perspective that limits the nature of the options that will be presented to ordinary citizens.

The second new funding device actually reinforces the disproportionate political power of the rich. Taking advantage of the distinction between expenditure and contribution, several enormously wealthy supporters of both candidates formed independent presidential campaign organizations in 2004, called 527s after the provision of the Internal Revenue Code that authorizes them. The wealthy supporters then poured massive sums into their 527s in an effort to affect the outcome of the election. Since the spending was avowedly electoral, 527s were obliged to disclose their finances and were forbidden to receive funds from corporations and labor unions. But, because 527s were ostensibly independent from the campaigns, and since the 527s *expended* money as opposed to *contributing* it, no restrictions existed on the size of the 527 spending or on the size of the funds funneled into the 527s. The result is a new vehicle for the rich to exercise disproportionate political power—this time through the vehicle of an independent 527 organization that acts as a surrogate for the wealthy supporter.

Closing the 527 loophole will be harder than the reforms effected by the McCain-Feingold law. Because 527s are funded by wealthy individuals with an absolute First Amendment right under *Buckley* to expend as much as they wish in support of a candidate (as long as they do so independently of the campaign), there is no obvious way to limit the amount of money a wealthy person (or a group of wealthy individuals acting jointly) may pour into the campaign via a 527.

One response to the current state of campaign finance law would be a frontal assault on *Buckley*. The questionable conflation of money and speech; the questionable distinction between expenditures and contributions; the rejection of electoral equality as a legitimate government purpose; the undefined nature of corruption; and the years of experience in seeking to make a supply-centered regulatory system work where demand cannot be capped—all argue for a serious reconsideration of the *Buckley* decision. Efforts to deal with 527s may create the necessary conditions for reconsideration.

A frontal attack on *Buckley* is, however, a gamble. While the case is an untidy compromise, one that may not be worth defending, what would replace it is unknown territory. If *Buckley* is a rotten tree just waiting to be pushed over, the question is: which way will it fall? A post-*Buckley* world could permit reasonable limits on campaign spending, thus dampening demand and making it possible to place effective limits on supply. But it could also reassert the link between money and speech, and recognize that contributions are just as protected by the First Amendment as expenditures, cementing the economically elite first tier as a permanent part of American democracy. For what it is worth, my guess is that a frontal attack on *Buckley* would result in greater regulatory authority and is worth pursuing; but then, I thought that John Kerry would win the 2004 presidential election.

A second response is to do the best we can within the constraints of *Buckley*. Nothing in *Buckley* impedes further development of the Internet as a source of large numbers of small contributions. Moreover, as the Supreme Court's positive response to the McCain-Feingold law attests, it is possible to achieve significant reform using a *Buckley* model. It may even be that the idea of the "appearance of corruption" has been pressed so far by the Court that it has morphed into a surrogate for "roughly equal political influence." If so, legislation designed to prevent members of the top tier from dominating access to government officials should be upheld.

Most important in the short run, the prominent role played by a few extremely wealthy supporters in the 527 process might create a strong suspicion that an official, after receiving such immense support, might be unduly beholden to the wealthy supporter after the election. If Kerry had won, what would he have owed to George Soros? What does George Bush owe to the wealthy supporters who bankrolled the 527-funded "Swift Boat" attacks on John Kerry? If the Supreme Court recognizes the power of Congress to act on such a suspicion in order to prevent the appearance of corruption, the influence of 527s could be regulated without a frontal assault on *Buckley*.

Most importantly, we can reject the idea that funding democracy is an off-the-books expense to be borne by volunteers. Nothing in *Buckley* or in any other constitutional theory would prevent us from eliminating the economically defined first tier entirely by recognizing that the funding of democracy is a communal responsibility. No one bats an eye today when the government pays for roads, schools, police, and the military. But the funding of each was once viewed as an off-the-books expense to be paid for by private interests. In the nineteenth century, roads were built by profit-making corporations, private police forces were the norm, and public schools were virtually unknown. Privateers once substituted for a Navy, and privately funded regiments fought in both the revolutionary and Civil wars. In fact, the running of the election itself, including the printing and counting of ballots, was long viewed as something to be privately funded by self-interested participants. In each instance, we came to regard public funding as preferable. No legal impediment exists to similarly viewing the necessary expenses of a well-conducted election campaign as an emerging public expense.

Buckley actually issues an invitation to subsidize weak voices as a constitutionally permissible means of advancing political equality. Virtually every other serious democracy subsidizes the campaign process, assuring that the rich do not exercise disproportionate political influence. A decision to subsidize some or all of the expense of running a campaign could take many forms, ranging from Bruce Ackerman's visionary call for redeemable campaign scrip distributed to everyone, to various schemes for tax credits keyed to political contributions, to targeted scrip redeemable by candidates for submarket access to the media, to calls for free or below-market access to the over-the-air broadcast media, to cash grants to qualifying candidates, to matching funds for private contributions. While issues will inevitably arise in deciding who is eligible for a subsidy, and whether and how much private spending can kick in once subsidized funds have been spent, the constitutional issues associated with campaign subsidies are relatively minor.

We already subsidize a portion of the presidential campaign. During the nomination process, once a candidate demonstrates widespread popular support by raising at least $5,000 from private donors in more than twenty states at not more than $250 per donor, the candidate is entitled to a one-to-one dollar match for all future contributions. In 2004, candidates accepting matching funds were required to agree to limit total nominating expenditures to just over $37 million, broken down state by state. The major party candidates declined to accept the matching funds, since they were able to raise far more on their own. For example, President Bush raised over $140 million during the nomination phase.

In 2004, the parties' nominating conventions were also heavily subsidized to the tune of just under $15 million each. Finally, each of the two candidates of the major parties in 2004 received a subsidy of $75 million for their presidential campaigns, with minor party candidates receiving a much smaller subsidy keyed to their respective performances in the last election. Although the general election campaign subsidy also carried with it a $75 million cap on campaign expenditures by each campaign, the spending cap was easily circumvented by funds raised by the political parties and other entities not directly connected with the campaign. The best estimate is that the Bush campaign, defined broadly, spent about $246 million and the Kerry campaign spent about $210 million, in addition to the $75 million subsidy available to each.[16]

Several states, including Maine and Arizona, have enacted comprehensive election subsidy plans. Some states, such as Arkansas, are experimenting with tax credits of up to $100 for small political contributions. Other states, notably North Carolina, subsidize campaigns for judicial office. Finally, New York City has successfully operated a broad subsidy program for elections to the City Council.

Given the widespread experimentation with varying forms of campaign subsidy plans, it seems clear that the obstacle to adopting one or more of the available campaign subsidy plans is not constitutional; it is political. The truth is that an economically defined first tier will remain in place and will continue to dominate American democracy until we decide to dismantle it.

B. The Constitution and the Third Tier: Bringing the Poor into the Voting Booth

If the first tier belongs to the rich, the third tier of American democracy is the political domain of the poor. Not too long ago, poor people did not vote because they could not afford the poll tax, because they were illiterate, because they were newcomers, or because they did not satisfy a property qualification. Today, although formal barriers no longer exist, the folks at the bottom of America's economic ladder still do not vote in any-thing like their actual numbers, virtually surrendering their ability to use politics to improve their lot.[17]

We could eliminate the third tier entirely by recognizing a civic duty to vote, similar to the duty to serve on juries or to cooperate with the census. Australia, among a number of democracies that view voting as a civic duty, boasts voter turnouts of 95 percent.[18] We have not reached 65 percent in a presidential election for more than a hundred years, and often fall below 50 percent. A 59 percent turnout was cause for celebration in 2004.

Alternatively, we could shrink the third tier dramatically by eliminating voter registration as a transaction cost for voting, either by delegating to the government the duty to register voters, a duty borne by virtually every other democracy; or by adopting same-day voter registration, enabling eligible voters to register and vote on Election Day. We could also move the election to the weekend, or to a holiday like Veteran's Day, enabling poor people to vote without missing work. We are the only democracy that insists on holding elections on a workday. Finally, we could upgrade the mechanics of voting in inner-city precincts to eliminate the numbingly long lines and appallingly inaccurate records.

Defenders of the current system argue that imposing a legal duty to vote would violate the First Amendment. Once formal barriers to voting have been removed, they argue, the decision not to vote is an individual's choice, entitled to as much respect as a decision to participate in the political process. It is, of course, true that any form of compulsory voting would risk forcing individuals to act inconsistently with their political beliefs. In order to avoid such an unpalatable result, any civic duty to vote must carry a convenient escape hatch, allowing an individual to opt out of voting merely by expressing a desire to do so. But once such an easy opt-out is made available, I see no constitutional problem in operating an opt-out voting process, as opposed to the current opt-in model. After all, a legal system that has rejected constitutional challenges to military conscription, compelled jury service, compulsory schooling, compulsory vaccination, compulsory cooperation with the census, and compulsory taxation to support programs with which the taxpayer profoundly disagrees can hardly draw a principled line at a civic duty to vote, especially one that can be so easily trumped by a convenient opt-out.

We know from our experience with activities ranging from joining class actions to participation in 401(k) retirement plans that opt-in systems tend to yield low turnouts, and that the turnout is lowest among the poor and less educated. When employers change from opt-in to opt-out partic-ipation in 401(k) retirement plans, participation rates among lower-rank-ing workers skyrocket. When the Supreme Court was asked to impose an opt-in system on class actions involving out-of-state class members having no minimum contacts with the forum, the Court declined to do so, recog-nizing that the diminished yield of an opt-in system would threaten the viability of the class mechanism.[19] And yet, we insist upon operating an opt-in system for voting. A switch to an opt-out system would virtually eliminate the third tier without violating anyone's First Amendment rights.

If the idea of compulsory voting is a little too Orwellian for your taste, the size of the third tier can be dramatically decreased by lowering the transaction costs associated with voting. No democracy makes it harder to vote than we do. We require prospective voters to carry out three prelimi-nary tasks before casting a ballot. First, a prospective voter must ascertain the place and method of registering and voting. In years past, officials bent on preventing blacks from voting made it as hard as possible to find the registration office. Nowadays, nobody actually hides the registration office, but the radically decentralized nature of our election administration often makes it difficult to identify exactly where to go to register to vote, much less where to go to actually cast your ballot. Our bewildering array of precincts, election districts, and assembly districts can create an electoral maze. While great progress has been made in simplifying registration—postcard registration is now widely available—the process of learning where to register and vote can seem daunting to a poor, unsophisticated person thinking about voting for the first time. And the easier we make it to fill out a registration postcard, the more likely it becomes that a techni-cal glitch—like listing the wrong precinct—will invalidate the process.

Second, in the United States the inertial burden of placing one's name on the registration rolls in advance of the election must be borne by the prospective voter. In most states, it is not enough to be motivated to vote on Election Day. The motivation must have caused the prospective voter to take the preliminary step of registering at least a month in advance of the election. No other democracy places such a preliminary inertial bur-den on the voter. The United States did not begin doing so until the first decade of the twentieth century, which not so coincidentally triggered a decline in voter participation from 75 percent in 1896 to 44 percent in 1924. In virtually every other democracy, the duty of assembling the voter registration rolls is placed on the government. In our system, the requirement of advance registration acts as an economic and social screening mechanism, disproportionately filtering less sophisticated, poorer voters out of the process. When we register young men for the draft, we do not count on voluntary compliance—we compel registration on pain of criminal sanction. When we enumerate the population for the census, we do not rely on voluntary registration—we use government officials to compile the data and compel cooperation with the process. When we register persons for jury service, we do not rely on voluntary registration—the government compiles the juror rolls. But when it comes to voting rolls, the government neither requires registration nor makes any effort to compile the necessary information.

Finally, once registration hurdles are surmounted, we require prospective voters to vote on a workday, using vintage voting equipment and appallingly outdated information technology, causing lines that can last for hours, especially in poor, black, and Latino inner-city precincts. Affluent election districts often have the resources to update their election technology, lowering the error rate and eliminating long waits to vote. Inner-city election districts, strapped for funds, often use the oldest, least reliable voting technology, and experience numbingly long lines to vote, which discourage all but the most highly motivated.

None of the three preliminary steps is insurmountable. To most of us, they constitute a minor annoyance. But to a poor, unsophisticated first-time voter, the preliminary steps can—and demonstrably do—act as a wall. Voter turnout in American elections is demonstrably lower than in virtually every other established democracy. Moreover, the percentage of poor people who vote in the United States is lower than comparable figures everywhere else. Finally, all agree that the nonvoting population in the United States is disproportionately poor. The explanation for the uniquely low voter participation in the United States lies not in some perverse form of American exceptionalism, but in the predictable cumulative impact of transaction costs that seem mere nuisances to a comfortable, well-educated voter, but which gnaw at the actual participation of poorly educated, economically marginal voters. No constitutional barrier stands in the way of eliminating these transaction costs.

First, the quaint tradition of delegating the administration of American democracy to thousands of local political subdivisions, each staffed by part-timers usually affiliated with the dominant political parties, has led to massive inefficiency, widespread confusion, and a hopelessly convoluted system that defies efforts at reform. The first step toward eliminating the third tier is to insist on a more efficient way to administer our elections. At a minimum, uniform rules, preferably national but at least statewide, should govern the eligibility to vote and the mechanics of registration. Election records should be computerized. Election workers should be held to a national standard of competence and receive national training. Such simplification and upgrading of the process for national elections would pose no constitutional problems. Indeed, *Bush v. Gore* suggests that our patchwork system, governed by radically different rules, may itself raise constitutional problems.

Second, no constitutional barrier prevents us from giving the government responsibility for preparing voter registration rolls. The simple expedient of automatically registering a voter every time the voter interacts with the government by graduating from high school, registering for the draft, filing a tax return, receiving unemployment insurance, disability, or welfare, getting a Social Security card, or obtaining a driver's license would eliminate the one transaction cost that impacts most severely on the poor. Every other democracy manages to compile a voter registration list, either independently or from existing sources of information. So should we.

Third, given modern technology, no reason exists to require voter registration long in advance of an election. One state, North Dakota, follows the nineteenth-century practice of eschewing voter registration entirely, relying on Election Day verification of a voter's eligibility, usually through the medium of a sworn statement backed up by penalties for false swearing. Six states permit Election Day registration without any reported increase in fraud or administrative difficulty, but with a marked increase in voter turnout.[20] In fact, given the technological capacity to assemble reliable voter lists, it may be unconstitutional to refuse to adopt same-day voter registration.

Finally, no constitutional barrier stands in the way of moving elections to a more convenient date and time. Oregon is experimenting with a two-week voting period. Michigan makes Election Day a holiday. Puerto Rico, which boasts a rate of election participation among the highest in the nation, turns the day into a fiesta of freedom. Every other democracy votes on a weekend, or makes Election Day a national holiday. We could move Election Day to Veterans' Day, already a national holiday, and honor by the simple act of voting the sacrifice of those who died to preserve democracy.

Were we to simplify election administration, require the government to assemble the voting rolls, permit Election Day registration, and make Election Day a holiday, the problem of a morally unacceptable third tier would cease to exist. Nonparticipation would, of course, continue. But it would be at a far lower rate; and most importantly, it would no longer be radically skewed by race and class.

III. Do We Want a Democracy That Overrepresents the Rich and Underrepresents the Poor?

Given the relative ease with which constitutional objections to the elimination of both the first and third tiers can be overcome, why do we continue to operate a democracy in which money plays such a dramatic role in the allocation of political power? One possible, though implausible, explanation is that, given its informal nature, the construction of the first and third tiers is not well understood. Once the consequences of the system are better understood, reformers hope that steps will be taken to eliminate, or at least ameliorate, the unequal allocation of political power based on wealth. A closely linked variant argues that constitutional objections have created a smokescreen that has shielded the existing system from searching review, since reformers fear nothing can be done without violating the constitution.

While I dearly wish to believe in the above explanations, they both ring hollow. The disproportionate political power of the rich and the political invisibility of the poor are not recent discoveries. Given the long-standing understanding of the issues and the weakness of constitutional objections to change, it is hard to believe that we leave the current system in place because we do not understand it, or think we lack the power to change it. I fear that the more persuasive answer is that we leave the system in place precisely because we do understand it and do not want to change it.

A plausible explanation is that we know how the system works but do not want to change it for principled reasons. One line of principled argument against change warns that any effort to impose legal reforms on the first or third tier invites government to regulate the core of the democratic process. Once government gets its nose in the democratic tent, skeptics warn, it will inevitably abuse its regulatory power by favoring its friends and handicapping its enemies. Anyone who watched Katherine Harris, the Secretary of State of Florida, twist and turn in 2000 in an effort to deliver the state's electoral votes to George Bush realizes the degree to which partisan officials can use regulatory authority to tilt the outcome of an election. Public subsidies, spending restrictions, contribution limits, compulsory voting, preparing the registration rolls, same-day registration—every one of these proposed reforms provides government regulators with a field of maneuver that may be abused. But doing nothing means the continued domination of American politics by the elite first tier and the continued marginalization of those in the third tier.

To my mind, the very real risk of abuse is outweighed by the need to minimize the degree to which wealth or poverty apportions political power in the United States. The risk of government abuse is, however, an important cautionary factor demanding careful attention to administrative procedure and review mechanisms.

A second principled line of argument reminds us that even if the government acts in good faith, a combination of bureaucratic ineptitude and the doctrine of unintended consequences may leave the system worse off after regulators get finished with it. Anyone who inspected the infamous "butterfly ballot" used in Palm Beach County in the 2000 presidential election knows that even the best-intentioned bureaucratic actions can be disastrous. And once we start fiddling with the spending and voting rules, we may discover a host of unintended consequences. For example, the timing of the presidential subsidy payments appears to have hampered George Bush's campaign in the spring of 1992, allowing Bill Clinton to gain a lead he never relinquished. Similarly, the Kerry campaign was hamstrung through the summer of 2004 by the timing of subsidy payments, which allowed the Bush campaign a precious opportunity for unrebutted advocacy.

Once again, though the risk of bureaucratic failure and the need to guard against unintended consequences necessitate caution in designing reforms, they do not argue dispositively in favor of retaining a manifestly unequal political system.

The third set of principled arguments against change rests not on the government's inability to carry out reform fairly and efficiently, but on a libertarian commitment to individual autonomy as society's prime value. Libertarians argue that if individuals choose to spend a lot of money on politics or to shop at Wal-Mart instead of voting, a society based on respect for individual choice should respect that choice, even when its exercise leads to a flawed democracy. Limiting spending on politics or forcing people to vote, they say, exalts political equality over individual autonomy, a recipe for overly paternalistic government.

The autonomy argument is often couched in constitutional terms, with the First Amendment deployed in defense of autonomy. But even if you reject the effort to codify a contested philosophical choice as binding constitutional law, as I do, the autonomy argument cannot be ignored. Our society does place a high value on respect for individual choice. Why should autonomy give way to equality in this setting?

I have spent a good deal of my career in defense of individual autonomy. If reforming the first and third tiers really posed an intractable collision between autonomy and equality, I would think long and hard before confidently preferring equality. But there is just no intractable collision. Moving to same-day voter registration is a clear gain for autonomy, as is moving the election to the weekend or a holiday. Even if we experimented with making voting a civic duty, providing a convenient opt-out would respect autonomy more effectively than we do in many other settings.

Similarly, the first tier can be reformed without undue loss of autonomy. Public funding has no autonomy costs. Moreover, while limiting campaign spending does circumscribe the autonomy of the very rich, it would actually enhance the autonomy of everyone else. It would free candidates from the current prisoner's dilemma that forces them to spend most of their time raising money because they fear that the other side will get ahead in the arms race. It would free voters from being manipulated by a financially skewed political marketplace of ideas where the candidate with the most money has the best chance of winning. And it would free donors from existing pressures from the boss or from the candidate to contribute more than they wish.

Thus, while principled arguments against reform exist, they do not persuade. Rather, I believe they are often deployed in defense of an unarticulated, unprincipled reason for favoring the three-tier system—the persistence of a belief that very rich people have earned the right to exercise greater political influence than the rest of us, and that the very poor cannot be trusted to exercise significant political influence.

IV. Conclusion

For most of its existence, democratic political theory has accepted the proposition that relative political power should vary with a citizen's wealth. Not until the egalitarian revolution of the late twentieth century did the wealth principle give way in America, at least formally, to an equality principle. The old system was justified by an assertion that since the rich had more at stake, they would be more responsible in exercising their political power. Freed from the desperation of economic want, the rich were said to be more likely to seek the general good than personal gain. That idea was reinforced in meritocracies like the early United States, where wealth was viewed as a rough proxy for talent. The obverse—that the very poor would be self-seeking and irresponsible in exercising their political power and that poverty was a proxy for personal inadequacy— fueled the formal exclusion of the very poor from the electorate. The persistence of property qualifications for voting, poll taxes, substantial filing fees for running for office, literacy tests, and extended durational residence requirements to keep out the riff-raff, coupled with a laissez-faire system of campaign financing and an onerous voter registration process, tilted the political system strongly toward the rich and even more strongly against the very poor.

The formal legal underpinnings of the old system have been swept away. As a formal matter, all eligible voters exercise equal political power. But the ways of thinking that fueled the old system are still alive. Many Americans continue to blame the very poor for their economic plight. Poverty is seen by many as a penalty for sloth, or as an indicium of moral failure. Poor people are generally viewed as less able than the rich, and as less likely to cast an informed, responsible ballot. Conversely, many Americans virtually worship the very wealthy, linking money with ability and viewing members of the propertied class as more trustworthy stewards of the nation's political future. The net result is a political system that quite purposefully re-creates de facto a good deal of the political inequality based on wealth that was once imposed by law. Until reformers confront this often unarticulated defense of the existing system, I fear that real reform of the first and third tiers will not take place.

Don't get me wrong. Dismantling the formal restrictions on political equality was worth the trouble. Many poor people do vote. Real limits have been placed on the ability of the rich to buy political influence. Moreover, even though many poor persons do not vote, their formal enfranchisement acts as a check on the first and second tiers, deterring them from policies that might galvanize the poor into voting in large numbers. In fact, I believe that many Americans think that we have backed into an ideal democratic structure, one in which political power is actually vested in the "better" segments of the population, but where the very poor retain the formal residual ability to rise up and vote if the governing classes abuse their power.

The easiest part of the argument to refute is the claim that the rich are entitled to greater political power. The size of their stake cuts both ways. They clearly have a lot to lose, but that may make them more irresponsible rather than more interested in the common good. Recent criminal behavior at the top of the corporate world should demolish any romantic notion that rich folks can be trusted to be faithful stewards of the democratic order because they have no need to be greedy. In fact, I believe that the mass of the public is no longer willing to cede disproportionate power to an economically elite first tier. That is why campaign finance reform proposals aimed at controlling the power and access of the first tier almost always win at the polls. The real challenge is to convert the diffuse sentiment in favor of campaign finance reform into a practical, politically attractive public funding program in the form of tax credits, targeted scrip redeemable for TV broadcast air time, matching grants, and direct subsidies to campaigns.

The harder part of the task is to break the link that continues to exist in the minds of many Americans between extreme poverty and personal untrustworthiness. Most importantly, we must remind the opponents of dismantling the third tier that elections are not tests, with voters being asked to find a "right" answer. Education does not necessarily translate into a "better" voter. Rather, elections allow voters to assure that their interests are being seriously considered in resolving social issues. We have already recognized formally that the interests of poor people are as worthy of electoral defense as the interests of the rich. We must now translate that formal recognition into practical reality by dismantling the existing opt-in system of registration and voting, a system that demonstrably minimizes the political power of the poor.

NOTES

1. *See* Christopher W. Blackwell, *Athenian Democracy: A Brief Overview, in* ATHENIAN LAW IN DEMOCRATIC CONTEXT (Adriann Lanni, ed., Center for Hellenic Studies On-Line Discussion Series, Feb. 28, 2003), *at* http://www.stoa.org/projects/demos/article_democracy_overview?page=4&greekEncoding=UnicodeC; *see also* MORGAN HERMAN HANSEN & J. A. CROOK, THE ATHENIAN DEMOCRACY IN THE AGE OF DEMOSTHENES (1999).

2. *See* FLORENTINE TUSCANY: STRUCTURES AND PRACTICES OF POWER (William J. Connell & Andrea Zorzi eds., 2004); JOHN JULIUS NORWICH, A HISTORY OF VENICE (1983).

3. A helpful chronological listing of British parliamentary reforms can be found at http://www.the caveonline.com/APEH/britishreforms.html.

4. *See* ALEX KEYSSAR, THE RIGHT TO VOTE: THE CONTESTED HISTORY OF DEMOCRACY IN THE UNITED STATES (2001).

5. *See also* Harper v. Virginia State Bd. of Elections, 383 U.S. 663 (1966) (invalidating state poll tax).

6. *See, e.g.*, Kramer v. Union Free Sch. Dist. No. 15, 395 U.S. 621 (1969); Phoenix v. Kolodziejski, 399 U.S. 204 (1970).

7. *See* Dunn v. Blumstein, 405 U.S. 330 (1972).

8. The richest source of data on the makeup of the voting population remains the U.S. Census Bureau. *See* http://www.census.gov/population/www/socdemo/ voting.html.

9. *See* website of the Center for Voting and Democracy particularly helpful at http://www.fairvote.org/turnout.

10. Raw data published by the Federal Elections Commission makes it possible to chart patterns in campaign spending. *See* www.fec.gov.

11. JOSEPH A. SCHUMPETER, CAPITALISM, SOCIALISM AND DEMOCRACY (1942).

12. 424 U.S. 1, 19, n.18 (1976).

13. Nixon v. Shrink Mo. Gov't PAC, 528 U.S. 377 (2000).

14. The ban on corporate political contributions was upheld in FEC v. Beaumont, 539 U.S. 146 (2003).

15. McConnell v. FEC, 540 U.S. 93 (2003).

16. Obviously, no subsidy plan designed to limit the disproportionate political power of the rich can work if it simply supplements vast sums raised from private sources. Thus, a major challenge facing proponents of campaign subsidies is to limit the extent of private funding so that the subsidy is not rendered meaningless as a device to equalize political power.

17. For a sample of the voluminous literature on voting and the poor, *see* MICHAEL J. AVERY, THE DEMOBILIZATION OF AMERICAN VOTERS: A COMPREHENSIVE THEORY OF VOTER TURNOUT (1989); RUY TEIXEIRA, WHY AMERICANS DON'T VOTE: TURNOUT DECLINE IN THE UNITED STATES, 1960–1984 (1987); WILLIAM CROTTY, POLITICAL PARTICIPATION AND AMERICAN DEMOCRACY (1991); *see also* Bill Winders, *The Roller Coaster of Class Conflict: Class Segments, Mass Mobilization and Voter Turnout in the U.S., 1840–1996*, 77 SOC. FORCES 833 (1999).

18. Compulsory voting exists in one form or another in thirty countries. For a listing, see Institute for Democracy and Electoral Assistance, *at* http://www.idea .int/vt/analysis/compulsory+voting.

19. Phillips Petroleum Co. v. Shutts, 472 U.S. 797 (1985).

20. Same-day voter registration exists in Minnesota, Maine, Wisconsin, New Hampshire, Wyoming, and Idaho. In 2000, turnout spiked by an average of 5.1 percent in same-day registration states, more than double the national average.

4

Contracting Civil Procedure

Judith Resnik

I. Shifting Paradigms: From the Process Due to the Bargain Made

During much of the twentieth century, civil processes in the United States relied on a conceptual framework anchored in the constitutional and common law of due process.[1] As judges and lawyers worked out rules for adjudication and faced questions about the standards to be applied when challenges were made to decisions, the inquiry focused on the opportunities for participation and the kind and quantum of information required in order for the state to put its force behind an outcome and enforce the resulting obligations. More recently, the law of process has turned to doctrines of contract and agency law as it enforces agreements that send disputants away from courts and as it encourages contractual settlements when cases are filed in courts.

Judges who were once skeptical of devolution of judicial authority to agency fact-finders now permit the reallocation of adjudication to government officials working outside courthouses in administrative offices. Further, federal judges who had once declined to enforce ex ante agreements to arbitrate federal statutory rights generally now insist on holding parties to such bargains—thereby outsourcing an array of claims. While "bargaining in the shadow of the law" is a phrase often invoked,[2] bargaining is increasingly a requirement *of* the law of conflict resolution. As a result, minicodes of civil procedure are being created by a multitude of public and private providers—all producing processes and outcomes not easily visible to the public.

With the predicate presumptions that parties' agreements validate outcomes and that using alternatives to courts is desirable, the attention paid to the quality and kind of process provided is waning. Instead of questions about the process "due," judges focus increasingly on whether an enforceable contract to preclude litigation has been entered, when a settlement has been achieved, who has the power to bind whom, whether any of the terms of the bargains struck ought not to be enforced, and which court has jurisdiction if postsettlement disputes arise. Moreover, the task of judging is itself changing as judges lay claim to the power to facilitate settlements by meeting informally with parties to encourage agreement.

As a consequence, the distinctive character of adjudication as a specific kind of "social ordering" that could be contrasted with others, such as contracts and elections (to borrow Lon Fuller's terminology and categories)[3] is diminishing. While the subject matter of procedure had been preoccupied with generating secondary rules by which to render judgment, today the task is to shape secondary rules for interpreting parties' agreements.

Below, I detail some of the history and analyze the import of this shift from one framework, *Due Process Procedure*, to this other—*Contract Procedure*.[4] My term *Contract Procedure* embraces both government-based encouragement of dispute resolution through contract and government enforcement of parties' agreements to contract out of litigation. As I explain, the two approaches have different normative assumptions about the state's role in responding to conflict. Contract Procedure may generate more outcomes and some at lower costs than does Due Process Procedure but, at present, it also entails less transparency and imposes fewer constraints on either litigants or jurists. Neither form of procedure responds well to the high demand for dispute resolution services nor solves the profound problems of inequality of power between disputants. But Due Process Procedure imposes more obligations on the state to justify its own exercises of power by reference to reasons other than acquiescence by disputants.

Yet the government's public accounting for its own power and its making patent the sources and nature of conflict—qualities that are emblematic of Due Process Procedure—are at risk. These features stem from traditions of publication of judgments and of reliance on trials held in courthouses to which the public and the press had ready access. These dimensions of Due Process Procedure are being eclipsed, in part by the pressures for production and in part by a lack of political commitment to support the enforcement of the rights to which women and men can now lay claim. Civil processes are thus both a site of conflict about the role of the state and a dynamic expression of government obligations to enable the pursuit and enforcement of rights and to be held accountable for its own actions.

II. Due Process Procedure: A Retrospective

In the 1920s, Congress began a century-long project to expand federal judicial capacity by increasing the number of judicial officers, the kind and array of federal rights, and the power of the federal judiciary to make national procedural rules.[5] In 1934, Congress delegated authority to the federal courts to create a national set of procedural rules that would displace the prior regime, under which federal judges conformed their court rules to the different states in which they sat.[6] In 1938, the Federal Rules of Civil Procedure came into being, providing federal judges with practices to share that helped them to develop their identity as a cadre of distinct government actors.[7] National rules of criminal procedure, appellate procedure, and evidence followed in the decades thereafter.

Lawyers and law professors shaped this trans-substantive code with the hopes of simplifying process, easing access to courts, and collapsing distinctions between law and equity. With their flexible, equity-based approach and their diminished formalism, the Federal Rules endowed trial judges with a good deal of discretion to tailor processes to the circumstances of a particular case. But the rules also channeled and constrained that discretion. As initially formulated, the rules did not involve judges much in supervising discovery, nor did they charge judges with structuring the timing of the filing of motions. Further, when parties sought judicial decision making, judges were required to apply standards set forth in rules (often amplified by case law) to determine whether cases could proceed to adjudication. Dispositive decisions were to be explained by findings of fact and conclusions of law.[8] While settlement was an expected outcome in many instances, the court-based process focused on the task of trying a case and imposed obligations on judges and lawyers to do so in a fashion formulated to be "fair" to adversaries and mostly transparent to the public.

These procedural rules did not stand alone. Rather, expressive of and coupled with an impressive investment in the infrastructure of the federal courts, they represented a normative commitment to federal regulatory power. In the wake of the Depression, many saw federal governance as a necessary and desirable response to political and economic conditions. The expansion of federal jurisdiction and uniform federal processes were mechanisms by which to shape a developing national legal regime. Time and again, Congress authorized government officials and private parties to bring lawsuits as a means of enforcing federal law. Federal procedure was thus part of a larger national constitutional project that relied in part on equipping individuals and groups to come to court as rights-seekers and upon judges to determine the obligations of disputants.[9]

That attitude toward process can be seen in the major wave of amendments to the Federal Rules that occurred in the 1960s and 1970s. The 1966 revision of the Rule governing class actions exemplified a widespread affection for entrepreneurial rights-seeking. Not only did the Rule invite "private attorneys' general" to file cases on behalf of groups to enforce public norms, but its approach was mirrored in a smorgasbord of other mechanisms. Congress gave government officials new authority to bring lawsuits, and private parties gained new incentives through fee-shifting statutes to pursue claims against both public and private wrongdoers.[10] The class action rule, complemented by statutes authorizing consolidation across federal district courts and fee-shifting provisions, reshaped ideas about what litigation might accomplish.[11]

The import of the changes—as a vehicle for adjudication's expansion— can be mapped through the growing sizes of dockets, as more and different kinds of cases were filed, and through the significant increases in funding for the federal courts. Congress authorized litigants to bring lawsuits aimed at enforcing civil rights, environmental rights, consumers' rights, and workers' rights. Between the 1960s and the 1990s, caseloads within the federal system tripled as hundreds of new statutory causes of action were enacted. In terms of budgets, Congress provided substantial resources to the federal courts, whose allocation grew from about $250 million in the early 1960s to about $4.2 billion in 2000.[12]

But even that largesse could not accommodate all the claimants eligible for adjudication under federal law. Further, neither Congress nor the leadership of the Article III judiciary were enthusiastic about augmenting the ranks of life-tenured Article III judges in numbers sufficient to decide the many kinds of cases that federal lawmakers had made possible. Instead, leaders of the bench and bar created new kinds of judges and new venues for judging, both within and outside the federal courts. Some of these auxiliary judges—magistrate and bankruptcy judges—are appointed by Article III judges, work inside Article III courts, and serve fixed and renewable terms.[13] Tens of hundreds of others work in administrative agencies that, beginning in the 1930s, have become important venues for federal adjudication.

III. Growing Criticisms and Alternative Processes

The volume of filings, the proliferation of adjudicatory processes, and the many forms of rights garnered praise from some quarters but also generated complaints. While the 1938 Federal Rules were once heralded as model solutions to many procedural challenges,[14] they are now identified as sources of problems. Some bemoan adjudication's failures to live up to its own promises; some think that the rights-seeking made available through adjudication is excessive,[15] and yet others believe that adjudication fails to provide a sufficient array of responses to human conflict.[16]

Within the federal courts during the second half of the twentieth century, a movement emerged to change the role of the judge and the rules under which judges operated. The leadership of the federal bench took on the task of teaching their peers to shift their focus from adjudication and opinion writing toward dispute resolution and case disposition. Classes for judges were geared toward persuading judges to become managerial in pursuit of settlement,[17] and Federal Rules were amended to delineate the new role.

Of course, the concept of settlement was not foreign to the 1930s rule drafters, who knew well that many cases ended without adjudication. But their 1938 Federal Rules of Civil Procedure neither used the term "settlement" nor charged judges with the task of promoting settlements. In contrast, the 2004 version of these Rules uses the word "settlement" in the texts of four rules—imposing obligations on lawyers (Rule 11),[18] specifying pretrial processes (Rule 16), creating class action possibilities (Rule 23),[19] and providing for discovery (Rule 26).[20]

Tracing the evolution of one of those rules—Rule 16 (initially denominated "Pre-Trial Procedure; Formulating Issues" and now called "Pretrial Conferences; Scheduling; Management")—provides insight into how the charter to federal judges was revised to urge them to press for settlement. The 1938 version had given judges discretion to convene a "pre-trial" meeting with lawyers.[21] The listed purposes of such a meeting included simplifying issues, amending pleadings, making admissions, limiting expert witnesses, referring matters to masters, and undertaking such "other matters as may aid in the disposition of the action." From judicial archives on committee and council meetings, we know that this rule was not used as much as its proponents hoped. Beginning in the 1950s, some federal judges (self-styled as "proselytizers") endeavored to convince their colleagues to "modernize" their justice by taking "control" of the pretrial phase of litigation.[22]

By 1983, their success could be seen in practice as well as in the promulgation of amendments to the Federal Rules. A mandate for judges to manage and to settle cases became codified, as the discretionary possibility of a pretrial conference became an obligatory requirement that judges enter scheduling orders to frame the pretrial process.[23] As the drafters noted, the purposes were to make "case management an express goal of pretrial procedure" and to move away from a pretrial "conference focused solely on the trial and toward a process of judicial management that embraces the entire pretrial phase, especially motions and discovery." One of the listed goals for Rule 16 was "facilitating the settlement of the case."

A decade later, in 1993, Rule 16 was again amended to detail more of the work and the power of the managerial judge, that authorized to direct "a party or its representative" to "be present or reasonably available by telephone in order to consider possible settlement of the dispute."[24] The 1993 amendments deleted the description of some conciliatory techniques as "extrajudicial" and instead called them "special procedures."[25] The text of the amendments added that the goal of such intervention was to "*assist* in resolving the dispute," in contrast to the prior statement that the aim was "to resolve the dispute." The changing language reflected changing aspirations—for resolution by negotiation in lieu of resolution by adjudication. As the drafters explained:

> Even if a case cannot be immediately settled, the judge and attorneys can explore possible use of alternative procedures such as mini-trials, summary jury trials, mediation, neutral evaluation, and nonbinding arbitration that can lead to the consensual resolution of the dispute without a full trial on the merits.[26]

The rule revisions also gave judges new authority to promote settlement. Although the notes explaining the 1983 amendment to Rule 16 had cautioned judges against imposing "settlement negotiations on unwilling litigants,"[27] the 1993 rule drafters gave judges power (unclear parameters)[28] to compel participation even when parties were reluctant to do so.[29]

The net result is a trial bench energetically promoting settlement. Examples include high-profile, large-scale cases such as the efforts to end the antitrust litigation against Microsoft with the help of the Honorable Richard Posner (of the U.S. Court of Appeals of the Seventh Circuit) serving as a mediator.[30] Less visible to the media but known to those reading reported decisions are ordinary disputes in which litigants protest judicial pressures to settle or to use alternative means of dispute resolution.[31]

The judicial embrace of a managerial role has been paralleled and sometimes prompted by an effort more generally to promote "alternative dispute resolution" (ADR). Bar associations and law schools have created programs and classes on negotiation, mediation, and arbitration; entrepreneurs have created new businesses providing dispute resolution services. Legislative changes also press for more and different forms of dispute resolution. ADR has became a feature of agencies and court processes in part through support from Congress, which has enacted statutes authorizing court-annexed arbitration programs[32] and has mandated or licensed the use of ADR in agencies as well.[33]

Surveying these various changes, one can see that several of the central concepts of Due Process Procedure have been displaced. The effort to simplify, unify, and enable enforcement of federal rights under a trans-substantive framework of rules has been altered from within. Rule amendments make discovery less liberal and processes more variable depending on the kind of case. In addition, whole categories of cases have been carved out for differential treatment. A prime example is prisoner litigation, with special statutes and rules limiting prisoner access and court remedies.[34] Further, both the judiciary and Congress have revisited class action practice with an eye toward imposing constraints. Congress has placed specific requirements on plaintiffs seeking to have securities claims certified as class actions.[35] In 2005, Congress created new provisions to federalize many state-based, large damage class actions.[36] Its proponents had argued that federalization was needed to curb lawyers too quick to file cases and state judges too hospitable toward such cases.

These various changes in statutes, doctrines, and court-based rules, coupled with educational programs for judges, have helped to redefine the "good judge" as a person focused on and able to achieve dispositions quickly. As one judge lectured his colleagues, "in most cases, the absolute result of a trial is not as high a quality of justice as is the freely negotiated, give a little, take a little settlement."[37] What is judicial (and judicious) is no longer equated with adjudication, with public processes, and with reasoned deliberation. In addition, judicial involvement in conciliation results in less appellate oversight of trial-level judges, which is (as Stephen Yeazell has put it) one of the "misunderstood consequences" of the 1930s reforms.[38] In short, managerial judges now exercise more discretion with less review.

Further, settlement pressures are not confined to the trial level. Appellate courts have also revamped their procedures to aim for more dispositions through conciliation. Federal rules now permit appellate courts to "direct the attorneys—and, when appropriate, the parties—to participate in one or more conferences to address any matter that may aid in disposing of the proceedings, including simplifying the issues and discussing settlement."[39] More than half of the federal circuits run such "civil appeals management programs" (CAMP) and oblige attorneys for disputants to meet with a staff member of the appellate court to negotiate settlements.[40]

IV. Contractual Divestment of Jurisdiction

In addition to the internalization of ADR within courts, judges have the means to promote ADR outside courts. An important technique is the judicial enforcement of predispute contracts stipulating that, if a conflict emerges, the parties agree to use dispute resolution systems other than courts. Some of these agreements are made between parties in long-term relationships or having specialized commercial interactions. But these mandatory arbitration clauses are now appearing in form contracts provided by manufacturers to consumers or by employers to employees.

American law once hesitated to enforce obligations to participate in private dispute resolution at the expense of access to public processes, and many jurists refused to enforce predispute arbitration contracts. But over the course of the twentieth century, the attitudes of legislators and court-based adjudicators changed. In 1925, Congress enacted the Federal Arbitration Act (FAA), requiring enforcement of parties' agreements in commercial contracts to use arbitration in lieu of litigation.[41] Yet judges sometimes declined enforcement in cases when plaintiffs brought claims based on rights—such as securities laws—created by Congress. Jurists found arbitration too flexible, too lawless, and too informal when contrasted with adjudication, esteemed for its regulatory role in monitoring adherence to national norms.[42]

However, in the 1980s, the U.S. Supreme Court revised its earlier rulings and upheld broad grants of authority to arbitrators, even when litigants relied on federal statutory rights when filing suit.[43] Further, the Court concluded that the federal commitment to arbitration embodied in the FAA preempted state laws authorizing judicial enforcement of statutory rights.

When articulating a federal commitment to arbitration, judges display attitudes toward both arbitration and adjudication that are very different than the views proffered by jurists in earlier decades. Instead of objecting to the informality of arbitration, judges now praise its flexibility and argue that this feature made arbitration preferable to adjudication. In turn, judges reposition adjudication as only one of several techniques appropriate for the resolution of disputes. Today, law often sends contracting parties (including employees and consumers) to mandatory arbitration programs created by employers, manufacturers, and the providers of goods and services.[44] Many of these disputants are strangers to each other rather than participants in long-term commercial relationships or in communities of affiliation.[45]

V. Conflicting Analytics

In some respects, the turn to and incorporation of ADR into federal adjudication represents the privatization of public processes—a development that is not unique to courts. Adjudication is predicated on public and disciplined fact-finding by judges and juries, licensed to inquire into specific problems to assess individual instances of alleged wrongdoing in order to enforce obligations. Both judges and litigants are confined to particular roles. As Lon Fuller famously explained, the presentation of proofs by litigants and the determination based on reasons by judges are the "distinguishing" characteristics of adjudication, which places individuals working within its strictures into "a peculiar form of participation."[46]

Support for adjudicatory procedure rests on a series of normative and political judgments: that the state is the appropriate central regulator of conduct, that norm enforcement through transparent decision making by state-empowered judges is desirable, that public resources ought to be spent upon individual complaints of alleged failures to comply with legal obligations, that litigants ought to be provided with opportunities to present proofs and reasoned arguments, that the power of adjudicators should and can be controlled by obliging them to rely on facts adduced on the record and to perform some of their duties in public, and that legitimate judgments thus result. While ad hoc juries have little by way of obligations of explanation, full-time judges are supposed to provide rationales for their application of law to fact, and those decisions are, at the parties' behest, subjected to appellate review. Direct participants and third parties benefit through the visible display of law's requirements applied to a myriad of specific situations.

The Contract Model of Procedure depends on analytic premises different from those of the Due Process Model. Just as the expansion of Due Process Procedure was part of a normative framework welcoming national regulation and rights-seeking, the shift to contract is nested in different social and political attitudes less hospitable to government oversight. Unlike adjudication's preference for adjudicators' pronouncements, ADR looks to the participants to validate outcomes through consensual agreements, sometimes fashioned by bilateral negotiation and sometimes facilitated through third parties.

But ADR has far fewer role constraints. It does not commonly build in rights to information held by adversaries nor does it require public explanation of the results or that outcomes be justified in relationship to legal norms. ADR practitioners are free to "get it done" and not obliged to explain how they "got it right." ADR is often chosen because it has the advantage of private decision making, made in the "shadow" rather than in the light. Public benefits are presumed to flow from the reduction of conflict and from the resolution predicated on parties' preferences.

Of the various enthusiastic constituencies for ADR, the support from federal judges is the most puzzling, as one might have thought that judges could be counted among adjudication's loyalists. Yet federal judges have used both their doctrinal authority and their dominant position as revisers of the Federal Rules of Civil Procedure to press toward disposition without adjudication. In the language of political economy, the question is: what incentives prompted judges, who could be understood to hold monopolistic power over adjudication, to risk their own status by minimizing reliance on their unique form of authority?

One explanation puts judges in the position of public servants, keenly aware that adjudication's utility had resulted in overload. Seeing too many cases, too long dockets, and too few decision makers, judges used their powers over process to try to accommodate more claimants. Under this analysis, judges are attempting a form of triage, modifying adjudicatory services in an effort to meet demand. As that demand outstripped the budgets provided by legislatures, judges helped to fabricate resolution services for as many as possible. ADR is not, under this thesis, a competitor but a "second-best" addendum, a short-form of judging that provides more claimants with more access.

A second interpretation identifies the changing attitudes as a form of backlash rather than accommodation, with a wing of the federal judiciary shaping doctrines and policies unwelcoming of rights-seekers. The procedural and substantive reforms that redistributed the power to use adjudication produced many institutional actors—including both governmental entities and private parties who were uncomfortable when labeled defendants. New kinds of claimants put such defendants to the burden of explaining their actions and, when victorious, obtained court mandates to improve conditions in prisons, desegregate schools, or provide money for harms from toxic wastes, dangerous products, and discriminatory behavior.[47] Some of those had the ability to "play for the rules," to borrow Marc Galanter's now classic explanation of why the "'haves' come out ahead."[48] Such "repeat players," with an advantage over "one-shot" participants, gained sufficient control in the federal government to install like-minded people as federal judges,[49] holding the authority to reframe procedural rules.

A third explanation is premised on adjudication's limitations, resulting in a failing faith in adjudicatory procedures. Critics come from a wide variety of vantages and raise very different kinds of complaints. Some attack the processes of courts because they are too easily exploited; others complain that adjudication is too labor-intensive and expensive, or too insensitive to the needs of disputants, and/or too unpredictable. Strategic manipulation, uncontrollable lawyers, and questionable outcomes have prompted judges, joined by many others, to rework liability and procedural rules to try to curb abuses and to mitigate structural weaknesses.

Increasingly, judicial commentary describes going to trial as a "failure of the system,"[50] but such "failures" are no longer commonplace. Rather "a full trial on the merits" has become a rare event. In the early 1940s, about 15 percent of federal civil cases ended with a trial.[51] In 1962, about 12 percent of the civil docket was resolved by trial. Today, trials are begun in about 2 percent of the civil docket. While filings and dispositions have risen significantly over these years (from, for example, 50,000 dispositions in 1962 to more than 260,000 in 2002), even the absolute number of federal civil trials has decreased, from about 5,800 in 1962 to about 4,700 in 2002.[52]

VI. Gains and Losses

In the 1970s, some commentators saw rising trial rates as a sign of law's capacity to empower, while others read the same data as evidence of unnecessary and wasteful conflict. Similarly, the information on falling trial rates and about the spread of ADR are met by some with celebration and by others with anxiety.

On the celebratory side, over the past four decades, Republican administrations have consistently identified litigation as harming economic innovation.[53] At both national and local levels, efforts have been undertaken under the umbrella of "tort reform" to limit or exempt manufacturers from liability, promote statutory caps on damages, and create alternatives to jury decision making.[54] Media campaigns, hoping to ignite hostility toward trial lawyers, have pointed to litigation as the source of a variety of ills, including the high cost of insurance.[55]

In addition to achieving some gains through legislation, opponents of ready access to courts have also succeeded in convincing judges to make rights-seeking more difficult. Several decisions of the U.S. Supreme Court have constrained the ability of individuals to rely on statutes, regulations, and the Constitution for redress. Other rulings have limited awards of attorneys' fees and upheld state prohibitions on lawyers seeking to approach victims of accidents.[56] As these changes have narrowed the opportunities for adjudication, courts and legislatures have also been mandating the use of ADR. As a result, the market in ADR appears to be flourishing—with conferences (on topics such as "Court ADR"), services (through firms with names such as "EndDispute" or "JAMS"—Judicial Arbitration and Mediation Services, Inc.), law school classes, model rules, and an ever-expanding literature addressing ADR's progress and challenges.

But questions are also now being raised about the wisdom of promoting widespread skepticism about adjudication. In the 1990s, Bryant Garth warned that the expansion of a private market for adjudication would put publicly funded judges at risk of losing "good" cases, described as those with interesting issues articulated by well-resourced litigants.[57] A few judges at both trial and appellate levels have started speaking out about the harm to the public sector from the antitrial movement. For example, William Young, Chief Judge of the U.S. District Court for the District of Massachusetts, warned that "for the first time in our history, business has a good chance of opting out of the legal system altogether."[58] Many academics have raised questions about the limitations on court access,[59] and in 2003, the Litigation Section of the American Bar Association funded a project called The Vanishing Trial to gather data on and assess the impact of declining trial rates.[60] The fact of decline has also proved a problem for judiciaries, trying to fend off fiscal cutbacks.[61]

Both state and federal judicial systems gained prominence over the last century because of legislative commitments, embodied in resources and statutory power, that endowed courts with the authority to hear hundreds of new kinds of claims of right. Further, the great edifice of "The Federal Courts" became an increasingly important aspect of the American polity over the course of the twentieth century because the congressional commitment of resources and obligations enabled the judiciary to expound on and expand access to rights. Over decades during the twentieth century, the American Bar Association, the American Law Institute, and the American Association of Law Schools (all elite institutions of the bench and bar) repeatedly undertook efforts that made federal lawmaking through courts both central and prestigious. Yet, the utility and the importance of this enterprise become questionable in a world in which Contract Procedure provides so many means to opt out of courts.

If one emerging line of critique about Contract Procedure comes from those vested in the continued flourishing of institutions that both brought forth and depend on Due Process Procedure, another set of criticisms stems from concerns that alternative dispute resolution can exacerbate problems of inequality among disputants. Resource disparities haunt all dispute resolution systems, for they raise the prospect that procedural systems could systematically benefit particular groups.[62] Beginning in the 1960s, many segments of the legal community took on these problems as they developed new laws about civil, criminal, and administrative litigation. The Supreme Court insisted that, as a matter of constitutional law, criminal defendants have rights to counsel and access to some investigatory services. But in more recent decades, the Court has been reluctant to enforce that mandate when faced with challenges to convictions based on poor lawyering.[63] On the civil side, with narrow exceptions,[64] the Court has left the problem of equipage of litigants to Congress. The federal legislature responded in 1974 with the creation of the Legal Services Corporation, designed to provide some civil services to the very poor and, as noted, with the enactment of some fee-shifting statutes and other mechanisms to permit groups of litigants to share the costs of litigation.

The rise of Contract Procedure has offered judges new opportunities that could—if judges wanted—be used to intervene on behalf of disputants less well equipped to bargain than their opponents. Indeed, in the 1950s, when the Supreme Court refused to enforce a clause mandating that a securities customer go to arbitration in lieu of the federal courts, one of its reasons was that the inequality of bargaining between customer and service provider undermined the fairness of the bargain made.[65] In contrast, since the 1980s the Supreme Court has repeatedly permitted enforcement of such predispute resolution clauses, even when those provisions appeared on forms proffered by service providers to consumers and by employers to employees. Emblematic of this approach is a 2001 case, *Circuit City Stores v. Adams*, involving an employee who alleged that a major store chain had discriminated against him in violation of state law. Nevertheless, the Supreme Court held that as long as the contractually mandated alternative dispute resolution process provides an adequate means to vindicate statutory rights (be they state or federal), contracts to arbitrate are to be enforced.[66]

Another body of doctrine, also tolerant of bargaining inequality, stems from a 1991 decision, *Carnival Cruise Lines, Inc. v. Shute*. There, the Supreme Court upheld a forum selection clause that sent two passengers from Washington State, alleging negligence against a cruise line, to litigate the dispute in Florida. The ticket that they had purchased included ("at its lower left-hand corner") a statement that its acceptance obliged passengers to agree to litigate claims in Florida.[67] While the Court reserved some modicum of "judicial scrutiny for fundamental fairness," the case before it—with unequally situated contracting parties, no evidence of any bargaining, and the provision of the forum clause only upon receipt of a purchased ticket—did not persuade the majority, who argued the utility of organizing and centralizing litigation.[68] What *Carnival Cruise* and *Circuit City* teach is that many judges are willing to rely on the concept of consent even when they know that individuals either do not really know that they have waived their rights or give consent under conditions of profound inequality.[69]

Yet a few lower court judges and some state courts have begun to question the adequacy of alternative dispute resolution programs and the validity of predispute arbitration clauses in contracts. Under the U.S. Supreme Court's current rules, an alternative dispute resolution system must permit a "prospective litigant" the opportunity to "effectively . . . vindicate [his or her] statutory cause of action."[70] Further, although the Court has imposed the burden of the showing of inadequacy on the party opposing arbitration, the Court has commented that "the existence of large arbitration costs could preclude a litigant" without resources from "effectively vindicating . . . federal statutory rights in the arbitral forum."[71] Some judges have relied on these parameters to stay arbitrations in order to permit discovery about how the costs of arbitration are allocated between the parties. A few judges have concluded that, when the costs of an alternative exceed what a disputant would have had to pay to proceed in court, that alternative is legally insufficient and a predispute contractual clause to use it is unenforceable. And some judges have also concluded that particular provisions on arbitration failed to provide clear notice or were unconscionable because they included specific terms favorable to the party drafting the agreement.[72]

Further, not all in Congress have been comfortable with the judiciary's embrace of mandatory arbitration. As Supreme Court decisions enforcing predispute arbitration clauses mounted in number and expanded in scope and as such clauses were placed on forms used for job applications and contracts for a range of consumer goods such as cell phones and credit cards,[73] members of Congress proposed legislation "to prevent the involuntary application of arbitration to claims" arising out of certain federal statutes (such as those dealing with discrimination based on sex, race, age, or disability) or for certain kinds of contracts (such as those involving consumer credit).[74] These bills address the problem of contracts of adhesion—proffered by one party without the other having a real opportunity to alter terms. The proposals generally make unenforceable the waiver of various litigation rights, including rights to obtain discovery of evidence in the possession of one's adversary, to aggregate claims through class actions, to jury trials, and to independent judges employed and paid by the state. Under these proposals, only waivers made after a specific conflict has arisen would be enforceable. Were these bills enacted, accession to postdispute arbitration would become a bargaining chip, perhaps facilitating some settlements once disputes arise.[75]

In general, these proposed pieces of legislation, aimed at protecting consumers and employees, have not become law. Yet one bill has, giving a set of unequal but otherwise better-situated disputants—franchisers buying cars from automobile manufacturers and then selling the cars to the public—a statutory exemption from the Federal Arbitration Act.[76] In a rider to an appropriations bill passed in 2002, Congress enacted a version of what had been called the Motor Vehicle Franchise Contract Arbitration Fairness Act.[77] This legislation makes unenforceable contractual arbitration clauses between car dealers and manufacturers unless consented to in writing after a controversy has arisen. Further, if arbitration is used, the arbitrator must "provide the parties to such contract with a written explanation for the factual and legal basis of the award."[78]

Car dealers can thus use courts to enforce their rights under state and federal laws, including specific provisions enacted in the 1950s aimed at controlling predatory practices by large commercial interests.[79] But, while most of the rationales supporting enactment of this legislation seem applicable to the bills proposed to protect many others (including the customers who buy cars from those automobile dealers), Congress has, thus far, acted only to protect one small subset.[80]

A third and related set of concerns casting shadows on Contract Procedure centers on the lack of transparency of ADR processes, whether conducted in or outside courts. For example, when using ADR programs, information generated may be protected from subsequent disclosure on the theory that a free exchange is more likely to lead to resolution; were statements admissible thereafter in litigation, parties would be unwilling to discuss relevant questions. Many states have created privileges for mediation; federal laws providing for mediation have a similar feature.[81] While protection of confidentiality stems from a desire to facilitate such frank exchanges in the hopes of resolving disputes, litigants can also try to use ADR rules strategically in an effort to prevent their opponents from obtaining otherwise discoverable facts. A few courts have concluded that statutes protecting against the disclosure of materials submitted during mediation do indeed create an immunity from production for documents.[82]

In addition to such legal rules limiting access, parties can also agree to confidentiality—either during the pendency of a dispute or at its conclusion. The resultant silence prevents others from learning about underlying patterns of wrongdoing or about how much compensation has been provided to victims. Some claims payment facilities created through mass tort settlements have also imposed confidentiality requirements.[83] Further, under current practices, privately created dispute resolution systems do not routinely publish public reports detailing the claims made or the dispositions provided.

Move then inside courts. If a litigation system is focused around trials, information is produced in front of third parties who have constitutional and common law rights of access to watch those proceedings.[84] When appellate courts hear oral argument and publish written decisions explaining their actions, public information is also disseminated. However, as the locus of activity has shifted from trials in courtrooms to pretrial settlement practices at both trial and appellate levels and as judges have stopped publishing all their decisions or have marked some of them "not for citation," public access to and use of information generated in courts has been constrained.[85]

Yet another issue is third-party access to materials that parties file in courts. In general, a presumption of public access, anchored in the First Amendment and in the Due Process Clause and coupled with common law rights, has persuaded judges to require that once documents are filed with a court, third parties can obtain them.[86] Further, given the constitutional and common law traditions of open court processes, the sealing of documents is not supposed to be routine. But a less exacting standard is applied for documents produced through discovery; documents can be sealed "for good cause."[87]

Even a presumption that court files are accessible does not, however, guarantee public knowledge. The question is what materials are filed with courts. Amendments in 2000 to Rule 5 of the Federal Rules of Civil Procedure provided that parties do not have to file in court what they exchange in discovery.[88] Unless such documents are appended to motions presented to judges, the information is unlikely to be placed in courthouse files. Moreover, parties may conclude agreements by dismissals and, in separate contracts that are neither filed with courts nor referenced in notices of dismissal, they may agree to terms that other people cannot readily find. They may also agree (in what are routinely called "confidentiality clauses") to refuse disclosure of the terms to others.

From reported disputes about settlement agreements and from proposals to amend ethics rules to prevent disputants from "burying" discovery or preventing lawyers from taking other clients with the same problems, we know that parties sometimes negotiate to limit others' access to information about particular settlements. Further, parties sometimes make agreements to keep hidden either data or expert witnesses who could substantiate wrongful actions.[89] The very secrecy of these agreements makes it difficult to know their typical content. One can assume, however, their widespread use from the frequency with which lawyers, judges, and judicial decisions mention the existence of "confidential settlement agreements." And thus far, most courts have not insisted on disclosure. As the

Second Circuit recently explained, "honoring the parties' express wish for confidentiality may facilitate settlement."[90]

But public protests have begun, often focused on "secret settlements" in cases involving sexual abuse of children by priests, exposure to toxic wastes, and injuries from design defects,[91] all instances in which hidden information might inform others about the existence of "substantial danger to the public health or safety."[92] In 1990, Florida created a statute—aptly named a "Sunshine in Litigation Act"[93]—that now is paralleled, with many variations, in some two dozen jurisdictions. Under such state statutes and rules of court, parties' confidentiality agreements may be overridden by laws requiring that professionals or insurance companies disclose settlements made for certain kinds of claims (such as those involving medical malpractice and settled for more than a fixed amount).[94] As for the federal system, comparable legislation has been proposed but has not been enacted.[95] A few districts have by local rule begun to take on "court secrecy."[96] For example, the District of South Carolina prohibits sealing of settlements filed in court,[97] while the Eastern District of Michigan limits the duration of time for which a document remains sealed.[98] Moreover, on occasion judges have ordered disclosure of an agreement when another litigant can show a specific need.

As these critiques of Contract Procedure emerge, they demonstrate the limits of bargaining as a response to conflict. Distress about certain terms in bargains has prompted some constraints, working at the margins and coming from provisions such as the federal statute sheltering automobile dealers from obligations to arbitrate and state statutes imposing disclosure requirements on certain kinds of professionals. In contrast to these legislative interventions, judges have generally treated settlements of conflicts as ordinary contracts and assumed the applicability of doctrines created when parties negotiated their own agreements without judicial pressures to accommodate. While judges have become a leading source of the growing obligation to bargain, they have not often reflected on what rules of law ought to be crafted especially for Contract Procedure, nor have judges offered means to improve the ability of litigants to bargain or insisted on transparency for the bargains reached.

Thus, the shift from Due Process to Contract Procedure raises new legal questions—ranging from whether disputants should be able, by contract, to alter the jurisdictional authority of courts (for example, to give more power to review arbitral awards than does federal law) to disputants' capacity to control the dissemination of information to third parties. Regulatory questions about the role of government are also posed in the wake of the recent reconfiguration of judicial power, empowering judges to promote a regime of bargained-for civil judgments. Needed now are norms about how managerial and settling judges are to behave. To conclude, I outline a few premises that I hope will inform the lawmaking to come.

First, rather than the current presumption that legal rules shaped for ordinary contracts ought to apply, judges and legislatures must develop doctrines and procedures that address how contracts crafted at the behest of judges are distinct kinds of agreements, worthy of special concern. Just as statutes, rules, and common law have mandated judicial oversight of settlements for class actions, for criminal plea bargains, for certain kinds of statutory claims, and for cases involving minors, lawmaking is needed to articulate how much judges ought to participate in bargaining, when judicial promotion of settlement becomes coercive, and whether judges who are involved in settlement agreements may subsequently participate in approving or enforcing the bargains made.

Second, lawmakers need to insist on the public dimension of government-based processing by mandating that records be made of judicial bargaining activities and by reimposing the presumption of public access to processes and outcomes generated through courts. If courts devolve their work to other institutions, the presumption of public access should flow with that devolution.

Third, turning to the problems of inequality of resources, the problem of unfairness should not to be hidden under the veneer of consent. Car dealers ought not to be the only litigants benefiting from concerns about form contracts precluding access to public processes. Rather, courts or legislatures ought to refuse enforcement of bargains about adjudication and its alternatives unless those agreements can be shaped by all parties to the contracts. In short, as Contract Procedure supplements and sometimes supplants Due Process Procedure, the rules of bargaining for state-enforced and binding judgments must identify what role judges are to take in shaping agreements and what bargains law cannot abide.

NOTES

1. All rights reserved. This chapter is closely related to the article, *Procedure as Contract*, 80 NOTRE DAME L. REV. 593 (2005), and builds as well on other aspects of my work, cited herein. Thanks are due to Paul Carrington for his suggestions as

well as for his lifelong devotion to the processes of justice; to Denny Curtis, Deborah Hensler, Lee Rosenthal, Jean Sternlight, and Peter Schuck for thoughtful exchanges on these topics; and to Johanna Kalb and Jennifer Peresie for able and generous research assistance.

2. *See* Robert H. Mnookin & Lewis Kornhauser, *Bargaining in the Shadow of the Law: The Case of Divorce*, 88 YALE L.J. 950, 950 (1979).

3. Lon L. Fuller, *The Forms and Limits of Adjudication*, 92 HARV. L. REV. 353, 363 (1978).

4. For further discussion, see Judith Resnik, *Procedure as Contract*, 80 NOTRE DAME L. REV. 593 (2005); Judith Resnik, *Trial as Error, Jurisdiction as Injury: Transforming the Meaning of Article III*, 113 HARV. L. REV. 924 (2000).

5. *See* Act of Sept. 14, 1922, ch. 306, Pub. L. No. 67-298, 42 Stat. 837.

6. *See* Rules Enabling Act, Pub. L. No. 73-415, 48 Stat. 1064 (1934) (codified as amended at 28 U.S.C. § 2072 (2000)).

7. Congress had given the Supreme Court the power to make rules, and the Court in turn appointed a committee of lawyers and law professors who did the drafting. *See* Appointment of Committee to Draft Unified System of Equity and Law Rules, 295 U.S. 774 (1935).

8. *See* FED. R. CIV. P. 12(b); FED. R. CIV. P. 56(d).

9. For more discussion, see Judith Resnik, *For Owen M. Fiss: Some Reflections on the Triumph and Death of Adjudication*, 58 U. MIAMI L. REV. 173 (2004).

10. *See generally* Judith Resnik, *Money Matters: Judicial Market Interventions Creating Subsidies and Awarding Fees and Costs in Individual and Aggregate Litigation*, 148 U. PA. L. REV. 2119 (2000).

11. *See* FED. R. CIV. P. 23 (1966); Multidistrict Litigation Act, Pub. L. No. 90-296, 82 Stat. 109 (1968) (codified as amended at 28 U.S.C. § 1407 (2000); *see generally* Judith Resnik, *From "Cases" to "Litigation,"* 54 LAW & CONTEMP. PROBS. 5 (1991).

12. *See* Marc Galanter, *The Vanishing Trial: An Examination of Trials and Related Matters in Federal and State Courts*, 1 J. EMPIRICAL LEGAL STUD. 459, 501, 505, and fig. 31 (2004). The amounts quoted in the text are in 1996 dollars.

13. *See* Judith Resnik, *"Uncle Sam Modernizes His Justice": Inventing the Federal District Courts of the Twentieth Century for the District of Columbia and the Nation*, 90 GEO. L.J. 607, 614–15 (2002).

14. *See*, e.g., Charles E. Clark, *The Role of the Supreme Court in Federal Rule-Making*, 46 J. AM. JUDICATURE SOC'Y 250, 254 (1963).

15. *See generally* ROBERT KAGAN, ADVERSARIAL LEGALISM: THE AMERICAN WAY OF LAW (2001). For analysis of how economic inequality diminishes the capacity of adversarial systems to produce results viewed as legitimate, see Judith Resnik, *Failing Faith: Adjudicatory Procedure in Decline*, 53 U. CHI. L. REV. 494 (1986).

16. *See* Carrie Menkel-Meadow, *From Legal Disputes to Conflict Resolution and Human Problem Solving: Legal Dispute Resolution in a Multidisciplinary Context*, 54 J. LEGAL EDUC. 7 (2004).

17. *See* Judith Resnik, *Managerial Judges*, 96 HARV. L. REV. 374 (1982).

18. *See* FED. R. CIV. P. 11(c)(2)(B); *see also* Advisory Committee Notes to the 1993 amendments to FED. R. CIV. P. 11.

19. The 1938 version, "Class Actions," prohibited dismissal or compromise without court approval. FED. R. CIV. P. 23(c), 1938 Federal Rules, 398 U.S. at 690. The 2004 Rule has a subsection entitled "Settlement, Voluntary Dismissal, or Compromise," and under that subsection, the process of settlement for class actions is detailed to some extent, with more discussion in the Advisory Committee Notes. *See* FED. R. CIV. P. 23(e).

20. The word settlement was first used in the context of Rule 26 in the 1970 Advisory Committee notes to amendments promulgated at that time. *See* Advisory Committee Notes to the 1970 amendments to Fed. R. Civ. P. 26 (noting that "discovery frequently provides evidence that would not otherwise be available to the parties and thereby makes for a fairer trial or settlement. On the other hand, no positive evidence is found that discovery promotes settlement."). In 1993, Rule 26 was again amended to provide that the parties must "confer to consider . . . the possibilities for a prompt settlement or resolution of the case . . ." FED. R. CIV. P. 26(f) (1993).

21. FED. R. CIV. P. 16, 1938 Federal Rules, 308 U.S. at 684 (1939).

22. The details are provided in Resnik, *"Uncle Sam Modernizes His Justice,"* *supra* note 13, at 651–55.

23. *See* FED. R. CIV. P. 16 (b) (1983); Robert F. Peckham, *The Federal Judges as a Case Manager: The New Role in Guiding a Case from Filing to Disposition*, 69 CAL. L. REV. 770 (1981).

24. FED. R. CIV. P. 16(c)(16) (1993).

25. FED. R. CIV. P. 16(c)(9).

26. Advisory Committee Notes to Paragraph 16(c)(9), FED. R. CIV. P. (1993).

27. Advisory Committee Notes to FED. R. CIV. P. 16(c)(7) (1983).

28. *See generally* Jeffrey A. Parness & Lance C. Cagle, *Guiding Civil Case Settlement Conferences and Their Aftermath: The Need to Amend Illinois Supreme Court Rule 218*, 35 LOY. U. CHI. L.J. 779 (2004).

29. *See* Advisory Committee Notes to FED. R. CIV. P. 16(b)(9) (1993).

30. *See* Steve Lohr, *U.S. vs. Microsoft: The Negotiations*, N.Y. TIMES, Apr. 4, 2000, at C1; Richard Posner, Mediation: Address for the Frank E. A. Sander Lecture given before the American Bar Association, Section on Dispute Resolution (July 8, 2000) (manuscript on file with author).

31. *See, e.g., In re* Atlantic Pipe Corp., 304 F.3d 135, 138 (1st Cir. 2002) (holding that a district court may order "an unwilling party to participate in, and share the costs of, non-binding mediation"); *In re* Novak, 932 F.2d 1397, 1407 (11th Cir. 1991) (concluding that courts have inherent authority to "direct parties to produce individuals with full settlement authority at pretrial settlement conferences"). The *Novak* court, however, reminded lower court judges that they lack the power to

compel parties to settle. *Id.* at 1405 (citing Kothe v. Smith, 771 F. 2d 667 (2d Cir. 1985)).

32. *See, e.g.,* Alternative Dispute Resolution Act of 1998, Pub. L. No. 105-315, 112 Stat. 2993 (codified at 28 U.S.C. §§ 651–58 (2000)).

33. *See* Administrative Dispute Resolution Act, Pub. L. No. 101-552, § 3(b)(1), 106 Stat. 944 (1990); Administrative Procedure Technical Amendments Act of 1991, Pub. L. No. 102-354, § 3(b)(1), 106 Stat. 944 (1992) (codified at 5 U.S.C. §§ 571–84 (2000)); *see also* JEFFREY M. SENGER, FEDERAL DISPUTE RESOLUTION: USING ADR WITH THE UNITED STATES GOVERNMENT 2 (2004) (citing examples of the government's growing reliance on ADR).

34. *See* Rules Governing Section 2254 Cases in the United States District Courts (eff. Feb. 1, 1977, Pub. L. 94-426, § 1, Sept. 28, 1976, 90 Stat. 1334, and as amended thereafter); Rules Governing Section 2255 Proceedings for the United States District Courts (eff. Feb. 1, 1977, Act of Sept. 28, 1976, Pub. L. 94-426, § 1, 90 Stat. 1334, and as amended thereafter), in 28 U.S.C. app (2000); The Prison Litigation Reform Act of 1995, Pub. L. No. 104-134, §§ 801–10 (codified at various parts of titles 18, 28, and 42, including 18 U.S.C. §§ 3634, 3636, and 42 U.S.C. §§ 1997-1997h (2000) and discussed in Margo Schlanger, *Inmate Litigation*, 116 HARV. L. REV. 1555 (2003)).

35. *See* FED. R. CIV. P. 23, as amended in 2003; Private Securities Litigation Reform Act of 1995, Pub. L. 104-67 109 Stat. 737 (codified as amended by the Securities Litigation Uniform Standards Act of 1998 at 15 U.S.C. § 77z-1, § 78a (2000).

36. *See* Class Action Fairness Act of 2005, Pub. L. No. 109-2. This bill, enacted by the 109th Congress was signed in February 2005, and gives federal courts jurisdiction over "any civil action in which the matter in controversy exceeds the sum or value of $5,000,000, exclusive of interest and costs," and is a class action in which the parties are generally of diverse citizenship. Section 4(a)(2), to be codified at 28 U.S.C. § 1332(d)(2).

37. Hubert L. Will, *Judicial Responsibility for the Disposition of Litigation, in Proceedings of the Seminar for Newly Appointed United States District Judges*, 75 F.R.D. 203, 203 (1976).

38. *See* Stephen C. Yeazell, *The Misunderstood Consequences of Modern Civil Process*, 1994 WIS. L. REV. 631.

39. *See* FED. R. APP. P. 33 (described as "entirely rewritten" in the early 1990s by the Advisory Committee Notes to the 1994 amendment).

40. *See, e.g.,* 1ST CIR. R. APP. P. 33(b)(1), and appendix (2004).

41. *See* Pub. L. No. 68-401, 43 Stat. 883 (1925) (codified at 9 U.S.C. §§ 1–14 (2000)). As first enacted, it was called the "U.S. Arbitration Act," but it is now commonly referred to as the Federal Arbitration Act.

42. *See, e.g.,* Wilko v. Swan, 346 U.S. 427 (1953). *See generally* Judith Resnik, *Many Doors? Closing Doors? Alternative Dispute Resolution and Adjudication*, 10 OHIO ST. J. ON DISP. RESOL. 211 (1995).

43. *See* Dean Witter Reynolds, Inc. v. Byrd, 470 U.S. 213 (1985); Mitsubishi

Motors Corp. v. Soler Chrysler-Plymouth, Inc., 473 U.S. 614 (1985) (both upholding *ex ante* arbitration agreements as sufficient despite claims of violation of federal securities and antitrust rights); *see also* Gilmer v. Interstate/Johnson Lane
Corp., 500 U.S. 20 (1991); Circuit City Stores, Inc. v. Adams, 532 U.S. 105 (2001). *See
generally* Paul D. Carrington & Paul H. Haagan, *Contract and Jurisdiction*, 1996
SUP. CT. REV. 331.

44. *See generally* Jeffrey W. Stempel, *Arbitration, Unconscionability, and Equilibrium: The Return of Unconscionability Analysis as a Counterweight to Arbitration
Formalism*, 19 OHIO ST. J. ON DISP. RESOL. 757 (2004); Richard C. Reuben, *Mandatory Arbitration: Democracy and Dispute Resolution*, 67 LAW & CONTEMP. PROBS.
279 (2004); Elizabeth G. Thornburg, *Contracting with Tortfeasors: Mandatory Arbitration Clauses and Personal Injury Claims*, 67 LAW & CONTEMP. PROBS. 253 (2004).

45. *Cf.* Owen M. Fiss, *The Social and Political Foundations of Adjudication*, 6
LAW AND HUM. BEHAV. 121 (1982).

46. Fuller, *supra* note 3, at 364.

47. *See* Theodore Eisenberg & Stephen C. Yeazell, *The Ordinary and the Extra-
ordinary in Institutional Litigation*, 93 HARV. L. REV. 465 (1980); Judith Resnik, *The
Rights of Remedies: Collective Accountings for and Insuring Against the Harms of
Sexual Harassment, in* DIRECTIONS IN SEXUAL HARASSMENT LAW 247 (Catharine
A. MacKinnon & Reva B. Siegel eds., 2003); Anna-Maria Marshall, *Injustice
Frames, Legality, and the Everyday Construction of Sexual Harassment*, 28 LAW &
SOC. INQUIRY 659 (2003).

48. *See* Marc Galanter, *Why the "Haves" Come Out Ahead: Speculations on the
Limits of Legal Change*, 9 LAW & SOC'Y REV. 95, 100 (1974).

49. *See* HERMAN SCHWARTZ, RIGHT WING JUSTICE: THE CONSERVATIVE CAM-
PAIGN TO TAKE OVER THE COURTS (2004); Dawn E. Johnsen, *Ronald Reagan and
the Rehnquist Court on Congressional Power: Presidential Influences on Constitutional Change*, 78 IND. L.J. 363 (2003).

50. *See* Resnik, *Trial as Error, supra* note 4.

51. Yeazell, *The Misunderstood Consequences of Modern Civil Process, supra* note
38, at 633.

52. Galanter, *Vanishing Trial, supra* note 12, at 460–65; Table C-4 U.S. District
Courts, Federal Judicial Caseload Statistics (March 31, 2002).

53. For example, President George W. Bush opened a conference on economic
issues by commenting that the "cost of lawsuits, relative to countries that we compete against, are high . . . [making] it more difficult for us," and that a "cornerstone
of any good program is legal reform" and specifically "meaningful liability reform
on asbestos, on class action and medical liability." *See President Discusses Lawsuit Abuse at White House Economy Conference*, Dec. 14, 2004, *available at* http://
www.whitehouse.gov/news/releases/2004/12/print/20041215-11html; *see also President Bush's Acceptance Speech to the Republican National Convention*, Sept. 2, 2004,
available at http://www.washingtonpost.com/wpdyn/articles/A57466-2004Sep2.htm

(expressing desire to protect "small-business owners and workers from the explosion of frivolous lawsuits that threaten jobs across our country").

54. *See generally* Jennifer H. Arlen, *Compensation Systems and Efficient Deterrence*, 52 Md. L. Rev. 1093 (1993).

55. *See* Marc Galanter, *An Oil Strike in Hell: Contemporary Legends about the Civil Justice System*, 40 Ariz. L. Rev. 717 (1998) (detailing various reports by the media misstating plaintiffs' problems and victories).

56. *See, e.g.*, Alexander v. Sandoval, 532 U.S. 275 (2001), Corr. Servs. v. Malesko, 534 U.S. 61 (2001); Buckhannon Bd. & Care Home v. W. Va. Dep't Health & Human Res., 532 U.S. 598 (2001); Fla. Bar v. Went For It, Inc., 515 U.S. 618 (1995). *See generally* Judith Resnik, *Constricting Remedies: The Rehnquist Judiciary, Congress, and Federal Power*, 78 Ind. L.J. 223 (2003).

57. *See* Bryant Garth, *From Civil Litigation to Private Justice: Legal Practice at War with the Profession and its Values*, 59 Brooklyn L. Rev. 931 (1993).

58. William G. Young, *An Open Letter to U.S. District Judges*, 50 Fed. Law. 30 (2003); *see also* Patrick E. Higginbotham, *Judge Robert A. Ainsworth, Jr. Memorial Lecture, Loyola University: So Why Do We Call Them Trial Courts?* 55 SMU L. Rev. 1405, 1409–13 (2002) (voicing concern about declining trial rates).

59. *See, e.g.*, Jean R. Sternlight, *The Rise and Spread of Mandatory Arbitration as a Substitute for the Jury Trial*, 38 U.S.F. L. Rev. 17 (2003).

60. *See* Galanter, *Vanishing Trial, supra* note 12; Judith Resnik, *Migrating, Morphing, and Vanishing: The Empirical and Normative Puzzles of Declining Trial Rates in Courts*, 1 J. Empirical Legal Stud. 783 (2004).

61. *See* Administrative Office of the U.S. Courts, 2002 Judicial Business of the United States Courts: Annual Report of the Director 23–24 (2003); Marcia Coyle, *This Time, Wolves at Justice's Door*, Nat'l L.J., Nov. 1, 2004, at S1; *FY 2004 Appropriations Finally Ok'd: But Courts Still Face Fiscal Threat*, 35 Third Branch 1 (Feb. 2004).

62. *See* Carrie Menkel-Meadow, *Do the "Haves" Come Out Ahead in Alternative Dispute Resolution Systems? Repeat Players in ADR*, 15 Ohio St. J. on Disp. Resol. 19 (1999).

63. *See, e.g.*, Dretke v. Haley, 541 U.S. 386 (2004); Wiggins v. Smith, 539 U.S. 510 (2003); Strickland v. Washington, 466 U.S. 668 (1984).

64. *See, e.g.*, Lassiter v. Dep't of Soc. Servs. of N.C., 452 U.S. 18 (1981); M.L.B. v. S.L.J., 519 U.S. 102 (1996).

65. *See* Wilko v. Swan, 346 U.S. 427, 435 (1953).

66. Circuit City Stores, Inc. v. Adams, 532 U.S. 105 (2001).

67. Carnival Cruise Lines, Inc. v. Shute, 499 U.S. 585, 587 (1991).

68. *Id.* at 595.

69. Decisions on the criminal side also acknowledge that prosecutors have "no shortage of in terrorem tools." *See* Blakely v. Washington, 124 S. Ct. 2531, 2542 (2004).

70. Gilmer v. Interstate/Johnson Lane Corp., 500 U.S. 20, 28 (1991) (quotation omitted).

71. Green Tree Fin. Corp. v. Randolph, 531 U.S. 79, 90 (2000). The Court has also concluded that interpretation of contracts to arbitrate—including whether aggregation of claims is permissible—generally is to be decided in the first instance by an arbitrator. *See* Green Tree Fin. Corp. v Bazzle, 539 U.S. 444 (2003).

72. *See, e.g.*, Circuit City Stores, Inc. v. Adams, 279 F.3d 889 (9th Cir. 2002); Penn v. Ryan's Family Steak Houses, Inc., 269 F.3d 753 (7th Cir. 2001); Armendariz v. Found. Health Psychcare Servs., Inc., 6 P.3d 669 (Cal. 2000).

73. *See, e.g.*, EEOC v. Waffle House, Inc., 534 U.S. 279 (2002). *See generally* Linda J. Demaine and Deborah R. Hensler, *"Volunteering" to Arbitrate through Predispute Arbitration Clauses: The Average Consumer's Experience*, 67 LAW & CONTEMP. PROBS. 55 (2004).

74. *See* Civil Rights Procedures Protection Act of 2001, H.R. 1489 (107th Cong. 1st Sess. 2001); Consumer Credit Fair Dispute Resolution Act of 2001, S. 192, 107th Cong., 1st Sess. (2001). Since 1994, Senator Feingold has proposed legislation addressing this issue. *See* Russell D. Feingold, *Mandatory Arbitration: What Process Is Due?* 39 HARV. J. ON LEGIS. 281, 292 (2002). Similarly, parallel protections have been proposed, and sometimes enacted, in states. However, these statutes are sometimes challenged as inconsistent with federal law. *See, e.g.*, Am. Fin. Servs. Ass'n v. Burke, 169 F. Supp. 2d 62 (D. Conn. 2001) (concluding that a Connecticut provision limiting the use of mandatory arbitration clauses in its Abusive Home Loan Lending Practices Act was preempted by federal law).

75. *See Motor Vehicle Franchise Contract Arbitration Fairness Act Report*, S. REP. No. 107-266 (2002); *Overview of Contractual Mandatory Binding Arbitration, Hearing before the Subcommittee on Administrative Oversight and the Courts of the Committee on the Judiciary*, U.S. Senate, 106th Cong., 2d Sess., Mar. 1, 2000.

76. According to Senator Feingold, by 2000 about 5,700 automobile dealers had contracts that mandated arbitration. *See* Feingold, *supra* note 74, at 293.

77. *See* 21st Century Department of Justice Appropriations Authorization Act, Pub. L. No. 107-273, 116 Stat. 1758 (including a provision, § 11028, labeled the "Motor Vehicle Franchise Contract Dispute Resolution Process," to be codified at 15 U.S.C. § 1226 (West Supp. 2004)).

78. *Id.* at § 11028 (a)(3).

79. See Automobile Dealers' Day in Court Act, 15 U.S.C. § 1221 et seq.; Paul D. Carrington, *Perspectives on Dispute Resolution in the Twenty-First Century; Self-Deregulation, the "National Polity" of the Supreme Court*, 3 NEV. L. J. 259, 266–69 (2002/2003).

80. Senator Grassley has proposed the Fair Contracts for Growers Act of 2003, S. 91, 108th Cong. 1st Sess. (Jan. 7, 2003), that would give livestock and poultry growers the protections accorded to automobile dealers. As he explained, it would "give farmers a choice of venues to resolve disputes" and "ensure that the decision

to arbitrate is truly voluntary." 149 Cong. Rec. S75 (daily ed. Jan. 7, 2003); *see also* Agriculture, Conservation, and Rural Enhancement Act of 2001, 147 Cong. Rec. S13,089-92 (daily ed. Dec. 13, 2001) (statement of Senator Grassley).

81. *See* 5 U.S.C. § 574 (2000); 28 U.S.C. § 652(d) (2000). *Compare* FDIC v. White, 76 F. Supp. 2d 736 (N.D. Tex. 1999) (concluding that this section does not prevent use of evidence disclosed at mediation to challenge a settlement agreement).

82. *See, e.g.*, Rojas v. Superior Court, 93 P.3d 260, 270–71 (Cal. 2004).

83. For example, the Dalkon Shield litigation concluded with a trust authorized to make payments to claimants. When it entered into individual agreements with claimaints, the Trust did not make public the amounts paid to individuals, so only those claimants represented by lawyers who appeared repeatedly could have gained a sense through informal networks about how the Trust was valuing various kinds of injuries.

84. *See generally* Judith Resnik, *Due Process: A Public Dimension*, 39 U. FLA. L. REV. 405 (1987).

85. This practice is under review. *See Appellate Rule Revision Postponed*, 72 U.S.L.W. 2767 (June 22, 2004) (describing a plan to study whether the Federal Rules of Appellate Procedure ought to prohibit the provision of opinions denominated "not for citation.").

86. *See* Jessup v. Luther, 277 F.3d 926 (7th Cir. 2002); Herrnreiter v. Chi. Housing Auth., 281 F.3d 634 (7th Cir. 2002); Enprotech Corp. v. Renda, 983 F.2d 17 (3d Cir. 1993); Bank of Am. Nat'l Trust & Sav. Ass'n. v. Hotel Rittenhouse Assocs., 800 F.2d 339 (3d Cir. 1986).

87. *See generally* Arthur R. Miller, *Confidentiality, Protective Orders and Public Access to Courts*, 105 HARV. L. REV. 427 (1991); Richard L. Marcus, *The Discovery Confidentiality Controversy*, 1991 U. ILL. L. REV. 457.

88. *See* FED. R. CIV. P. 5(d) (amended in 2000).

89. *See, e.g.*, Baker v. Gen. Motors, 522 U.S. 22 (1997) (discussing a Michigan injunction, entered in the course of a settlement that provided that the former employee could not in general testify without the written prior consent of his employer, General Motors); Kate Kelly & Colleen Debaise, *Morgan Stanley Settles Bias Suit for $54 Million*, WALL ST. J., July 13, 2004, at A1 (describing agreement that prevented dissemination of data on hiring practices).

90. *See, e.g.*, Gambale v. Deutsche Bank AG, 377 F.3d 133, 143–44 (2d Cir. 2004).

91. *See* Joseph F. Anderson, Jr., *Hidden from the Public by Order of the Court: The Case against Government-Enforced Secrecy*, 55 S.C. L. REV. 711 (2004).

92. This phrase can be found in some legislation and has been proffered by one commentator urging that ethical rules prevent lawyers from entering into such bargains. *See* Richard A. Zitrin, "Written Testimony to the American Bar Association's Center for Professional Responsibility" (Oct. 5, 2001), *available at* http://www.abanet.org/cpr/zitrin.html.

93. *See* Fla. Stat. Ann. § 69.081 (West 2004).

94. *See, e.g.*, Conn. Gen. Stat. § 19a-17a (2003) (requiring disclosure for certain medical malpractice claims). Efforts to block New Jersey's statute providing for public disclosure of the dates and amounts of malpractice judgments were recently refused in *Medical Society of New Jersey v. Mottola*, 320 F. Supp. 2d 254 (D.N.J. 2004).

95. *See* Sunshine in Litigation Act of 2003, S. 817, 108th Cong. (2003).

96. *See generally* Symposium, *Court-Enforced Secrecy*, 55 S.C. L. REV. 711–905 (2004).

97. *See* D. S.C. L. R. 5.03(E) (2004).

98. *See* E.D. MICH. L.R. 5.4. (2003).

5

Skybox Lawyering

Marc Galanter

I. The Arrival of the Big Firm

The multiplication and flourishing of corporations as engines of economic growth in the late nineteenth century transformed the American legal profession.[1] A new kind of law firm was invented, an integrated, durable, and hierarchical organization rather than a loose and often transient collection of lawyers. At the core of these firms was a device that proved successful in coordinating senior and junior lawyers as they provided complex and continuous legal services to growing businesses. This device, later named the promotion-to-partnership tournament (PPT), entailed the hiring of highly qualified but inexperienced young lawyers who worked for the firm's clients (not their own) under the supervision of seniors. The PPT held out the promise of regular progression to greater responsibility and, for the most productive and promising juniors, eventual admission to partnership. These firms flourished in a setting where there were clients with great bundles of legal work, like the new corporations and their promoters. Lawyers who earned the trust of such clients had a valuable piece of human capital, which could be shared with other lawyers, and the PPT proved an effective way of sharing this capital while minimizing the risks of shirking, grabbing, and spoiling.[2]

Firms built around the partnership tournament became the standard way of organizing the delivery of continuous and comprehensive legal services. The older patterns of fluid partnership, casual apprenticeship, and nepotism gradually gave way to the promotion-to-partnership template. Since promotions entailed the addition of more junior lawyers and eventually more promotions and even more juniors, in an unending spiral, adoption of the tournament device launched the firm on a trajectory of exponential growth.

The great aggregations of corporate wealth and legal business not only changed the way that lawyers related to one another, but also the way they related to clients. Lawyers in the new firms turned from courtroom advocacy to office practice; they abandoned the stance of independent advocates and embraced the role of client–caretakers, a term employed (and very likely coined) by Roscoe Pound in 1908. According to Pound, leading American lawyers

> are not primarily practitioners in the courts. They are chiefly client caretakers. . . . Their best work is done in the office, not in the forum. They devote themselves to study of the interests of particular clients, urging and defending those interests in all their varying forms, before legislatures, councils, administrative boards and commissions quite as much as in the courts. Their interest centers wholly in an individual client or set of clients, not in the general administration of justice.[3]

Theron G. Strong, a New York lawyer who kept a wonderful journal during the period of transition to corporate practice, observed in 1914 that relations with clients had

> undergone a complete and marvelous change. The advent of the captains of industry, the multi-millionaires, the mighty corporations and the tremendous business enterprises, with all the pride of wealth and luxury which have followed in their train, have reversed their relative positions, and the lawyer, with a more cultivated intellect than ever and as worthy of deference and respect as formerly, is not treated with the deference and respect of early days. This is accounted for to some extent by the keen competition which exists in the profession, placing the lawyer in the attitude of reaching out for retainers, instead of being regarded as conferring a favour by accepting them.[4]

Lawyers on annual retainers to corporations, Strong thought,

> become little more than a paid employee bound hand and foot to the service of [the corporation]. . . . [The lawyer] is almost completely deprived of free moral agency and is open to at least the inference that he is virtually owned and controlled by the client he serves.[5]

Although the large firm has frequently been portrayed as the exemplary site of legal professionalism, where lawyers exercise their autonomy to restrain the unreasonable or antisocial demands of clients, there is considerable evidence to support Strong's conclusions. Research suggests that large corporate firm lawyers may have less autonomy vis-à-vis their clients than lawyers in smaller practices. Robert Nelson concluded that "the notion that lawyers struggle with clients over fundamental questions about the common good is simply wrong. . . [I]n general[,] large-firm lawyers strive to maximize the substantive interest of their clients within the boundaries of legal ethics."[6] The work of leading law firms in arranging the deals that gave rise to the corporate scandals of recent years does not allay concern about the independence of lawyers from the magnetic field of powerful clients.

II. Lawyering in Two Hemispheres: Corporate v. Individual Representation

While the representation of corporate actors is done largely by large firms built around the promotion-to-partnership tournament, the representation of individuals and small businesses is conducted by solo practitioners or small firms. The bifurcation of the profession became so evident that in 1921 Alfred Z. Reed, in a report to the Carnegie Endowment that many hoped would be the Flexner report of legal education, proposed institutionalizing it. Reed proposed formation of an Inner Bar made up of those of superior attainments and broader vision, as distinguished from a less highly trained General Body of Practitioners. The Inner Bar would address large issues of policy, while the General Body would administer the law as it stood.[7] In spite of intensified specialization and stratification, ideology and politics weighed against division and the facade of a unitary profession was maintained.

A long series of studies nonetheless point to the persistence of a bifurcated structure, with lawyers from different social and educational backgrounds providing different services to different sorts of clients.[8] With due allowance for exceptions, the upper strata of the bar consist mostly of large firms whose members are recruited mainly from elite schools and who serve corporate clients; the lower strata consist of individual or small-firm practitioners who are drawn from less prestigious schools, and who service individual clients. Much of the variation within the profession, John Heinz and Edward Laumann conclude, is accounted for by

> one fundamental distinction—the distinction between lawyers who represent large organizations (corporations, labor unions, or government) and those who represent individuals. The two kinds of law practice are two hemispheres of the profession. Most lawyers reside exclusively in one hemisphere or the other and seldom, if ever, cross the equator.[9]

In the corporate hemisphere, a wider range of services is supplied over a longer duration; there is more specialization and coordination; research and investigation are more elaborate; and tactics can be more innovative and less routine.[10]

III. The Flourishing of the Corporate Sector

In post-World War II American society, there was a dramatic enlargement of virtually every aspect of the legal world: the amount and complexity of legal regulation; the frequency of litigation; the amount of authoritative legal material; the number, coordination, and productivity of lawyers; the number of legal actors and the resources they devote to legal activity; the amount of information about the law and the presence of the law in public consciousness.[11] Starting around 1970, the proportion of lawyers in the population increased steeply. By the end of the twentieth century, the number of lawyers had tripled. During this period of sustained growth, the large firm sector grew much more rapidly than the remainder of the profession. The incomes of large-firm lawyers increased substantially, while the income of other lawyers stagnated.[12] Large corporate firms loomed much larger as a presence on the legal stage. At midcentury, elite large-firm practice involved only a few thousand lawyers. By the end of the century there were over 130,000 lawyers in firms of fifty or more.

The increasing predominance of organizations as users of the law is dramatically displayed in Heinz and Laumann's studies of the Chicago bar. They estimated that in 1975 "more than half (53 percent) of the total effort of Chicago's bar was devoted to the corporate client sector, and a smaller but still substantial proportion (40 percent) was expended on the personal client sector.[13] When the researchers returned to the field twenty years later, they found that there were roughly twice as many lawyers working in Chicago. But in 1995, about 61 percent of the total effort of all

Chicago lawyers was devoted to the corporate client sector and only 29 percent to the personal/small business sector.[14] Since the number of lawyers in Chicago had doubled, this meant that the total effort devoted to the personal sector had increased by 45 percent while the corporate sector had grown by 126 percent. To the extent that lawyers serving the corporate sector were able to command more staff and support services, these figures understate the gap in services delivered.

This pattern is not peculiar to Chicago. Census data show that as the size of the legal services "pie" was increasing, businesses were buying a greater share of that pie. In 1967, individuals bought 55 percent of the product of the legal services industry, and businesses bought 39 percent. With each subsequent five-year period, the business portion increased and the share consumed by individuals declined. By 1992, the share bought by businesses had increased from 39 percent to 51 percent and the share bought by individuals had dropped from 55 percent to 40 percent.

In the quarter century from 1967 to 1992, individuals' expenditures on legal services increased 261 percent, while law firms' receipts from businesses increased by 555 percent. This more than double rate of growth understates the growth of business expenditures, for it includes only outside lawyers and does not include in-house legal expenditures, which also increased greatly during this period.

Among individuals, the share of those persons least able to pay decreased in both absolute and relative terms. In constant dollars, funding for the Legal Services Corporation (LSC) in 2003 was less than half of its 1979 high.[15] And Congress had restricted LSC's scope to focus on a client's day-to-day legal problems rather than on broader efforts to address the more general systemic problems of the client community.[16]

The regressive trend in the provision of legal services—more for businesses, relatively less for individuals, and absolutely less for the worst off—reflects a much wider turn in the law that began in the mid-1970s. After a generation of expanding remedies and broadening accountability, the prevailing critique of the legal order shifted from accusations of too little justice to laments about too much law.[17] Policy makers began to acquiesce to demands for deregulation, privatization, and reduction of remedies; courts embraced the avoidance of trial and judicial tutelage in early stages of cases—all of which accentuated the regressive distribution of legal services. This distribution is mirrored in other locations (e.g., incomes, tax rates, educational funding, and health care) where the most affluent have flourished and those in the lower ranges of the distribution have suffered.

"[T]he market for lawyers," Gillian Hadfield observes, "overwhelmingly allocates legal resources to clients with interests backed by corporate aggregations of wealth."[18] "The aspects of the legal system most responsive to the needs and aspirations of individuals absorb less energy and attention as the legal system prices itself out of the reach of all individuals except those with a claim on corporate wealth."[19] So the system is "heavily, and it seems increasingly, skewed toward managing the economy rather than safeguarding relationships and democratic institutions."[20]

IV. Cracks and Fissures: Portents of Change in the Distribution of Legal Services

One might be tempted to conclude that corporate domination of the legal system is inexorable and there is no hope that the system will be accessible and responsive to ordinary persons and their concerns. But the development of the modern legal profession reveals cracks and fissures that suggest some rearrangement of elements could take place. I confine myself here to two developments intimately related to the growth and transformation of large law firms.

Within the large firm sector, the 1970s saw the dissolution of a world of assured tenure, little lateral movement, and enduring retainer relationships with loyal long-term clients. In its place arose a world of rapid growth, mergers and breakups, overt competition, aggressive marketing, attorney movement from firm to firm, fears of defection, and pervasive insecurity.[21] Throughout the industry, relationships became more fluid: the mobility of clients was matched by mergers and breakups of firms and by the increased mobility of individual lawyers. Within the firm, there was more hierarchy and the tournament was prolonged.

In the old world, the fortunate few who gained partnership in a sizable firm acquired a kind of tenure. Partners could anticipate billing fewer hours with the passing years and could expect to stay at the same firm until they achieved a dignified, often gradual and partial, retirement beginning in their late sixties. These expectations have been shattered by the intersection of changes in the competitive environment with a major demographic transition. In the 1960s, the annual number of law school graduates doubled and it continued to rise for another twenty years. At first, the profession became much younger: the smaller numbers of older lawyers were joined by much larger cohorts of young lawyers. The profession formed an age pyramid with a wide base of younger lawyers and a smaller peak of senior lawyers. As time passed and the new large cohorts of lawyers aged, the number of older lawyers underwent a similar dramatic increase, while the number of new entrants (and thus of younger lawyers) remained more or less steady. The total body of lawyers continues to grow, but now virtually all the net growth is in lawyers over fifty years of age. In 2000 there were about 308,000 lawyers aged fifty or more, a bit less than one third of all lawyers. In 2020 it is estimated that there will be some 569,000 lawyers over fifty, some 45 percent of all lawyers. In contrast, the number of lawyers under age fifty will increase by only 50,000 or so.[22]

The arrival of a much greater number of older lawyers will radically change the shape of lawyers' careers. But the impact will be quite different in the two hemispheres of the practicing bar. Solo and small-firm practitioners, who serve individual and small business clients, will face an increasingly competitive environment as their numbers grow, new technologies make them more proficient, and powerful interests act to constrain the legal initiatives of individuals. In the large-firm sector, the total amount of business is likely to increase more rapidly. But the structure of these firms generates pressure for more hires to bill more hours and pressure to promote the most productive associates to partnership, for such promotion is the prize that energizes the tournament and enables the firm to compete in the market for new talent. There is a limit to how many partners a firm can support at a level that maintains the expectations of those in power. If firms are constrained in their ability to limit promotion, the pressure to curtail the size of the partnership will fall on those who are already partners. These partners will have to leave gracefully, take early retirement, or hang on with diminished status and income. In consequence, the shape of a career in large law firm practice will change from a lifelong trajectory culminating in the position of respected elder to a compressed period of intense and lucrative involvement followed by a long retirement.

Many of the much larger number of over-fifty lawyers that will soon populate the profession will be involuntary retirees, underemployed, or otherwise inclined to forsake their practices. Many of these people will be financially secure and in good health. They form an immense and rapidly growing pool of human capital that is in danger of being underutilized. Might some significant fraction be diverted into second careers of public service lawyering in existing legal services organizations, in free-standing firms, or in the pro bono department of their old firms? There are formidable organizational and cultural problems in engineering such a transition. But the coming wave of late-career lawyers is a wonderful resource that might bring the shrinking public services sector an infusion of lawyers able to act independently and assertively on behalf of clients, free of career and command pressures. These lawyers will also bring an enlarged repertoire of expertise and new political support. Some entrepreneurs have shown that such a transition is possible, but it remains to be seen whether the organizational resources are available to replicate this on a large scale.

Another possible source of augmentation of the public service sector is the prospect of greatly increased pro bono activity on the part of the practicing bar. Already in place is a standard requiring that every lawyer aspire "to devote fifty hours a year to pro bono public service," of which a substantial majority should go to the poor and to organizations that help the poor. And hundreds of law firms have pledged to donate 3 or more percent of their billable hours to free services for the poor. Whether the profession will move beyond aspirational standards and embrace mandatory pro bono remains an open question. A mandatory program could produce optimum benefit if it included a provision for the transferability of pro bono credits, so that lawyers are free to provide services directly or to pay other lawyers to provide them.[23] If pro bono credits are transferable not only within firms but between them, there could be an effective market in pro bono credits. Existing legal services organizations or start-ups organized by service-minded lawyers could contract to do the pro bono work of firms that found it burdensome or uncongenial to do it themselves. Such providers could hire full-time attorneys who would become expert in the legal problems of particular disadvantaged constituencies, for example the elderly poor or AIDS victims. Enjoying the advantages of scale and continuity, such providers would be able to make investments in specialized expertise that would not be feasible for a one-of-a-kind excursion into an unfamiliar area of the law. At best they might succeed in addressing their clientele's problems in a comprehensive and strategic fashion rather than as a series of disconnected emergencies. Were they to succeed in becoming institutionalized, such pro bono providers could seed the profession with a set of durable firms made up of dedicated advocates with specialized competence. This would expand opportunities for idealistic lawyers to practice law on behalf of the disadvantaged and even to build careers on such service.

Are these initiatives feasible? Lawyers in large firms are not only in the best financial position to undertake and support these sorts of activities, but there is evidence that large numbers of them would find this congenial. Financial rewards aside, large-firm lawyers are less fulfilled professionally than lawyers in every other practice setting.[24] For example, the percentage of Chicago large-firm lawyers "very satisfied" with their jobs is lower than in every other practice setting. Public-interest lawyers, on the other hand, enjoy the highest levels of professional satisfaction. Also, the bar, targeted by twenty years of attacks and acutely aware of its fall in public estimation, has a strong incentive to support pro bono initiatives.

A significant number of second-career recruits and institutionalized pro bono provider firms could supply a welcome enlargement of the pro bono sector in the near term. But these schemes would not resolve the great structural disparity in our legal system. Corporate players are, crudely, sized right to access, in a routine and continuous way, our complex, sophisticated, and expensive system. Individuals are not. Not surprisingly, corporations are more effective players over time. Addressing this division and all its implications would require an ambitious restructuring—a restructuring that would involve redefining the place of corporate entities as players in the legal system and curbing the advantages of their law firm representatives. If and when these issues come to the fore, the presence of a vigorous public service bar will be a great asset in the struggle to democratize the legal system.

NOTES

1. My assignment here provided an opportunity to weave together themes that are explored in more detail in earlier writings. These writings are available at www.marcgalanter.net.

2. The arrival of big firms and the dynamics of the promotion-to-partnership tournament are analyzed in MARC GALANTER & THOMAS PALAY, TOURNAMENT OF LAWYERS: THE TRANSFORMATION OF THE BIG LAW FIRM (1991). Important emendations are in David B. Wilkins & G. Mitu Gulati, *Reconceiving the Tournament of Lawyers: Tracking, Seeding and Information Control in the Internal Labor Markets of Elite Law Firms*, 84 VA. L. REV. 1581 (1998); Marc Galanter & Thomas Palay, *A Little Jousting about the Big Law Firm Tournament*, 84 VA. L. REV. 1683 (1998); Bruce M. Price, *How Green Was My Valley? An Examination of Tournament Theory as a Governance Mechanism in Silicon Valley Law Firms*, 37 LAW & SOC'Y REV. 731 (2003).

3. Roscoe Pound, *The Etiquette of Justice*, 3 NEB. ST. B. ASS'N PROC. 231, 235 (1909).

4. THERON G. STRONG, LANDMARKS OF A LAWYER'S LIFETIME 378 (1914).

5. *Id.*

6. Robert L. Nelson, *Ideology, Practice and Professional Autonomy: Social Values and Client Relationships in the Large Law Firm*, 37 STAN. L. REV. 503 (1985).

7. ALFRED Z. REED, TRAINING FOR THE PUBLIC PROFESSION OF THE LAW 237–38 (1921).

8. *E.g.*, JEROME E. CARLIN, LAWYER'S ETHICS: A SURVEY OF THE NEW YORK CITY BAR (1966).

9. JOHN P. HEINZ & EDWARD O. LAUMANN, CHICAGO LAWYERS: THE SOCIAL STRUCTURE OF THE BAR 319 (1982).

10. On the contrasting styles of ordinary lawyering and mega-lawyering, see Marc Galanter, *Mega-Law and Mega-Lawyering in the Contemporary United States in* THE SOCIOLOGY OF THE PROFESSIONS: LAWYERS, DOCTORS AND OTHERS 152 (R. Dingwall & P. Lewis eds., 1983).

11. Marc Galanter, *Law Abounding: Legalisation around the North Atlantic*, 55 MODERN L. REV. 1 (1992).

12. Richard Sander & Douglas Williams, *Why Are There So Many Lawyers? Perspectives on a Turbulent Market*, 14 LAW & SOC. INQUIRY 431 (1989).

13. HEINZ AND LAUMANN, *supra* note 9, at 42.

14. JOHN P. HEINZ ET AL., URBAN LAWYERS: THE NEW SOCIAL STRUCTURE OF THE BAR 43 (2005).

15. ALAN W. HOUSEMAN & LINDA E. PERLE, SECURING EQUAL JUSTICE FOR ALL: A BRIEF HISTORY OF CIVIL LEGAL ASSISTANCE IN THE UNITED STATES 36 (2003).

16. *Id.* at 37.

17. Marc Galanter, *The Turn against Law: The Recoil against Expanding Accountability*, 81 TEX. L. REV. 285 (2002). On the decline of trials in favor of managerial judging and Alternative Dispute Resolution, see Marc Galanter, *The Vanishing Trial: An Examination of Trials and Related Matters in Federal and State Courts*, 1 J. EMPIRICAL LEGAL STUD. 459 (2004).

18. Gillian Hadfield, *The Price of Law: How the Market for Lawyers Distorts the Justice System*, 98 MICH. L. REV. 953, 998 (2000).

19. *Id.*

20. *Id.* at 1004.

21. GALANTER & PALAY, TOURNAMENT OF LAWYERS, *supra* note 2, at 47–68.

22. These estimates are taken from Marc Galanter, *"Old and in the Way": The Coming Demographic Transformation of the Legal Profession and Its Implications for the Provision of Legal Services*, 1999 WIS. L. REV. 1081.

23. Marc Galanter & Thomas Palay, *Let Firms Buy and Sell Credit for Pro Bono*, NAT'L L.J., Sept. 6, 1993, at 17–18.

24. John P. Heinz et al., *Lawyers and Their Discontents: Findings from a Survey of the Chicago Bar*, 74 IND. L.J. 735, 744 (1999). A similar pattern among University of Michigan graduates is displayed in Kenneth G. Dau-Schmit & Kaushik Mukhopadhyay, *The Fruits of Our Labors: An Empirical Study of the Distribution of Income and Job Satisfaction across the Legal Profession*, 49 J. LEGAL EDUC. 342 (1999).

Consequences

More for Those in the Skyboxes

Fair Pay for Chief Executive Officers

James D. Cox

I. Income Disparity in America

Given the choice, it is better to be the company's CEO than its average
worker.[1] A whole lot better! With the burdens of leadership come not only
manicured fingers, monogrammed shirts, and a big office, but also a
significant compensation package, one that clearly separates the CEO from
his workforce and the public at large.

> [I]n 1970, the average CEO at an S&P 500 company made roughly 30 times
> more than a production worker. By 1996, this gap had widened to 210 times
> the average earnings of a production worker.
>
> The magnitude of these pay differentials can be further illustrated by
> comparing executive pay increases with the growth in other workers' pay.
> From 1982 to 1994, the average CEO's pay increased 175% or approximately
> 8.8% per year. If total wealth increases are measured by including the
> change in the value of stock options, then average CEO wealth increased by
> 269.7% or 11.5% annually. By contrast, the rate of increase for average com-
> pensation for all workers during that same time period was only 0.6% a
> year. . . . Only Major League Baseball players and National Basketball Asso-
> ciation players achieved annual increases of similar size to those of CEOs.
>
> The pay gap between CEOs and line workers is . . . many times greater in
> the U.S. than elsewhere. At large Japanese firms, the average CEO earns only
> 17 times more than the average worker. German and French firm CEOs make
> about 24 times more than those firms' average worker.[2]

Although the differential in compensation between the CEO and the average worker is large in all societies, it is significantly greater in the United

States than in comparable western societies. Scholars explain that the disparity between the American experience and that of other countries is due to greater reliance in the United States on stock options as a core feature of the executive's compensation package.[3] But this explanation is not totally convincing. In the United States, but not in Europe, 60 percent of the average CEO's compensation is derived from gains garnered in the exercise of stock options, or some other stock-based compensation.[4] If this factor were removed entirely from the comparisons, the American CEO's compensation is still approximately ninety times that of the average worker; this means that American CEOs are compensated more than five times that of their French or German counterparts relative to the pay of their average worker. This suggests that something more is at work here than just the popularity of stock-based compensation.

The disproportion of CEO compensation reflects the growing income disparity within the United States. It is a component of a larger societal development—the growing economic gulf between the top 10 percent and the 90 percent income strata. This is illustrated in the following graph.[5]

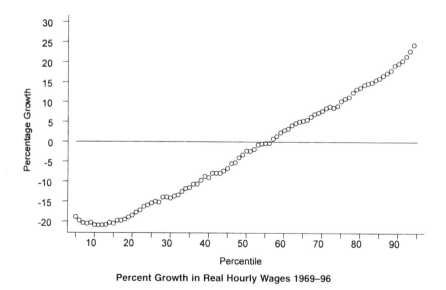

Percent Growth in Real Hourly Wages 1969–96

This graph reports growth in hourly wages adjusted for inflation between 1969 and 1996 as a function of income strata. Several points are to be observed. First, during this period income has actually declined for about one half the workforce. That is, to the question "Are you better off today than you were when President Nixon was first elected?" one-half of the workforce should answer "No." Second, the growth in inequality among workers of different income strata is pervasive. The income growth for those in the top 10 percent grew at a faster rate than that of the next 10 percent, and so forth, all down the scale. This is not a bimodal situation where one half of the households are pulling away from the other half. What we see are multiple sets of households pulling away from others, only to discover that the income of those above them is growing faster than their own. A rising tide is not lifting all boats; the tides are placing some boats at very safe anchorages while stranding others on tough economic shoals.

II. The Rise of Stock Options

It would be unfair to investment bankers, doctors, and Donald Trump to attribute the top 10 percent of the graph solely to well-compensated CEOs or to the enriching effects of their stock options. There certainly are a good many vocations that place one in the top echelons. But we expect to find today's CEO in the top deciles of such a graph and stock options can explain the momentum placing executives there.

Like so many questionable commercial developments, the initial impetus for stock options was the Internal Revenue Code. In an era where capital gains were taxed at a substantially lower rate than ordinary income, the stock option was a means for executives to receive compensation at a much lower effective tax rate.[6] But the real impetus for stock options came from the academy. In a highly influential article, Professors Michael Jensen and William Meckling[7] provide a rigorous and universal description of the separation of ownership from management in public companies.[8] Jensen and Meckling identify *agency costs* as the central problem of public companies. That is, because managers customarily have a small ownership percentage of the public companies they manage, their natural tendency is to maximize their own utility, for example, by shirking, and not that of the firm's owners.

Managerial shirking is not the sole concern. Managers were also said to be often reluctant to undertake high risk, high return projects that could maximize the company's value and increase shareholders' wealth. Jensen's and Meckling's proposal to align more perfectly the interests of managers and owners is performance-based compensation, particularly arrangements that link executive pay to positive changes in shareholder wealth.[9] At the time of their article, stock options were not a significant component of the CEO's compensation package.[10] When Jensen and Meckling put forth their model of the firm, it was possible to point toward the dramatic example of the power of performance-based compensation existing in leveraged buyouts. In leveraged buyouts, public companies were being converted into private ones by sophisticated buyers who perceived that the targets of their takeovers were undervalued by the stock market. Such buyouts were funded by large lenders. High-level managers were then generally rewarded with large equity positions to provide incentives to increase the value of the newly privatized firm. Evidence indicated that the assets of firms "bought out" in this way were managed more successfully after the buyout. The chief difference was said to be the improvement in the incentive structure for managers.[11] From this experience with the leveraged buyout, one could see stock-based compensation as at least a partial remedy for the agency problem. Today, stock-based compensation is generally a significant component of the CEO's compensation package and the chief mechanism for linking CEO compensation to firm performance.

Current data suggest that 98 percent of the correlation between CEO pay and firm performance is attributable to stock options or other stock-based rewards.[12] But today we can more appropriately conclude that performance-based compensation is both a remedy for the classic agency problem, and too frequently a glaring manifestation of the agency problem itself.[13] Furthermore, no strong empirical support has emerged for the proposition that high compensation or stock-based compensation is correlated with above-average performance of the firm.[14]

Further momentum for compensation by stock options was provided in the 1980s and 1990s by the increasing acceptance of the premise that corporations are but a web of contractual relations among owners and managers, to which other constituencies are only occasional parties.[15] The agency costs thesis wed easily to this contractual perspective of the firm: if the firm is a mere nexus of contracts, compensation should naturally enough be linked to the performance of the contract. Monitoring efforts by owners or their stewards to reduce the agency costs of managerial self-aggrandizement cannot be expected to reduce those costs to zero. So a useful complement to monitoring is to structure the executives' incentives in such a way as to increase the costs to themselves of shirking.

Jensen's and Meckling's description of agency costs and the emerging "nexus of contracts" definition of the firm each helped explain the rise of another contemporary development, namely, the movement to include more outside directors on the boards of public companies. A central purpose of the outside director is to monitor management's stewardship of the firm. Poorly performing managers are presumably more likely to be removed when the board is "independent" of management than when it is not. From this, it is but a small step to the conclusion that independent directors will represent stockholders' interests by contracting with management to provide optimal incentives for managers to overcome their natural aversion to risk and to pursue promising projects, and otherwise to dedicate themselves to maximization of the firm's value.

This vision of a vigilant, supervisory board of directors assumes that independent directors do not themselves suffer from the same agency problems as the managers they are charged with monitoring. The pecuniary and nonpecuniary rewards of being a director are well understood and their realization is dependent on a measure of support from the CEO.[16] This dependency results from the importance of the CEO in the selection of the independent directors who are nominated to sit on the board.[17] Monitoring can thus be understood as akin to managers and their monitors each looking into the same mirror and assessing their joint reflection.

The pervasive use of stock options cannot be attributed merely to the force of intellectual perspectives of the firm advanced by academics. An important if unintended nudge came from Congress when it addressed the problem of executive compensation. In 1993, in response to the growing furor over the size of executive pay packages, Congress enacted section 162(m) of the Internal Revenue Code, which prohibits the deduction of compensation in excess of $1 million per year for any of the top five executives of any corporation.[18] Importantly, that provision does not apply to "performance-based arrangements." A natural, but unexpected, consequence of section 162(m) was a broad movement toward pay packages that are performance-based.

Although the work of academics and experience with leveraged buyouts provided a theoretical and empirical framework for incentive pay, the question presented by the congressional reform of the tax laws was: what should be the device to assure performance-based compensation? There are a good many possible mechanisms to link the executive's compensation to changes in firm value, for example, through cash bonuses tied to changes in the firm's value or a grant of shares of stock upon meeting certain performance levels or achieving specified objectives.

Stock options became the prevalent means to link pay and performance in large part because of their favorable accounting treatment. When a firm pays a cash bonus to its executive for meeting some reward benchmark, accounting principles require the full amount of the bonus to be reported as an expense on the company's financial statements. The same treatment occurs if the executive is awarded shares of the company's stock; this is seen by the tax collector as merely a substitution of one form of payment—stock—for another—cash. In either case, an accruing expense results in a reduction of reported net income in the fiscal period when the bonus is paid or the shares are issued. In contrast, the alchemy of stock options sweeps the accounting of the grant of options into the footnotes of the firm's financial statements. Within the footnotes one can glean an estimate of the ultimate value of the options to the employee and the forgone opportunity of the corporation to have received cash equal to their future worth at the exercise date. But this can best be seen as delayed pain to the corporation. Importantly, no reduction in net income occurs when the option is granted to the executive. Simply put, by issuing stock options in place of cash, firms reduce their compensation expense and thereby increase their current apparent profitability above what could have been claimed had another form of compensation been used.[19]

It was this powerful alchemy that prompted efforts in the mid-1990s by the Financial Accounting Standards Board (FASB) to require that stock options conferred on management be reported as an expense.[20] Instead, the Senate passed a sense-of-the-Senate resolution, sponsored by Senator Joseph Lieberman, opposing such a requirement. The Senate's action reflected the disturbing effects of pressure by executives who feared that the FASB was about to take away a good thing, something that enabled corporations to seem more profitable than in fact they were and that resulted in a general inflation of the stock market. Contemporary estimates are that expensing options would reduce 2004 earnings per share for the S&P 500 by 7.4 percent.[21] We might reasonably conclude that treating managers' stock options as expenses would correct by 7.4 percent the amount by which public companies have systematically overstated their earnings.

Stock options as a form of executive compensation act as a one-way street for the corporation. The executive incurs no diminution in her net worth if the firm's price declines so that the option is "out of the money."

When the value of the firm declines, the executive is disappointed but her compensation is not diminished. Thus, accounting practices that prevailed until recently led to the perverse result that the actual expense of management was not measured. Management compensation was therefore poorly managed.

Another harmful feature of poorly designed stock options is the strong incentive they create to massage the financial reports or other activities of the firm to enhance the options' value on their exercise date.[22] Unexercised options near or past their exercise date, or substantial shareholdings that arise via options, both provide perverse incentives to the executives who hold them. Thus, the executive whose options are exercisable on April 1st and who is not limited as to when she can resell her shares has a conflict regarding whether to announce the loss of a major customer on or before April 1st. Similarly, the executive has a special interest in finding, say, another $.05 per share of earnings for the first fiscal quarter so as to surpass the earnings forecast by outside analysts. Indeed, the executive may adopt a more buoyant tone in her discussions with analysts if she has just received valuable stock per options recently exercised.[23]

III. Who's Minding the Store?

How is it that the absence of accounting metrics explains the failure of companies to manage their executive pay packages? A central feature of today's corporate governance model is a critical mass of outside directors and increasing reliance upon a committee system within the boardroom. Under the received model the most important charge for the independent directors is evaluation of management's stewardship of the firm. A central component of this evaluation is rewarding or penalizing the executive based on his performance via the compensation approved by the board or one of its committees. In light of the wide condemnation of executive compensation, even from executives themselves, and the absence of visible support for the status quo, it is easy to conclude that the model is not working. Why is this so?

The responsibility to determine the amount and components of the executive's pay package rests with the board of directors. This task is customarily delegated to the board's compensation committee, composed of outside directors, giving it an aura of independence from the CEO whose pay the committee regulates. But the work of the committee is compromised in a number of ways. The compensation committee is not expected to devote a lot of time to its task, and it seldom disappoints in this regard.[24] Moreover, compensation committees are rarely proactive; they customarily react to proposals by managers or the compensation consultant retained to guide the committee. The role of the compensation consultant is fraught with conflicting interests because he sees himself as representing both the executive and the committee.[25] He is customarily retained or recommended by the CEO and is often also a vendor to the corporation of a wider range of human resource consulting services.[26] This tightly tethers the economic interests of the compensation consultant to the CEO. It is not unusual for the compensation consultant to garner revenues from the firm for other services that are several orders of magnitude greater than the revenues received for advising the compensation committee regarding the CEO's pay package.[27] This no doubt explains why there is not a rich history of compensation consultants opining that the CEO is overpaid or is compensated at just the right level. If the compensation consultant's recommendations do not further the CEO's quest to earn more money, the consultant will be rapidly shown the door.[28]

Compensation consultants have a variety of strategies they can employ to gerrymander the process of setting, or more likely raising, an executive's compensation. Evidence reveals that when firms have been performing well, compensation consultants compare compensation levels to those at less well-performing firms to justify awarding greater executive compensation. But when a firm has not performed well, the reference group is not selected on the basis of relative performance. Instead, a peer group that the consultant opines is within a comparable industry group is used.[29] Consultants seldom recommend, and boards seldom approve, executive compensation packages that compare unfavorably with those of executives in rival firms.

Boardrooms continue to be congenial locations and a critical consideration for board membership continues to be a board nominee's ability to work within a group to reach a consensus. For this reason the use of board committees to nominate new directors has not removed the CEO from the nomination process. This is also the reason that more than 16,000 comment letters were received by the Securities and Exchange Commission when it proposed modestly to reform the nominating process; its proposals identify fairly narrow instances in which stockholders owning 5 percent of the company's shares would be able to nominate for election a distinct minority of the board.[30]

IV. From Shaming to Lake Wobegon

The problems of setting CEO compensation were exacerbated in 1992 when the SEC amended Item 402 of Regulation S-K in order to expand the disclosure requirements of public companies regarding executive compensation. The new requirements mandate: (1) disclosure of the amounts awarded, (2) disclosure of the types of compensation (cash, bonus, stock option), (3) an elucidation of the company's general compensation policies, (4) discussion of the relationship between company performance and executive compensation awarded in the most recent fiscal year, and (5) a five-year line graph of company performance comparing executive compensation to cumulative returns to shareholders, which in turn is compared to a broad market index. These rules seek the disclosure of useful information to investors, but also seek to stimulate self-regulation. We can see in the Commission's disclosure requirements the wisdom of Louis Brandeis: "Sunlight is said to be the best of disinfectants; electric light the most efficient policeman."[31]

Theoretically, the benefits should occur on several levels. First, they provide a template for directors approaching compensation decisions. This process could, it might be hoped, lead to thoughtful decisions. At a minimum, when directors are required to gather information to fulfill their disclosure obligations they might be assembling and analyzing information they otherwise would not have before them. So the increased disclosure obligation might cause directors to monitor executive compensation from a different perspective than otherwise.[32] You manage, we are told, what gets measured.[33]

Second, the compensation report required by Item 402 includes the names of directors who serve on the compensation committee. Thus, the disclosure regulations can give rise to a fair amount of shaming of compensation committee members who brazenly award the underperforming CEO scandalously high compensation. Thus, facing the humiliation of failing to link compensation to the firm's performance, directors might more closely hew the compensation of the individual executive to his contributions to their firm.

Finally, shareholders armed with information can see when a disconnect exists between the firm's (and therefore its executives') performance and its executives' compensation, and can withhold their support for the directors in the next annual election.[34] It is pertinent that on the same day that Item 402 was amended the Commission greatly liberalized its proxy rules to permit stockholders to communicate among themselves. This reform enables stockholders more easily to encourage their fellow holders to withhold their votes for management's nominees to the board.[35]

But what actually has happened in the wake of the 1992 amendments to Item 402 is to the contrary. To meet their obligations under Item 402, the compensation committees needed guidance. Therefore, the enhanced disclosures made reliance on compensation consultants even more prevalent. Whatever misgivings may have existed regarding the role of compensation consultants prior to the amendment of Item 402 were heightened in the wake of the enhanced disclosures. Item 402 made benchmarking the order of the day for compensation committees. Executives who eyed their rivals' Item 402 disclosures became competitive with respect to salaries. And, more importantly, boards did not feel comfortable learning from their consultant that the firm's CEO's compensation was in the bottom half of a cohort of peer firms. A CEO compensated within the top half or quartile of his peers is believed to make the company appear strong.[36] Paying the CEO below the average strikes a blow to institutional pride. Thus, a significant percentage of the firms whose consultants use peer groups in setting executive compensation place their executives' compensation at or above the fiftieth percentile level.[37] Thus, CEOs were transformed by Item 402 to children of Lake Wobegon—whether CEO or Wobegon child, each was above average.

A final feature in the apparent failure of Item 402 was the booming economy. Warren Buffet observed that even scrawny ducks that can't swim or quack rise in a swollen pond.[38] Executives with stock options found their wealth skyrocketing with the unprecedented rise in the stock market in the second half of the 1990s. A survey of Fortune 200 firms found that between 1992 and 1997 CEO compensation nearly doubled, with most of the increase being related to stock options exercised in the booming market.[39] Thus, any imbalance between performance and pay was exacerbated by the rapid rise in stock prices.

Nevertheless, boards and their compensation committees do not appear to be totally immune from the publicity that can surround executive compensation. For example, executives receive smaller pay increases and their pay becomes more sensitive to the firm's financial performance following negative media coverage regarding their executives' compensation arrangements.[40] Moreover, executives of firms that experienced shareholder proposals critical of executive pay found their pay packages reduced in the years following the shareholder proponent's efforts.[41] But such events are episodic and can be seen as focusing more attention on the compensation arrangement than the more bland disclosures compelled by Item 402.

V. Is There a Referee for This Game?

The courts have not only failed to be a restraining force on executive compensation, but they have in their wayward tact contributed to the insularity of the compensation-setting process. A review of the history of the courts' interface with executive compensation reveals that excessive executive compensation has long been a subject of public debate. During the Great Depression there were many judicial attacks on executive compensation, especially bonus and incentive compensation arrangements. The concerns of these suits and reactions to compensation-related abuses were captured in extensive congressional hearings leading up to the enactment of the federal securities laws.[42]

The most famous of the suits attacked the bonus awarded the executives and directors of the American Tobacco Company. The CEO of American Tobacco, in addition to receiving an annual salary in excess of $1 million, had been granted an immediate option to purchase shares for an amount $1,169,000 below their then current market value. As part of the same option arrangement, the approving directors awarded themselves handsome options as well. The case ended triumphantly for the plaintiff in the U.S. Supreme Court. The Court concluded that even though the arrangement had been approved by the stockholders and was therefore "supported by the presumption of regularity," that presumption nevertheless would not

> justify payments of sums as salaries so large as in substance and effect to amount to spoliation or waste of corporate property. . . . If a bonus payment has no relation to the value of services for which it is given, it is in reality a gift in part, and the majority stockholders have no power to give away corporate property against the protest of the minority.[43]

The substantive reasonableness focus embodied in the American Tobacco case has since been replaced by an emphasis on process. The result of the shift from substance to process is that suits against executive compensation have their highest chance for success in close corporations and a much lower probability of success in public corporations. This is because process is more likely overlooked in close corporations whereas process is almost always present in public corporations due to their ability to retain talented and compulsive counsel. Consider that, in their study of all litigated compensation disputes between 1912 and 2000, Professors Thomas and Martin report that plaintiffs' success is about 50 percent greater in close corporations than it is in public corporations when the complaint is substantively based and 100 percent greater when the complaint focuses on process.[44] Because Thomas and Martin do not identify the 124 cases captured in their study, it is only possible to state that it is likely that the public company cases are typical of the time period of their study and therefore do not reflect the more contemporary emphasis on process over substance. If their data are so skewed, which this author believes is highly likely, then, even though their data reflect slim odds of success to be enjoyed by plaintiffs attacking compensation decisions in public companies, those slim odds would be even slimmer today when the emphasis on process produces even greater insularity for compensation decision making.

The greatest barrier a plaintiff faces in litigating executive compensation claims is satisfying the "demand requirement." Under Delaware law, for example, a shareholder may not begin most derivative suits before making a demand on the board, which can refer the matter to a committee of disinterested and independent directors that is empowered to dismiss the suit as harmful to the corporation's best interests. This demand requirement is excused if the shareholder can allege facts establishing a reasonable doubt either that the directors were disinterested and independent or that the action challenged was facially harmful to the corporation.

A leading Delaware case, *Aronson v. Lewis*,[45] reflects how high a hurdle the demand requirement places in the path of the derivative suit plaintiff when the focus is executive compensation. *Aronson* involved a challenge to the employment contract awarded to Leo Fink, the owner of 47 percent of the firm's voting stock. When Fink was seventy-five years old, the firm granted him an employment contract that would pay him $150,000 a year (plus 5 percent of the firm's pretax profits above $2.4 million). Fink could terminate the contract at any time and would receive a six-figure consulting payment for the remainder of his life; the payments would be made even if he became incapacitated. The board also approved interest-free loans to Fink that totaled $225,000. The Delaware Supreme Court dismissed the action, announcing that the suit could proceed without approval by Fink's handpicked board only if the plaintiff's complaint alleged facts that created "reasonable doubt" regarding the board's independence or the reasonableness of the compensation arrangement. Neither the dominant stockholdings of Fink nor the one-sided employment and loan agreements were sufficient to raise a reasonable doubt about either issue.[46] Post-*Aronson* decisions support the view that the decision was not a mere aberration.[47] One observable impact of *Aronson* is the greater prominence of the demand requirement in Delaware post-*Aronson*. Prior to *Aronson*, defendants made motions to dismiss the derivative suit challenging executive compensation for failure to make a demand on the board in roughly the same percentage of cases in Delaware (14 percent) as outside Delaware (18 percent). After *Aronson*, such motions in executive compensation cases are made in 75 percent of the Delaware cases compared with only 14 percent of non-Delaware cases.[48]

In re The Walt Disney Co. Derivative Litigation[49] might be seen as an important first step toward closer judicial scrutiny of executive compensation decisions. This recent (2003) case arose from the Disney board's approval of an executive compensation contract with Michael Ovitz and its implied approval of a no-fault termination of Ovitz resulting in his receiving in excess of $140 million after barely one year of employment. The Chancery Court held, based on facts set forth in the complaint that could not have been more egregious, that the plaintiff's complaint withstood the defendant's motion to dismiss. The facts alleged in the complaint include, among other things, the following:

- Ovitz was hired pursuant to pressure from Disney's CEO, Michael Eisner;
- Eisner and Ovitz had been close friends for twenty-five years;
- Ovitz had never been an executive for a publicly owned entertainment company;
- Internal documents had warned that Ovitz was unqualified;
- A member of the compensation committee received a $250,000 fee to secure Ovitz's employment with Disney;
- Neither the compensation committee nor the board had received, or had an opportunity to review, either the draft or final employment contract with Ovitz;
- The compensation committee and the board had devoted hardly any time at their meetings to reviewing and approving the employment of Ovitz;

- The compensation committee and the board had delegated the details of the transaction to Eisner;
- The board did not condition the employment contract becoming effective upon their final review or approval;
- The final version of the employment contract varied significantly from the drafts earlier summarized for the compensation committee;
- From the outset of his employment Ovitz performed poorly;
- No experts were consulted at any time in either the employment or termination of Ovitz;
- The terms for Orvitz's departure were entered into without express committee or board approval; and
- The severance agreement entered into by Eisner, acting for Disney, awarded significant financial benefits to Ovitz more quickly than if he had remained with Disney.

The Chancellor observed:

> These facts, if true, do more than portray directors who, in a negligent or grossly negligent manner, merely failed to inform themselves or to deliberate adequately about an issue of material importance to their corporation. Instead, the facts . . . suggest that the defendant directors consciously and intentionally disregarded their responsibilities, adopting a "we don't care about the risks" attitude concerning a material corporate decision. Knowing or deliberate indifference by a director to his or her duty to act faithfully and with appropriate care is conduct, in my opinion, that may not have been taken honestly and in good faith to advance the best interests of the company. Put differently, all of the alleged facts, if true, imply that the defendant directors knew that they were making material decisions without adequate information and without adequate deliberation, and that they simply did not care if the decisions caused the corporation and its stockholders to suffer injury or loss. Viewed in this light . . . [the] complaint sufficiently alleges a breach of the directors' obligation to act honestly and in good faith in the corporation's best interests for a Court to conclude, if the facts are true, that the defendant directors' conduct fell outside the protection of the business judgment rule.[50]

The facts alleged in *Disney* reflect not just sloppy procedures, but nothing less than an abdication of the board's monitoring role. It is not to be expected that in most instances the flagrantly dominating CEO, perhaps supplemented by cronyism as appears to have been the case in *Disney*, will be present. Instead, the record will be painfully constructed to support results that may not be far from the windfall garnered by Ovitz. The facts alleged in *Disney* served up a nice softball for the Chancery Court to knock beyond the park's typical walls. It remains to be seen whether that court or any other court can make contact with the curve balls that are more frequently pitched.

Courts have insulated pay challenges from meaningful attack through shareholder suit by fallacious obeisance to the demand requirement. Even in the rare case where demand is excused, the court's focus is on process so that only in the truly extreme situation immune to the contrivances introduced by lawyers and other consultants to the board, exemplified by *Disney*, will the compensation decision be subject to review. By devoting their scrutiny to process rather than substance, courts provide a compelling incentive for compensation committees to rely upon the advice of compensation consultants whose own interests, as noted, conflict.

Another and more important consequence of the courts' emphasis on process is that there is no legal standard by which compensation decisions are to be judged. To be sure, compensation is to be "fair" and not "wasteful." But these are merely code words for "deliberate," "thoughtful," and "reasonably examined." These are expressions of process devoid of substance. In analogous areas where the courts are called on to assess the fairness of transactions because they involve obvious self-dealing on the part of officers or even directors, their inquiry is more substantive. Thus, whether a building rented from a company controlled by the lessee's CEO is fair to the lessee is determined by comparing the lease's terms with leases of comparable properties.[51]

This approach works poorly for CEO compensation. It entails the risk of the same mischief presented by the compensation committee's encounters with their consultants. And compensation practices within an industry or across many referent industries may be so out of line that the resulting reference is untrustworthy. But the greatest concern simply is that CEOs are not like apples or even prime real estate among which crisp comparisons can be made. When challenging an executive's compensation the issue is complicated by the unique endowments of the executive as well as the equally unique challenges that confront the firm. Third-party reference points may prove helpful, but only as a starting point. In the end, the courts are likely to defer to the compensation committee's judgment regarding just how myriad intangible variables are to be weighed in setting executive compensation.

VI. Is There a Standard to Be Found? Maximizing Firm Value by Minimizing Income Disparities

Post-Enron, much attention has been paid to strengthening the corporate governance of public companies by enhancing the independence of their boards of directors. Listed companies now are required to have a majority of their directors be independent and their compensation committees are to be composed of independent directors. One proposed additional reform is the institution of a rule requiring the nomination of directors to be insulated from the CEO. This may occur, but the earlier response to more modest Commission proposals suggests that this is not likely.

It may be that the heightened board independence and post-Enron ethos will cause boards to turn away executives' requests for ever fatter paychecks. But determining what is excessive is not easy in the abstract. Indeed, the indeterminateness of the fairness of executive compensation remains a problem at the root of the matter. Some rigor is needed in the establishment of substantive standards against which executive compensation decisions could be made. Lacking that, we have only process to assure fair treatment of the corporation's interests.

It might help to focus more attention than is presently customary among American boards on the impact of a new compensation package on the gap between the compensation of average workers and those in the higher reaches of management. The aim would not be wealth redistribution but maximizing for the firm's owners the value of the services it is buying. There is a fairly consistent body of scholarship, both empirical and theoretical, tending to confirm that increased wage disparities between executives and other workers result in greater personnel turnover, lower employee morale, poorer product quality, and lower productivity.[52] Therefore, take note: an astonishing disparity between the average worker's compensation and that of executives may tend not to maximize the value of the firm. So even we who favor the shareholder primacy model, which obligates directors to maximize profits, may perceive that a failure to fairly reward those down the hierarchy is not in the shareholders' best interest.

NOTES

1. The author is grateful for the research assistance of Messrs. Paul Castle and Raegan Watchman, and Ms. Yi Wang.

2. Randall S. Thomas, *Should Directors Reduce Executive Pay?* 54 HASTINGS L. J. 437, 454–55 (2002). Broad-based concern regarding the rapid rise of executive pay exists even in countries whose pay differentials are substantially lower than those in the United States. *See* Brian R. Cheffins and Randall S. Thomas, *Should Shareholders Have a Greater Say over Executive Pay? Learning from the U.S. Experience*, 1 J. CORP. LAW STUDIES 277, 279, 280–84 (2001) (examining executive pay in the United Kingdom).

3. *See generally*, Brian R. Cheffins, *The Metamorphosis of "Germany, Inc.": The Case of Executive Pay*, 49 AM. J. COMP. L. 497, 506–16 (2001).

4. *See* Paul Meyer, *What's Wrong with Executive Compensation*, 81 HARV. BUS. REV., Jan. 2003, at 68. The total amount of stock covered by executive options is staggering. A study by the Investor Responsibility Research Council estimated that the average potential dilution posed by stock option plans in existence in 1998 equaled 12.7 percent of the firms' outstanding shares. *See* DREW HAMBLY & ALESANDRA MONACO, POTENTIAL DILUTION 1998 1 (1999).

5. Kevin M. Murphy & Finis Welch, *Wage Differentials in the 1990s: Is the Glass Half-Full or Half-Empty? in* CAUSES AND CONSEQUENCES OF INCREASING INEQUALITY 341, 347 (Finis Welch ed., 2001).

6. *See, e.g.*, Mark A. Clawson & Thomas C. Klein, *Indexed Stock Options: A Proposal for Compensation Commensurate with Performance*, 3 STAN. J. BUS. & FIN. 31, 34 (1997).

7. *See* Michael C. Jensen & William H. Meckling, *Theory of the Firm: Managerial Behavior, Agency Cost, and Ownership Structure*, 3 J. FIN. ECON. 305 (1976).

8. Adolf Berle and Gardner Means identified this general problem four decades earlier. *See* ADOLF A. BERLE & GARDNER C. MEANS, THE MODERN CORPORATION AND PRIVATE PROPERTY (1932).

9. Jensen & Meckling, *supra* note 7, at 353.

10. *See* Michael C. Jensen & Kevin J. Murphy, *Performance Pay and Top-Management Incentives*, 98 J. POL. ECON. 225 (1990).

11. *See* PAUL MILGROM & JOHN ROBERTS, ECONOMICS, ORGANIZATION AND MANAGEMENT 425, 435 (1992); Kevin J. Murphy, *Executive Compensation, in* 3 HANDBOOK OF LABOR ECONOMICS 2485, 2542 (O. Ashenfelter & D. Cards eds., 1999); Bill Gross, *The New Math of Ownership*, 76 HARV. BUS. REV., Nov.–Dec. 1998, at 69.

12. *See* Brian J. Hall & Jeffrey B. Liebman, *Are CEOs Really Paid Like Bureaucrats?* 113 Q. J. ECON. 653 (1998) (analyzing data from 1980–1994 and finding, among other things, that for every 10 percent increase in firm value the average

CEO garners $1.25 million via stock options or other stock-based rewards, and this amount is 53 times greater than increases reaped via salary increase or a bonus as a result of positive changes in the firm's value).

13. *See, e.g.*, Lucian A. Bebchuk & Jesse M. Fried, *Executive Compensation as an Agency Problem*, 17 J. ECON. PERSP. 71 (Summer 2003); Lucian A. Bebchuk et al., *Managerial Power and Rent Extraction in the Design of Executive Compensation*, 69 U. CHI. L. REV. 751 (2002).

14. *See* GLASS LEWIS & CO., PAY DIRT: A REVIEW OF 2003 EXECUTIVE COMPENSATION (Apr. 30, 2004) (reviewing numerous illustrations of companies whose executives received substantial compensation but whose firms performed poorly and vice versa).

15. *See* Symposium, *Contractual Freedom in Corporate Law*, 89 COLUM. L. REV. 1395–1774 (1989).

16. *See generally* James D. Cox & Harry L. Munsinger, *Bias in the Boardroom: Psychological Foundations and Legal Implications of Corporate Cohesion*, 48 LAW & CONTEMP. PROBS. 83 (1985).

17. Even when public companies have nominating committees composed exclusively of outside directors, the committee is sensitive to the CEO's views of what qualities are sought in new board nominees and who on the present board should be retained. There is no requirement presently for public companies to advance or even receive nominations from their shareholders, regardless of the ownership interest of any requesting owner. To be sure, dissatisfied owners can launch their own solicitation process to support a nominee or nominees, but they face significant logistical obstacles and incur substantial expenses in doing so. *See* Lucian A. Bebchuk & Marcel Kahan, *A Framework for Analyzing Legal Policy toward Proxy Contests*, 78 CAL. L. REV. 1073 (1990).

18. *See* I.R.C. § 162(m).

19. *See, e.g.*, U.S. CONGRESSIONAL BUDGET OFFICE, ACCOUNTING FOR EMPLOYEE STOCK OPTIONS 4, 11 (Apr. 2004).

20. *See generally* Floyd Norris, *Accounting Board Yields on Stock Options*, N.Y. TIMES, Dec. 15, 1994, at D1.

21. *See* WATSON WYATT, HOW DO EMPLOYEES VALUE STOCK OPTIONS? RESULTS FROM A SPECIAL SURVEY (2004).

22. *See* JAP EFFENDI ET AL., WHY DO CORPORATE MANAGERS MISSTATE FINANCIAL STATEMENTS? THE ROLE OF OPTION COMPENSATION, CORPORATE GOVERNANCE, AND OTHER FACTORS (Working Paper, May 2004); Carmelita Troy et al., Violator Firms Research (2003) (unpublished research, *available at* http://www.rhsmith.umd.edu/pr/secstudy03.html).

23. *See* Deborah Solomon, *Open Secrets: SEC Probes Options Grants Made as Company News Boosts Stock*, WALL ST. J., Mar. 30, 2004, at A1; David Aboody & Ron Kasznik, *CEO Stock Option Awards and the Timing of Corporate Voluntary Disclosure*, 29 J. ACCT. & ECON., Feb. 2000, at 73.

24. *See* GRAEF S. CRYSTAL, IN SEARCH OF EXCESS: THE OVERCOMPENSATION OF AMERICAN EXECUTIVES 16 (1991).

25. *See* Roundtable (Charles Elson, Moderator), *What's Wrong with Executive Compensation*, HARV. BUS. REV., Jan. 2003, at 5, 7 ("Good consulting practice is to provide counsel assuming that we're 51% working for the board and 49% working for management. . . .").

26. Further evidence of the incestuous environment of the compensation consultant and the entire compensation-setting procedure is that the CEO customarily takes the lead in nudging director compensation upward. This process begins by the same compensation consultant benchmarking the board's current pay against appropriate peer institutions. Thus, the board can eagerly greet the approach of the compensation consultant with the expectation that this will lead to a rising tide that lifts all boats. *See id.* at 20–21.

27. *See id.* at 13.

28. *See id.* at 12.

29. *See* Stuart L. Gillan, *Has Pay for Performance Gone Awry? Views from a Corporate Governance Forum*, 68 RES. DIALOGUE, July 2001, at 1. This process is referred to as "survey database gerrymandering." *See* Graef S. Crystal, *Why CEO Compensation Is So High*, 34 MGMT. REV., Fall 1991, at 9.

30. *See* SEC, SECURITY HOLDER DIRECTOR NOMINATIONS, EXCHANGE ACT. REL. No. 48626 (Oct. 14, 2003).

31. LOUIS D. BRANDEIS, OTHER PEOPLE'S MONEY AND HOW BANKERS USE IT 92 (1933). In approving the new rules, SEC Chairman Breeden paraphrases Brandeis, remarking, "the best protection against abuses in executive compensation is a simple weapon—the cleansing power of sunlight and the power of an informed shareholder base. . . ." Exchange Act Rel. No. 31326 in [1992 Transfer Binder] Fed. Sec. L. Rep. ¶ 85,051 at 83,354.

32. *See* Merritt B. Fox, *Required Disclosure and Corporate Governance, in* COMPARATIVE CORPORATE GOVERNANCE—THE STATE OF THE ART OF EMERGING RESEARCH 701, 713–14 (Klaus J. Hopt et al. eds., 1998).

33. *See generally* Louis Lowenstein, *Financial Transparency and Corporate Governance: You Manage What You Measure*, 96 COLUM. L. REV. 1335 (1996).

34. Post-1992 there has been an increase in stockholder proposals on a wide variety of compensation-related issues, such as linking pay to the company's stock price. However, one study found that only 12.8 percent of the shares were voted in favor of compensation proposals. This compares with 53.7 percent supporting proposals to redeem the company's poison pill. *See* Randall S. Thomas & Kenneth J. Martin, *Should Labor Be Allowed to Make Shareholder Proposals*, 73 WASH. L. REV. 41, 76 (1998) (study of results in the 1994 proxy season).

35. *See* SEC, Regulation of Communications among Shareholders, Exchange Act Rel. No. 31326 (Oct. 16, 1992).

36. *See* Brian Hall & Ed Woolard, Jr., *What's Wrong with Executive Compensation?* 81 Harv. Bus. Rev., Jan. 2003, at 68.

37. *See* Kevin J. Murphy, *Executive Compensation in* Handbook of Labor Economics 2485 (Orley Ashenfelter & David Card eds., 1999); Kevin J. Murphy, *Politics, Economics, and Executive Compensation*, 63 U. Cin. L. Rev. 713, 736 (1995); John M. Bizjak et al., Has the Use of Peer Groups Contributed to Higher Levels of Executive Compensation? 2 (Portland State University, Working Paper, 2000).

38. *See* Shawn Tully, *Raising the Bar*, Fortune, June 8, 1998, at 272.

39. *See id.*

40. *See* Marilyn F. Johnson et al., Stakeholder Pressure and the Structure of Executive Compensation (Social Science Research Network, Working Paper Series, 1997).

41. *See* Thomas & Martin, *supra* note 34.

42. *See* James D. Cox & Thomas Lee Hazen, Cox and Hazen on Corporations § 11.05 at 567–68 (2d ed. 2003).

43. Rogers v. Hill, 289 U.S. 582, 591–92 (1933).

44. *See* Randall S. Thomas & Kenneth J. Martin, *Litigating Challenges to Executive Pay: An Exercise in Futility?* 79 Wash. U. L. Q. 569, 608, 610 tbls. 4 & 8 (2001).

45. 473 A.2d 805 (Del. 1984).

46. The plaintiff was allowed to amend his complaint and as amended withstood the defendants' motion to dismiss. *See* Lewis v. Aronson, 1985 WL 11553, 11 Del. J. Corp. L. 243 (Del. Ch. May 1, 1985). However, even this subsequent opinion held that demand was not excused by the allegation that Fink controlled a *majority* of the shares, that the board nominees were his nominees, or that a majority of the directors served in subservient officer positions that could be terminated as a result of Fink's financial interests in various firms. What permitted the complaint to withstand a motion to dismiss was the allegation that the compensation arrangement was a means of addressing Fink's concern that he had received too low a price for shares he sold to companies in which seven of the Meyers directors were officers or directors. Thus, the complaint alleged that the consulting contract with Fink was a ruse, being merely a means to use the assets of Meyers to compensate Fink for his sale of these shares. So alleged, the court believed that a demand on the board could be excused since a majority of the Meyers directors were interested in the outcome of the suit. The court also believed reasonable doubt was raised in the amended complaint as to whether the contract with Fink was the product of a reasonable business judgment, given that Meyer's operations and Fink's residence were in different states and given that Fink may have been bound under a second contract to provide managerial services to Meyers.

47. *See, e.g.*, Levine v. Smith, 591 A.2d 194 (Del. 1991) (requiring demand because at least twelve of the twenty-one directors of General Motors were believed to be independent).

Fair Pay for Chief Executive Officers   119

48. *See* Thomas & Martin, *supra* note 44 at 579.

49. 825 A.2d 275 (Del. Ch. 2003).

50. 825 A.2d at 289.

51. *See, e.g.*, Lewis v. S.L.& E., Inc., 629 F.2d 764 (2d Cir. 1980). More generally, related party transactions are evaluated from a host of metrics to assess their over-all fairness to the corporation, with the central inquiry being whether the transac-tion compares reasonably with what would have occurred in arms-length negotiations. *See, e.g.*, Oberly v. Kirby, 592 A.2d 445 (Del. 1991); General Dynamics v. Torres, 915 S.W.2d 45 (Tex. App. 1995).

52. For the theory on why such disparities will cause harmful side effects within an organization, *see, e.g.*, Leon Festinger, *A Theory of Social Comparison Process*, 7 HUM. REL. 117 (1954). For empirical support of this proposition in business set-tings, *see, e.g.*, Charles A. O'Reilly, III, et al., Overpaid CEOS and Underpaid Man-agers: Equity and Executive Compensation (GSB Research Paper No. 140, Stanford University, Nov. 1996); Jeffery Pfeffer & Nancy Langton, *The Effect of Wage Disper-sion on Satisfaction, Productivity, and Working Collaboratively: Evidence from Col-lege and University Faculty*, 38 ADMIN. SCI. Q. 382 (1993); Matt Bloom & John G. Michel, *The Relationships among Organizational Context, Pay Dispersion, and Managerial Turnover* (2000), 45 ACAD. MGMT. 33 (2002).

7

The Antitrust "Revolution" and Small Business
On "The Turnpike to Efficiencyville"

Thomas E. Kauper

Trade or commerce under . . . [unreasonably low prices] may nonetheless be badly and unfortunately restrained by driving out of business the small dealers and worthy men whose lives have been spent therein, and who might be unable to readjust themselves to their altered surroundings.[1]

Defendant's concern for the weakest among them has a quaint, Rawlesian charm to it, but we find it hard to square with the competitive philosophy of our antitrust laws. Inefficiency is precisely what the market aims to weed out. The Sherman Act, to put it bluntly, contemplates some road kill on the turnpike to Efficiencyville.[2]

These two quotations, taken from opinions one hundred and six years apart, are indicative of the new revolution in antitrust analysis, a revolution that focuses on consumer welfare and economic efficiency, and places little or no emphasis on the preservation of small entrepreneurs or anything else that cannot be put in efficiency terms. Change began in the 1970s and continues today, with the Supreme Court directly overruling its own precedents and with the lower courts, taking the cue, proceeding on the "turnpike to Efficiencyville." The revolution has been directed by the courts and federal enforcement agencies, without any substantive legislative change. The Robinson-Patman Act,[3] which forbids some forms of price discrimination and is particularly focused on the preservation of small entrepreneurs, now stands alone in today's antitrust world and is seldom invoked. There is little doubt that many small businesses have fallen by the wayside over the past several decades.

It does not follow, however, that the changes in antitrust law over the past thirty years have much to do with growing disparities between haves and have-nots, or between large and small enterprises. In evaluating the impact of antitrust changes on what might be broadly described as class war, a critical question immediately appears: Who are the classes we use to measure have and have-nots? Is the focus on small (however we define "small") as opposed to large, business enterprises? Or are we talking about individuals? If preservation of small enterprises is an end, it is entirely possible that favoritism toward them works to the detriment of consumer citizens, and vice versa.

A simple example makes the point. The manufacturers in a given market contemplate entering into a price fixing agreement, raising prices to their purchasers. The harsh *per se* rule against price fixing[4] is a means of prohibiting harm to purchasers caused by this conduct. To the extent price fixing is deterred, purchasers benefit. Among these purchasers may be small enterprises, who benefit just as any other purchasers, large or small. On the other hand price fixing may work to the advantage of smaller, less efficient manufacturers because it creates an increased price umbrella under which they may profitably operate. Thus we have small enterprises on both sides of the equation. Does a *per se* prohibition harm some small businesses more than it benefits others? Moreover, enforcement of such a *per se* rule also is likely to benefit individual consumers. In short, who are the haves and have-nots in this example? This chapter will focus on small enterprises. In the ultimate accounting, as we shall see, changes in antitrust law since the 1970s have worked to the *benefit* of those have-nots who are consumers.

I. Antitrust Law and Small Business: 1900–1970

Concern over the protection of small enterprises could impact antitrust doctrine in two very different ways. First, conduct by firms that is not otherwise anticompetitive could be found unlawful *because* it impacts small

enterprises. This is the approach of the Robinson-Patman Act, for example, where price discrimination may be *condemned* simply because it is
detrimental to small firms. Second, conduct by private firms that is otherwise anticompetitive and therefore illegal may be *upheld* because small
businesses are benefited. In the first case, a violation is found because of
an adverse impact on small firms. In the second, no violation is found
because the conduct benefits such firms. In the first, the protection is the
result of enforcement. In the second, it is the result of forbearance.

American antitrust has from time to time favored both antitrust intervention and antitrust forbearance as a means of protecting small businesses, or at least so courts have said. But with changes beginning in the
1970s and continuing today, these earlier pronouncements articulating a
special concern for the preservation of small enterprises are a thing of the
past (except in the rare case brought under the Robinson-Patman Act).

Small businesses benefit from a variety of antitrust rules just as larger
businesses do. Price fixing may injure purchasers large or small. The same
is true of some horizontal mergers, which may cause damage to all of a
merging firm's customers. Where a monopoly firm excludes rivals without
legitimate justification, the elimination of the exclusionary conduct
benefits all its rivals, whatever their size. These cases involve no special
protection to businesses simply because they are small. But are there
instances where antitrust has protected small enterprises as an end value
in itself, where antitrust rules either condemn conduct that adversely
affects small enterprises, the harm to such firms becoming the role measure of competitive harm, or where we might tolerate the actions in question because small enterprises gain from it?

In the period between 1900 and 1960 antitrust cases were far less
numerous than today. The major antitrust cases were resolved against
defendants in the first two decades of the twentieth century.[5] Antitrust
enforcement died out during World War I and was slow to resume during
the probusiness euphoria of the 1920s. Antitrust was virtually abandoned
during the first New Deal.[6] It was resumed with a vengeance under the
direction of Thurman Arnold during the second New Deal, with most of
the cases brought during that period involving price fixing. Antitrust
enforcement was again abandoned during World War II. Private actions
seeking treble damages or injunctive relief, actions that are commonplace
today, and indeed now far outnumber government enforcement, were not
common until well after World War II.[7] There were few cases in which the
policies underlying the Sherman Act, which condemns contracts "in

restraint of trade" and monopolies,[8] were carefully analyzed. Nevertheless, the protection of small enterprises as one of many values incorporated into the Sherman Act seems to have been recognized in a small number of cases. I say "seems" because in most of these cases the discussion of small enterprises was not central to the decision and thus appears secondary.

One might think that the legislative history of the Sherman Act would provide some guidance where the statute itself does not. This is not the case. A. D. Neale observed that much has been written about "what was in the minds of the authors and sponsors of the Sherman Act, and it is not always easy to trace a clear and consistent story, as different schools of thought about what antitrust ought to be tend to seek support for their views in selected quotations from contemporary writings and speeches."[9] Neale's statement remains accurate today. Support can be found in the legislative history for an antitrust policy based solely on consumer welfare, meaning an antitrust policy focused entirely on allocative and productive efficiency. Support can also be found for an antitrust policy that takes into account wealth distribution, or one that reflects more populist concerns such as limitation of economic, social, or political power, and the preservation of business opportunities, particularly for small entrepreneurs. Thus Robert Bork could assert that the Act was meant to be confined to efficiency concerns,[10] and Hans Thorelli could assert that "the immediate beneficiary legislators had in mind . . . was in all probability the small business proprietor or tradesman whose opportunities were to be safeguarded from the dangers emanating from those recently-evolving elements of business that seemed so strange, gigantic, ruthless and awe-inspiring."[11] The dispute over legislative goals will not be resolved here.[12] Suffice it to say that no single-minded, clearly articulated purpose emerges. There is enough, however, to indicate that in some ill-defined and vague way the Congress was concerned with the continued well-being of small enterprises, both as purchasers and as rivals, without indicating how this concern was to be implemented.

In *Board of Trade of Chicago v. United States*,[13] the Court, speaking through Justice Brandeis, upheld a rule of the Chicago Board of Exchange that essentially fixed prices every day between sessions of the Exchange. The opinion recites a number of reasons for upholding the rule, one of which was that by providing both buyers and sellers with full information it was particularly protective of "country dealers and farmers."[14] Justice Brandeis returned to this theme in *Maple Flooring Manufacturers Ass'n v. United States*.[15] In both cases joint undertakings were upheld, with the protection of small country dealers accepted as one justification. In neither case was this critical to the outcome. The most significant of these "small enterprises" opinions is that of Judge Hand in *United States v. Aluminum Co. of America*,[16] a monopolization case. Alcoa had argued that because over time it had made only a 10 percent return on its invested capital, it could not be viewed as a monopolist. Judge Hand's well-known response came in two parts. First, because a monopolist may be slothful ("immunity from competition is a narcotic"),[17] it is likely to have higher costs than would be incurred in a competitive market. To conclude based on these costs that the rate of return precluded a finding of monopoly would clearly be inappropriate. Second, Congress may have forbidden monopoly not for economic reasons, but in order "to prefer a system of small producers, each dependent for his success upon his own skill and character."[18] Judge Hand went on to assert that one of the purposes of the antitrust laws was to preserve "for its own sake, *and in spite of possible cost*, an organization of industry in small units."[19] Noteworthy is the reference to cost; small firms should be preserved even if inefficient. This result seemed to Judge Hand to be something "constantly assumed" from 1890 on, relying on a statement by Senator Sherman as the underlying basis for the assumption. But none of these small business references were critical to the decision.

By 1950, antitrust law had some clear rules. Cartels were illegal *per se*,[20] as was resale price maintenance.[21] Tying arrangements were highly suspect, if not *per se* illegal.[22] Concerted refusals to deal were arguably *per se* illegal.[23] The *Alcoa* case began the focus in monopolization cases on the use of exclusionary conduct as the measure of illegality. Merger cases were virtually nonexistent; merger rules had to await the amendment of Section 7 of the Clayton Act in 1950.[24] Some of these rules undoubtedly benefited small enterprises, but not necessarily in the same way they benefited similarly situated large firms. The Supreme Court's ruling that resale price maintenance was illegal may have worked to the detriment of small dealers, whose margins were protected by the practice.[25]

But statements in opinions that preservation of small firms was a purpose of the Sherman Act in most cases did not address the critical issue, namely, whether such a purpose would overcome other goals in the case of conflict.[26] In each instance, recognized values all pointed in the same direction. With one notable exception, there was little to suggest that the protection of small firms was an end value in itself, an end value that could lead a court to condemn conduct not otherwise anticompetitive and where such protection conflicted with other recognized goals, such as competitive pricing. The notable exception was the Robinson-Patman Act, passed to protect small entrepreneurs from the discriminatory effects of large discounts being given to chain stores and other sizable buyers who competed with the disfavored small firms, a purpose that is made abundantly clear in its legislative history.[27] The Robinson-Patman Act was predicated on Congress's assessment that the then-existing antitrust laws were *not* adequately recognizing the need to preserve these small and independent businesses.

The decades of the 1960s and 1970s were periods of major change in the direction of a more populist antitrust policy, a policy emphasizing the protection of individual initiative, equality of opportunity and the preservation of small firms, particularly independent distributors. As I noted in 1968, the Warren Court era in the development of antitrust standards moved in the direction of a policy based more on the "rights" of individual firms than on any economic concept of competition.[28] These "rights" included the right to exercise independent judgment and to be free of discrimination.[29] Dealer termination cases flourished as small distributors sought antitrust relief against termination by their suppliers, usually much larger firms. Most of the shift in emphasis came in cases involving restraints imposed on distributors or mergers. The past thirty years have been in large part the undoing of what was done in the period between 1960 and 1975, at least in result, albeit with a different analytical bent.

In a real sense, the shift in emphasis began in earnest in 1962 with *Brown Shoe Co. v. United States*,[30] the first Supreme Court decision interpreting Section 7 of the Clayton Act, the merger control statute, as amended in 1950. *Brown Shoe* is a remarkable opinion. On its face it is the picture of the rule of reason carried over into merger policy. What is startling by today's standards is the outcome. The Court found a violation in the merging of two retailers who in the same market had a combined market share somewhat in excess of 5 percent. The Court asserted that if this merger were permitted it would then be required to approve further mergers by the defendant's rivals at that level, exacerbating what it perceived to be a trend toward oligopoly. *Brown Shoe* has been severely criticized, primarily on economic grounds.[31] Of direct relevance here is the assertion that one of the anticompetitive effects of the acquisition arose from the fact that the defendant was an integrated manufacturer-retailer. The acquired stores would thus gain the cost advantages of integration, allowing them to undersell their rivals. But Congress meant to promote competition by protecting "viable, small, locally owned business,"[32] even while it recognized that higher costs and prices might result. In an article preceding *Brown Shoe*, Derek Bok interpreted the legislative history in 1950 as giving Section 7 "a strong socio-political connotation which centered on the virtues of the small entrepreneur to an extent seldom duplicated in economic literature."[33] Whatever else may be said of *Brown Shoe*, its language is consistent with this interpretation.

Brown Shoe was followed by a series of horizontal merger cases developing numerical standards as to concentration and market share needed to create a presumption, based on numbers, of illegality.[34] The end, in a sense, came with *United States v. Von's Grocery Co.*,[35] a case involving two retail grocery chains with a combined market share of 7.5 percent. Prior to their merger, each of the partners had been steadily expanding. The most remarkable part of the decision was its reliance on statistics showing a significant decline in the number of single stores, stores that typically were merged into chains. Quoting from *Trans-Missouri* and *Alcoa*, the Court clearly thought it was somehow protecting small enterprises. It was as though the best way to keep them in the market was to close the exit door (thereby making it difficult for these enterprises to recover their invested capital).

Brown Shoe's willingness to impose higher costs if necessary to preserve small businesses led, in turn, to the next logical step, namely, the conclusion that mergers enhancing efficiency might be condemned for that reason, since the merged firm thus acquired an advantage over its smaller, less efficient rivals. The Court seemed to so hold in *Federal Trade Commission v. Proctor & Gamble Co.*[36] The so-called deep pocket and entrenchment theories developed in the lower courts were similarly based on the availability to the acquired firm of the assets of the larger acquiring firm, enabling it to use those resources to the detriment of its smaller rivals.[37]

These developments in the approach to mergers seem highly protective of smaller rivals, even if efficiencies are forgone and prices rise (thus of course injuring small firms that purchase the goods or services in question). But it is in a series of decisions involving vertical restraints, particularly restraints imposed by manufacturers on their distributors, that the "rights" approach to antitrust and the concerns over equality of opportunity, independent judgment, and small businesses generally were most apparent.[38] The *per se* prohibition against resale price maintenance was extended by a greater judicial willingness to expand the concept of agreement, finding a broader range of conduct to be actionable vertical agreements.[39] In *Albrecht v. The Herald Co.*,[40] the *per se* rule was extended to maximum resale price fixing, on the ground, inter alia, that a manufacturer who imposed a ceiling on resale price would tend to channel sales away from smaller (presumably less efficient) distributors to much larger distributors. Vertical territorial and customer allocations imposed on distributors were declared *per se* illegal in *United States v. Arnold, Schwinn & Co.*,[41] by application to such practices of "the ancient rule against restraints on alienation," a rule applicable because the distributor took title to the goods in question. In *Simpson v. Union Oil Co.*, an attempt by Union Oil to convert its distributors to consignees, and thereby permit Union to control the "resale" price by making it Union's own price, was found to violate the Sherman Act because it took from independent businesses their primary indicator of independence, namely, their power over their own price.[42]

Running through all these cases is a common theme. Each finds to be illegal restraints that deprive dealers of their ability to make judgments about where, to whom, and at what price they sell, restraints imposed by manufacturers on what in most cases are far smaller enterprises. The same theme appears in *Klor's, Inc. v. Broadway-Hale Stores, Inc.*,[43] imposing a *per se* rule (or so it is generally interpreted) against a boycott by an appliance store and a group of manufacturers against a small competing appliance store. Such a boycott deprived the plaintiff of its ability to buy in an open market, and was "not to be tolerated merely because the victim is just one merchant whose business is so small that his destruction makes little difference to the economy."[44] Monopoly can arise by the elimination of small firms one at a time.

No discussions of the 1960s would be complete without reference to the Robinson-Patman Act. In that decade the Federal Trade Commission initiated a large number of cases, finding against the seller in most cases.[45] Most involved price discrimination between competing buyers, so-called secondary line cases where injury is presumed from the fact of the discrimination itself.[46] Private Robinson-Patman cases became common. The Supreme Court upheld a number of FTC orders, consistently ruling in the commission's favor on such issues as when goods are of like grade and quality, and the meeting competition defense.[47] The effect of these decisions was the expansion of the Act and, therefore, of the protection extended to small firms who paid discriminatorily high prices. And in *Utah Pie*,[48] a primary line injury case, the Court found a violation based on territorial price differences that injured a rival in the low price local market, despite the fact that the allegedly injured party, a firm significantly smaller than its rivals, held a monopoly in the local market before the challenged pricing conduct began. These decisions reflected the broader "populist" concerns of the 1960s, although it must be said that they were to a substantial degree in conformity with the legislative history of the Act.[49]

On the face of it, these decisions benefited small dealers, who were freed from manufacturer-imposed restrictions and protected from collective refusals to deal and discriminatory prices. Dealer termination cases proliferated and some met with success. But did small dealers actually benefit? They could effectively compete with other dealers, and were given the opportunity to do so. But in terms of actual, measurable benefits, the answer is not clear. Small dealers may gain from being insulated by resale price maintenance and vertical territorial restrictions from competing head-to-head with more efficient rivals. But the independent grocery stores in *Von's Grocery* could also have been harmed if they could not sell their businesses to firms with a greater number of stores, the very firms likely to pay the most for their assets. To the degree that any or all of these practices impaired efficiency and resulted in higher prices, all purchasers, large and small, were harmed. In any event, the winds of change were blowing.

II. Antitrust Law and Small Business: 1970–2005

As we turn to changes in antitrust policy and law from the mid-1970s on, changes often characterized as revolutionary, one is struck by the fact that virtually nothing in the preceding five paragraphs reflects the law or enforcement policy as it exists today. As we have said, the last thirty years were in large part an undoing of the rulings of the 1960s and early 1970s and a return to the law as it existed in the preceding period. Except in the case of mergers, where there were very few rulings prior to the 1960s, policy may be seen as reverting to an earlier time.

The changes of the past thirty years were rooted in severe academic criticism, not only from members of the Chicago School, such as Robert Bork[50] and Richard Posner,[51] but from others as well.[52] The 1977 decision in *Continental T.V. v. GTE Sylvania*[53] marked the turning point. The particular issue before the Court was whether a manufacturer could restrict its retailers' sales to particular store locations—hardly a matter of major functional importance. But the decision marks the first overruling of a decision of the 1960s, the *Schwinn* case. The outcome in *Sylvania* was never in doubt. *Schwinn* with its holding based on the doctrine of unlawful restraints on alienation was a particular target of criticism.[54] What is significant in *Sylvania* is not the result but the methodology used to reach it. First, the Court appeared to adopt the efficiency, or consumer welfare, standard as the primary, if not sole goal of antitrust policy. To the argument that restrictions on where and to whom a retailer could resell because they impinged on "the autonomy of independent businesses," even if there was no price, quality, or output effect, the Court responded that "an antitrust policy divorced from market considerations would lack any objective benchmarks."[55] With that, the primary rationale in the *Simpson* case was gone. Second, in determining whether a *per se* rule should apply, the issue became whether the practice could, in a significant number of cases, enhance efficiency; if so, a *per se* rule was inappropriate. Efficiency gains and output restrictions were determined through the use of price theory, a methodology now thought of as commonplace.

Sylvania opened the floodgates, leading not only to a curtailment of the rules concerning restrictions on dealers but, ultimately, to virtually exclusive reliance on economic analysis in all antitrust cases, ranging from mergers to tying arrangements. In the twenty-seven years since the *Sylvania* case, antitrust has become the domain of economists, not lawyers. In the case of dealer restrictions, *Sylvania* ultimately led to a focus on interbrand effects rather than solely upon intrabrand effects which were the focus of an earlier time.[56] As a result, vertical territorial and customer restrictions are virtually *per se* legal.[57] The *per se* rule against resale price maintenance has been sharply curtailed, not by elimination of the rule itself but by making proof of the requisite agreement increasingly difficult.[58] The *Albrecht* decision, applying a *per se* rule against *maximum* vertical price fixing, was explicitly overruled in 1997.[59] Tying cases moved away from any concern about the buyer, often smaller businesses, and the notion that the buyer was being forced to take something it did not want, and instead focused on foreclosure of the seller's competitors.[60] Modification of the approach to concerted refusals to deal significantly weakened the new "*per se*" approach of the 1960s.[61] Taken together, these developments lessened protection of dealers from what might be seen as particular forms of arbitrary termination, and dealer termination antitrust cases have become virtually nonexistent. A well-known plaintiff's antitrust lawyer allegedly advised his office receptionist that if a prospective plaintiff arrived with a dealer termination case she should validate her parking and send her on her way. Apocryphal or not, the story makes a point.

While dealers may have lost some of the protections of the 1960s, the Robinson-Patman Act, unamended despite many attacks upon it, remains. Today it affords little protection to direct rivals from predatory pricing. Given the requirements for a predatory pricing claim set forth in *Brooke Group, Ltd. v. Brown and Williamson Tobacco Corp.*,[62] requirements that plaintiffs, often smaller rivals of the defendant, have been almost uniformly unsuccessful in meeting,[63] the protection afforded by earlier cases in the 1950s and 1960s is largely gone. But the heart of the Robinson-Patman Act, the very reason for its existence, was to guard smaller retailers from discriminatory prices, discounts, and rebates granted by sellers to larger competing firms. On the face of it, this protection remains. While the meeting competition defense has been expanded through rejection of some of the limitations placed upon it in the 1960s,[64] small firms victimized by discriminatory pricing do win from time to time.[65] While an occasional court has tried to restrict the application of the Act by insisting that the plaintiff must prove an actual injury to competition, the majority have continued to apply the presumption of injury created in 1948, one that arises simply from proof of significant, sustained price discrimination among competing buyers.[66]

Yet it is clear that Robinson-Patman has seen relatively little use over the past three decades. This may seem odd, given that private plaintiffs do win on occasion. But the cost of litigation makes it highly unlikely that a single small firm would even attempt a suit under the Act. The Federal Trade Commission, the sole federal agency involved in the Act's enforcement, has brought only two significant cases in some twenty years,[67] a dramatic reduction from the number of filings in the 1950s and 1960s. Both the FTC and the Justice Department have been critical of the Act,[68] and the FTC's virtual nonenforcement of the Act rests squarely on its view that the Act itself is inconsistent with the antitrust laws generally, facilitating collusion by banning the discriminatory rebates and discounts that are likely to break down a cartel or oligopolistic pricing system.

Nowhere has the change of the last twenty-five years been greater than with respect to merger policy. We have gone from condemnation of a horizontal merger where the parties' combined market share was 7.5 percent[69] to upholding a merger where the combined share was over 70 percent (based on a showing of ease of entry).[70] The Supreme Court's 1974 *General Dynamics* opinion[71] marked the initial retreat from the almost mechanical application of market share and concentration numbers seen in cases like *Von's Grocery* and opened the door to a radical revision of earlier standards. Most of the change has come, however, without the Court's leadership. The Court has not decided a merger case on the merits since 1974.[72]

Lower courts, taking guidance from Supreme Court opinions in other than merger cases, began to move in the direction of a purely efficiency-based set of criteria. With the issuance in 1982 of the revised Department of Justice Merger Guidelines,[73] guidelines that are cast purely in economic efficiency terms, the two federal enforcement agencies not only committed themselves to the efficiency standard but, as it turned out, led the federal courts in the same direction. Over the ensuing years these courts have come to rely heavily on the guidelines as though they were authoritative.[74] Today, it is hard to conceive that in the absence in the market of one truly dominating firm a horizontal merger with a combined market share of less than 40 percent could be successfully attacked in court, or would bring any objection from federal agencies.[75] Vertical merger cases are virtually nonexistent, and there is little basis left for questioning conglomerate mergers.[76] Decisions of the 1960s that relied on the creation of efficiencies through the merger as a basis for finding illegality are today discredited. Courts and agencies are moving toward acceptance of a full-blown efficiencies defense that would uphold even an otherwise anticompetitive merger. Nothing remains of the language in earlier opinions that recognized any special place under the Clayton Act for the protection of small firms.

This dramatic shift in merger policy has been accompanied by (and may to some extent be the result of) changes in the manner in which federal agencies consider pending mergers. Since 1976, the two federal agencies are to be notified of significant mergers.[77] The parties may not consummate the transaction for a minimum of thirty days. In theory, the agencies then have time to get a preliminary injunction against the transaction. In practice, the result has been to turn the process into a highly regulatory one. Agency objections are generally resolved through negotiation, with a consent decree then entered. There is disagreement over the impact of premerger notification and whether it has worked to the benefit of the public.[78] Very few cases are litigated today, a fact that bothers commentators who favor greater judicial involvement.[79] It is too late, however, for such involvement to reincorporate the historic concern for small firms.

Both substantively and procedurally, changes in the treatment of vertical restraints and mergers have been dramatic. There are some standards, however, that have not changed significantly since the 1950s and 1960s. This has been true with respect to monopolization cases under Section 2 of the Sherman Act, where the use of economic analysis has become central but the basic standards remain much the same as they were fifty years ago. Although a monopolist may be expected to charge a monopoly price, not all monopolies are condemned. Monopoly is condemned only when created or maintained through conduct characterized as "predatory" or "deliberate" and "exclusionary." More specifically, the issue is whether the monopolist has excluded rivals, usually firms smaller than it, without a legitimate justification. Such justifications might include a legal grant of the monopoly, as with a patent, historical accident, or the achievement of greater efficiency.[80] This rather vague conduct standard has been severely criticized,[81] and the courts may be moving toward a more specific sacrifice standard requiring a showing that the monopolist has sacrificed profits or goodwill that can be recouped only through harm to a rival. This evolution, however, is far from complete.[82]

On its face, a monopoly, like a cartel, will charge a sufficiently high price that smaller, less efficient rivals can survive under the umbrella of the monopolist's higher price. For this reason, Richard Posner has argued that if the preservation of small firms were the goal the best antitrust policy would be no antitrust policy at all.[83] Posner's argument fails to recognize the harm caused to rivals excluded from the market by conduct that is not legitimately justified. For example, one of the Section 2 violations found in the *Microsoft*[84] case was the exclusion of Sun Microsystems, a much smaller firm, from the market. In short, much as small rivals might like to function in a monopoly market, they do not want to be eliminated as the monopolist drives to its monopoly position. Section 2 protects this interest, as it has for over fifty years.

The most important substantive non-change, however, has been the continued application of the severe *per se* rule against cartels as it was set out in 1940. Cartels are viewed as an evil now as they were then. The cartel story is not one of rule change, but of far more effective enforcement. In 1974, criminal violations of the Sherman Act were elevated from misdemeanors to felonies with an increase in maximum jail sentences and fines.[85] Both have been significantly increased in the ensuing years.[86] In the 1990s, we saw corporate fines in hundreds of millions of dollars, and sentences, to be served, of the statutory three-year maximum. Enforcement has been dramatically increased through the Justice Department's formal leniency policy, which, in a sense, rewards through a grant of amnesty the first member of a cartel to notify the Department about it.[87] These changes, coupled with the commitment of greater resources by the Department, have made anticartel efforts far more effective. This may have hurt small firms in the cartelized market, while benefiting others who are purchasers.

There also have been significant procedural changes since the 1970s that have imposed limits on the use of treble damage actions that may, in some cases, work to the detriment of smaller enterprises. The *Illinois Brick* doctrine, permitting only direct purchasers from the level at which the competitive harm occurs to recover damages, has effectively eliminated suits by retailers, often small firms, who purchase through middlemen.[88] While this is so, there will be cases where small firms are direct purchasers, sometimes as middlemen or sometimes as direct buying retailers. Moreover, so long as *someone* can sue, the deterrent effect of the threat of suit will work to the benefit of all purchasers. The antitrust injury requirement, first enunciated in 1977[89] (as was *Illinois Brick*) also has operated to curtail treble damage litigation, although there is no reason to believe that it has had a peculiar effect on small enterprises. Because both of these doctrines work to limit litigation, there may a perception by some that they benefit larger enterprises, who are likely to be the defendants, at the cost of smaller plaintiffs.

III. Why the Revolution?

The changes in antitrust law and policy beginning in 1977 have been dramatic. Virtually all of the changes have been the result of the view that the primary, if not sole goal of antitrust is economic efficiency. In the case of vertical restraints the result, in large part, has been a return to the law as it stood before the 1960s. In a sense that is even true with respect to merger policy. All that remains to provide *particularized* protection to small firms is the seldom enforced Robinson-Patman Act.

How are these changes—the "revolution" if you like—to be explained? Because most, but not all, of the changes appear to favor putative defendants there is a temptation to assert that they simply reflect a big business orientation, either judicially, or politically, or both. An attitude, in the words of Charles Wilson, that "what's good for General Motors is good for the country." This is far too simple.

There is a common perception that the modern shift in antitrust is a legacy of the Reagan administration, an administration that stressed individual initiative and responsibility, as well as the reduction of government, and curtailed, or attempted to curtail, social welfare and other government programs that represented a societal assumption of responsibility for the well-being of some of society's members. Economic progress would follow from a minimization of government regulation and unfettered individual initiatives. Thus, business generally should be left alone and to its own devices. The deregulation movement is often described as the result, with antitrust thought of not as the antithesis of regulation, the historical view, but as just another form of it. This legacy continued in later years through Reagan appointees to the federal bench.

This perception clearly has some truth to it. Conservative judges appointed by President Reagan (and his successor) have undoubtedly played a significant role. Some received economics training that to a substantial degree reflected the views of the so-called Chicago School. The Antitrust Division of the Reagan years promulgated the 1982 Merger Guidelines, guidelines that reflected an efficiency-only approach and opened the door to horizontal mergers of a significantly greater size than would have been acceptable in the 1960s. At the same time, the Antitrust Division led the move to overturn earlier precedent with respect to vertical restraints.[90] And the Reagan administration did seek deregulation of the economic regulatory regimes of an earlier day. But it was this same Antitrust Division that insisted on the far-reaching consent decree that broke up AT&T.[91] Reagan appointees to the federal bench have not always been antiplaintiff. And the deregulation movement actually began in earnest when the Ford administration sought airline deregulation.

I do not minimize the impact of the philosophy of the Reagan administration, but other factors were also at work in spurring the shifts we identify over the past twenty-eight years (measured from the *Sylvania* case in 1977). First, until the 1960s antitrust doctrine had been relatively conservative. It was the decisions of the 1960s that were the first to suffer. There was a pre-1960s base to which to return. Those earlier decisions recited the need to preserve small enterprises, but seldom was that a real basis for decision making.

Second, decisions like *Schwinn*, *Simpson*, and *Von's Grocery*, decisions that placed more emphasis on the need to preserve the independence and autonomy of small firms, were simply intellectually unsustainable. They had been criticized to the point of ridicule, and had contributed to a growing cynicism about the utility of antitrust.[92] These rules became easy targets once a sounder approach was understood and presented.

Third, by the 1970s a clear, well-articulated, and comprehensive approach was available to fill this intellectual void. The views of the Chicago School have never been fully accepted,[93] and modern economic analysis, having built upon them, has moved some distance away.[94] But it is hard to underestimate the impact of those views in the 1970s and 1980s. Their analysis dealt with virtually all antitrust issues and exposed the costs of the policies of the 1960s. Policy decisions required measurements of political power, or how much preference should be given to small firms. To entrust such decisions to the courts, the least democratic of the branches of government, was seen as giving courts what amounted to legislative power. It was fine for the Congress to determine how much subsidy should be given to particular economic players, but it ought not to be done by the courts. To build such values into antitrust policy would, in the Supreme Court's words, "lack any objective benchmarks."[95]

Fourth, and perhaps most important, beginning in the 1970s, American firms were confronted for the first time since World War II with the loss of sales to foreign firms, both at home and abroad. The confrontation with "Japan, Inc." brought a steady drumbeat of demands that American firms become more efficient and that efficiency-impairing regulation, including at least some antitrust constraints, be eliminated. This, of course, was at the heart of many of the policies of the Reagan administration, but the requirement of greater efficiency predated the election of 1980.

These elements came together in the *Sylvania* case. Confronted with an indefensible earlier decision, the Court adopted much of the approach of the Chicago School in overturning it. On its face, the decision simply corrected the excess of the 1960s. The Court's commitment to an efficiency-driven consumer welfare standard put the camel's nose in the tent, and that standard has since been applied in virtually all antitrust cases. There is no place in this regime for the protection of small businesses absent a showing that there is an economic case for doing so. If small businesses were generally more efficient, or more innovative, or necessary to preserve entry as a deterrent to monopoly power, special protection for such firms might be recognized even in the current climate, but such a case has never been successfully made. The identification of small firms as "small" is of course itself an impediment to special recognition. And, in an antitrust world now willing to accept the consequences of an efficiency-driven policy, special protection simply has no place. While the pre-1960s saw references to such recognition, these were usually make-weights. Except for the peculiarities of the 1960s, antitrust *never* really extended *special* protection of any consequence to small enterprises.

As it now stands, antitrust rules are directed toward regulating conduct that enhances market power (or is likely to do so), conduct that brings a reduction in output and increase in price. The emphasis is on horizontal transactions, such as cartels and large horizontal mergers, and on conduct that adds to or maintains monopoly power by driving rivals, usually smaller rivals, from the market. Vertical restrictions and mergers raise few antitrust concerns.

So, we might ask, who benefits and who loses as a result of the changes of the past thirty years? Deterrence of cartels, large horizontal mergers, and unlawful monopolies benefits consumers and purchasers, many of whom are small businesses. When prices are held at competitive levels and efficiencies are gained, lower prices are of greater benefit to the less advantaged since their dollars are of higher marginal utility. Small enterprises may have some protection against exclusionary conduct by putative monopolists although as the law is developing it may protect only those rivals that are, or absent the exclusionary conduct would be, as efficient as the monopolist. Removal of prohibitions against vertical restrictions that do not enhance market power presumably also benefits purchasers, although it also eliminates protection of smaller dealers against arbitrary termination and permits vertical restrictions that may reduce their independence. And because small firms are often antitrust *defendants*, they may be benefited by an easing of antitrust restrictions. Balancing of the effects of these changes on small firms is virtually impossible. The benefit to consumers, however, is relatively clear.

While consumers do benefit in purely economic terms, there seems to be a growing sense of consumer powerlessness in the face of large corporate enterprises, and a dissatisfaction with what is perceived to be increasing abuses and misconduct by them. The consumer may have lost choices and be forced to confront the frustrations of dealing with large and seemingly unresponsive corporate bureaucracies. Most of us have likely been frustrated in our dealings with larger and larger banks or television cable companies, for example. Fabrication of financial records and misuse of corporate funds seem almost commonplace. Many of these large enterprises are the result of corporate acquisitions that are not subject to attack on antitrust grounds because they are the result of efficiencies or present no significant risk of increase in consumer prices. What creates these frustrations is not increasing market power in the antitrust sense, but mounting corporate size, size that breeds indifference and lack of accountability. But antitrust, which from the beginning has been market oriented, is not concerned with corporate size.[96] Even under the policies of the 1960s, size unrelated to market power was not targeted.

In the end, is antitrust worth the effort and the costs of applying it? Those who suggest that it is not argue that monopolies and cartels cannot long exist in the face of freedom of entry and rapid innovation. Fragility is their hallmark. Any transient harm they cause to consumers prior to collapse is more than offset by the costs of enforcement, costs that are relatively high. The historical record, however, suggests that neither cartels nor monopolies are as fragile as this argument suggests.[97] And the harm caused, at least in some instances, seems to far exceed the costs of the antitrust system, although concededly both costs and benefits are difficult to measure. Justice Scalia has recently said that "the benefits of antitrust are worth its sometimes considerable disadvantages."[98] Even with antitrust in its present form, this is clearly correct.

Notes

1. United States v. Trans-Missouri Freight Ass'n, 166 U.S. 290, 323 (1897).

2. Freeman v. San Diego Ass'n of Realtors, 322 F.3d 1133, 1154 (9th Cir. 2003).

3. The Robinson-Patman Act, enacted in 1936, is technically an amendment to Section 2 of the Clayton Act, 15 U.S.C. 13(a)-(p).

4. The rule applies to any agreement among competitors to fix prices, allocate markets, or reduce output. United States v. Socony Vacuum Oil Co., 310 U.S. 150, 224 n.59 (1940).

5. *See, e.g.*, United States v. Am. Tobacco Co., 221 U.S. 106 (1911); Standard Oil Co. v. United States, 221 U.S. 1 (1911).

6. The 1933 National Industrial Recovery Act, 48 Stat. 195 (1933), authorized a variety of forms of cartel conduct. Key provisions of the Act were declared unconstitutional in *Panama Refining Co. v. Ryan*, 293 U.S. 388 (1935).

7. Between 1937 and 1954 the annual average of such cases was 104. In 1972 alone, 1,203 private cases were filed. RICHARD A. POSNER, ANTITRUST LAW 34 (1976). By 1980 the number of private cases had declined, so that by 1999 the number was 608. RICHARD A. POSNER, ANTITRUST LAW 46 (2d ed. 2001) [hereinafter POSNER 2001].

8. U.S.C. § 1–2.

9. A. D. NEALE, THE ANTITRUST LAW OF THE U.S.A. 12–13 (2d ed. 1970).

10. ROBERT H. BORK, THE ANTITRUST PARADOX 50–66 (1978).

11. HANS B. THORELLI, THE FEDERAL ANTITRUST POLICY 226–27 (1954).

12. A comprehensive discussion may be found in PHILIP E. AREEDA & HERBERT HOVENKAMP, ANTITRUST LAW 41–124 (2d ed. 2000); *see also* references cited in Peter J. Hammer, *Antitrust beyond Competition: Market Failures, Total Welfare, and the Challenge of Intramarket Second-Best Tradeoffs*, 98 MICH. L. REV. 849, 905 n.150 (2000).

13. 246 U.S. 231 (1918).

14. *Id.* at 240.

15. 268 U.S. 563 (1925).

16. 148 F.2d 416 (2d Cir. 1945).

17. *Id.* at 427.

18. *Id.*

19. *Id.* at 429 (emphasis added).

20. United States v. Socony Vacuum Oil Co., 310 U.S. 150 (1940).

21. Doctor Miles Med. Co. v. John D. Park & Sons, 220 U.S. 373 (1911). While *Doctor Miles* does not use *per se* terminology, it has consistently been so interpreted. *See, e.g.*, Bus. Elecs. Corp. v. Sharp Elecs. Corp., 485 U.S. 717 (1988).

22. Int'l Salt Co. v. United States, 332 U.S. 392 (1947).

23. Fashion Originators' Guild of Am. v. Fed. Trade Comm'n, 312 U.S. 457 (1941).

24. 15 U.S.C. § 18. The Celler-Kefauver amendments of 1950 expanded the reach of Section 7, putting the statute largely in the form applied today.

25. Doctor Miles Med. Co. v. John D. Park & Sons, 220 U.S. 373 (1911).

26. In *Chicago Board of Trade*, the protection of small country dealers was but one of a whole list of factors found by the Court to justify the restraint. And in *Alcoa*, the statements about small businesses is but a secondary reason for not permitting a "good monopoly" defense. Moreover, the court's suggestion that perhaps the interest of small producers may trump efficiency concerns ("in spite of possible cost") seems inconsistent with its later recognition that monopoly resulting from the firm's "skill, foresight and industry" is not unlawful. *Trans-Missouri* could be read to adopt a special small business protection in its discussion of the fixing of *low* prices, but the case focused primarily on *high* cartel prices.

27. *See* discussions in Fed. Trade Comm'n v. Morton Salt Co., 334 U.S. 37 (1948); Chroma Lighting v. GTE Prods. Corp., 113 F.3d 693 (9th Cir. 1997); Boise Cascade Corp. v. Fed. Trade Comm'n, 837 F.2d 1127 (D.C. Cir. 1988) (particularly dissent of Judge Mikva).

28. Thomas E. Kauper, *The "Warren Court" and the Antitrust Laws: Of Economics, Populism and Cynicism*, 67 MICH. L. REV. 325 (1968).

29. *See, e.g.*, Simpson v. Union Oil Co., 377 U.S. 13 (1964).

30. 370 U.S. 294 (1962).

31. *See, e.g.*, HERBERT HOVENKAMP, FEDERAL ANTITRUST POLICY 451–52 (1994); POSNER 2001, *supra* note 7, at 122–26.

32. 370 U.S. at 344.

33. Derek Bok, *Section 7 of the Clayton Act and the Merging of Law and Economics*, 74 HARV. L. REV. 226, 236–37 (1960); *see also* HOVENKAMP, *supra* note 31, at 451.

34. *See* United States v. Philadelphia National Bank, 374 U.S. 321 (1963); *see also* United States v. Pabst Brewing Co., 384 U.S. 546 (1966); United States v. Von's Grocery Co., 384 U.S. 270 (1966); United States v. Aluminum Co. of America (Rome Cable), 377 U.S. 271 (1964) (predating *Philadelphia Bank*).

35. United States v. Von's Grocery Co., 384 U.S. 270 (1966).

36. 386 U.S. 568 (1967).

37. *See, e.g.*, Reynolds Metals Co. v. Fed. Trade Comm'n, 309 F.2d 223 (D.C. Cir. 1962).

38. *See* Kauper, *supra* note 28, at 331–33.

39. *See* Albrecht v. The Herald Co., 390 U.S. 145 (1968); United States v. Parke, Davis & Co., 362 U.S. 29 (1960).

40. 390 U.S. 145 (1968).

41. 388 U.S. 365 (1967).

42. Simpson v. Union Oil Co., 377 U.S. 13 (1964).

43. 359 U.S. 207 (1959).

44. *Id.* at 213.

45. Many of these cases are collected in Thomas E. Kauper, *Cease and Desist: The History, Effect, and Scope of Clayton Act Orders of the Federal Trade Commission*, 66 MICH. L. REV. 1095, 1173–78 (1968).

46. *See* Fed. Trade Comm'n v. Morton Salt Co., 334 U.S. 37 (1948); *see also* Texaco Co. v. Hasbrouck, 496 U.S. 543 (1990); Chroma Lighting v. GTE Prods. Corp., 113 F.3d 693 (9th Cir. 1997).

47. Fed. Trade Comm'n v. Borden Co., 383 U.S. 637 (1966); Fed. Trade Comm'n v. Sun Oil Co., 371 U.S. 505 (1963).

48. Utah Pie Co. v. Cont'l Baking Co., 386 U.S. 685, *reh'g denied*, 387 U.S. 949 (1967).

49. *See* HOVENKAMP, *supra* note 31, at 523; *see also* cases cited in *supra* note 27.

50. *See* BORK, *supra* note 10.

51. *See* POSNER 2001, *supra* note 7.

52. There are scores of such critiques from persons not identified with the Chicago School. Among them was Professor Phillip E. Areeda, whose multivolume antitrust treatise is consistently critical of virtually all the decisions of the 1960s.

53. 433 U.S. 36 (1977).

54. Much of this criticism is expressly referred to by the Court in *Sylvania*. *See id.* at 48 nn. 13–14.

55. *Id.* at 53 n.21.

56. *See, e.g.*, Crane & Shovel Sales Corp. v. Bucyrus Erie Co., 854 F.2d 802 (6th Cir. 1988); Jayco Sys. Inc. v. Savin Bus. Machs. Corp., 777 F.2d 306 (5th Cir. 1985). Adverse intrabrand effects involve restriction of competition between dealers of the same brand.

57. HOVENKAMP, *supra* note 31, at 431.

58. *See, e.g.*, Monsanto Co. v. Spray-Rite Serv. Corp., 465 U.S. 752 (1984); Bus. Elecs. Corp., v. Sharp Elecs. Corp., 485 U.S. 717 (1988).

59. State Oil Co. v. Khan, 522 U.S. 3, 18 (1997).

60. *See* Jefferson Parish Hosp. Dist. No. 2 v. Hyde, 466 U.S. 2 (1984); United States Steel Corp. v. Fortner Enters., Inc., 429 U.S. 610 (1977).

61. *See* Fed. Trade Comm'n v. Ind. Fed'n of Dentists, 476 U.S. 447 (1986); Northwest Wholesale Stationers, Inc. v. Pacific Stationery & Printing Co., 472 U.S. 284 (1985).

62. 509 U.S. 209 (1993).

63. *See, e.g.*, Taylor Publ'g Co. v. Jostens, Inc., 216 F.3d 465 (5th Cir. 2000); Nat'l Parcel Servs., Inc. v. J. B. Hunt Logistics, Inc., 150 F.3d 170 (8th Cir. 1998); Israel Travel Advisory Serv., Inc. v. Israel Identity Tours, 61 F.3d 1250 (7th Cir. 1995). The Justice Department has fared no better. *See* United States v. AMR Corp., 335 F.2d 1109 (10th Cir. 2003).

64. In *Falls City Industries, Inc. v. Vanco Beverage, Inc.*, 460 U.S. 428 (1983) (rejecting the contention that the defense must be proven on a customer-to-customer basis and also finding that the defense was not confined to meeting the offers by competitors to *existing* customers).

65. *See, e.g.*, Coastal Fuels of P. R., Inc. v. Caribbean Petroleum Co., 79 F.3d 182 (1st Cir. 1996).

66. *Compare* Boise Cascade Corp. v. Fed. Trade Comm'n, 837 F.2d 1127 (D.C. Cir. 1988) (requiring an evaluation of market effects), *with* Chroma Lighting v. GTE Prods. Corp., 111 F.3d 653 (9th Cir. 1997) (rejecting the approach of *Boise Cascade*), *and* George Haug Co., Inc. v. Rolls Royce Motor Cars, Inc., 148 F.3d 136 (2d Cir. 1998).

67. *See Boise Cascade*, 837 U.S. 1127; McCormick & Co., 5 CCH TRADE REG. REP. § 24, 711 (FTC 2000) (consent).

68. *See, e.g.*, U.S. DEP'T OF JUSTICE, REPORT ON THE ROBINSON-PATMAN ACT (1977).

69. United States v. Von's Grocery Co., 384 U.S. 270 (1966).

70. United States v. Baker Hughes, Inc., 908 F.2d 981 (D.C. Cir. 1990).

71. United States v. Gen. Dynamics Corp., 415 U.S. 486 (1974).

72. *United States v. Citizens & S. Nat'l Bank*, 422 U.S. 86 (1975), involved a very peculiar set of facts and makes no contribution to substantive merger standards.

73. The 1982, 1984, and 1992 Merger Guidelines may be found in 4 CCH TRADE REG. REP. §§ 13, 101–104.

74. *See, e.g.*, United States v. Waste Mgmt., Inc., 743 F.2d 976 (2d Cir. 1984); Fed. Trade Comm'n v. Staples, Inc., 970 F. Supp. 1066 (D.D.C. 1997); Fed. Trade Comm'n v. Butterworth Hosp. Corp., 946 F. Supp. 1285 (W. D. Mich. 1996), *aff'd*, 121 F.3d 708 (6th Cir. 1997).

75. In *Federal Trade Commission v. H. J. Heinz Co.*, 246 F.3d 708 (D.C. Cir. 2001), a merger of firms with a combined market share of under 40 percent was enjoined, but the only remaining firm had a market share in excess of 65 percent.

76. As Professor Hovenkamp has put it, "most of the theories under which conglomerate mergers are challenged have either fallen into disrepute or have been characterized as unmanageable or excessively speculative." HOVENKAMP, *supra* note 31, at 502.

77. Clayton Act, § 7A, 15 U.S.C. § 18A.

78. *Compare* Joe Sims & Deborah P. Herman, *The Effect of Twenty Years of Hart-Scott-Rodino on Merger Practice: A Case in the Law of Unintended Consequences Applied to Antitrust Litigation*, 65 ANTITRUST L.J. 865 (1997).

79. *See* Stephen Calkins, *In Praise of Antitrust Litigation: the Second Annual Bernstein Lecture*, 72 ST. JOHN'S L. REV. 1 (1998).

80. *See* United States v. Grinnell Corp., 384 U.S. 563 (1966); *see also* Verizon Communications, Inc. v. Law Offices of Curtis V. Trinko, 540 U.S. 398 (2004); United States v. Microsoft Corp., 253 F.3d 34 (D.C. Cir.), *cert. denied*, 534 U.S. 952 (2001).

81. *See* Einer Elhauge, *Defining Better Monopolization Standards*, 56 STAN. L. REV. 253, 261 (2003).

82. *See* Symposium, *Predatory Behavior in the Marketplace*, 18 ANTITRUST 7 (2003).

83. POSNER 2001, *supra* note 7, at 26.

84. United States v. Microsoft Corp., 253 F.3d 34 (2001).

85. 15 U.S.C. Sec. 1. As a result of 2004 legislation, the maximum corporate fine under the Sherman Act is now 100 million dollars, the maximum individual fine is one million dollars and the maximum jail sentence is ten years. H.R. 1086, Act of June 22, 2004. This represents a tenfold increase in the maximum corporate fine over the prior level.

86. The maximum corporate fine to date is 500 million dollars assessed against F. Hoffman LaRoche in the vitamins cartel case. These fines are assessed under the Criminal Fines Improvement Act of 1987, 18 U.S.C. 3571 (1994). On length of jail sentences imposed, see United States v. Andreas, 216 F.3d 645 (7th Cir. 2000).

87. The Corporate and Individual Leniency Policies may be found in 4 TRADE REG. REP. (CCH) ¶ 13, 113.

88. Ill. Brick Co. v. Illinois, 431 U.S. 720 (1977).

89. Brunswick Corp. v. Pueblo Bowl-O-Mat, Inc., 429 U.S. 477 (1977).

90. The Vertical Restraints Guidelines issued in 1985 by the Department were a substantial departure from the existing law on nonprice vertical restraints. These guidelines, withdrawn in 1993, may be found in 4 CCH TRADE REG. REP. § 13, 105.

91. United States v. AT&T, 552 F. Supp. 131 (D.D.C. 1982), *aff'd mem. sub. nom.*, Maryland v. United States, 460 U.S. 1001 (1983).

92. *See* Kauper, *supra* note 28.

93. For example, the *per se* prohibition against resale price maintenance has remained in effect.

94. *See* Symposium, *Post-Chicago Economics*, 63 ANTITRUST L.J. 445 (1995).

95. Cont'l T.V., Inc. v. GTE Sylvania Inc., 433 U.S. 36, 53 n.21 (1977).

96. *See* United States v. United States Steel Corp., 251 U.S. 417, 451 (1920) (stating "the law does not make mere size an offence").

97. The recently prosecuted vitamins cartel lasted for years. Monopoly power has existed for decades in some cases. *See, e.g.*, United States v. Aluminum Co. of America, 148 F.2d 416 (2d Cir. 1945); United States v. United Shoe Mach. Corp., 110 F. Supp. 295 (D. Mass. 1953), *aff'd per curiam*, 347 U.S. 521 (1954). Indeed, Microsoft's monopoly with respects to computer operating systems has now lasted well over a decade.

98. Verizon Communications, Inc. v. Law Offices of Curtis v. Trinko, 540 U.S. 398, 412 (2004).

8

Residential Privilege
The Advent of the Guarded Subdivision

David L. Callies and Paula A. Franzese[1]

In the classic science fiction movie, "Soylent Green," the world is divided into a rabblelike proletariat and the rich and powerful. The former live largely in the streets or in dilapidated multifamily, presumably subsidized, housing and receive minimal public services, including the distribution of food substitutes such as soylent green. The rich and powerful live in walled-off communities and enjoy a variety of perquisites, among which is real food. We are, of course, nowhere near such bleak evolution. But a variety of trends over the past thirty years has culminated in rather a lot of exclusion, primarily in the single-family residential market. Primary among these trends is the exponential increase in common interest or covenanted communities loosely governed by homeowners' associations, and in particular the gated version of such communities. This chapter traces the growth of gated communities, examining the values they represent and some of their less desirable consequences. The chapter also considers whether certain legal principles and other legislative tools may be used effectively to curb the segregating effects of these communities.

I. Gated Communities

A. The Growth of Gated Communities

In all areas of the United States now experiencing an increase in residential construction, common interest communities ("CICs") are increasing in number. Florida, California, and Texas are home to the greatest proportion of homeowner associations, followed by New Jersey, New York, Virginia, Pennsylvania, Maryland, and Hawai'i.[2] More than 30 million Americans, or 12 percent of the country's population, live in approximately one hundred fifty thousand CICs. Once considered the domain only of the most affluent, today CICs represent the main staple of suburban and metropolitan residential development.[3]

The latter part of the twentieth century witnessed record growth in gated and walled communities, a subset of all CICs. It is estimated that eight out of ten new residential housing developments in urban centers are gated.[4] Gated communities are proliferating in suburban areas as well, across all regions and price classes, from New York to California.[5] New homes in more than 40 percent of planned developments are gated throughout the South, the West, and the southeastern United States.[6] With the boom in gated and walled CICs, these communities now house about 8 million Americans.[7]

Gated and walled CICs include condominiums, cooperatives, and planned communities. In many ways, these developments closely approximate small municipal governments. Through homeowner associations,[8] they maintain private streets and parks, provide homeowner security, collect homeowner assessments for the purpose of financing the aforesaid activities, and by means of walls and gates, keep all but homeowners and their invited guests from the precincts of the community. Those living in the more than twenty thousand gated communities[9] cite safety, status, lifestyle enhancement, and the preservation of property values as prime motivators. The desire for safe, secure housing has only intensified in the wake of the tragic events of September 11, 2001.

Gated and walled communities have been described as being "as old as city-building itself."[10] Still, the first "purely residential gated neighborhoods" did not appear in the United States until the latter half of the nineteenth century.

> Upper-income gated developments like New York's Tuxedo Park and the private streets of St. Louis were built in the late 1800s by wealthy citizens to insulate themselves from the troublesome aspects of rapidly industrializing cities. During the twentieth century more gated, fenced compounds were built by members of the East Coast and Hollywood aristocracies for privacy, protection, and prestige. But these early gated preserves were different from

the gated subdivisions of today. They were uncommon places for uncommon people.[11]

Gated communities became more commonplace in the 1960s, as retirement communities allowed "average Americans to wall themselves off." These retirement areas were located predominantly in the Southeast and Southwest. Later, "[i]n the 1980s, upscale real estate speculation and the trend to conspicuous consumption saw the proliferation of gated communities around golf courses that were designed for exclusivity, prestige and leisure."[12] At the same time, gated communities became accessible to the middle class, and emerged in urban and suburban settings throughout the Northeast, Midwest, and Northwest, largely as a response to rising crime rates.[13] "In absolute numbers, California and Florida are home to the most gated communities, with Texas running a distant third. Gated communities are also common around New York City, Chicago, and other major metropolitan areas, but they are found nearly everywhere."[14]

The sense of exclusion does not by any means end with the gated residential community, however. Vacation communities also perpetuate notions of exclusivity. While there have always been exclusive retreats for the most rich and powerful (presidential retreats like Camp David spring to mind as well as the Kennedy compound at Hyannisport, Ted Turner's huge ranches, and entire islands owned by the likes of the Rockefellers), the trend is moving down into the ranks of the merely well-to-do and/or well-known. Most of these retreats are gated, with private recreational facilities which include golfing, skiing, and hunting. Most require hefty membership fees or deposits ranging from hundreds of thousands of dollars to over a million dollars. Membership is, of course, limited.

B. Gated Communities as Presently Structured and the Values They Reflect

Today, gated communities in the United States fall into one of three categories: so-called "lifestyle communities, prestige communities, and security zone communities."[15] Lifestyle communities include retirement communities, "developed for middle and upper-middle class retirees who want structure, recreation, and a built-in social life in their early retirement years."[16] Prestige or elite communities flaunt social status, using gates to "symbolize distinction and prestige and create and protect a secure place on the social ladder. . . . The gates are motivated by a desire to project an image, protect current investments, and control housing values."[17] In security zone communities, now proliferating in both metropolitan as well as suburban settings, residents erect the gates to protect against crime and enhance the sense of community and control in their neighborhood. "Security zone gatings and street closures occur at all income levels and in all areas. . . . Affluent neighborhoods in Los Angeles and public housing projects in Washington, D.C., among many others, have erected gates."[18] All three categories of gated communities reflect several social values: (1) a sense of community; (2) exclusion; and (3) privatization.

1. A Sense of Community

"Sense of community" has become important to understanding the motivations and aspirations of gated community residents. The term itself is taken from the field of community psychology and has been defined as the feeling an individual has about belonging to a group and involves the strength of the attachment people feel for their communities or neighborhoods. It is primarily a psychological construct: the presence or absence of a sense of community is experienced as an abstract concept in the human mind.[19]

Prior to the twentieth-century phenomena of urbanization and industrialization, sense of community was an intrinsic and natural aspect of everyday life in the United States. Postindustrial changes eliminated many community building blocks, so that the consensus from a myriad of disciplines is that today "sense of community is no longer a natural by-product of daily life; sense of community must be consciously defined and understood if it is to be maintained and enhanced in modern society."[20]

In this twenty-first century of increasing depersonalization and isolation, gated communities offer the promise of shared values, a shared destiny, connection, friendship, and cooperation. Sadly, as presently designed, gated communities rarely fulfill these goals either within the communities themselves or between the communities and their surrounding areas. The creation of exclusive neighborhoods "carries with it the possibility that those affluent enough to live in CIDs will become increasingly segregated from the rest of society."[21] When large groups of people remove themselves from the greater community, they fail to note their integral connection with that larger community, even on the external level of relying on public infrastructure and services beyond their gates. Instead they tend to focus on what they pay for—their private infrastructures within the gated communities—and feel overburdened by public taxes that benefit the general public. Thus, gated community homeowners tend to further disassociate themselves from the general public by being resentful for having to "pay twice." This can manifest itself through lower voter participation, less volunteerism, and a basic lack of interest in municipal concerns. In short, private community homeowners see themselves more as taxpayers than as citizens connected to a larger public.[22]

Even within gated communities, the desired sense of community is often lacking. Gated communities overemphasize covenants, conditions, and restrictions as planning and control devices, favoring regulation and enforcement to the detriment of social networks and leadership by consensus. Homeowner or community associations are formed, and a governing board is elected to oversee and enforce the restrictions privately.[23] Increasingly, these associations may become rigid, uninspired, and excessively concerned with compliance and control.[24] In a significant indictment of gated and walled communities' essential default, two experts observe that:

> They employ walls and guards to prevent crime rather than applying integrated, holistic solutions that encourage community participation to ward off destructive elements. Gated communities do not undertake strategies to acquire and maintain adequate education, jobs, and public services—fundamental civic goals that are the first crucial step in crime prevention. Instead of rich and vibrant public spaces, they contain, at best, private recreational facilities and clubhouses that serve a limited membership and offer a narrow range of activities rather than the entire spectrum of community needs.[25]

These fundamental shortcomings have led to tensions within gated communities, as members balk at overzealous restrictiveness and rules that are perceived to be heavy-handed.[26] Outside the enclaves themselves, gates and walls have engendered considerable resentment and protest.[27] Anti-gating organizations argue that gated communities inherently deepen divisions and differences, thereby escalating conflicts between the "haves" and the "have-nots."[28]

Whether the neighborhoods segregate on the basis of wealth, interest, or fear, the continued fragmentation of municipalities erodes the original concept of community.[29] Even so, as a society Americans have segregated themselves and been segregated for centuries. "It might be argued that residential associations simply embody in design what high-priced suburbs achieve in practice. Yet while expensive housing markets may prevent certain individuals from living in certain areas, residential associations have the additional power to prevent such individuals from even entering these areas."[30]

2. THE POLITICS OF EXCLUSION

Gated communities are, by definition, exclusionary. Such exclusivity is characterized by the establishment of boundaries that delineate and mark the given community as separate and distinct from the world at large.[31] Boundaries can contribute to a sense of community or shared destiny within the delineated area. But boundaries by themselves cannot build neighborhood attachment amongst those inside the development without the additional presence of "social bonding and behavioral rootedness." Gates do not actively cultivate these determinants of community.

Because gated communities are exclusionary in their practices—staking out boundaries and rendering access physically as well as economically prohibitive—those outside the gates assail gated and walled communities. Walled communities have been described as "the means of continuing the housing industry's and the federal government's decades-old policies that segregated residential areas by income, social class, and race."[32] Gates and walls have been likened to the "walled cities of the medieval world, constructed to keep the hordes at bay."[33] Some argue that their very existence "causes harms to nonmembers by developing exclusive communities, by gating formerly public streets and neighborhoods, and by increasing the fiscal burdens of cities and states."[34]

Exclusionary measures breed distrust on both sides of the gate. Those inside tend to accentuate their fear of the outside, while those outside may assume distrust by those inside and respond accordingly. When private security agencies decide who is allowed inside the gates, the chances of what would normally be considered illegal segregation increase. Such isolation, protection, and fragmentation does little to promote social and economic opportunity, solve problems facing today's municipalities, or work toward healthy societies.[35]

At least one court has found that a gated community's segregating effects, whether overtly intentional or not, can harm minority communities. In *Huntington Branch, NAACP v. Huntington,*[36] the Second Circuit invalidated a zoning ordinance that prohibited private construction of a subsidized multifamily apartment complex in a virtually all-white neighborhood. The construction was limited to an urban renewal area predominantly occupied by minority residents. In determining that the facially neutral regulation violated the federal Fair Housing Act, the court applied a disparate impact analysis. The plaintiff needed to prove only discriminatory effect, and not discriminatory intent. One might consider extending the same analysis to gated communities that, for example, charge 20 percent more for housing than comparable residential areas, and argue that these communities are effectively excluding blacks and Hispanics who generally earn 20 to 30 percent less than whites.[37]

The homogeneity of private communities leads to an enforced isolation that does not promote interest in or understanding of surrounding municipalities. The isolation of such communities lowers interaction among various ethnic, racial, social, and economic groups, and thus lessens the experience level of one with the other, with a concomitant loss of empathy. Some have argued that the large number of people choosing the gated or private community lifestyle proves that it has much to offer, and that such communities should be opened to a variety of other, typically disenfranchised, groups.[38] According to this view, private communities should not be forced to open their gates to a wider variety of people, but rather a wider variety of private communities should be made available, including some in the inner city.

3. Privatization and Fiscal Responsibility

"Privatization" describes the "shift of government functions from the public to the private sector."[39] Gated communities contribute to privatization by tempting the wealthy out of the cities, "siphoning off their tax dollars, their expertise and participation, and their sense of identification with a community," in essence creating a "secession of the successful."[40] With enough of these communities, the surrounding cities and counties could find themselves bereft of much of their population and resources, so that "the city could become financially untenable for the many and socially unnecessary for the few."[41]

Critics observe that by living in a gated community, residents are not supporting the public services that support the community at large.[42] However, homeowners in a community development must still pay local property taxes for local government services, whether or not they avail themselves of such services, and even though they already pay extra for their private community's services.[43] As a result, members of homeowner associations have begun requesting tax deductions for their dues. Indeed, in California, in the aftermath of Proposition 13, obtaining a rebate for providing their own segment of public services is a major political goal of people living in planned communities.[44] Proposition 13 effectively limited the amount of public services provided by local government. To compensate for the absence of certain amenities, private developments began including their own streets, drainage, parks, recreation facilities, and streetlights. Where the communities were not gated, the general public had access to these privately funded infrastructures, for which the public paid nothing. Meanwhile, the relevant municipality still taxed private community homeowners to provide the same infrastructures for the public as well. These homeowners balked, arguing that they pay for their own public services (e.g., garbage collection, street maintenance, security, and recreation) and see no need to pay for services to others, especially if they do not partake of those services elsewhere.[45]

The problem with this argument is that people living in private communities do use some public services and it would be difficult to determine exact percentages of what each homeowner uses. The opposition also argues that one rarely pays taxes for only what one uses or receives. In addition, when a private community provides some of its own public services, the municipality can withdraw from those areas in an effort to save money and manpower, thereby effectively lowering everyone's costs.

Regardless of the merits of their claims, as a group, people living in planned communities are an easily mobilized bloc that will vote to protect property values, to lower property taxes, and to seek tax equity. Considering that more than 30 million Americans live in private communities, with 8 million in gated communities, that can be a large, local voting bloc.

II. Zoning: A More Traditional Method of Exclusion

Zoning and city planning also bear some of the responsibility for exclusionary tendencies. Zoning was meant to be exclusionary in some sense, as the Supreme Court acknowledged in 1923 when it upheld the exercise of such power by local governments in the celebrated *Euclid* case.[46] Under traditional zoning practices, "homes are with homes; business is with business; factories are with factories."[47] This segregation of uses is by definition exclusionary. Indeed, in one of the more famous pre-*Euclid* decisions upholding early zoning, the California Supreme Court said:

In addition to all that has been said in support of the constitutionality of residential zoning as part of a comprehensive plan, we think it may be safely and sensibly said that justification for residential zoning may, in the last analysis, be rested upon the protection of the civic and social values of the American home. The establishment of such districts is for the general welfare because it tends to promote and perpetuate the American home. It is axiomatic that the welfare, and indeed the very existence, of a nation depend upon the character and caliber of its citizenry. The character and quality of manhood and womanhood are in a large measure the result of home environment. The home and its intrinsic influences are the very foundation of good citizenship and any factor contributing to the establishment of homes and the fostering of home life doubtless tends to the enhancement, not only of community life, but the life of the nation as a whole.[48]

This is not an exceptional statement. According to Alfred Bettman, counsel for the Village of Euclid, of the eleven state high court decisions upholding zoning prior to the *Euclid* decision, "every one of these decisions upheld the creation of exclusively residential districts and the exclusion of non-nuisance industries and businesses therefrom, and many of them upheld the creation of exclusively single family home districts from which apartment houses were excluded."[49]

That such districting could lead to segregation and exclusion on the basis of race and class was certainly a concern of the early proponents of zoning. This concern was well founded because zoning was often used as an exclusionary tool, both racially and economically. As one commentator at the time put it:

City planning and zoning experts were appealing to their clientele with promises that the new controls would protect them from "undesirable neighbors." In fact, all the arguments adduced to show that zoning protects property values are meaningless unless they imply this important element in the determination of values. No height restriction, street width, or unbuilt lot area will prevent prices from tottering in a good residential neighborhood unless it helps at the same time to keep out Negroes, Japanese, Armenians, or whatever race most jars on the natives.[50]

Consistent with these views, a prominent zoning consultant in Atlanta allegedly prepared a zoning ordinance in which residential districts were divided into three types—white, colored, and undetermined—for the reason that "race zoning . . . is simply a common sense method of dealing with facts as they are."[51] The same consultant was equally happy with the economic segregation zoning might perpetuate.

While the Supreme Court made relatively short work of outlawing explicit zoning by race in *Buchanan v. Warley*,[52] there remained the matter of economic discrimination among residential classifications. If minorities could not afford to live in particular communities, it would not be due to racial discrimination per se, but to the inherent constraints of wealth, or lack thereof. Thus, in the 1940s and 1950s, local governments began touting the importance of preserving community character and controlling growth, and implemented ever-expanding requirements for minimum floor space, setbacks, and lot sizes.[53] As housing requirements became more demanding, low- and moderate-income housing became less viable. The effects of "exclusionary zoning," that is, zoning practices that tend to segregate people along economic, social, and racial lines, became increasingly common. Nevertheless, courts overwhelmingly upheld these ordinances as legitimate exercises of the general welfare police power. This practice was particularly notable in the Northeast, where judges were known to cite the "quiet beauty of rural surroundings"[54] and the value of "nice houses."[55] In New Jersey, the state court approved a residential five-acre minimum lot size on such grounds.[56]

Ironically, it was the New Jersey Supreme Court that later struck the hardest blow to exclusionary zoning tactics with its landmark decision in *Southern Burlington County NAACP v. Township of Mount Laurel*.[57] In *Mount Laurel*, over half the township was restricted to single-family homes, with minimum lot sizes of one-half acre, one acre, or three acres. Garden apartments and multifamily housing, which had been anticipated by poor, mostly black, residents in the area, were expressly prohibited.[58] Finding that housing is one of "the most basic human needs," the court held that available housing is an essential element of the general welfare, and must therefore be promoted by the state and its municipalities pursuant to the state's police power. Furthermore, the court declared that New Jersey's state constitution, which is stricter than its federal counterpart, guarantees equal protection for the poor and extends substantive due process protection to housing. Because Mount Laurel's zoning ordinances did neither, and because its stated interest (to collect enough property taxes to cover municipal governmental and educational costs) did not meet constitutional standards, the court invalidated the ordinance.

In the end, the New Jersey court imposed a duty on developing municipalities like Mount Laurel to "affirmatively . . . plan and provide, by [their] land use regulations, the *reasonable opportunity* for an appropriate variety and choice of housing, including . . . low and moderate cost housing, to meet the needs, desires and resources of *all categories of people* who may desire to live within [their] boundaries."[59] Henceforth, developing municipalities would be required to "make all reasonable efforts to encourage and facilitate" their "fair share" of low- and moderate-income housing.[60] These concepts were later codified in the New Jersey Fair Housing Act of 1985.[61]

In the years following *Mount Laurel*, several other courts interpreted their state constitutions to require affordable housing on a regional basis.[62] Other states took a different approach, adopting "inclusionary" zoning ordinances to combat the long-standing history of exclusionary practices; these were either voluntary or mandatory, with or without incentives. A prime example is California's Density Bonus Statute, which grants developers an automatic bonus if their plans set aside certain percentages of the property for low-income, very-low-income, and senior citizen housing.[63] By statute, the inclusionary units are required to maintain exterior designs consistent with surrounding noninclusionary units, so low-income residents are less identifiable and less stigmatized than they might be otherwise. While some courts and legislatures recognize the need to provide for affordable housing, courts continue to take a hands-off approach to local zoning ordinances, especially where the municipality's asserted justification is preservation of family and community, along with keeping the "city beautiful," as the following section demonstrates.

III. The Role of Law in Perpetuating Class Exclusion

A. Constitutional Claims

Plaintiffs challenging the segregating effects of gated communities have no viable constitutional claims under the federal Constitution. First, private developers are not "state actors," placing their conduct beyond the reach of the Fourteenth Amendment's due process and equal protection provisions. Second, even if private developers were considered state actors, discrimination based on class raises no heightened level of judicial scrutiny because wealth is not a suspect class.

To the extent that gated communities mimic municipalities in the lives of everyday people, perhaps they should be considered state actors. As suggested in Part I.A, in many ways gated communities and their governing homeowners' associations function as "private governments."[64] For this reason, some scholars have argued that gated communities should qualify as de facto state actors[65] and should be required to satisfy the Constitution's due process and equal protection guarantees.

Although this contention has not been squarely litigated before the U.S. Supreme Court, lower courts have for the most part resisted applying constitutional safeguards to common interest community functions.[66] These courts are ambivalent, if not somewhat confused, about whether to characterize privately owned gated communities as the sort of state actors that would be subject to certain constitutional requirements.

Even if a plaintiff succeeded in persuading a court to find a gated community developer to be a state actor (thus subjecting it to the constitutional requirements of due process and equal protection), there still remains a strong likelihood that the constitutional challenge would fail. As noted earlier, discrimination based on wealth, or lack thereof, does not merit heightened judicial scrutiny. In the landmark case of *San Antonio Independent School District v. Rodriguez*,[67] the U.S. Supreme Court stated "at least where wealth is involved, the Equal Protection Clause does not require absolute equality or precisely equal advantages."[68] The Court then held that the poor do not constitute a suspect class under the Fourteenth Amendment, noting:

> The system of alleged discrimination and the class it defines have none of the traditional indicia of suspectness: the class is not saddled with such disabilities, or subjected to such a history of purposeful unequal treatment, or relegated to such a position of political powerlessness as to command extraordinary protection from the majoritarian political process.[69]

Thus, the Constitution provides no remedy for a low-income plaintiff suing over the exclusionary and segregating effects of a gated community.

B. Statutory Claims

Plaintiffs may have a statutory claim under the Fair Housing Act ("FHA")[70] if a gated community's income requirement produces a disparate impact upon a protected class. The FHA prohibits discrimination in the sale or lease of dwellings on the basis of race, color, religion, sex, handicap, familial status, and national origin.[71] Wealth is not a protected class under the Act. Thus, a low-income plaintiff suing a gated community developer for discrimination under the FHA would need to prove that the developer's methods of selecting homebuyers by income also disproportionately affected some other class of people protected under the FHA.

To make a claim for "disparate impact," a plaintiff must show that a facially neutral policy had an adverse effect on one (or more) protected classes under the FHA. The plaintiff need not prove intent to discriminate. Several appellate courts have found that local zoning restrictions, whether overtly intentional or not, can result in segregating effects that harm minority communities.[72] As we suggested earlier in discussing *Huntington*, this analysis could be applied to gated communities. Those charging 20 percent more for housing than comparable residential areas may be effectively excluding blacks and Hispanics who generally earn 20 to 30 percent less than whites.[73] In this way, income requirements that disproportionately exclude potential residents on the basis of race, a protected class, would violate the FHA.

A gated community developer may rebut a plaintiff's prima facie case by showing that the plaintiff was denied a home for business reasons that were neither discriminatory nor a pretext (i.e., a cover) for discrimination. There are two different standards of "business reasons": (a) "reasonable" or "legitimate" business reasons and (b) "business necessity." Additionally, a municipal government alleged to have violated the FHA (e.g., through zoning ordinances that disproportionately impact protected classes) may rebut a plaintiff's prima facie case by showing that there were "no less restrictive means" to accomplish whatever action it has taken. The following cases do not squarely deal with an income requirement's disproportionate impact upon protected classes under the FHA, but they illustrate how such a claim might progress through the various U.S. Circuit Courts.

Holding developers to the "reasonable" or "legitimate" business reasons test, the Ninth Circuit in *Pfaff v. U.S. Dept. of Housing & Urban Development*[74] held that a numerical limitation on the number of occupants in a home did disproportionately impact potential occupants based on familial status, but that the landlord's business reason for the classification— preservation of property values—was reasonable and legitimate.[75] Using the same reasonableness test, as opposed to the more stringent "business necessity" test, yet reaching a different result, the Eighth Circuit in *U.S. v. Badgett*,[76] held that an occupancy limitation (one person per one bedroom apartment) discriminated against a potential renter on the basis of familial status. Further, the court did not accept the landlord's proffered business reason—that the limited availability of parking spaces justified the occupancy cap. At least in the Eighth and Ninth Circuits, this lower level of scrutiny, applying the "business reasons" test, while not entirely hostile to plaintiffs, may mean that plaintiffs are generally less likely to prevail on a disparate impact claim against a gated community developer than might be the case if the "business necessity" test were applied.

Illustrating the "business necessity test," the Tenth Circuit in *Mountain Side Mobile Estates v. Secretary of Housing and Urban Development*[77] held that an occupancy limit in a mobile home estate (no more than three occupants per mobile home) disproportionately impacted buyers based on familial status. The court held developers to an intermediate level of scrutiny, meaning that the developers would have to prove that "the discriminatory practice has a manifest relationship to the housing in question."[78] In this case, the court found that the business necessity reasons given for the occupancy limit, namely, sewer capacity and quality of life, were legitimate.[79] However, the "business necessity" standard is a more demanding one than the "reasonableness" standard. Accordingly, plaintiffs generally have a better chance of prevailing on an FHA claim in the Tenth Circuit.

When municipal governments pass ordinances that disproportionately impact protected classes and violate the FHA, they must also proffer justifications for doing so. The Second Circuit, in *Huntington*,[80] articulated a "no less restrictive means" test for assessing the validity of such justifications. In *Huntington*, the court found that a zoning ordinance restricting multifamily housing to nonwhite areas of the town violated the FHA by disproportionately impacting minority populations and perpetuating the effects of segregation.[81] The court held the town to a heightened level of scrutiny, requiring it to rebut plaintiff's prima facie case with "bona fide and legitimate justifications for its action with no less discriminatory alternatives available."[82] Thus, in this circuit, plaintiffs have the best chance of suing municipal governments for class discrimination by linking their claims to disproportionate impact claims under the FHA.

We may conclude that a claim under the FHA against a gated community developer's income requirements due to disparate impacts on other protected classes might succeed, depending upon a court's willingness to scrutinize the developer's or government's proffered justifications. Such a claim has yet to be squarely litigated.

IV. Conclusion

This chapter has shown how both government and homeowner associations use land use controls to foster a measure of exclusivity. Such use is arguably part of a larger problem, that of elitism in the ecology movement generally, an elitism that has eroded any possible sense of community. The late Dick Babcock wrote about this brand of elitism in the context of affordable housing with typical verve and bluntness—and with a little help from a coauthor of this chapter—in 1973.[83] Generally, the "ecology first" enthusiast has a low opinion of his fellow man, which is why he may be willing to consign a goodly portion of mankind (usually that portion to which he does not belong) to a less fortunate position. In such a context, ecology is indeed elitist. Jon Margolis wrote about it for *Esquire Magazine*, dealing with the cry of the ecologists for an end to growth and the effect that would have on housing:

> Stop growing? But growing is the secret of our success. We have mass affluence, to the extent we have it, not because we took from the rich and gave to the poor but because we became—*we grew*—so much richer that even most of the poor live tolerably. They still get the short end of the stick, but the stick is so long now that one can get at least a fingerhold on the end.
>
> . . . the conservationists are not on that end. They are not steelworkers or assembly-line workers or small farmers or hotel clerks. They are Wall Street lawyers and junior faculty and editors and writers and corporate vice-presidents. One does not become a conservationist until one has had the time and learning to care about whether there are eagles or Everglades. . . . The suburbs are open to them, as Vermont is to the more affluent, because of technology, because draining swamps and dirtying streams and damming rivers and polluting the air gave them high-paying jobs. True, as Ian McHarg said, ecological planning can give any given area more high-paying jobs and more profits plus good environment. But for the nation as a whole, for the economy, the conservationist's dichotomy remains, and he has not faced up to it: if we do not stop expanding, we ruin the environment; if we do, we condemn the lower middle classes to their present fate.[84]

As Richard Neuhaus has made clear in his *In Defense of People*, it is often a matter of the rich man's politics of choice versus the poor man's politics of necessity:

To whom, politically speaking, does the environmental issue belong? To the aristocrats, certainly. To the monied, misanthropic aristocrats who live in the city as much as need compels but find their "real life" in getting away from it all. The presumably radical ecotacticians of the 1970s are in large part the heirs of a conservationist history that, in a thousand variations, has peddled the proposition that "only man is vile."[85]

Our point is not that ecology is unimportant—or even that gated communities are evil by definition. We simply wish to draw attention to some of the assumptions that underlie judicial decisions—beautiful homes with lots of space around them are inherently good—and suggest that, just as analysis of the consequences of those assumptions reveals negative impact on the poor, we may need to expand our understanding of the social consequences of some compelling ecological truisms—growth is bad, the environment should be protected. Social critics of the ecological renaissance find themselves being cozied up to by some suspect characters who, as in the cartoons, have dollar signs where their eyes ought to be. But other goals of a *social* nature are *also* important. And surely it must be worthwhile to devote some serious thought to the development of a model that will include social justice in thinking about land use, growth, and the environment. The notion of raising ecology to the dignity of a moral principle and then declaring it to be a matter of *survival* is aptly skewered by Neuhaus: "Who has time for programs of social justice if indeed survival is at stake?"[86]

<h4 style="text-align:center">NOTES</h4>

1. The authors wish to thank Adrienne Iwamoto Suarez, a past editor of the University of Hawai'i Law Review, for her able research assistance.

2. EVAN McKENZIE, PRIVATOPIA: HOMEOWNER ASSOCIATIONS AND THE RISE OF RESIDENTIAL PRIVATE GOVERNMENT 11 (1994).

3. *See* James L. Winokur, *Critical Assessment: The Financial Role of Community Associations*, 38 SANTA CLARA L. REV. 1135, 1138 (1998).

4. EDWARD J. BLAKELY AND MARY GAIL SNYDER, FORTRESS AMERICA: GATED COMMUNITIES IN THE UNITED STATES 7 (1997).

5. *Id.* at 7; Lois M. Baron, *The Great Gate Debate*, 21 BUILDER 92, 92–96 (Mar. 1998).

6. BLAKELY & SNYDER, *supra* note 4, at 7.

7. Douglas S. Bible & Chengho Hsieh, *Gated Communities and Residential*

Property Values, 69 APPRAISAL J. 140, 140 (April 2001); Baron, *supra* note 5, at 92–100.

8. Michael Halberg, *Gated Communities: Do They Raise Residents' Expectations and Increase Liability for Associations?* 4 CAI's J. COMMUNITY ASS'N L. 5, 6 (2001).

9. *See* Bible & Hsieh, *supra* note 7, at 140.

10. BLAKELY & SNYDER, *supra* note 4, at 3.

11. Maria Burnham, *Gated Homes a Trend, Expert Declares*, COM. APPEAL, Mar. 10, 2002, at 4.

12. BLAKELY & SNYDER, *supra* note 4, at 4; *see also* David Dillon, *Fortress America: More and More of Us Are Living behind Locked Gates*, PLANNING 8 (June 1994).

13. BLAKELY & SNYDER, *supra* note 4, at 5; *see also* Georjeanna Wilson-Doenges, *An Exploration of Sense of Community and Fear of Crime in Gated Communities*, 32 ENV'T AND BEHAV. 597 (Sept. 2000); Robert Atlas & W. G. LeBlanc, *The Impact on Crime of Street Closures and Barricades*, 5 SECURITY J. 140 (1994).

14. BLAKELY & SNYDER, *supra* note 4, at 5.

15. *Id.* at 38.

16. *Id.* at 39.

17. *Id.* at 40–41.

18. *Id.* at 42–43.

19. Stephen E. Cochrun, *Understanding and Enhancing Neighborhood Sense of Community*, 9 J. PLAN. LITERATURE 92, 93 (1994); *see also* W. J. Goudy, *The Ideal and the Actual Community: Evaluations from Small Town Residents*, 18 AM. J. COMMUNITY PSYCHOL. 277, 285 (1990).

20. Cochrun, *supra* note 19, at 92.

21. *Id.* at 22.

22. Sheryll D. Cashin, *Privatized Communities and the "Secession of the Successful": Democracy and Fairness beyond the Gate*, 28 FORDHAM URB. L. J. 1675, 1677 (2001); *see also* Paula A. Franzese, *Does It Take a Village? Privatization, Patterns of Restrictiveness and the Demise of Community*, 47 VILL. L. REV. 553, 588 (2002); Richard Damstra, *Don't Fence Us Out: The Municipal Power to Ban Gated Communities and the Federal Takings Clause*, 35 VAL. U. L. REV. 525, 539 (2001).

23. *See RCA Characteristics and Issues, in* RESIDENTIAL COMMUNITY ASSOCIATIONS: PRIVATE GOVERNMENTS IN THE INTERGOVERNMENTAL SYSTEM? 9, 15 (U.S. Advisory Comm'n on Intergovernmental Relations ed., 1989).

24. *See, e.g.*, Robert E. Lang & Karen A. Danielson, *Gated Communities in America: Walling Out the World?* 8 HOUSING POL'Y DEBATE 867, 873 (1997).

25. BLAKELY & SNYDER, *supra* note 4, at 169.

26. *See* Dennis R. Judd, *The Rise of the New Walled Cities, in* SPATIAL PRACTICES: CRITICAL EXPLORATIONS IN SOCIAL/SPATIAL THEORY 144, 158 (Helen Liggett & David C. Perry eds., 1995); Tim Vanderpool, *But Isn't This My Yard? Revolt against Neighborhood Rules*, CHRISTIAN SCI. MONITOR, Aug. 18, 1999, at 2; Harvey Rice, *Flurry of Lawsuits Divides Carriage Hill Neighbors*, HOUS. CHRON.,

Sept. 3, 2000, at A43; Maureen Feighan, *Fight Over Rights Gets Unneighborly, Lawsuits Grow as Homeowner Groups Enforce Rules*, DETROIT NEWS, Dec. 22, 2000, at A1.

27. *See* Citizens against Gated Enclaves v. Whitley Heights Civic Ass'n, 28 Cal. Rptr. 2d 451, 453 (Cal. Ct. App. 1994); *see also* Sacha Pfeiffer, *Fence Called a Barrier to Community*, BOSTON GLOBE, Nov. 8, 1998, at B1.

28. *See* Bob Campbell, *Subdivision Security Plan Is Critiqued*, ST. PETERSBURG TIMES, Mar. 11, 1992, sec. 1, at 1; Ina Jaffe, *Gated Communities Controversy in Los Angeles* (All Things Considered, Nat'l Pub. Radio, Aug. 11, 1992) *cited in* BLAKELY & SNYDER, *supra* note 4, at 159.

29. Damstra, *supra* note 22, at 536–37.

30. David J. Kennedy, Note, *Residential Associations as State Actors: Regulating the Impact of Gated Communities on Nonmembers*, 105 YALE L.J. 761, 771 (1995).

31. *See* David W. McMillan & David M. Chavis, *Sense of Community: A Definition and Theory*, 14 AM. J. COMMUNITY PSYCHOL. 6, 9–11 (1986).

32. Judd, *supra* note 26, at 155.

33. *Id.* at 160.

34. Kennedy, *supra* note 30, at 763.

35. Damstra, *supra* note 22, at 537.

36. Huntington Branch, NAACP v. Huntington, 844 F.2d 926, 937 (2d Cir. 1988).

37. Angel M. Traub, *The Wall Is Down, Now We Build More: The Exclusionary Effects of Gated Communities Demand Stricter Burdens under the FHA*, 34 J. MARSHALL L. REV. 379, 400 (2000).

38. Robert H. Nelson, *Privatizing the Neighborhood: A Proposal to Replace Zoning with Private Collective Property Rights to Existing Neighborhoods*, 7 GEO. MASON L. REV. 827, 865 (1999).

39. George L. Priest, *Introduction: The Aims of Privatization*, 6 YALE L. & POL'Y REV. 1, 5 (1988).

40. MCKENZIE, *supra* note 2, at 23; *see also* Robert Reich, *Secession of the Successful*, N.Y. TIMES MAG., Jan. 20, 1991, at 42.

41. *Id.* at 186.

42. Baron, *supra* note 5.

43. MCKENZIE, *supra* note 2, at 188.

44. *Id.*

45. Andrew Stark, *America, the Gated?* 22 WILSON Q. 98 (1998).

46. In *Village of Euclid v. Ambler Reality Co.*, 272 U.S. 365 (1926), the U.S. Supreme Court held that zoning was a valid exercise of the police power.

47. JAMES METZENBAUM, THE LAW OF ZONING 60 (1955).

48. Miller v. Bd. of Pub. Works, 234 P. 381, 386–87 (Cal. 1925).

49. ALFRED BETTMAN, CITY AND REGIONAL PLANNING PAPERS 166 (Arthur C. Comey ed., 1946).

50. SEYMOUR I. TOLL, ZONED AMERICAN 261–62 (1969) (quoting Lasker).

51. *Id.* at 262.

52. 245 U.S. 60 (1917) (upholding a contract right to sell to a willing black buyer despite zoning restriction of that part of St. Louis to whites only).

53. Lionshead Lake, Inc. v. Township of Wayne, 89 A.2d 693 (N.J. 1952) (minimum floor space); City of Dallas v. Lively, 161 S.W.2d 895 (Tex. 1942) (minimum setbacks); Caruthers v. Bd. of Adjustment, 290 S.W.2d 340 (Tex. 1956) (minimum lot size).

54. Simon v. Town of Needham, 42 N.E.2d 516, 518 (Mass. 1942).

55. Flora Realty & Inv. Co. v. City of Ladue, 246 S.W.2d 771 (Mo. 1952).

56. Fischer v. Township of Bedminster, 93 A.2d 378 (N.J. 1952).

57. 336 A.2d 713 (N.J. 1975).

58. David L. Kirp et al., Our Town: Race, Housing, and the Soul of Suburbia 1–3 (1995).

59. *Mount Laurel*, 336 A.2d at 728 (emphasis added).

60. *Id.*

61. *See* N.J. Stat. Ann. Sec. 52:27D–311 to 329 (2001). Compare this statute with the federal Fair Housing Act, 42 U.S.C. § 3601, which was first enacted in 1968.

62. *See* Berenson v. Town of New Castle, 415 N.Y.S.2d 669 (1979); Surrick v. Zoning Hearing Bd. of Upper Providence, 382 A.2d 105, 108 (Pa. 1977).

63. Nadia I. El Mallakh, *Does the Costa-Hawkins Act Prohibit Local Inclusionary Zoning Programs?* 89 Cal. L. Rev. at 1847, 1860 (2001).

64. McKenzie, *supra* note 2, at 122; *see also* Robert H. Nelson, *supra* note 38, at 828–29 (1999) (suggesting legislation to allow public neighborhood developments to be recast as private neighborhood associations); Harvey Rishikof & Alexander Wohl, *Private Communities or Public Governments: The State Will Make the Call*, 30 Val. U. L. Rev. 509, 511–16 (1996) (exploring propriety of state action designation to homeowners' associations); Wayne S. Hyatt & Jo Anne P. Stubblefield, *The Identity Crisis of Community Associations: In Search of the Appropriate Analogy*, 27 Real Prop. Prob. & Tr. J. 589, 634–41 (1993) (describing community association as quasi-government, with many of the powers and duties of municipal government).

65. *See* Steven Siegel, *The Constitution and Private Government: Toward the Recognition of Constitutional Rights in Private Residential Communities Fifty Years after* Marsh v. Alabama, 6 Wm. & Mary Bill Rts. J. 461, 462 (1998); *see also* Kennedy, *supra* note 30.

66. *See, e.g.*, Brock v. Watergate Mobile Home Park Ass'n, 502 So.2d 1380 (Fla. Dist. Ct. App. 1987); but see *Committee for a Better Twin Rivers v. Twin Rivers Homeowners' Ass'n*, 2006 N.J. Super. Lexis 29, for a contrary view, holding homeowning associations to be state actors.

67. 411 U.S. 1 (1973) (finding that Texas was under no constitutional obligation to equalize school spending among its richer and poorer school districts).

68. *Id.* at 24.

69. *Id.* at 28.

70. 42 U.S.C. § 3601 et seq.

71. *Id.* § 3604.

72. *See, e.g.*, Huntington Branch, NAACP v. Town of Huntington, 844 F.2d 926, 937 (2d. Cir. 1988); Metro. Hous. Dev. Corp. v. Vill. of Arlington Heights, 558 F.2d 1283, 1288–90 (7th Cir. 1977).

73. Traub, *supra* note 37, at 400.

74. 88 F.3d 739 (9th Cir. 1996).

75. *Id.* at 750.

76. 976 F.2d 1176 (8th Cir. 1992) (holding that business reason of "limited availability of parking" was unreasonable and pretextual).

77. 56 F.3d 1243 (10th Cir. 1995).

78. *Id.* at 1254.

79. *Id.*

80. 844 F.2d 926 (2d Cir. 1988).

81. *Id.* at 938.

82. *Id.* at 939.

83. Richard Babcock & David Callies, *Ecology and Housing: Virtues in Conflict*, *in* MODERNIZING URBAN LAND POLICY (Marion Clawson ed., 1973).

84. Jon Margolis, *Land of Ecology*, ESQUIRE, Mar. 1970 (emphasis added).

85. RICHARD NEUHAUS, IN DEFENSE OF PEOPLE: ECOLOGY AND THE SEDUCTION OF RADICALISM 30 (1971).

86. *Id.* at 114.

9

The Declining Progressivity of the Federal Income Tax

Lawrence A. Zelenak

Politicians proposing tax cuts seldom, if ever, want those cuts to be viewed as favoring the rich.[1] Whether a tax cut disproportionately benefits high-income taxpayers may depend, however, on the chosen framework for distributional analysis. From one perspective, a tax cut may be skewed in favor of the rich, while from another perspective the same tax cut may be proportional or even progressive. Thus, a politician who can control the analytical framework may improve the chances that his proposed tax cuts will be enacted.

This chapter examines how the income tax reductions enacted during the presidency of George W. Bush appear under several different distributional frameworks.[2] The chapter begins with the framework advocated by the Bush Treasury Department, under which analysis the distribution of the Bush-era tax cuts has actually been somewhat skewed *against* the rich. The chapter then turns, however, to several alternative frameworks—all of them more defensible than the Treasury's—and shows how the cuts heavily favor the rich under each alternative framework. Following discussion of how the Bush cuts appear under the several analytical perspectives, the chapter turns to three aspects of the cuts with particularly disturbing distributional implications, namely, the impact of the alternative minimum tax on the tax cuts for middle-income taxpayers, the relationship between the income tax cuts for the rich and the Social Security system, and the fact that the tax cuts for the rich have been enacted at a time of remarkable growth in the pretax inequality of income. The chapter concludes with some thoughts as to why the American public has been supportive of

© 2003. All Rights Reserved. Originally published in the Louisville Courier-Journal.
Reprint permission provided by Nick Anderson in conjunction with the
Washington Post Writers Group and the Cartoonist Group.

the Bush tax cuts, despite the skewing of those cuts in favor of high-income taxpayers.

I. The Bush Administration Frameworks and Some Alternatives

A. Distributional Effects of Changes in Tax Rates: A Narrow Focus

Debates on fairness in taxation tend to focus on the distribution of the *changes* in tax burdens caused by new (or proposed) legislation, rather than on the *absolute levels* of tax burdens under the new law. The assumption (seldom stated) must be that prior law "got it right" distributionally, and that the law is being changed only because the government's revenue requirement has changed. Thus, the benefit of the tax cut (or the burden of the tax increase) should fall proportionately on taxpayers throughout the income distribution. In keeping with the usual assumption, the focus of this chapter is on what it means to distribute a tax cut (or tax increase) proportionately.

This is a narrow focus, and it is always possible to argue that prior law "got it wrong." If, for example, prior law overburdened the rich, proponents of tax cuts for the rich could defend those cuts despite the fact—really, *because of* the fact—that the cuts disproportionately benefit the rich. The proponents of the tax cuts have not pursued this avenue of defense. Rather, they have claimed that the distribution of the changes in tax burdens does not favor the rich. However, their argument in favor of that claim is seriously flawed.

B. The Administration's Preferred Frame: Percentage Changes in Tax Liability

To simplify the question of distributional effects of tax cuts it is useful to imagine a country with just two types of citizens, the Highs and the Lows, with an equal number of each. Each High has a pretax income of $100,000 per year, and each Low has a pretax income of $50,000. At the beginning of the story, each High pays $20,000 tax (for an average rate of 20 percent), and each Low pays $5,000 tax (for an average rate of 10 percent). As a result of tax cut legislation, the tax liability of each High is then reduced to $16,000 (average rate of 16 percent) and the tax liability of each Low to $4,000 (average rate of 8 percent).

In 2001 and again in 2003, the Bush Treasury Department measured the distributional effects of income tax cuts by focusing on percentage reductions in income tax liabilities for taxpayers at various points in the income distribution.[3] The implicit assumption of the two Treasury analyses is that a tax cut is distributionally neutral if it results in the same percentage reduction in income tax liability for taxpayers in all income classes. Any such across-the-board, equal-percentage reduction leaves unchanged the percentage of total income taxes paid by each income class—a seemingly neutral result. In using this framework, the Bush Treasury was following the approach used successfully by Ronald Reagan in promoting and defending major tax cut legislation in 1981:

> Now, of course, those having a larger tax will get a larger reduction in the number of dollars. The fellow paying a $10,000 tax will get a $1,000 reduction. The fellow paying a $1,000 tax will get $100 off. But the first one will still be paying 10 times as much as the other one. The tax rate reduction is the same percentage across the board.[4]

In 2001 and again in 2003, the Treasury announced that the year's tax legislation produced the smallest percentage reduction in income tax liability for the highest income group.[5] By Treasury's standard, then, both the 2001 and 2003 cuts were progressive.[6] With respect to the 2003 cuts, for example, Treasury remarked:

> Because the percentage reduction in income taxes is greatest for families with incomes under $50,000, these families will pay a smaller share of the total income tax burden under the Act than they do under current law. . . . Conversely, families with incomes of $100,000 or more receive a smaller than average percentage reduction in income taxes so they will pay a larger share of the total income tax burden under the Act than they do under current law.[7]

Returning to the country of the Highs and the Lows, the hypothetical tax cut would be viewed by the Bush Treasury as distributionally neutral, since it reduced the tax liability of each High by 20 percent ($4,000/$20,000), and that of each Low by the same 20 percent ($1,000/$5,000). It also left unchanged the percentage of the total tax paid by each income group. The Highs paid 80 percent of all tax before the cut ($20,000/$25,000), and they paid 80 percent of all tax after the cut ($16,000/$20,000). The Lows, of course, paid 20 percent of all tax both before and after the cut.

That this is a dubious measure of distributional neutrality is suggested by a *reductio ad absurdum*. Suppose the income tax were virtually repealed, so that the Lows paid no tax and each High paid $1 of tax. According to the Bush Treasury, this would be a highly progressive change, since the Highs paid 100 percent of the tax after the change, compared with only 80 percent before. Yet "highly progressive" does not seem to be a fair description of that hypothetical cut. By the same token, "distributionally neutral" may not be a fair description of the across-the-board 20 percent cut for the Highs and the Lows, and "progressive" may not be a fair description of the actual Bush tax cuts. We turn then to the alternative frameworks for distributional analysis.

C. A First Alternative Frame: Percentage Changes in After-Tax Income

How is the distributional analysis of the hypothetical tax cut affected if we focus on percentage increases in aftertax incomes instead of percentage reductions in tax liabilities? The tax cut increases the aftertax income of a

High from $80,000 to $84,000—an increase of 5 percent. At the same time, the cut increases the aftertax income of a Low from $45,000 to $46,000—an increase of only 2.22 percent. By this measure, the tax cut—which would be proportional to the Bush Treasury—appears regressive. As a matter of arithmetic, if the starting point is an existing progressive tax, then any tax cut which reduces all tax liabilities by the same percentage (i.e., which is proportional in the Bush Treasury sense), will result in a larger percentage increase in aftertax income for higher-income taxpayers.[8] In fact, it is possible for a tax cut to be progressive from the Bush Treasury's percentage-of-tax-liability perspective, and regressive from the percentage-of-after-tax-income perspective.[9]

Given the differing—even contradictory—results produced by the two frameworks, the choice between them has obvious policy significance. A comprehensive review of tax distributional analysis methodology, prepared by the Treasury Department's Office of Tax Analysis during the Clinton administration, concluded that the aftertax income framework was clearly superior:

> The only tax burden measure with some theoretical basis is the percentage change in after-tax income. It alone provides some indication of a family's change in welfare, because after-tax income represents the family's consumption possibilities in either the current or future years. In contrast, the share of the total change in tax burdens, which is often quoted in the popular press, does not convey information on a family's relative welfare gains because it does not recognize the importance of a family's initial welfare position.[10]

In this view, the important distributional question with respect to tax cuts is how they affect the well-being of taxpayers at various points in the income distribution. And the effect of tax cuts on well-being cannot be determined without reference to the effect of tax cuts on aftertax incomes.

As the Bush Treasury Department has abandoned analysis of the effect of tax cuts on aftertax income, the Tax Policy Center (a joint undertaking of the Urban Institute and the Brookings Institution) has stepped into the breach. Analyzing the effect on aftertax income of all the tax cuts (individual income, corporate income, and estate and gift) enacted during the Bush administration, the Tax Policy Center found—unsurprisingly—that the percentage increases were smallest for the lowest-income taxpayers and largest for the highest-income taxpayers.[11] The increases ranged from

0.2 percent for taxpayers in the lowest-income quintile to 3.5 percent for taxpayers in the top quintile; within the top quintile, the increase was 4.3 percent for taxpayers in the top 1 percent of the overall income distribution and 5.4 percent for taxpayers in the top 0.1 percent.

By calculating the effects of the tax cuts on the top 1 percent and the top 0.1 percent of the income distribution, the Tax Policy Center's analysis provides a much sharper focus on rich taxpayers than does the Treasury Department's lumping of all taxpayers with incomes of $200,000 or above into a single class. An even narrower focus, on the fabulously rich, is available. In 2003, the Statistics of Income Division of the Internal Revenue Service released a detailed analysis of the 400 tax returns with the highest adjusted gross incomes (AGIs) in each of the years from 1992 to 2000.[12] In 2000, the minimum AGI required for membership in the "Fortunate 400"[13] was $86.63 million, and the average AGI for the 400 was $173.9 million.[14] The average tax rate for these 400 returns in 2000 (as a percentage of AGI) was 22.29 percent.[15] The *New York Times* has calculated that current law (reflecting the 2001 and 2003 tax cuts), if applied to the 2000 incomes of the Fortunate 400, would produce an average tax rate of only 17.5 percent.[16] Based on an average pretax income of $173.9 million, the effect of the rate reduction from 22.29 percent to 17.5 percent would be to increase aftertax income by 6.2 percent.[17] Thus, the percentage increase in the aftertax income of the top 0.000003 percent exceeds even the percentage increase for the top 0.1 percent.

D. A Second Alternative Frame: The Distribution of Dollars of Tax Cuts

The quoted 1999 Report of the Treasury Department's Office of Tax Analysis was clearly correct in its insistence that distributional analysis of tax law changes must center on aftertax incomes. The Report is not so clearly correct, however, in its view that *percentage* changes in aftertax income are the appropriate focus, and in its implicit suggestion that a distributionally neutral tax cut is one which increases aftertax income by the same percentage for taxpayers at all points in the income distribution. If a tax cut is neutral when it increases all aftertax incomes by the same percentage, then a neutral tax cut will always provide more dollars of tax reduction for richer taxpayers than for poorer. Under that definition of neutrality, the rich should get bigger tax cuts in terms of dollars, simply because they had more dollars of aftertax income before the cuts. This is a rich-get-richer sort of "neutrality," which will not be self-evident to all, and may even strike some as perverse. This critique of the percentage-of-after-tax-income approach suggests yet another framework for analysis—a focus, simply enough, on absolute dollars of tax cuts, with the suggestion that a neutral tax cut would reduce the tax liabilities of all taxpayers by the same dollar amount, regardless of pretax income level. This version of neutrality will be unattainable (except for very small tax cuts) if a taxpayer's precut tax liability is taken as the ceiling on the possible tax cut for that taxpayer. But there is no technical impediment to achieving this form of neutrality if negative tax rates are permitted—or, equivalently, if transfer payments can be used as well as tax cuts, so that each person receives tax-cuts-plus-transfer-payments of the same dollar amount.

It is clear that this form of neutrality was not in the minds of the architects of the Bush tax cuts. According to the Tax Policy Center's analysis, the average dollars of tax reductions from the combined effect of the 2001 and 2003 tax legislation increased dramatically with income: from $17 for taxpayers in the lowest-income quintile, to $4,374 for taxpayers in the highest quintile, to $28,187 for the top 1 percent of taxpayers, to $149,516 for the top 0.1 percent.[18] As for the Fortunate 400, application of the Bush tax cuts to their returns for the year 2000 would produce an average tax cut of about $8.4 million a year.[19]

A variation on comparing the average dollars of tax cuts going to different taxpayers is to consider the percentages of the total dollars of tax reductions received by taxpayers at various income levels. By this standard too, the Bush cuts are heavily skewed in favor of the rich. The bottom quintile of taxpayers received 0.3 percent of the total tax cuts (1.5 percent of their pro-rata share), while the top quintile received 68.7 percent of all cuts (more than 3.4 times their pro-rata share), the top 1 percent received 22.1 percent of the cuts (more than 22 times their pro-rata share), and the top 0.1 percent received 11.7 percent of the cuts (117 times their pro-rata share).[20]

E. A Third Alternative Frame: Accounting for Reductions in Government Spending as Well as for Reductions in Tax Liabilities

None of the three three prior analytical frameworks—the Bush Treasury's and the two alternatives—pay any attention to the effect of decreased tax revenues on the operations of government. The distributional effects of tax cuts are considered (from one perspective or another), but the distributional effects of reduced government spending (or increased borrowing, or both) are disregarded. The third alternative frame corrects that omission by adopting a unified tax-and-spending distributional analysis. Of the possible frameworks for distributional analysis, this one is theoretically the most attractive, because it alone can provide a complete account of the distributional effects of tax changes. It is also the most challenging analysis to perform, because of the difficulty of determining how the burden of spending cuts (and borrowing increases) has been distributed among the citizenry.[21]

To understand how, in general terms, results under this approach will differ from those under the other analytical frameworks, return to the imaginary nation of the Highs and the Lows. Before the tax cut, each High taxpayer has $100,000 pretax income and pays $20,000 tax, and each Low taxpayer has $50,000 pretax income and pays $5,000 tax. This gives the government $25,000 of tax revenue, the spending of which was ignored in the previous analyses. This time, however, assume that the government expenditures financed with the $25,000 provide $12,500 of benefits for each High taxpayer, and also $12,500 of benefits for each Low. Although no one knows for sure, educated speculation suggests that this distributional pattern—roughly equal benefits across the income spectrum—is reflective of the United States today.[22]

Notice that the overall effect of this tax-and-spending program is progressively redistributive, transferring $7,500 from High to Low. High pays $20,000 tax and receives $12,500 of spending benefits, while Low pays $5,000 tax and receives $12,500 of benefits. Now suppose a tax cut is enacted which is designed to increase the aftertax income of both High and Low by the same percentage (and thus is not regressive under the percentage-of-after-tax-income framework). For example, High's average rate could be reduced from 20 percent to 16 percent, and Low's average rate from 10 percent to 5.5 percent. This would increase High's aftertax income by 5 percent (from $80,000 to $84,000), and Low's also by 5 percent (from $45,000 to $47,250). This tax cut would be described as progressive by the Bush Treasury (because Low's tax liability is reduced by 45 percent, while High's is reduced by only 20 percent), and as proportional by a proponent of the percentage-of-after-tax-income approach.

But how does the cut fare under tax-and-spending analysis? That depends, of course, on how the government adjusts to the decrease (of $6,250) in its revenue. The initial response may be to maintain current spending levels by borrowing, but that approach cannot be maintained indefinitely. Sooner or later, government spending must be decreased. The spending cuts might be distributed in any number of ways, but a reasonable starting point might be to assume that the burden of the spending cuts will be distributed in proportion to the benefits of pre–tax cut spending. If so, half of the burden of the $6,250 reduction in spending would be borne by High, and half by Low. High's postcut benefit from government spending would then be $9,375 (i.e., $12,500—$3,125), and Low's benefit would be the same. The tax-and-spending cuts would have decreased High's tax by $4,000 while decreasing High's benefits by $3,125, and would have decreased Low's tax by $2,250 while reducing his benefits by $3,125. The net effect of the changes would be regressive, conferring a benefit of $875 on High at a cost of $875 to Low. These results are summarized in the accompanying table.

Distributional Effects of Hypothetical Tax-and-Spending Cuts

	a. Pretax income	b. Precut tax liability	c. Precut benefit from government spending	d. Postcut tax liability	e. Postcut benefit from government spending	f. Tax decrease (b – d)	g. Benefit decrease (c – e)	h. Net gain (loss) from tax-and-spending decrease
High	100,000	20,000	12,500	16,000	9,375	4,000	3,125	875
Low	50,000	5,000	12,500	2,750	9,375	2,250	3,125	(875)

Thus a tax cut which appears progressive under the Bush Treasury's percentage-reduction-in-tax-liability approach, and proportional under the percentage-increase-in-after-tax-income approach, is actually regressive under a comprehensive tax-and-spending analysis. While the example is hypothetical, the Center on Budget Policy and Priorities has concluded that the Bush tax cuts are significantly regressive under this analytical framework. The CBPP study considered the distributional effects of the 2001 and 2003 tax cuts (when fully in effect and assuming they are made permanent) on the assumption that the cuts are financed by reducing the benefit of government expenditures by an equal dollar amount ($1,520) for each family, regardless of income level.[23] Under this scenario, the net effect of the tax cuts and spending cuts is to reduce aftertax income by 21.1 percent for the bottom quintile of the income distribution, by 7.0 percent for the second quintile, by 3.1 percent for the middle quintile, and by 0.8 percent for the fourth quintile.[24] The only winning quintile is the top one, where aftertax income increases by 3.2 percent. Within the top quintile the biggest winners are in the top 0.1 percent of the income distribution, where aftertax income increases by 7.3 percent. In dollar terms, the net effect is to transfer $113 billion from the bottom 80 percent of the income distribution to the top 20 percent, with $35 billion of the $113 billion going to households with incomes of more than $1 million.[25]

II. Beyond the Framework Question: Some Particular Distributional Aspects of the Bush Tax Cuts

A. The Tax Cuts, the Alternative Minimum Tax, and Middle-Income Taxpayers

By the later years of this decade, much of the skewing of the Bush tax cuts in favor of the rich will be attributable to the alternative minimum tax (AMT).[26] The AMT will make the Bush cuts in the regular income tax largely illusory for many middle-income taxpayers, but will have little effect on the income tax cuts for the rich. The AMT functions as a shadow income tax, running alongside the regular tax. The base of the tax is "alternative minimum taxable income" (AMTI), which is defined so as to disallow many of the exclusions and deductions permitted under the regular income tax. After allowance of a substantial exemption amount,[27] the remaining AMTI (the "taxable excess") is subject to an almost-flat tax (with rates of 26 percent and 28 percent), to produce a "tentative minimum tax." If the tentative minimum tax exceeds a taxpayer's liability under the regular income tax, the taxpayer must pay both the regular tax and the amount by which the tentative minimum tax exceeds the regular tax. The effect is the same as requiring the taxpayer to pay the greater of the regular tax or the tentative minimum tax.

Congress enacted the first AMT in 1969, and extensively revised it in the Tax Reform Act of 1986.[28] As the Senate Finance Committee explained in connection with the 1986 revisions, the purpose of the tax was "to ensure that no taxpayer with substantial economic income can avoid significant tax liability by using exclusions, deductions, and credits."[29] The current and projected future impact of the AMT bears little resemblance, however, to the historic purpose of the tax. The tax now functions primarily as a tax on the upper-middle class rather than on the rich, and by 2010 it will be a tax on the middle-middle class as well. According to a study by the Tax Policy Center, 55.3 percent of taxpayers with AGIs from $200,000 to $500,000 were subject to the AMT in 2003.[30] By contrast, only 28.9 percent of taxpayers with AGIs from $500,000 to $1 million owed the tax, and only 19.3 percent of taxpayers with AGIs above $1 million.[31] Absent new legislation, by 2010 more than one-third (36.6 percent) of taxpayers with AGIs from $50,000 to $75,000 will be subject to the AMT, as will almost three-quarters (72.9 percent) of taxpayers with AGIs from $75,000 to $100,000, and over nine-tenths of taxpayers in both the $100,000 to $200,000 (92.0 percent) and $200,000 to $500,000 (96.2 percent) AGI ranges.[32] Richer taxpayers, however, will mostly avoid the tax. In 2010, the AMT will apply to slightly fewer than half (49.3 percent) of taxpayers in the AGI range of $500,000 to $1 million, and to fewer than one-quarter (24.1 percent) of income millionaires.[33] Thus, taxpayers with incomes from $50,000 to $100,000 will be substantially more likely to owe the AMT than taxpayers with seven-figure incomes. In her 2003 Annual Report to Congress, National Taxpayer Advocate Nina E. Olson identified "the growing reach" of the AMT as the most serious problem facing taxpayers, and described the AMT as functioning "randomly, no longer with any logical basis in sound tax administration or any connection with its original purpose of taxing the very wealthy who escape taxation."[34]

The incidence of AMT liability is low for the highest income taxpayers because the 35 percent marginal rate applicable to most of their income under the regular tax is substantially higher than their 28 percent rate under the AMT. As a result of this rate differential, they are subject to the AMT only if their AMTI is considerably greater than their regular taxable income. By contrast, AMT marginal rates are actually higher than regular income tax marginal rates for many middle-class taxpayers. Three additional factors help explain the large and growing impact of the AMT on nonwealthy taxpayers. First, the rate structure and exemption amounts of the regular tax are indexed for inflation while the AMT is not; thus inflation pushes more taxpayers into the AMT each year.

Second, a number of tax benefits disallowed by the AMT are not tax preferences enjoyed by wealthy investors, but rather are run-of-the-mill deductions of the middle class. Perhaps the best evidence of how far the AMT has strayed from its original purpose is the fact that the special 15 percent tax rate on capital gains and on dividends applies under the AMT as under the regular tax, but dependency exemptions and the deduction for state and local taxes are disallowed by the AMT.[35] Third, the cuts in the regular income tax enacted during the Bush administration have not been accompanied by corresponding cuts in the AMT.[36] Combine the effects of all these factors, and the Bush-era cuts in the regular income tax will prove largely illusory for middle- and upper-middle-income taxpayers; what Congress appears to give away through the regular tax it takes back through the AMT.

The above explains the growing reach of the AMT as a technical matter, but what is the political explanation? One possibility is that the architects of the Bush tax cuts used the AMT to achieve eventually, through a two-step process, a larger tax cut than would have been politically possible if the AMT had been reduced (and indexed for inflation) when the regular tax was reduced. The failure to adjust the AMT held down the official revenue cost of the cuts,[37] thus attracting crucial support for the cuts from legislators concerned about their revenue effect. But (so this explanation goes) tax cut proponents expect that in a few years those same legislators will accept whatever revenue loss is required—no matter how large—to avoid the prospect of millions of middle-income taxpayers becoming angry about their AMT liabilities.[38]

The other possible explanation is that the Bush administration and Congressional Republicans cared deeply only about tax cuts for the rich, and they would be happy to forgo the second step in the two-step process if it turned out that middle-income taxpayers did not insist on AMT relief.

One technical feature of the AMT—the nondeductibility of state and local income and property taxes—makes it particularly plausible that Republicans may have little interest in providing relief to the middle-income victims of the AMT. Because of this feature, in 2010 the AMT will apply to a significantly higher percentage of taxpayers in high-tax states than in low-tax states,[39] and the AMT liability per affected taxpayer will be higher in high-tax states than in low.[40] As Daniel Gross pointed out, high-tax states tend to be "resolutely Democratic."[41] Gross speculated before the 2004 election that Republican lack of concern about the growing reach of the AMT might be "because those most likely to fall prey to the AMT live in states that Bush-Cheney '04 has already written off."[42]

B. Social Security Taxes, Social Security Benefits, and the Bush Tax Cuts

The Social Security payroll tax is imposed, at the rate of 12.4 percent, on the first $87,900 of a worker's annual earnings.[43] The tax is nominally bifurcated, with half the tax imposed on the employee and half on the employer. Economists agree, however, that the bifurcation of the tax has no economic significance and that virtually the entire burden of the tax is borne by wage earners in the form of reduced wages.[44]

Viewing the payroll tax solely as a tax—rather than as part of an overall Social Security tax-and-transfer program—a flat rate tax on the first $87,900 of wages is decidedly regressive. Moreover, if Social Security benefits are disregarded and the combined effects of the Social Security tax and the income tax are considered, the payroll tax severely undermines the apparent progressivity of the income tax. The standard justification for disaggregating the income and Social Security taxes for purposes of distributional analysis is that Social Security constitutes a self-contained tax-and-transfer system. Social Security taxes are used to pay Social Security benefits, and the apparent regressivity of Social Security taxes is offset—or more than offset—by the progressivity of the Social Security benefits formula.[45] However, this justification is only as good as its premise—that Social Security tax receipts are dedicated to the payment of Social Security benefits. Developments in recent years threaten to undermine that premise. Indeed, it is arguable that a significant portion of the Social Security tax is now being used to finance the Bush tax cuts for the wealthy.

Understanding the argument requires a little historical background. Until the late 1970s, Social Security was conceived and operated on a pay-as-you-go basis. Social Security taxes collected during any given year approximately equaled Social Security benefits paid during that year, and Social Security trust fund accumulations were minimal. Foreseeing the difficulty the retirement of the baby boomers would pose for pay-as-you-go Social Security (because of the anticipated low ratio of workers paying tax to retirees receiving benefits), in 1977 Congress enacted legislation providing for future increases in Social Security tax rates.[46] In the decades preceding the boomers' retirement, the increased tax receipts would exceed benefit payments, the excess would be used to create a substantial Social Security trust fund, and the trust fund would be drawn down during the boomers' retirement (so that benefit payments could then exceed current tax receipts). It quickly became apparent that the 1977 legislation was inadequate to ensure the long-term solvency of Social Security. A National Commission on Social Security Reform, chaired by Alan Greenspan, was appointed to make recommendations, and its 1983 Report[47] proposed a number of measures—including partial income taxation of Social Security benefits, acceleration of the future payroll tax increases called for by the 1977 Act, and a phased-in increase in the normal retirement age—designed to make Social Security solvent for the next seventy-five years.[48] Congress quickly followed the Commission's advice by enacting the Social Security Amendments of 1983.[49]

As a result of the 1977 and 1983 legislation, annual Social Security tax receipts now greatly exceed annual benefit payments, with the excess going to the Social Security trust fund. By the end of 2004, the trust fund had accumulated $1.69 trillion,[50] and the trust fund is expected to continue to grow until 2017.[51] In 2004, Social Security taxes of $553 billion exceeded net Social Security benefits (i.e., benefits net of income taxes on benefits) of $477.6 billion by $75.4 billion; thus only 86 percent of Social Security taxes collected in 2004 were needed to pay 2004 benefits.[52]

The trust fund assets consist of federal government bonds. Each year the trust fund lends the year's cash flow surplus to the federal government to help finance the regular (i.e., non-Social Security) activities of the government, and the trust fund receives federal debt obligations in return. When current benefits begin to exceed current tax receipts (in or around 2017), and the trust fund begins to spend down its assets to make benefit payments, the Treasury will have to make cash payments to the trust fund. Those cash payments will have to be financed by general tax revenues, by new government borrowing, or a combination of the two.

The combination of the fact that Social Security taxes exceed Social Security benefit payments, and the fact that the excess is financing the general operations of the federal government, does not necessarily undermine the view that Social Security taxes are dedicated to the payment of Social Security benefits. Since the 1977 and 1983 amendments, Social Security taxpayers have been told that they are paying higher taxes now so that the system will be able to pay their benefits when they retire. It is true that the taxes in excess of current benefit payments have been loaned to the federal government, but that is not inconsistent with the dedication of the excess taxes to Social Security, *if* the government repays the loans as the boomers retire. The trust fund can be understood as a loan from Social Security taxpayers to income taxpayers, to be repaid beginning around 2017.

The problem with this view is that there are now serious rumblings that income taxpayers will not repay the loan—indeed, cannot repay the loan—if the Bush tax cuts (most of which are currently scheduled to expire at the end of 2010) are made permanent as the Bush administration and most Congressional Republicans desire. In widely reported and remarked-on testimony to Congress in February 2004, Alan Greenspan, chairman of the Federal Reserve and of the 1983 Social Security Commission, suggested that income tax revenues would not be sufficient for the government to repay its debt to the trust fund, and that Congress should renege on its promise to future retirees by further raising the normal retirement age and by not fully adjusting Social Security benefits for inflation.[53] If Greenspan's suggestions are adopted by Congress, the overall effect—of the 1977 and 1983 Social Security legislation, the Bush tax cuts, and the enactment of Greenspan's proposed benefit reductions—will be the failure of wealthy-income taxpayers to repay a massive loan from Social Security taxpayers of much more modest means. From a slightly different perspective, enactment of Greenspan's proposals would mean that Social Security taxpayers have been paying hundreds of billions of dollars of extra taxes for the past several decades not so that they could receive promised Social Security benefits in retirement, but so that the rich could receive massive income tax reductions. A number of commentators have noticed the implications of Greenspan's remarks and have reacted with understandable outrage.[54]

The bottom line is simple enough. If Social Security taxes are being used to finance general governmental operations (as they clearly are), and if that turns out to be permanent financing rather than a loan to be repaid (as it will turn out if Congress follows Greenspan's advice), then the justification disappears for viewing the distributional effect of the still somewhat-progressive income tax in isolation from the regressive Social Security tax. As Robert S. McIntyre recently wrote:

> There's no doubt that as a quasi-pension system, Social Security is very progressive, offering benefits that are a much higher share of contributions to lower-income workers than to higher-income workers. But if the Social Security tax is used to pay for the government's regular activities, it's about as regressive a tax as one can imagine—one that rich people are nearly exempt from paying, even though they get the biggest benefits from the way we structure our society.[55]

The relationship between the Bush tax cuts and Social Security also has implications for the analysis of the tax cuts under the administration's preferred framework (based on percentage changes in tax liabilities, or, equivalently, on shares of the total tax burden borne by different income classes). A report by the Congressional Budget Office, issued in August 2004, supported the Treasury's conclusion that the Bush tax cuts had modestly increased the percentage share of the total federal income tax burden borne by upper-income taxpayers.[56] On the other hand, the report also concluded that the Bush tax cuts had modestly *decreased* upper-income taxpayers' share of the overall federal tax burden (including payroll tax and excise tax, in addition to individual and corporate income tax).

The explanation for these seemingly contradictory results is that the tax cuts had two relevant effects. They made the income tax more progressive (within the Bush Treasury's analytical framework), but they also made the income tax less significant—and the regressive payroll tax more significant—in the overall federal tax picture. As it happened, because the second effect was larger than the first, the tax cuts were regressive—even under the Treasury's framework—with respect to federal taxes in their entirety. For the Bush tax cuts to be viewed as progressive, then, it is not enough to grant Treasury its choice of analytical framework; one must also grant Treasury its focus on the income tax in isolation.

This is where the Social Security story becomes relevant. The more Social Security taxes are used to finance income tax cuts, rather than to finance Social Security benefits, the weaker the argument becomes for not including payroll taxes in the distributional analysis of the Bush tax cuts. And the weaker that argument becomes, the weaker grows the administration's claim that the tax cuts were progressive by any standard.

C. The Bush Tax Cuts against a Backdrop of Increasing Inequality of Pretax Income

The Congressional Budget Office (CBO) recently published a study that included a detailed analysis of changes in the distribution of pretax income from 1979 to 2001.[57] The accompanying table, based on the CBO study, shows that the pretax income share of the top quintile of the pretax income distribution increased substantially from 1979 to 2001, while the pretax income shares of all four other quintiles decreased. In fact, the bottom half of the top quintile also saw its share decrease over that period, and even the bottom half of the top decile realized only a minor increase in its share. The only big winner was the top 1 percent of the income distribution, whose share increased from 9.3 percent to 14.8 percent—an increase of nearly 57 percent. In 1979, the top 1 percent had only (so to speak) 1.6 times the income share of the bottom quintile, but by 2001 the share of the top 1 percent was 3.5 times the size of the bottom quintile's share. In 2001, the average pretax income of a member of the top 1 percent was seventy times that of the average pretax income of a member of the bottom quintile, and the top 1 percent of the income distribution had a larger share of pretax income (14.8 percent) than the two lowest quintiles combined (13.4 percent).

Percentage Shares of Pretax Income, 1979 and 2001[58]

Pretax Income Category	Category's Percentage Share of Total Pretax Income, 1979	Category's Percentage Share of Total Pretax Income, 2001	Increase (Decrease) in Percentage Share of Pretax Income, 1979 to 2001
Lowest Quintile	5.8	4.2	(1.6)
Second Quintile	11.1	9.2	(1.9)
Middle Quintile	15.8	14.2	(1.6)
Fourth Quintile	22.0	20.7	(1.3)
Highest Quintile	45.5	52.4	6.9
Ninth Decile (80% to 90%)	15.0	14.8	(0.2)
Bottom Half of Top Decile (90% to 95%)	9.8	10.1	0.3
95% to 99%	11.4	12.7	1.3
Top 1%	9.3	14.8	5.5

The CBO study indicates that in 2001 the minimum pretax income required for membership in the top 1 percent pretax income category was $238,000, while the average income in the top 1 percent was $1,050,100.[59] The tremendous difference between the group minimum and the group average suggests that disaggregating the top 1 percent would produce some interesting information. Although the CBO study does not break down the top 1 percent into smaller groups, two other studies provide more detail on how the highest income Americans have fared over the past few decades.

One of those studies, by Thomas Piketty and Emmanuel Saez, covers 1913 to 1998 and includes data for (among other categories) the top 0.1 percent and the top 0.01 percent of the income distribution.[60] Piketty and Saez found that in 1998 the threshold for membership in the top 0.01 percent of the income distribution (a group consisting of 13,100 taxpaying units) was income of $3,620,500, and the average income within the group was $9,970,000.[61] This group had 2.57 percent of all income in 1998 (257 times the group's pro-rata share).[62] The group's share had more than quadrupled since 1979, when it was only 0.62 percent of all income.[63] Although the group's share of income did not increase every year between 1979 and 1998, the overall story for those two decades was of an increasing income share for the richest taxpayers—a "smooth increase in inequality," in the words of Piketty and Saez.[64]

But even the top 13,100 (0.01 percent) of all taxpayers is not the most exclusive group imaginable. For an even thinner slice of the truly rich, one can return to consideration of the Fortunate 400, mentioned earlier.[65] These Fortunate 400 constitute the top 0.000003 percent of the income distribution; one tax return in 323,434 made the cut in 2000. Recall that the minimum AGI for membership in the top 400 in 2000 was $86,830,000, and the average AGI for the group was $173,915,610.[66] The top 400 had 1.09 percent of all AGI in 2000, which was more than 360,000 times their pro-rata share. The Fortunate 400 for 1992, by contrast, had only (again, so to speak) 0.52 percent of all AGI. Thus, the AGI share of the top 400 had more than doubled in just eight years. In constant dollars, the AGI threshold for the top 400 nearly tripled over that same period, and the average AGI within the group slightly more than tripled.

Because the AGI of the Fortunate 400 in 2000 consisted largely of capital gains eligible for preferential rates,[67] the average tax rate (as a percentage of AGI) within the group was only 22.29 percent. This was only moderately higher than the average tax rate for all income taxpayers in 2000—as indicated by the fact that the Fortunate 400's share of all tax liability (1.58 percent) did not greatly exceed the group's share of all AGI (1.09 percent). The 22.29 percent average tax rate was actually slightly less than the 2000 average tax rates calculated by the IRS (using the same methodology) for taxpayers with AGIs from $200,000 to $500,000 (23.9 percent), and substantially less than the average tax rate for taxpayers with AGIs from $500,000 to $1,000,000 (28.3 percent).[68]

At the beginning of the Bush administration, then, Congress was faced with a dramatic long-term trend toward greater income inequality, and with an income tax system which was actually regressive at the top of the income distribution. Congress might have responded to this situation by increasing the progressivity of the income tax—to decrease the inequality of the distribution of *after*-tax income, and to correct the high-end regressivity of the income tax. As we have seen, however, the legislative response was exactly the opposite; Congress enacted tax cuts skewed in favor of the rich generally, and in favor of the superrich in particular.

As noted earlier, if the 2003 income tax law—with the Bush tax cuts in effect—were applied to the 2000 tax returns of the Fortunate 400, the average tax rate would fall from 22.29 percent to 17.5 percent.[69] (For comparison, the average tax rate in 2003 for an unmarried taxpayer with no dependents, $100,000 AGI, and claiming the standard deduction, would be 20.6 percent.)

As Joel Slemrod and Jon Bakija have explained, under optimal income tax theory the proper response to growing inequality of pretax income would be to increase the progressivity of the income tax.[70] Optimal income tax analysis, as originated by James Mirrlees[71] and developed by Mirrlees and others, considers what form of tax-and-transfer system would maximize social welfare under various sets of assumptions. The insight at the heart of optimal income tax theory is that taxation for the purpose of redistribution has countervailing effects on social welfare. On the one hand, the transfer of a dollar from a richer person to a poorer person increases social welfare because the gain of a dollar increases the poorer person's utility more than the loss of the dollar decreases the utility of the richer person. On the other hand, the taxation of the rich person's income needed to finance the redistribution decreases welfare because of the efficiency loss associated with the labor-discouraging effect of the tax. Optimal tax analysis furnishes mathematical techniques for balancing the welfare gains from redistribution against the deadweight loss from taxation, so as to maximize social welfare. The optimal tax-and-transfer system design depends on a number of assumptions—about behavioral responses to the system, about societal "taste" for redistribution (i.e., the social welfare function), and about the distribution of income-earning abilities (i.e., wage rates) in society.

Slemrod and Bakija focus on Mirrlees's finding that the greater the inequality of the distribution of income-earning abilities in society, the higher the marginal tax rates called for by optimal income tax analysis.[72] The intuition behind this result is that the gains from redistribution become greater, relative to the efficiency cost of taxation, as the dispersion of economic skills increases.[73] Writing in 2000—shortly before the Bush tax cuts of 2001—Slemrod and Bakija noted "an apparent inconsistency between the theory of optimal income taxation and actual U.S. tax-and-transfer policy of the past two decades: the degree of progressivity has hardly budged, may have decreased, and certainly has not increased substantially in the face of apparently massive increases in the degree of pretax income inequality."[74] They speculated that perhaps the "political system produces outcomes in a way that is unrelated, or even opposite, from what would be predicted by the artificial construct of constrained social welfare maximization."[75] Of course, optimal tax theory was not intended as a predictive tool. It tells us how legislators interested in maximizing social welfare would respond to increasing inequality of pretax income, but it takes no position as to whether legislators are interested in social welfare.

Events since 2000 suggest that Congress and the Bush administration are not interested in maximizing the welfare of Americans as a whole, but only in maximizing the welfare of the richest Americans.

III. The Politics of Tax Cuts for the Wealthy: Buying Off the Middle Class

If the American public was not clamoring in the streets for the Bush tax cuts, at the least it did not object to them. In fact, public opinion was quite favorable to both the 2001 and 2003 legislation.[76] What explains the public's acceptance of tax cuts heavily skewed in favor of a small and rich segment of the population? The Bush Treasury's framing of tax cut distributional analysis may be part of the explanation: to the extent that the public is persuaded that distributional neutrality in tax cuts means decreasing everyone's tax liability by the same percentage, the public will be content to have the highest income taxpayers receive the bulk of the tax cut dollars. A recent paper by Larry M. Bartels, however, suggests a simpler—and perhaps more discouraging—explanation.[77] Bartels concludes that most people form their views on tax policy issues largely "on the basis of simple-minded and sometimes misguided considerations of self-interest."[78] The implication is that people are generally willing to accept large tax cuts for the rich as long as those cuts are accompanied by small tax cuts for themselves.

Bartels's analysis is based on his detailed examination of opinion polling from the 2002 National Election Study (NES) survey.[79] Respondents were asked whether they favored the 2001 tax cut legislation. They were also asked for their opinions on a number of related issues, including: whether they believed the rich were under- or overtaxed; whether they believed the poor were under- or overtaxed; whether they believed they personally were under- or overtaxed; whether they would like to see more or less spent on government programs; whether they considered themselves conservative or liberal; and whether they considered themselves Democrats or Republicans. Even after controlling for government spending preferences, ideology, and political party, respondents who viewed their own tax burdens as too high were significantly more likely to support the tax cut than those who did not.[80] In striking contrast, respondents' attitudes toward the tax burden of the rich had no effect on their support for the 2001 tax cut, after controlling for spending preferences, ideology, and party identification.[81]

A politician could reasonably conclude from Bartels's analysis that a taxpayer who believes his own federal income tax burden is too high (which is the case with almost half of all taxpayers)[82] will support *any* income tax cut, no matter how skewed it may be in favor of the rich, as long as the taxpayer perceives that there is some small tax reduction for himself. If that is correct, the Bush tax cuts were well designed to take advantage of that phenomenon. In order to ensure that the bulk of taxpayers received *some* tax reduction, the Bush cuts included three provisions, a significant portion of the benefits of which inured to the middle class—the carving out of the 10 percent bracket from the 15 percent bracket, the increase in the amount of the child tax credit, and marriage penalty relief. These three provisions constituted the vast majority of the Bush tax cuts for the bottom 80 percent of the income distribution; for example, the three provisions accounted for all but $100 of the $647 average 2004 tax cut for taxpayers in the middle-income quintile.[83] These same three provisions, however, accounted for only 3.8 percent of the 2004 tax reduction for the top 1 percent of taxpayers (on average, $1,320 out of $33,672), and for only 1.2 percent of the 2004 tax reduction for taxpayers with incomes above $1 million (on average, $1,439 out of $123,592).[84] When one excludes the three middle-class provisions, more than 40 percent of the dollars of tax reduction in 2004 go to the top 1 percent of the income distribution.[85] The 2004 revenue cost of the three middle-class provisions is less than one-third of the total 2004 revenue cost of the Bush tax cuts.[86] The bulk of the Bush tax cuts, for the bulk of the taxpaying population, thus could have been provided at less than one-third of the total revenue cost of the overall legislation. But to put it that way may be to get the politics exactly backwards—perhaps the revenue loss from the middle-class tax cuts was the cost the tax cut proponents had to accept in order to achieve their goal of massive tax cuts for the rich.

Bartels considers whether education might affect the public's tendency to support large tax cuts for the rich when packaged with small cuts for the rest of the population. Finding that the least politically informed respondents in the NES survey overwhelmingly supported the 2001 tax cut, while the best informed respondents were about evenly divided on the merits of the cut, Bartels remarks: "If we are willing to take this cross-sectional difference in views as indicative of the impact of information on political preferences, it appears that the strong plurality support of Bush's tax cut . . . is attributable to simple ignorance."[87] It is one thing to conclude that the politics of tax cuts would be different if the electorate were better informed; it is a different and much more difficult thing to accomplish the necessary education, especially when a great deal of political power is held by those with a vested interest in continuation of the status quo. Bartels himself sums up the prospects for the electorate's achieving enlightened self-interest on matters of tax policy in two words: "Not likely."[88]

Middle-class taxpayers are not demanding tax cuts—not even for themselves, let alone for the rich. Politicians do not *need* to enact tax cuts to satisfy the electorate. But if politicians *want* to enact tax cuts for the rich, they will not face hostility from their nonrich constituents as long as the big tax cut dollars for the rich are accompanied by a few dollars for the masses. There may come a time when voters will rebel at the budget deficits resulting from those cuts—especially if they perceive the deficits as threatening their Social Security benefits—but until that time, the only limits on the ability of Congress to cut taxes for the rich may be those imposed by the consciences of its members.

NOTES

1. A slightly different version of this chapter appeared previously in *Tax Notes*. Lawrence Zelenak, *Framing the Distributional Effects of the Bush Tax Cuts*, 105 TAX NOTES 83 (Oct. 4, 2004).

2. The major cuts in the individual income tax were made by the Economic Growth and Tax Relief Reconciliation Act of 2001, Pub. L. No. 107-16, 115 Stat. 38 (2001), and by the Jobs and Growth Tax Relief Act of 2003, Pub. L. No. 108-27, 117 Stat. 764 (2003). A third piece of tax legislation enacted during the Bush administration had only a minor impact on the income tax liabilities of individuals. Job Creation and Worker Assistance Act of 2002, Pub. L. No. 107-147, 116 Stat. 21 (2002). This chapter does not examine the distributional effects of two items of tax legislation enacted in the fall of 2004. The Working Families Tax Relief Act of 2004, Pub. L. No. 108-311, 118 Stat. 1166 (2004), repealed scheduled post-2004 reductions in the child tax credit, marriage penalty relief, and the 10 percent rate bracket, and provided limited alternative minimum tax relief for 2005. The American Jobs Creation Act of 2004, Pub. L. No. 108-357, 118 Stat. 1418 (2004), made major changes in the taxation of business income (in a roughly revenue-neutral manner), but its distributional effects are modest compared with those of the 2001 and 2003 legislation.

3. U.S. Dep't of the Treasury, Distribution Table for the President's Tax Relief Plan (Mar. 8, 2001), *available at* 2001 Tax Notes Today 47–19 (Mar. 9, 2001) [hereinafter Treasury 2001]; U.S. Dep't of the Treasury, Distributional Table for the Jobs and Growth Tax Relief Reconciliation Act of 2003 (May 22, 2003), *available at* 2003 Tax Notes Today 100–17 (May 22, 2003) [hereinafter Treasury 2003].

4. Ronald Reagan, *Excerpts from Reagan Talk to Carpenters' Union*, N.Y. Times, Sept. 4, 1981, at A10.

5. Treasury 2001, *supra* note 3; Treasury 2003, *supra* note 3. The table below summarizes Treasury's analyses of the two tax cuts. (Note that the 2001 analysis is with respect to the president's proposal, which was similar but not identical to the changes actually enacted. The 2003 analysis is with respect to the cuts actually enacted in 2003.)

Cash Income Class (in thousands of dollars)	Percent Change in Individual Income Taxes, 2001	Percent Change in Individual Income Taxes, 2003
0–30	− 136.2	− 15.5
30–40	− 38.3	− 19.3
40–50	− 28.0	− 14.0
50–75	− 20.8	− 11.1
75–100	− 16.3	− 12.7
100–200	− 10.7	− 11.0
200 and over	− 8.7	− 10.8

The highest income group, in both analyses, is taxpayers with pretax cash income of $200,000 or more. As discussed in Part I.B of this chapter, use of such a broad income category masks the effect of the tax cuts on very high income taxpayers.

6. A report of the Congressional Budget Office, released in August 2004, confirmed the Treasury's claims by showing that the combined effect of the 2001 and 2003 tax cuts was to reduce the percentage of total income tax paid by each of the four lowest quintiles, while increasing (by 3.8 percentage points) the percentage paid by the highest quintile. Cong. Budget Office, Effective Federal Tax Rates under Current Law, 2001 to 2014, at 13 tbl. 4 (2004). The report also noted, however, that the combined effect of the 2001 and 2003 tax cuts on shares of *total* federal tax liability (individual and corporate income tax, payroll tax, and excise tax) was quite different; the top quintile's share decreased slightly (with the greatest decrease enjoyed by the top 1 percent of the income distribution), while the shares of the middle and fourth quintiles increased slightly. *Id.*

7. Treasury 2003, *supra* note 3.

8. Let H signify High's pretax income, L signify Low's pretax income, t_H signify High's average tax rate before the tax cut, and t_L signify Low's average tax rate before the tax cut. Before the tax cut, High's aftertax income is H $(1 - t_H)$, and Low's aftertax income is L $(1 - t_L)$. Now suppose a tax cut reduces the average tax

rate of both High and Low by the same percentage. We can indicate the effect of this cut by multiplying both t_H and t_L by c, where $0 < c < 1$ (for example, $c = .8$ would indicate the effect of a 20 percent tax rate cut). With the tax cut in effect, High's aftertax income is now $H (1 - c \times t_H)$, and Low's aftertax income is now $L (1 - c \times t_L)$. The percentage increase in High's aftertax income as a result of the tax cut is equal to $[H (1 - c \times t_H) - H (1 - t_H)] / H (1 - t_H)$, which can be restated as $t_H (1 - c) / (1 - t_H)$. Similarly, the percentage increase in Low's aftertax income as a result of the tax cut is equal to $[L (1 - c \times t_L) - L (1 - t_L)] / L (1 - t_L)$, which can be restated as $t_L (1 - c) / (1 - t_L)$. In comparing the two ratios (in their restated forms), notice first that if $t_H > t_L$, and $0 < c < 1$, then $t_H (1 - c) > t_L (1 - c)$. Also notice that, if $t_H > t_L$, then $(1 - t_H) < (1 - t_L)$. Since the percentage increase in High's aftertax income has both a larger numerator and a smaller denominator than the percentage increase in Low's aftertax income, it is necessarily a larger percentage increase.

9. For example, suppose High's tax on $100,000 was reduced from $20,000 to $17,000, while Low's tax on $50,000 was reduced from $5,000 to $4,000. The Bush Treasury would consider the tax cut progressive, because High's tax was reduced by 15 percent while Low's was reduced by 20 percent. On the other hand, High's aftertax income increased by 3.75 percent ($3,000/$80,000), while Low's increased by only 2.22 percent ($1,000/$45,000).

10. JULIE-ANNE CRONIN, U.S. TREASURY DISTRIBUTIONAL ANALYSIS METHOD-OLOGY 34 (OTA Paper 85, Sept. 1999).

11. TAX POLICY CTR., DISTRIBUTION OF ENACTED BUSH INDIVIDUAL INCOME TAX CUTS BY PERCENTAGE CHANGE IN AFTER-TAX INCOME, 2004 tbl. 04-0009 (Mar. 18, 2004), *available at* http://www.taxpolicycenter.org. The TPC numbers are not directly comparable to the Bush Treasury Department's figures on percentage changes in tax liabilities because the TPC numbers do not separately analyze the effects of the 2001 and 2003 tax cuts.

12. STATISTICS OF INCOME DIV., I.R.S., DATA RELEASE, THE 400 INDIVIDUAL INCOME TAX RETURNS REPORTING THE HIGHEST ADJUSTED GROSS INCOMES EACH YEAR, 1992–2000, I.R.S. STAT. INCOME BULL. 7 (Spring 2003), *available at* http://www.irs.gov/pub/irs-soi/00in400h.pdf.

13. Credit for the label belongs to Joel Slemrod. *See* Joel Slemrod, *The Fortunate 400*, 100 TAX NOTES 935 (Aug. 18, 2003).

14. DATA RELEASE, *supra* note 12, tbl. 1 (minimum AGI), and author's calculation based on tbl. 1 (average AGI).

15. *Id.*, tbl. 1. The average rate was far below the then-prevailing top marginal rate of 39.6 percent, primarily because 64 percent of the AGI of the Fortunate 400 consisted of long-term capital gains taxed at a maximum rate of 20 percent. *Id.*

16. David Cay Johnston, *Very Richest's Share of Income Grew Even Bigger, Data Show*, N.Y. TIMES, June 26, 2003, at A1. The major factors causing the reduction in the average tax rate are the reduction in the top marginal tax rate from 39.6 percent to 35 percent, the reduction in the rate on most long-term capital gains from

20 percent to 15 percent, and the taxation of most dividends at the 15 percent rate generally applicable to long-term capital gains.

17. Average aftertax income for the Fortunate 400 in 2000, under then-existing law, was $173.9 million x (1 - .2229) = $135.1 million. With the Bush tax cuts, average aftertax income would be $173.9 million x (1 - .175) = $143.5 million. The $8.4 million increase in aftertax income is 6.2 percent of $135.1 million.

18. TAX POLICY CTR., DISTRIBUTION OF ENACTED BUSH INDIVIDUAL INCOME TAX CUTS BY DOLLARS, 2004 tbl. 04-0009 (Mar. 18, 2004), *available at* http://tax-policycenter.org.

19. *See* calculations, *supra* note 17.

20. Tax Policy Ctr., Distribution of Enacted Bush Individual Income Tax Cuts by Percentage of Total Tax Cuts, 2004 tbl. 04-0009 (Mar. 18, 2004), *available at* http://www.taxpolicycenter.org.

21. To the extent that a reduction in cash transfer payments, or easily valued in-kind transfers (such as food stamps), is clearly associated with a tax cut, the distributional analysis of the spending cuts is easy. In many cases, however, life will not be so simple—because the relationship between tax cuts and spending cuts is unclear, or because the burden of the spending cuts is difficult to allocate (as with cuts in spending on education, for example), or for both reasons.

22. Gene Steuerle, *Can the Progressivity of Tax Changes Be Measured in Isolation?* 100 TAX NOTES 1187 (2003) (suggesting that the benefits of government expenditures may increase slightly with income); William G. Gale et al., *The Ultimate Burden of the Tax Cuts* 13–14 (2004), available at http://www.cbpp.org/6-2-04tax.htm (suggesting that the benefits of government expenditures are roughly equal across income categories).

23. Gale et al., *supra* note 22, at 8–10. The study also considers the distributional effects of the tax cuts under the alternative assumption that they are financed by a combination of spending cuts and progressive tax increases. *Id.* at 10–12. The latter scenario seems unlikely, since progressive tax increases would largely defeat the purpose of the 2001 and 2003 tax cuts.

24. *Id.* at 17, app. tbl. 3.

25. *Id.* at 4, tbl. 3.

26. IRC §§ 55–58.

27. For 2004 and 2005, the AMT exemption amount is $58,000 for joint returns and $45,000 for unmarried taxpayers. IRC § 55(d)(1).

28. Tax Reform Act of 1969, Pub. L. No. 91-172, 83 Stat. 487; Tax Reform Act of 1986, Pub. L. No. 99-514, 100 Stat. 2085.

29. S. Rep. No. 99-313, at 518–19 (1986).

30. Leonard E. Burman et al., *The AMT: Projections and Problems*, 100 TAX NOTES 104, 110 tbl. 2 (2003).

31. *Id.*

32. *Id.*

33. *Id.*; *see also* DANIEL FEENBERG AND JAMES POTERBA, THE ALTERNATIVE MINIMUM TAX AND EFFECTIVE MARGINAL TAX RATES 26, tbl. 4 (Nat'l Bureau of Econ. Research, Working Paper No. 10072, 2003) (producing results similar to that of the Tax Policy Center).

34. NINA E. OLSON, NATIONAL TAXPAYER ADVOCATE ANNUAL REPORT TO CONGRESS iv (2003).

35. I.R.C. §§ 55(b)(3) (applying the 15 percent rate for purposes of the AMT as well as the regular tax), 56(b)(1)(E) (disallowing dependency exemptions under the AMT), 56(d)(1)(A)(ii) (disallowing itemized deductions for state and local taxes under the AMT).

36. There is one exception. The AMT exemption amounts were increased for 2003 through 2005, but in 2006 they are scheduled to revert to their prior levels. I.R.C. § 55(d)(1).

37. *See* Burman et al., *supra* note 30, at 107 tbl. 1, indicating that from 2003 through 2010 the AMT is expected to raise $660.2 billion of revenue, compared with the $364.9 billion revenue it would have raised over the same period without the Bush reductions in the regular tax. The difference between those two amounts—$295.3 billion—is the amount by which failure to cut the AMT along with the regular tax has held down the revenue cost of the Bush tax cuts.

38. *See* David Cay Johnston, *Even for Wealthy, Tax Plan's Benefits Could Vary Widely*, N.Y. TIMES, May 15, 2001, at C1.

39. *See* Burman et al., *supra* note 30, at 110 tbl. 2.

40. *Id.* at 112 tbl. 3.

41. Daniel Gross, *Bush's Secret Tax on Democrats*, SLATE, Apr. 13, 2004.

42. *Id.*

43. IRC §§ 3101(a) (imposing 6.2 percent tax on employees), 3111(a) (imposing 6.2 percent tax on employers). The ceiling is adjusted annually for inflation.

44. JOEL SLEMROD & JON BAKIJA, TAXING OURSELVES: A CITIZEN'S GUIDE TO THE GREAT DEBATE OVER TAX REFORM 67–68 (2d ed. 2000).

45. For the benefits formula, see 42 USC § 415 (providing a schedule under which the first dollars of "average indexed monthly earnings" (AIME) are replaced at the rate of 90 percent, additional dollars of AIME are replaced at the rate of 32 percent, and the last dollars of AIME are replaced at the rate of only 15 percent).

46. Social Security Amendments of 1977, Pub. L. No. 95-216, 91 Stat. 1509 (1977).

47. Report of the National Commission on Social Security Reform (1983), *available at* http://www.ssa.gov/history/reports/gspan.html.

48. Despite legislative adoption of the Commission's recommendations, the exhaustion of the trust fund, with resulting inability to pay full scheduled benefits, is now expected in 2041. 2005 ANNUAL REPORT OF THE BOARD OF TRUSTEES OF THE FEDERAL OLD-AGE AND SURVIVORS INSURANCE AND DISABILITY INSURANCE TRUST FUNDS 8 (2005).

49. Social Security Amendments of 1983, Pub. L. No. 98-21, 97 Stat. 65 (1983).

50. 2005 Annual Report, *supra* note 48, at 132 (Appendix A).

51. *Id.* at 8.

52. *Id.* at 4 tbl. II.B1. The trust fund earned $89 billion of interest income in 2003. *Id.* If that interest is viewed as available to pay current benefits, then only $388.6 billion ($477.6 billion minus $89 billion) of taxes (approximately 70% of total tax receipts) was needed to finance current benefits, and the remaining $164.4 billion augmented the trust fund.

53. Edmund L. Andrews, *To Trim Deficit, Greenspan Urges Social Security and Medicare Cuts*, N.Y. TIMES, Feb. 26, 2004, at A1.

54. *See, e.g.*, Robert S. McIntyre, *Social Security's Zealous Raider*, AM. PROSPECT, Apr. 2004, at 16; William Greider, *Greenspan's Con Job*, NATION, Mar. 22, 2004, at 6; David Cay Johnston, *The Social Security Promise Not Yet Kept*, N.Y. TIMES, Feb. 29, 2004, at sec. 4, p. 5; Gilbert E. Metcalf, *Fooled by the Shell Game*, BOSTON GLOBE, Mar. 1, 2004, at A15.

55. McIntyre, *supra* note 54.

56. CONG. BUDGET OFFICE, EFFECTIVE FEDERAL TAX RATES: 1979–2001 (Apr. 2004).

57. *Id.* at 13 tbl. 4.

58. Quintile and top 1 percent data are directly from a CBO table labeled "Share of Income (Percent), Pretax Income." *See id.* Other data are derived from the author from the same CBO table.

59. *Id.*, tables labeled "Average Income (2001 dollars), Pretax Income" and "Minimum Adjusted Income (2001 dollars)."

60. Thomas Piketty & Emmanuel Saez, *Income Inequality in the United States, 1913–1998*, 2003 Q. J. ECON. 1 (2003).

61. *Id.* at 5 tbl. I. These figures are based on a definition of income which excludes capital gains. With capital gains included in income, the 1998 income threshold for the top 0.01 percent was $6,184,855, and the average income within the group was $17,030,999. THOMAS PIKETTY & EMMANUEL SAEZ, INCOME INEQUALITY IN THE UNITED STATES, 1913–1998 tbl. A6 (Nat'l Bureau of Econ. Research, Working Paper No. 8467, 2001).

62. Piketty & Saez (2003), *supra* note 60, at 10 tbl. II. This is based on a definition of income which excludes capital gains.

63. Piketty & Saez (2003), *supra* note 60, at 10 tbl. II. The group's 1979 share was itself an increase from the 1973 low point of 0.50 percent. Again, these figures are based on income excluding capital gains.

64. Piketty & Saez (2003), *supra* note 60, at 11.

65. I.R.S. DATA RELEASE, *supra* note 12.

66. *Id.* at tbl. 1.

67. Capital gains eligible for preferential rates constituted 64.01 percent of the AGI of the Fortunate 400 in 2000. *Id.*

68. David Campbell & Michael Parisi, *Individual Income Tax Returns and Tax*

Shares, 2000, 2002 STAT. INCOME BULL. 6, 8 fig. B (Winter 2002–2003); *see also* Martin A. Sullivan, *The Rich Get Soaked While the Super Rich Slide,* 101 TAX NOTES 581, 582 fig. 1 (2003).

69. Johnston, *supra* note 54.

70. JOEL SLEMROD & JON BAKIJA, DOES GROWING INEQUALITY REDUCE TAX PROGRESSIVITY? SHOULD IT? (Nat'l Bureau of Econ. Research, Working Paper No. 7576, 2000).

71. *See, e.g.,* James A. Mirrlees, *An Exploration in the Theory of Optimum Income Taxation,* 38 REV. ECON. STUD. 175 (1971).

72. SLEMROD & BAKIJA, *supra* note 70, at 4, citing Mirrlees, *supra* note 70, at 207.

73. Mirrlees, *supra* note 71, at 207.

74. SLEMROD & BAKIJA, *supra* note 70, at 6.

75. *Id.*

76. *See, e.g.* , Richard L. Berke & Janet Elder, *60% in Poll Favor Bush, But Economy Is Major Concern,* N.Y. TIMES, Mar. 14, 2001, at A1; Humphrey Taylor, *Lukewarm Support for Bush Tax Cut,* THE HARRIS POLL No. 35 (June 20, 2003), *available at* http://www.harrisinteractive.com/harris_poll/index.asp?PID=384.

77. Larry M. Bartels, *Homer Gets a Tax Cut: Inequality and Public Policy in the American Mind* (2003), *available at* http://www.wws.princeton.edu/~policybriefs/bartels_taxcut.pdf.

78. *Id.* at 21.

79. Detailed information about the survey is available at http://www.umich.edu/~nes.

80. *Id.* at 28, 47 tbl. 10.

81. *Id.* at 28–29, 47 tbl. 10. A bizarre finding was that favoring increased spending on government programs had strong *positive* association with support for the tax cut. *Id.* at 28.

82. *Id.* at 42 tbl. 3.

83. ISAAC SHAPIRO & JOEL FRIEDMAN, CENTER ON BUDGET & POL'Y PRIORITIES, TAX RETURNS: A COMPREHENSIVE ASSESSMENT OF THE BUSH ADMINISTRATION TAX CUTS 20–22, 55 app. tbl. 6 (2004). Shapiro's and Friedman's analysis considers the effects of cuts in the estate and gift taxes, and the corporate income tax, as well as the individual income tax.

84. *Id.* at 55 app. tbl. 6.

85. *Id.* at 21.

86. *Id.* at 51 tbl. 3. The estimated cost of the three provisions is $91 billion, and the estimated total revenue cost is $276 billion.

87. Bartels, *supra* note 77, at 33.

88. *Id.* at 37.

10

Class War and the Estate Tax
Have the Troops Gone AWOL?

Richard L. Schmalbeck

One might naively think that democracy would be a comprehensive anti-dote to class warfare of the traditional rich-versus-the-masses sort.[1] Even in developed societies, the lower and middle classes vastly outnumber the wealthy[2] and can outvote them at will.[3] That being the case, it would seem that when an issue pits the interests of the wealthy against the interests of the vastly more numerous lower and middle classes, the latter would invariably prevail. After all, as George Bernard Shaw once observed: A government which robs Peter to pay Paul can always count on the support of Paul.[4]

The apparent lack of popular support for the U.S. estate tax, however, is enough to cause one to despair of democracy. From a populist perspective, the estate tax would seem to have a lot going for it. By the most generous estimates, it burdens the estates of less than 5 percent of all decedents; by doing so, it undoubtedly contributes an element of progressivity to a tax system that has few such elements. It raises a sizable amount of revenue[5] and also results in substantial charitable bequests, at least some of which would not likely be made in the absence of the tax.[6] Perhaps most importantly, it mildly retards the growth of dynastic wealth, offsetting to some degree a natural tendency in a market economy for wealth to accumulate in the hands of the relatively few.[7] Despite these characteristics, which would seem to make the estate tax attractive to most ordinary Americans, the American public appears strongly to support its repeal. Two well-respected recent polls show that either 70 percent[8] or 57 percent[9] of respondents favor permanent repeal of the tax. This essay explores the reasons why this might be so, and if indeed it is.

A number of explanations are theoretically available, some of which cast our democratic processes in more favorable light than others. They can be divided into five broad categories:

1. Perhaps voters do indeed understand that they are unlikely to be burdened by the tax, but nevertheless regard it as inefficient or unfair. Under this view, citizens are, in opposing the estate tax, giving expression to their better natures, reflecting a sound sense of public policy rather than mere self-interest.

2. Alternatively, perhaps citizens *are* acting out of self-interest. Believing that they will become wealthier over the course of their remaining lives, they have adopted viewpoints consistent with the interests they hope to hold, rather than the ones they hold now.

3. Perhaps the opposition to the estate tax is simply part of a broader antitax, antigovernment stance that has captured some significant part of the electorate in recent years. Some Americans, it would seem, would reflexively favor repeal of *any* tax, if given half a chance to express that view.

4. Or maybe the American public is simply inert, insensible to the whole idea of class warfare, and sees no useful role to be played by a tax aimed exclusively at wealthy households. Or, in a variant on this theme, perhaps there is class warfare being waged, but the battle lines have been drawn differently: instead of the rich versus the rest, perhaps it is the comfortable majority versus those who are seen by that majority as the undeserving recipients of disproportionate governmental support.

5. Or, finally, perhaps the public simply does not understand this tax, and so opposes it mistakenly. In fact, there appears to be, as will be discussed, substantial evidence that the estate tax is poorly understood and that this explains much, but not all, of the apparent opposition to it.

For the most part, these are not mutually inconsistent explanations, and any particular citizen could conceivably hold anti–estate tax views for several of these reasons. It is also true that each of the views expressed could be held by only a small minority; but if each is in itself a sufficient cause for opposing the estate tax, the cumulative effect of small slices of the electorate adopting each position would be enough to explain an overall opposition to the tax. In any case, each of these possibilities will be explored in detail below. Before they are considered, however, a brief description of the estate tax, and the recent attempts to repeal it, is offered as background for the later analysis.

I. The U.S. Estate Tax: A Brief Overview

A. The Structure

The U.S. estate tax[10] has been continuously in force since it was first enacted in 1916. It imposes a tax on the transfer of assets from an estate to a decedent's heirs and beneficiaries to the extent that the value so transferred exceeds a generous exemption.[11] Since 1932, a counterpart federal gift tax has been imposed on gifts made during the donor's life.[12] As will be explained in a moment, while the gift tax remains intact, there are presently two versions of the estate tax rules: one set could be called the "permanent" rules, which remained in effect until 2001 and will be effective again in 2011. The other set consists of the temporary rules governing the tax years from 2002 through 2010.

The permanent rules—now in the background—were set out in their basic form by the Tax Reform Act of 1976 (TRA 76), and most recently modified by the Taxpayer Relief Act of 1997 (TRA 97). TRA 97 raised the exemption to $625,000 for estates of decedents dying in 1998, with a series of further increases to be phased in gradually over the succeeding years until an exemption of $1,000,000 was to have been reached for decedents dying in 2006 or later years.

These rules were supplanted, but only temporarily, by the Economic Growth and Tax Relief Reconciliation Act of 2001 (EGTRRA), which amended the Code in several respects, including important changes to the estate tax provisions.[13] In particular, after a series of steps that would lower the rate of tax and increase the exemption amount between the years 2002 and 2009, EGTRRA purports to "repeal" the estate tax altogether in 2010. However, because EGTRRA includes a provision sunsetting the entire Act at midnight, December 31, 2010, its rules will, unless Congress acts further, lose effect at that time, thus resurrecting the estate tax in the form of the permanent rules as enacted in TRA 76 and TRA 97.

Under both the permanent and temporary provisions, Congress has tried to give the estate tax a fairly broad reach, so that assets may be included in an estate for purposes of the estate tax even if they are not in the probate estate, and even if the decedent enjoys less than full ownership of those assets at the time of death. On the other hand, the reach of the tax is circumscribed by a number of deductions, of which two are particularly important: there is an unlimited marital deduction, so that any part of the estate left to a surviving spouse may be deducted in full;[14] and there is an unlimited charitable deduction, allowing deduction in full of any testamentary gifts to charitable organizations or governmental units.[15] These deductions significantly lessen the impact of the tax: for estate tax returns filed in 2001, the aggregate value of the assets listed on estate tax returns was nearly $216 billion; however, the net asset value subject to tax was only a little more than half of that amount—$123 billion.[16] The difference between the gross and net was largely the consequence of allowing marital deductions totaling $63 billion and charitable deductions totaling $16 billion.[17]

A significant aspect of the unlimited marital deduction is that it makes it relatively easy for a married couple, in effect, to double the estate tax exemption. Full elaboration of the techniques used to achieve this result is beyond the scope of this essay; but, roughly, the first spouse to die passes an amount equal to her exemption down to the next generation of the family without tax, since it is sheltered by her exemption.[18] When the second spouse dies, he uses his own exemption. Thus, for example, the current exemption of $2,000,000 (the amount provided by EGTRRA for 2006–08) should be thought of as the equivalent of a $3,000,000 exemption for married couples—plenty large enough, one would think, to shelter most Mom and Pop businesses, or family farms, from exposure to the estate tax.

The charitable deduction has a significant and positive effect on both the sources and the uses side of tax policy: it removes money from the fund of dynastic wealth that can be passed to the next generation (which is certainly one of the important justifications of an estate tax) and devotes it instead to charitable purposes.[19]

B. The Reach of the Estate Tax

Perhaps the most important point about the estate tax for present purposes is its extremely limited reach. Although over two million Americans died in each of the last several years,[20] only about 100,000 estates each year had assets of sufficient value that they were obligated to file an estate tax return.[21] Because many of those estates were able to claim marital and/or charitable deductions large enough to eliminate any estate tax liability, only about 50,000 estates actually paid any estate tax.[22] The decedents were, on average, quite wealthy individuals, having—in the case of returns filed in 2001—a mean gross estate of about $2.4 million, on which they paid a mean estate tax of about $450,000.[23]

These numbers are based on the estate tax as it existed prior to EGTRRA 2001, which significantly increased the exemption.[24] Extrapolating a bit from the historical data, it seems reasonable to expect that since the exemption amount has by now increased to $1,500,000 for estates of decedents dying in 2004–05, fewer than 25,000 estates in each of those years will likely pay any estate tax.[25] And by the time the exemption amount reaches $3,500,000 in 2009, fewer than 10,000 estates will likely be subject to the tax, though of course the group still remaining in the estate-tax web by that point will be much wealthier, on average, than the 2001 group.[26] At that point, fewer than one in two hundred estates would actually pay any estate tax. But those would be the wealthiest of the wealthy, and they would still pay tens of billions of dollars annually in transfer taxes, and would transfer additional tens of billions to charitable organizations, in part because of the presence of the estate tax.[27]

Then, of course, it all comes to an end, with the repeal of the estate tax in 2010. But, as noted, the estate tax will spring back to life, with a $1,000,000 exemption, in 2011.[28] At that time, it is estimated that the estate tax may produce as much as $52 billion in revenue.[29]

C. The Future of the Estate Tax

Of course, no one expects that the temporary provisions put in place by EGTRRA 2001 will be allowed to run their full course. The purported repeal of the estate tax in 2010, followed by its return to life in full force in 2011, is so lunatic that some have referred to this set of provisions as the Throw Momma from the Train Act. Proposals for permanent change in the estate tax have been introduced several times since 2001. The Republicans, with very few exceptions, seek permanent repeal of the estate tax. The Democrats, with similarly few exceptions, seek to retain the tax, but with a more generous exemption than the current permanent provisions contain. (Proposals have varied, but an exemption from $2,000,000 to $5,000,000 captures the range.) Congress, however, has reached an impasse on this issue, and it is difficult to predict exactly what could happen.

The impasse, in fact, explains why the 2001 legislation phased in the estate tax cuts only gradually and made the repeal only temporary. Congressional Republicans—and the White House—were reasonably united, and they would have liked to repeal the estate tax immediately and permanently. But they could not do it *immediately*, because immediate repeal would have been too costly, sacrificing at least $410 billion of federal revenue over the ten-year revenue projection window from 2001–2010.[30] Congress, slightly constrained by the Democratic minority, was working within a budget resolution that permitted a total revenue loss of only (!) $1.35 trillion over the 2001–2010 period. If the Republican majorities that designed the bill (with the help of the White House) had spent a third of that on estate tax repeal, they would not have had enough left to make the changes they planned for income tax. The solution? Hold off the biggest jump in the estate tax exemption until 2009, and absorb the full measure of the revenue loss resulting from complete repeal for only one year— 2010. This strategy permitted them to claim that they had repealed the estate tax, while for budget purposes recognizing only a fraction of the true revenue loss associated with repeal. In certain other contexts, this sort of three-card monte would be criminal; in the context of congressional tax and budgetary politics of late, it seems to be fairly routine.

The Democratic minority also stood in the way of making the repeal *permanent*. The so-called "Byrd Amendment" of the 1974 Budget Act provides that any senator may object to any bill that would lose revenue in years beyond the ten-year-period used for revenue estimates (the out years). Such procedural objections are to be sustained under the Act unless at least sixty senators vote to waive the Byrd amendment. The Republican leadership decided—correctly, it would appear—that they did not have sixty votes in the Senate for retaining a number of the EGTRRA provisions, including estate tax repeal. They could have compromised on a less sweeping bill, but they chose instead to enact a slow phase-in of a disappearing repeal.

Congress has done no better in subsequent legislative sessions. On several occasions, bills have been introduced to make repeal of the estate tax permanent, or to void the provisions of EGTRRA in favor of a revised version of the permanent estate tax with a higher exemption. Republicans have voted for the former, but they have lacked sufficient numbers to overcome the Byrd amendment. Democrats have voted for the latter, but they are outnumbered in both houses, and have had little success persuading Republicans to join them in this cause.

This may change in the new Congress elected in the fall of 2004. Republicans now hold fifty-five seats in the Senate. Most of those senators would vote to repeal the estate tax. In addition, seven Democratic senators have in the past voted for repeal. This brings the Senate very close to the point at which it could count sixty votes for repeal. However, past votes for repeal were cast in situations in which it seemed that actual repeal was unlikely; it is entirely possible that if actual repeal were threatened, some of the Democrats, and even some of the Republicans, would reconsider their positions. All that can be said with certainty as this book goes to press is that the issue will closely divide the Senate, with all possible outcomes (repeal, reform, or continued impasse) still very much in play.

II. Why Does Repeal Appeal?

The foregoing background makes clear that there is indeed something of a class war—or at least a partisan war—going on over the future of the estate tax, but largely at the congressional level. Public participation has been minimal and, where it exists, largely in support of repeal. As noted in the introduction, survey data suggest that a substantial majority of the populace favors repeal of the estate tax. The introduction also offered some tentative explanations of this somewhat counterintuitive phenomenon. Each of these explanations is considered separately below.

A. The Merits of the Estate Tax

To suggest that broad public support for repeal of the estate tax is counterintuitive may require the assumption that American voters would support any tax that exclusively burdens people other than themselves. Indeed, many economists and political scientists routinely make assumptions rather like this, in using models that assume that self-interest is the prime motivator of economic and political decision making. Yet, ordinary Americans have been leery of tax structures that are explicitly designed to "soak the rich"; we managed, after all, to get through the first 124 years of our national history without having either income or wealth taxes, which are prerequisites to any serious soaking based on income or wealth.[31]

Reticence about soaking the rich seemed to dissolve, however, shortly after the income tax and the estate tax (which is essentially a wealth tax imposed once each generation)[32] were put in place in 1913 and 1916, respectively. Evidence of a class-war approach to those taxes was borne out in breathtakingly high rates for most of the following fifty years or more:

as recently as 1963, the highest marginal income tax rate was 91 percent, and until 1976, the highest marginal estate tax rate was 77 percent.

Since the 1980s, however, we have witnessed something of a rebirth of restraint in tax rates, with income tax rates generally not exceeding 40 percent, and estate and gift tax rates not exceeding 55 percent. Perhaps this simply reflects that lower- and middle-income taxpayers are losing the war. It may, however, also reflect a degree of enlightened self-interest. For example, it now seems clear that a marginal income tax rate of 91 percent is likely to be counterproductive from everyone's viewpoint: certainly in the view of the taxpayer burdened with that rate, but even from the perspective of total revenue, in which all taxpayers have a stake. Rates that high are likely to discourage generation of income in the first place. The Treasury is thus denied revenue that would have been yielded by some lower rate that would not have discouraged production of that increment of income.

1. THE EFFICIENCY ARGUMENT

Arguments resembling the one that brought down marginal tax rates have been made in support of repealing the estate tax. The estate tax, it is asserted, is inefficient because it discourages the most productive members of society from continuing to accumulate wealth at some marginal point. The productive acts so discouraged would have generated income (and income tax revenues) and would also have contributed to national savings, aggregate capital accumulation, and, ultimately, productivity growth throughout the economy.[33]

Though this argument is theoretically subject to empirical verification, this is inherently a difficult matter to study, especially given the absence of significant changes in the estate tax in recent decades. The existing empirical evidence is scanty on both sides of the argument.[34] Absent hard evidence, one is left with mere analysis of probable tendencies. In that regard, I would note that people accumulate wealth for a number of reasons, only one of which—to pass wealth onto one's heirs—is significantly impacted by the estate tax. People accumulate wealth in order to fund their own consumption opportunities, to provide for their own economic security, and to augment their economic power. They accumulate wealth to do the same things for a spouse. They accumulate wealth in order to advance charitable objectives. Sometimes, especially in the case of extremely wealthy individuals, they accumulate because they can hardly help but do so.[35] None of these motivations is affected at all by the estate tax. The estate tax obviously does not burden the taxpayer directly during his own life, so continued accumulation of economic power and security continue to benefit the individual doing the accumulation. The unlimited marital and charitable deductions likewise preclude estate tax influences as to transfers to recipients qualifying for those deductions. And no influences matter with respect to accidental accumulations.

Even as to accumulations intended to enrich one's heirs, the incentive effects created by an estate tax are ambiguous. It may be that the benefactor has a target amount that he would like to leave to his heirs. In that case, an estate tax would spur *greater* efforts in order to achieve the fixed goal in aftertax terms. And, if an estate tax does blunt the benefactor's incentives, that may be offset by an opposite incentive effect on the heirs, who, after imposition of an estate tax, would no longer be able to rely on receipt of their great expectations undiminished by taxes. If *they* have in mind a target accumulation of wealth, they may need to contribute more of their own output to the pool in order to achieve it.

All in all, then, the estate tax may be a relatively efficient tax, in that those subject to the tax can avoid its sting indefinitely simply by remaining alive, or by writing wills that leave all or most of the estate to a spouse or to charity. And if they can avoid or defer its incidence, they may very well be able to put it out of their minds, in which case its influence on productive behavior will be very modest. It is difficult to know with any certainty, but in light of the foregoing, it would seem that the burden of demonstrating the inefficient consequences of the adverse incentives created by the tax should be on those who claim that such consequences exist and are sizable.

Even if there is not much substance to the inefficiency argument, it is possible that some people could be swayed by it, and that it could account for some of the popular opposition to the estate tax. There is some evidence of this in some quarters: surveys taken among small business owners suggest that they have indeed adopted this as one of their primary arguments in opposition to the tax.[36] However, as individuals whose estates are likely to be burdened, they are obviously self-interested in repeal of the tax; the more interesting question in this regard is whether the very large majority of individuals whose estates are unlikely to be burdened by the tax adopt efficiency as grounds for opposing the tax. I am aware of no evidence that would suggest that this is the case.

2. THE FAIRNESS ARGUMENT

In the context of the estate tax, the most common form of fairness argument is that the estate tax represents a form of double taxation, taxing savings that have already been subject to an income tax when they were first earned. One notes at the outset that the premise of this argument is frequently flawed: many wealthy individuals have portfolios the value of which is largely in the form of unrealized appreciation of investment assets. Many of the contemporary superrich, in fact, are founders of successful companies whose wealth consists in large part of the highly appreciated stock of those companies. If they continue to hold that stock until their deaths, they will never be subject to an income tax on those values because they will have had no realization event; and their heirs will not be subject to tax on those values because they will receive a basis in those assets equal to the fair market value of the decedents' assets at the date of death.[37]

Even if there is double taxation in some cases, it is far from clear that this is objectionable, or even exceptional. If, for example, a wealthy person were deciding between spending $250,000 on a Ferrari, or accumulating that amount for eventual passage to her heirs, she would be wrong if she thought the former course would not be burdened with a tax. In fact, she would, depending on the jurisdiction and date of purchase, be likely to pay a state sales tax, and federal excise taxes on gas guzzlers, tires, and, at some times, luxury automobiles.[38] In subsequent periods, she would likely pay a state personal property tax each year, and federal excise taxes on gasoline and replacement tires, as well as quasi-taxes like road tolls, and sales taxes on ancillary purchases of parking, repairs, and the like, as the car is used.

In fact, as a general matter, the *number* of times a particular flow of income is taxed is of no consequence; what matters is the total tax burden so imposed. Two 15 percent taxes are no worse than a single 30 percent tax. That does not answer the fairness objection to the estate tax, but it does shift it to a different question: is the estate tax, especially when viewed together with the income and other taxes that may have been imposed, excessive? There can be no objective answer to that question, but it may help to note that although the bite of the estate tax is significant, its frequency is very limited. It is imposed on wealthy individuals only once, and at the end of their lives. From the perspective of a very wealthy dynastic family, it could be viewed as imposed on the family once each generation, or about once every twenty-five to thirty years. It has been estimated that the estate tax imposes a tax burden that is roughly the equivalent of an additional income tax increment of 2 or 3 percent during the time that the wealth is accumulating.[39] Whether or not one agrees that such an incremental burden would have been precisely appropriate, it would not seem to be outside the bounds of fairness.

Regardless of its substantive merits, there is some reason to believe that this argument resonates with at least some people. For example, in a survey done by a consortium of National Public Radio, the Kaiser Family Foundation, and the Kennedy School of Government at Harvard University, respondents were asked whether they favored or opposed repeal of the estate tax.[40] Those who favored repeal were offered several possible explanations for their position. One of those was: the money was already taxed once and it should not be taxed again.[41] Fully 92 percent of those respondents favoring repeal (52 percent of the entire sample) indicated that this was indeed one of their reasons for supporting repeal, far outdistancing the next most popular answer.[42]

Many voters do hold, at least implicitly, a view that aftertax income should be exactly that: after any and all taxes. As the foregoing suggests, the variety of consumption taxes that may apply to one's use of so-called aftertax income show that this view is not well-founded. Still, it persists. The solution may lie along one of two paths. The first would be to repeal the estate tax, but as part of a package of tax changes that replicated the distributional consequences of the estate tax through an additional marginal income tax surcharge that applied only to very large incomes. Alternatively, one might address taxpayer misconceptions via survey data that compiled taxpayer preferences and consequences in trade-offs between the income tax and the estate tax. It could be noted, for example, that the federal wealth transfer taxes were raising about $30 billion per year, prior to EGTRRA.[43] Since there are about 100 million taxable income tax returns filed per year in recent years, this comes to about $300 per return. Voters could plausibly be asked if they would prefer to preserve the estate tax in something resembling its pre-EGTRRA form, or have an average increase in income tax bills of $300 per taxpayer. My sense is that such a question would elicit much more support for the estate tax than we have seen in recent years.

B. Greeting Miss Rosy Scenario: Can't Stop Thinkin' about Tomorrow

Is it possible that many Americans imagine that they will die wealthy, no matter what their means at any particular moment? If so, it would provide a self-interested explanation of their aversion to the estate tax. The data, of course, suggest that expectations of achieving great wealth will be disappointed in almost all cases. It is not simply that we know that only one in twenty, or fifty, or two hundred (depending on the exemption amount chosen) will in fact die with enough wealth to be exposed to the estate tax. It is also that we have a pretty good sense of who those people will be. They will tend to be people who are born into wealth, or those whose educational backgrounds or spectacular talents give them access to the best business and employment opportunities. There is some income mobility—by which I mean a possibility of moving from a relatively low income in percentile terms to a much higher one, or the reverse—but, even in this land of opportunity, the numbers are not encouraging.[44] Poor and middle-income people can become suddenly wealthy, by, for example, winning a multimillion dollar lottery. Or by . . . well, actually, winning the lottery just about exhausts the range of possibilities. There may be, for all I know, scores, or even hundreds, of multimillion dollar winners each year; but even the most optimistic person cannot reasonably *expect* to be one of those, among the millions of buyers of lottery tickets. At most, one can entertain the faintest of hopes. Could that possibly be enough to influence voters to abandon assessments of their self-interest based on their actual status, in favor of a perspective based on a faint hope?

It is just possible that this is so, at least for some people. The thought that views on important public policy issues such as the estate tax could be warped by the faint hope of winning a huge lottery prize would in that case be one more reason to oppose (but pointlessly, by this time) the spread of the lottery mania. But in any event, one cannot dismiss the possibility that some voters' views on the estate tax are indeed shaped to some extent by unrealistic expectations regarding the size of the estate that they will themselves leave behind.

There is some evidence that opposition to the estate tax may be at least partly explained by this misplaced optimism about one's prospects. The NPR et al. survey noted above[45] offered those who favored repeal another explanation for that position: "It [the estate tax] might affect YOU someday." Sixty-nine percent of these respondents (39 percent of the entire sample) indicated that this was among their reasons for supporting repeal of the estate tax.[46] It is unclear, however, whether this view is based on an expectation that the respondents' economic status will dramatically improve at some subsequent point in their lives, or upon their misunderstanding of the incidence of the estate tax.[47] As will be discussed below, most voters do not have a good sense of the threshold wealth level that exposes an estate to the estate tax; so this question is irredeemably ambiguous as to whether it is unrealistic expectations or ignorance of the tax threshold that causes voters to imagine that their own estates will be exposed to it.

C. Antitax, Antigovernment Views

Some of the negative responses to survey questions about the estate tax may simply reflect generally negative views of any and all taxes. Some citizens believe that governments at all levels, but especially at the federal level, do very little that adds value to their lives. Yet they encounter tax burdens everywhere they look. Some evidence that this attitude influences choices about the estate tax is found in the substantial correlation between a taxpayer's sense that his own taxes are too high, and his support of estate tax repeal.[48]

Larry M. Bartels attributes these findings to what he calls variously "unenlightened self-interest" or "misplaced self-interest," the point in either case being that people are unhappy with their own tax burdens, and as a consequence reflexively support virtually *any* measure that would reduce or eliminate *any* tax. The problem, of course, is that such indiscriminate opposition is highly counterproductive for most individuals who, by supporting repeal of a tax that will never burden them, increase the likelihood that some other tax (to which they more probably would be exposed) will need to be increased. As in the previous category (unrealistic expectations of wealth increase), this explanation begins to shade toward an explanation based more on ignorance than on deeply held belief. Accordingly, it will be discussed further below in Section II.E.

D. What Class War?

We Americans like to think of ourselves as free of class consciousness and snobbery, at least relative to European cultures. We like to think that we are a country in which the absence of pedigree is no bar to advancement, even in the most socially elite institutions. Although this self-image is patently inaccurate, we nonetheless embrace it.[49] Importantly, this self-image may influence views about the desirability of the estate tax. That tax seems so obviously an assault on the nameless rich that it may have come to embody a certain quaintness rather like the feel of the society films of the 1930s and 1940s by Frank Capra and others. Perhaps, in this view, the estate tax is just an artifact of the era when Lodges spoke only to Cabots, an artifact that is unnecessary and slightly anachronistic in today's more fluid society.

While I detect a bit of this view in at least some expressed sentiments about the estate tax, there is little direct evidence bearing on this question one way or the other. What is somewhat clearer is that social class has in recent decades become more complex: it is not simply a matter any more of the very wealthy versus the rest of the citizenry. The popular sociology of the new millennium emphasizes the existence of competing elites, consisting on one side of so-called knowledge workers: scientists, lawyers, educators, journalists, who are by and large well-off but rarely truly wealthy,[50] and a business elite, which consists of successful businesspeople of a variety of sorts, including those whose immense financial success has put them squarely in the crosshairs of the estate tax. Each elite aspires to leadership positions in the political hierarchy, and each has achieved some success. Oversimplifying grandly, the knowledge workers seem to have the support of racial and ethnic minorities, and what remains of the true working class. It is a coalition, one might say, of those who think they might be beneficiaries of governmental transfer programs, and those who think that such programs are a good idea. On the other hand, the business elites have been able to erect a façade of ordinariness that seems congenial to many members of the middle class, who may in contrast be put off by the intellectual pretensions of the knowledge workers, and are also likely to view themselves as funding transfer payments rather than receiving them.

The estate tax can thus be seen as a very minor pawn in a larger stakes contest for total control of the polity. The wealthy are in a position to finance political campaigns, and many of them care deeply about repeal of the estate tax. The rest of the right-of-center coalition merely goes along with the platform, which appeals overall to them primarily because they see it as containing other, more important planks to their liking, primarily on a variety of social issues.[51] This explanation of estate tax opposition again has elements of voter ignorance at its roots: it is much easier to obtain support for estate tax repeal from a large slice of the electorate if most of the members of that slice do not realize the degree to which their own financial interests may diverge from the interests of others in the right-of-center coalition. By itself, however, the explanation set forth above fails because the divide described in this section is roughly even in numerical terms; yet, the divide on the estate tax appears to be far more heavily tilted toward repeal.

E. Ignorance: What We Don't Know May Hurt Us

So most roads, if not all of them, lead to what is probably the central problem in developing public support for the estate tax: citizens by and large do not understand what the tax is intended to do, nor—and this is even more critical—how narrow its incidence truly is. Some respondents to the surveys on this question confess to their ignorance of the tax: fully 28 percent of the respondents to the NPR survey selected "don't know enough to say" as their response to the question of whether the estate tax should be repealed.[52] At least these respondents knew their limitations. Fully 49 percent of respondents in the same survey, when asked how many families would have to pay the estate tax when someone died, indicated their belief that most families have to pay.[53] This was patently untrue at the time of the survey (April 2003) and has been untrue for the entire history of the estate tax in this country.

Even more revealing for present purposes, only 56 percent of those initially opposed to the estate tax indicated that they would maintain the same position even if the estate tax were imposed only on estates worth $1 million or more.[54] But this survey was undertaken at a time when the estate tax exemption was exactly that figure. (The $1 million exemption level is also the exemption level that the permanent estate tax rules will revert to in 2011 if Congress does nothing further in this area.) Putting these numbers together yields a particularly interesting insight: while this survey found that 57 percent of the respondents favored repeal of the estate tax when asked that simple question, only about 46 percent favored repeal of a tax whose features were in fact those embodied in the law extant at the time of the survey![55]

Those who indicated that they would still favor repeal even if the exemption were $1 million were asked further if they would favor repeal if the exemption were $5 million; and those who said they still favored repeal at that level were asked if they would still favor repeal if the exemption were $25 million. The responses to those further questions indicated that only 34 percent of all respondents would favor repeal if the exemption were set at $5 million, and only about 26 percent of the total sample would favor repeal if the exemption were set at the $25 million level. This does not, of course, mean that the remainder of the respondents necessarily support an estate tax at those various levels.[56] As noted, 28 percent of the sample expressed no view on the initial question, and additional undecided respondents appear at each subsequent step in the survey. What we can say, however, is that the initial result, that 57 percent of the survey respondents favor repeal of the estate tax, is highly misleading. Many of those would seem to have been prepared to support the tax had they been aware of even the current exemption level, and many more would appear to have preferred retention of the tax, but with a somewhat higher exemption level, which is essentially the position of the Congressional Democrats. In fact, it is possible to say from the detailed data in the NPR survey that fully 51 percent of respondents would favor an estate tax that was only imposed on estates exceeding $5 million in assets.[57]

Support for some type of estate tax may be even broader than that, in light of the fact that there are two further sources of prorepeal bias reflected in the survey numbers. First, both surveys split their samples into groups whose questions, while substantively identical, were expressed slightly differently. One group within each sample was asked for their views on repeal of the estate tax, while the other group was asked for their views on the death tax or the estate tax that some people call the death tax.[58] This appears to have made a modest, but nontrivial, difference in responses. For example, in the NPR survey, the figure of 57 percent overall support for repealing the tax is composed of the 60 percent support among those who received the death tax wording, and 54 percent support from those who were asked about the estate tax, unmodified by the death tax label. The death tax pejorative is misleading, and apparently consciously so.[59] It suggests that death is the triggering event for the tax, and that the tax so imposed might be quite general. But, as has been noted elsewhere, death is neither a necessary nor a sufficient cause to impose a wealth transfer tax under current law.[60] Many very wealthy people routinely pay gift taxes on their gratuitous transfers during their lives, and most people die without leaving estates of sufficient size to give rise to an estate tax liability. If a legislator is honestly trying to determine the views of voters on this question, those views provided on the "death tax" should be simply disregarded.

A second source of prorepeal bias lies in the failure to mention that bequests to spouses and charitable organizations are not subject to the estate tax. This is understandable, given limitations on the design of survey questions. It can nevertheless produce misleading results in circumstances where the respondents have little background information about the estate tax. One presumes that at least some respondents have in mind the notion that a surviving spouse's living standards should not be burdened by an estate tax, and may favor repeal on that (erroneous) basis. The best wording might be something like: Do you think that a tax should be imposed on estates of decedents who leave more than $1 million to their descendants? That is a question that more or less accurately embodies what the current permanent provisions of the estate tax would do. If that is the tax Congress proposes to repeal, that is what constituents ought to be asked about.

The degree to which the oft-repeated survey results are misleading may be lamentable, but one should keep in mind that the fate of the estate tax will not be decided by a plebiscite: there is no provision for any direct vote by the public on any matter of federal law. Surveys are of interest only insofar as they inform Congress of the likely positions of the electorate on public policy issues on which the Congress will or may vote. Congress can and should give these surveys close, and somewhat skeptical, inspection along the lines suggested. If they do so, they will see that, while many people would like to see the complete repeal of the estate tax, most are reasonably satisfied with the estate tax we actually have, or at most would like to see modest increases in the exemption levels.

III. Conclusion: Mobilizing the Troops

Repealing the estate tax is the sort of issue with which democracies have trouble. A small number of people care deeply about repeal, and have the resources to mount an impressive campaign to that end. A much broader segment of the population either favors retention of the tax, or would favor retention of the tax if the tax were described to them accurately. Many people are not even aware of the degree to which the current tax is in accord with their views. In any event, their views are typically not as intensely felt as those who favor repeal, at least in part because less is at stake for them than for those whose estates may retain millions more dollars if the estate tax were repealed.

Proponents of repeal have developed a soundly structured lobbying effort. They have orchestrated letters to Congress from a large number of middling-wealthy individuals who claim that the tax inhibits their incentives to produce wealth (and jobs, and so on). They have offered sympathetic, though apparently spurious, cases of family businesses or family farms that have allegedly been liquidated due to the estate tax.[61] They have managed to attach a pejorative label—the death tax—to a tax that is not accurately so described. They have created an impression of a grassroots movement to repeal the estate tax, a movement that, if it exists, is based largely on misinformation, and only as a result of said misinformation gives the appearance of strongly supporting repeal. And they have even engaged a handful of academics who have, somewhat contrary to the weight of academic opinion, given some intellectual respectability to the idea of repealing the estate tax. Finally, they have backed up their efforts with a nearly inexhaustible supply of money that can be mobilized for direct lobbying expenses as well as for the financing of political campaigns of candidates favoring repeal. They are a formidable foe.

But resistance is not yet futile. Congress can be urged to remember that there is no free lunch when it comes to funding government programs. The permanent estate and gift tax rules provide a potent revenue-generating machine, capable of producing $30 billion or more of revenue each year. That is more than the federal government has spent in recent years on all law enforcement, litigation, and judicial activities, to choose just one example.[62] The estate tax also stimulates charitable giving. Both the tax collections themselves and the charitable gifts they stimulate serve to remove some funds from families of great wealth and devote them to purposes more generally advancing the welfare of our nation. And, finally, despite superficial appearances to the contrary, it is not the case that the majority of American voters want to repeal the estate tax we actually have.

Perhaps the single datum that best summarizes the case for the estate tax is derived from speculating, as I did in section II.A.2 above, about how our tax system would generate an equivalent amount of revenue from some other source. The logical source would be additional income taxes, since any other tax imaginable would replace a highly progressive tax with one that is likely to be seriously regressive (such as payroll taxes). But if we want to collect an additional $30 billion each year from the income tax, it would mean that the average income tax bill would have to be increased by about $300 per taxpayer, per year. One wonders what the poll results would be if the question asked were: Would you, as an average American taxpayer, be willing to pay $300 more income tax each year, for the rest of your life, so that millionaires would be able to pass unlimited millions or billions of dollars down to the next generation free of any estate tax?" In truth, that is the question we face in thinking about the estate tax. I doubt that more than a small minority of Americans would endorse such a plan if it were offered to them honestly.

N O T E S

1. The author is grateful for the insights offered by Lawrence Zelenak and Jay Soled on an earlier draft of this work, but of course retains responsibility for any errors.

2. Only 3.4 percent of the adult population in 1998 had personal wealth exceeding $625,000, the threshold in that year of potential exposure to the U.S. estate tax. Barry W. Johnson & Lisa M. Schreiber, *Personal Wealth, 1998*, STAT. INCOME BULL., Jan. 1, 2002, at 87, 99.

3. The supposition is naive because it is now commonplace to observe, in the fashion of public choice theorists, that small but organized and passionate groups can easily dominate large but diffuse ones. *See, e.g.*, MANCUR OLSON, THE LOGIC OF COLLECTIVE ACTION: PUBLIC GOODS AND THE THEORY OF GROUPS 29 (1971). But this essay is not about why the estate tax might be repealed, but rather why so many people who are not likely to be burdened by the tax nevertheless find the tax distasteful.

4. GEORGE BERNARD SHAW, EVERYBODY'S POLITICAL WHAT'S WHAT? 256 (1944). (I am indebted to Ronald Pearlman for this gem.)

5. In fiscal year 2000, the last year preceding adjustments in the estate tax that reduced its revenue capacity, total estate and gift tax collections were $29.7 billion. IRS, INTERNAL REVENUE GROSS COLLECTIONS, BY TYPE OF TAX, FISCAL YEARS 1973–2003, *available at* http://www.irs.gov/pub/irs-soi/03db07co.xls [hereinafter INTERNAL REVENUE GROSS COLLECTIONS].

6. Over $16 billion in charitable bequests were reported on estate tax returns filed in 2001. IRS, ESTATE TAX RETURNS FILED IN 2001 tbl.1 (unpublished statistics, *available at* http://www.irs.gov/pub/irs-soi/01eso1gr.xls) [hereinafter 2001 ESTATE TAX RETURNS]. It has been estimated that the decline in charitable giving due to repeal of the estate tax would likely be in a range from 24–44 percent. Charles T. Clotfelter & Richard Schmalbeck, *The Impact of Fundamental Tax Reform on Non-profit Organizations, in* THE ECONOMIC EFFECTS OF FUNDAMENTAL TAX REFORM 211, 233–35 (Henry J. Aaron & William G. Gale eds., 1996).

7. For an important contribution to the analysis of income and wealth distribution and the role played by the tax system in controlling excesses, see Martin J. McMahon, Jr., *The Matthew Effect and Federal Taxation*, 45 B.C. L. REV. 993 (2005).

8. See the University of Michigan's 2002 National Election Survey (NES), *available at* http://www.umich.edu/~nes. Some of the data reflected in this chapter are based on the analysis of the NES data by Larry M. Bartels. *See* Larry M. Bartels, Homer Gets a Tax Cut: Inequality and Public Policy in the American Mind 14 (Aug. 2003), *available at* http://www.princeton.edu/~csdp/research/pdfs/homer.pdf.

9. NAT'L PUB. RADIO ET AL., NATIONAL SURVEY OF AMERICANS' VIEWS ON TAXES (Apr. 2003), *available at* http://www.kff.org/kaiserpolls/ [hereinafter NPR SURVEY]. There may be many explanations for the discrepancy between the two surveys, but one obvious possibility is that the NES survey, by offering an opportunity to express either "strong" or "not strong" views on repeal, was more inviting to people who otherwise might have expressed no opinion. The NPR survey, on the other hand, offered only the choice of repeal, not repeal, or no opinion. See further discussion of survey results *infra* in section B.5 of this chapter.

10. 26 I.R.C. § 2001 et seq. (1986).

11. Technically, the exemption is achieved by allowing a credit equal to the amount of the tax on an estate of precisely the size of what I have called the exemption. For example, the estate of a decedent dying in 2000 would have had a federal unified estate and gift tax credit of $220,550. This amount is precisely equal to the tentative tax computed with respect to a taxable estate of $675,000. Thus, by offsetting the tax on an estate of that size, the credit effectively exempts estates of that size or smaller from any actual estate tax incidence. There are some technical differences between an exemption and a credit, but they are irrelevant to the purposes of this essay.

12. Although initially conceived primarily to protect the integrity of the estate tax, it is now thought that the gift tax also protects the integrity of the income tax to a considerable degree. As such, the gift tax is likely to be preserved even if the estate tax is eventually repealed.

13. It did not, however, significantly change the gift tax, for reasons explained in *supra* note 12.

14. I.R.C. § 2056. The marital deduction only applies in this way if the donee is a U.S. citizen.

15. I.R.C. § 2055.

16. 2001 ESTATE TAX RETURNS, *supra* note 6.

17. *Id.*

18. *See* Richard Schmalbeck, *Avoiding Federal Wealth Transfer Taxes, in* RETHINKING ESTATE AND GIFT TAXATION 113, 128–30 (William G. Gale et al. eds., 2001).

19. In some ways, the $16 billion passing to charity at death in 2001 understates the impact of the tax because it does not count the value of gifts made during the decedent's lifetime in order to avoid the estate tax. When a wealthy person decides that she would rather give some of her estate to charity than expose that value to an estate tax, there is a fair chance that she will decide to do so during life rather

than waiting until death because doing so gets the assets out of the estate (saving estate taxes), and also yields valuable income tax deductions that can shelter income during the individual's life. On the other hand, the $16 billion overestimates the effect in another sense: there would no doubt continue to be some charitable bequests even if there were no estate tax.

20. U.S. Census Bureau, Statistical Abstract of the United States, 2003, at 86 tbl.108, *available at* http://www.census.gov/prod/2004pubs/03statab/vitstat .pdf.

21. 2001 Estate Tax Returns, *supra* note 6, at tbl.1.

22. *Id.*

23. *Id.* As always in cases involving the extremes of a normal statistical distribution, those arithmetic means are a bit misleading. Even among the taxable estates, most are relatively small, with assets of less than $2.5 million. (Of the 52,000 taxable estates, about 43,000, or about five-sixths, had gross asset valuations of less than $2.5 million.) And those estates pay relatively little tax. In contrast, at the far end of the estate-tax exposed population (which is itself at the far end of the total population of decedents) are the very small number of estates representing great wealth, and paying a greatly disproportionate share of the tax. In 2001, nearly $8 billion of estate tax was paid by just 1,317 taxable estates that had gross assets in excess of $10 million each. That rarified group had an average gross estate of $29 million, and paid an average estate tax of about $6 million. *Id.*

24. The data are for estate tax returns filed in 2001, which mostly represent estates of individuals who died in either 1999 or 2000.

25. About 8,000 taxable returns filed in 2001 showed assets exceeding $2.5 million, and about 25,000 showed assets between $1 million and $2.5 million. It thus seems reasonable to expect that all of the former, and no more than 60 percent of the latter, would have had to file had the exemption been $1.5 million in the years of their deaths. 2001 Estate Tax Returns, *supra* note 6, at tbl.1.

26. For taxable estate tax returns filed in 2001, only about 8,000 showed gross estates exceeding $2,500,000; but those estates had a mean gross estate of nearly $8,000,000.

27. Estates with more than $2.5 million in gross assets paid about $17 billion of estate taxes in 2001; some of that revenue would be lost under a $3.5 million exemption because some estates would then be below the threshold, and even those above the threshold would have more of their estates sheltered by the larger exemption. There would also, however, be some growth in the decedent population, and in wealth, between now and 2009. In all, it seems highly likely that even in that year, estate tax collections will exceed $10 billion.

28. Although the exemption was only $675,000 when EGTRRA was passed, the permanent rules called for increasing exemptions over the years between 2001 and 2006. When the EGTRRA provisions expire, the 2006 exemption will be left standing.

29. Cong. Budget Office, The Budget and Economic Outlook: Fiscal Years 2002–2011 tbl.3-11 (Jan. 2001), *available at* http://www.cbo.gov/showdoc .cfm?index=2727&sequence=4#Table#3-11.

30. The Joint Committee on Taxation estimated informally that immediate repeal of the estate and gift taxes at the end of 2001 would have cost $410 to $662 billion. Heidi Glenn, *W[ays] + M[eans] Clears $193 Billion Estate Tax Repeal with Antiavoidance Rules*, Tax Notes, Apr. 2, 2001, at 7.

31. There was briefly an income tax during the Civil War, but it was repealed following the war. Congress enacted another in 1894 that was declared unconstitutional by the Supreme Court in *Pollock v. Farmers' Loan & Trust Co.*, 157 U.S. 429, 601 (1895).

32. I believe the characterization in the text is accurate as a practical matter; however, the estate tax has been explicitly found to be an excise tax on the passage of wealth for constitutional purposes, not a direct tax on wealth. New York Trust Co. v. Eisner, 256 U.S. 345 (1921).

33. Edward J. McCaffery, *The Uneasy Case for Wealth Transfer Taxation*, 104 Yale L.J. 283 (1994).

34. For a nice summary, see William G. Gale & Joel Slemrod, *Overview, in* Rethinking Estate and Gift Taxation 1, 32–37 (William G. Gale et al. eds., 2001).

35. A pool of wealth of $1 billion will generate, when conservatively invested to produce a 5 percent return, an income of some $137,000 per day. It is very difficult to literally consume such an amount; one tends instead (I have to imagine) to buy things with it: yachts, apartments in Paris, and the like. But even those things may appreciate, or at least hold their value reasonably well, adding to one's wealth in subsequent time periods.

36. *See, e.g.*, Joseph H. Astrachan & Roger Tutterow, *The Effects of Estate Taxes on Family Business: Survey Results*, 9 Fam. Bus. Rev. 303 (1996).

37. An executor can choose instead to value the assets as of a date exactly six months after the date of death, in which case that date is used as the basis at which the heirs take in the assets. Note also that, under the temporary EGTRRA provisions, taxpayers who inherit property from a decedent who dies in 2010 may have to take the decedent's own basis as their basis, rather than getting a basis that has been stepped up to fair market value. There are, however, a number of exceptions to this rule.

38. The luxury automobile tax expired at the end of 2002; but the point is that Congress did not feel constrained from imposing such a tax simply because the funds to purchase the car typically would come from income that had previously been taxed.

39. James Poterba, *The Estate Tax and After-Tax Investment Returns, in* Does Atlas Shrug? The Economic Consequences of Taxing the Rich 345 (Joel Slemrod ed., 2000).

40. NPR Survey, *supra* note 9.

41. *Id.* at question 49.

42. The next most popular answer was "It might force the sale of small businesses and family farms," which was cited by 74 percent of these respondents. *Id.*

43. In fiscal year 2000 (the year ending on 9/30/00), the federal government collected $25.6 billion in estate tax and $4.1 billion in gift tax. Internal Revenue Gross Collections, *supra* note 5.

44. *See* McMahon, *supra* note 7, at 1010–12.

45. NPR Survey, *supra* note 9.

46. *Id.* at question 49.

47. Some light on this is shed by the last of the explanations for support of repeal offered by the survey (in addition to the double-tax and small business explanations mentioned in Section II.A.1). Sixty-two percent of respondents who favored repeal (36 percent of the whole sample) listed the belief that it [the estate tax] affects too many people among their reasons for supporting repeal. It seems doubtful that so many people would have used this rationale had they known that less than 5 percent of estates are even obligated to file a return, and that fewer than half of those returns result in estate tax liability.

48. Bartels, *supra* note 8 tbl.4 (placing the correlation coefficient at .413, and at .324 after controlling for ideology, party identification, and spending preferences).

49. Joseph Epstein, Snobbery: The American Version 62–72 (2002).

50. *See, e.g.*, David Brooks, Bobos in Paradise: The New Upper Class and How They Got There (2001).

51. Thomas Frank develops variations on this theme throughout his recent book What's the Matter with Kansas? How Conservatives Won the Heart of America (2004).

52. NPR Survey, *supra* note 9, questions 47 and 48.

53. *Id.* at question 51.

54. Both the 57 percent who favored repeal, and the 28 percent who expressed no opinion on the initial question, were asked if they would favor repeal if the exemption level were set at $1 million. Of that group, some 85 percent of the total sample, 56 percent would still favor repeal at the $1 million level, 31 percent would oppose repeal, and 18 percent would have no opinion. *Id.* at question 52.

55. There are some minor discrepancies in the NPR data report that cannot be explained by simple rounding error. For example, they reported that their initial sample of 1,339 split among three groups: 57 percent who favored repeal, 28 percent who had no opinion, and 15 percent who did not favor repeal. The first two groups—which should have numbered between 1,124 and 1,151—were then asked if they would favor repeal with a $1 million exemption, but the subsample size shown for this question was only 1,104. Of that group, 56 percent, or about 618 respondents, would have favored repeal even with that exemption level. That number, 618, is 46 percent of the total sample of 1,339. Similar modest discrepan-

cies infect the subsequent derived percentages as well, but will not be fully detailed in these notes.

56. *E.g.*, it should not be inferred that 77 percent of respondents would favor an estate tax with a $5 million exemption, simply because only 23 percent of respondents would favor repeal even with an exemption that high.

57. There is a certain amount of rounding error in the public report released by the NPR consortium, but it appears that about 15 percent of the survey sample favored retention of the tax without further information; an additional 26 percent would favor retention at a $1 million exemption level; and an additional 11 percent would favor retention of the tax at a $5 million exemption level. Finally, another 7 percent would favor retention at a $25 million level, indicating that a full 59 percent of the survey sample favored retention of *some* estate tax, with differences among this sample as to the appropriate threshold.

58. This is the wording of the NPR Survey, *supra* note 9, question 48.

59. David Cay Johnston, Perfectly Legal 80–81 (2003).

60. Gale & Slemrod, *supra* note 34.

61. *See* Johnston, *supra* note 59, at 71

62. *See, e.g.*, Budget of the United States Government, Fiscal Year 2000, at 341 tbl.34-2 (showing a total outlay in Account No. 750, "Administration of Justice," of $26.7 billion in fiscal year 2000—which was chosen because that is the last year preceding the temporary changes to the estate tax imposed by EGTRRA).

And Less for Those in the Cheap Seats

Trade Law, Labor, and Global Inequality

David M. Trubek and Lance Compa

Globalization is transforming the conditions of labor around the world. These changes are facilitated by developments in trade law and the larger trade and investment regime of which it is a part. While trade law has done a great deal to foster economic integration and increase cross-border flows of goods and services, workers in many countries and in many industries have suffered job losses, declining wages, and abusive conditions that can be attributed at least in part to trade pressures.

This chapter examines the effects of globalization on labor and what is being done to offset its negative consequences. We show that the benefits of globalization are not evenly spread, and that workers are often losers in the trade game. We explain how globalization can weaken domestic labor protections and indicate that the trade regime has yet to provide compensating protection. We suggest that there is a way to construct a transnational labor regime to maintain labor standards and protect labor rights in a globalized economy. We show how negative effects might be counteracted by coordinated action at domestic, regional, and global levels and suggest that the lack of a clear vision of how transnational labor law might operate is hampering progress toward an effective transnational labor regime.

I. The Scope of Trade Law

Trade law sets the legal framework for cross-border commercial transactions. Trade law takes shape in global, regional, and subregional arrangements among governments. At the same time, all countries maintain domestic laws on trade, and much of trade law's application involves reconciling conflicting supranational rules and domestic statutes.

Domestically, the United States has an extensive system of law governing international trade. First and most simply, U.S. laws set tariffs on imports into the United States. Many people are not aware that the infamous and high Smoot-Hawley tariffs of the 1930s are still on the books. They are superseded by application of the WTO's most-favored-nation (MFN) rule, which requires that WTO members must extend to all trading partners the tariff levels granted to their single "most-favored" partner. This is why MFN status for China was such a contentious issue through much of the 1990s, when China was not a WTO member and Congress had to act annually to grant MFN status to China. If MFN were not granted, tariffs on imports from China would snap to Smoot-Hawley levels, making Chinese products prohibitively expensive.

Congress finally granted permanent MFN status to China to avoid the annual dust-up, though in the process proponents changed the nomenclature from "most-favored-nation" to "normal trade relations" (NTR) to avoid giving the impression that China was getting some kind of favorable treatment. NTR has now become the term of art in U.S. trade discourse for the MFN principle, and is catching on in the rest of the world.

In 2002 Congress granted trade negotiating authority to President Bush under what used to be called "fast track" terms, by which the executive negotiates a complete trade agreement with a trading partner or group of partners, and Congress quickly votes yes or no, without amendments, on the final deal. Fast-track authority had earlier been denied to President Clinton largely over concerns that labor standards and environmental protection were inadequately addressed in the legislation.[1]

The Bush administration renamed fast-track "trade promotion authority" (TPA)—another nomenclature change, this time to avoid the implications of "pulling a fast one" that critics had used to derail fast track for Clinton. In the 2002 TPA, Congress included a labor clause making enforcement of labor standards a required objective in any trade deal.[2] The United States also has labor rights clauses in statutes governing preferential trade arrangements with developing countries, such as the Generalized System of Preferences (GSP), about which more below.

Bilaterally, the United States has negotiated several trade agreements, notably with Jordan, Chile, Singapore, and Australia, opening selected product and service markets and reducing tariffs and nontariff barriers. These agreements also contain labor rights clauses requiring the parties to effectively enforce their labor laws. Many labor advocates view the Jordan agreement in particular as a strong template for trade-labor linkage. It sets out International Labour Organization ("ILO") core labor standards as relevant norms and incorporates labor standards into the text of the agreement, rather than standing as a separate "side agreement," and it subjects labor violations to the same dispute settlement regime as commercial violations. One problem, however, is that the U.S.-Jordan agreement only contemplates "complaints" by one of the governments against the other, not a complaint system open to submissions by unions, human rights groups, or other civil society forces. These entities would have to lobby their government to launch a complaint, making government willingness, not citizen initiative, the trigger for investigating workers' rights violations.

One innovative bilateral trade-labor arrangement should be noted here. The U.S.-Cambodia textile trade agreement provides positive incentives for garment manufacturing firms in Cambodia to comply with international labor standards. Under the agreement, compliance—certified by an equally innovative monitoring system run by the ILO—brings increased quota opportunities to export products to the United States. In fact, firms and workers in Cambodia made substantial gains under this accord.[3] The quota system providing the incentive ended with the demise of the Multi-Fibre Arrangement as of January 1, 2005; nonetheless, Cambodia hopes to retain its export industry based on its reputation for fair treatment of workers built up under the agreement.

Regionally, the United States is party to the North American Free Trade Agreement (NAFTA), which constructs a detailed set of trading rules among Canada, Mexico, and the United States. In the wake of NAFTA, the United States has negotiated with other Western Hemisphere nations for a U.S.-Central America Free Trade Agreement (CAFTA—still subject to ratification, and a subject of controversy in the House of Representatives as we write). Negotiations have also proceeded on a Free Trade Agreement of the Americas (FTAA), but talks are stalled, largely over disputes over agricultural subsidy policies.[4]

The United States also participates in the Asia-Pacific Economic Cooperation (APEC), a much looser trade coordinating body so oddly named precisely because the countries want to avoid suggesting that they have created an "organization" setting rules for trade. Other countries have their own regional trade arrangements, notably the European Union (which is much more than a simple trading area) and the Common Market of the South (Mercosur), which includes Argentina, Brazil, Paraguay, and Uruguay, with Chile, Bolivia, and Peru as associate members, who are likely to be joined by Mexico.

At the multilateral level, the United States is involved in global trade law matters through participation in the World Trade Organization (WTO) and, to a lesser extent, the Organization for Economic Cooperation and Development (OECD). The WTO has a complex rule-making and adjudicative system. As in any such system, parties win and lose cases. The WTO does not have the power directly to force a country to change its trade laws or regulations, but can authorize the prevailing party in a WTO case to take trade countermeasures against the violating party. Such sanctions are used rarely. Most WTO rulings push contending parties into negotiations to settle the dispute before sanctions are imposed or soon after sanctions begin to pinch. Settlements usually lead to a change in the violating party's offending law or practice. However, these WTO disciplines do not extend to labor rights violations.

II. Trade and Labor Standards

Labor law, broadly defined, involves measures to provide social protection and offset negative effects of an unconstrained market. It includes industrial relations regimes allowing (and regulating) workers' collective action such as trade union organizing, collective bargaining, and strikes. It sets labor standards like minimum wage, overtime limits, child labor restrictions, nondiscrimination protections, and more. What most of the world calls "social security law" provides programs like health insurance, pensions, unemployment benefits, and workers' compensation for job-related injuries.

In the predominantly national frameworks that characterized most of the twentieth century, workers could achieve bargaining rights, fair labor standards, and social protection through class-based political action in local and national legislatures. They made such gains both in the industrial countries then doing most of the world's high-value-added production and in larger developing countries that protected leading national sectors under import substitution industrialization (ISI) policies.

These standards could be maintained in part because national economies were not subject to major shocks from outside their borders. But global competition that arose in the last part of the twentieth century—where, for example, auto workers in Mexico and electronics workers in Malaysia could produce cars and computer hardware with high levels of quality and productivity at a fraction of wage costs in developed countries—put enormous downward pressure on collective bargaining, labor standards, and social protection systems everywhere. This happened regardless of the geography of competition: North-North, North-South, or South-South.

The results of global competition vary in different countries and regions, but much of the effect on labor conditions is to reduce effective protection. Workers in the United States have seen job losses, wage and benefit cuts, and accelerated trade union decline. Even in Europe, which has tried to resist such pressures, the European social model is now under siege as pressures mount for longer hours, less job security, and fewer benefits in many countries.[5] To a degree, Europe has sought to adjust to these pressures while creating new approaches to providing security and protection under the ungainly rubric of "flexicurity," but in many cases there has been a net loss for labor.[6]

In developing countries, race-to-the-bottom competition, especially in labor-intensive sectors like garment and electronics manufacturing, results in worsening conditions as governments seek to lure investors with promises of low labor costs and no unions. Where unions are allowed to exist, they are often government-dominated unions that serve as a labor discipline mechanism, not as workers' representatives. Such is the case in two of the largest exporting countries, Mexico and China.[7]

Many mainstream economists, government officials, corporate spokespersons, and pundits assume that free trade creates net gains in wealth for society as a whole—and it may. But society as a whole is an intellectual construct, not real people in the real world. In real economies, there are winners and losers, and workers are often the losers. While trade clearly benefits multinational corporations and those that serve them, its effect on workers is varied and often negative. To be sure, workers in some sectors and some industries in some countries gain jobs. In the United States, workers handling imports from Asia at Pacific coast ports are an example. But many more workers suffer lost jobs, lower wages, and reduced social protection. Even those workers in developing countries who have gained employment as a result of globalization may be working under abusive conditions and earning subsistence wages.[8]

The proclaimed "net gains" mask a small number of winners and huge number of losers in the globalized economy. And if the many losers get no recompense from the winners, the results are unjust. For example, in the North American context, U.S. workers have inadequate unemployment insurance and a scandalous lack of health insurance when they lose their jobs; Mexican workers have no unemployment insurance; and Mexican farmers thrown off their land by the effects under NAFTA of imported U.S. corn receive no help from transition programs. Indeed, migrating illegally to the United States is their adjustment program.

Imbalance between the power of labor and that of capital preserves the injustice. We are seeing on a global scale a repeat of the situation that prevailed in domestic markets a century ago, when the power of capital often crushed workers' aspirations. Workers in the global economy face the same challenge now that workers in national economies faced then: how to halt race-to-the-bottom competition among states, provinces, and regions with differing levels of economic development and natural endowments. The response a century ago, taking decades to advance (and still not fully accomplished) was to set a rules-based floor of labor standards which subnational jurisdictions and firms were not permitted to undercut. The solution today must be to construct an international system that has a similar effect.

Within the economy of the United States, the process of constructing a uniform labor standards "floor" started in the early twentieth century with states-based initiatives like the first workers' compensation and child labor laws. Regulation moved to the federal level in the 1930s with New Deal legislation like the National Labor Relations Act and the Fair Labor Standards Act. Later came equal pay laws, nondiscrimination laws, occupational safety and health laws, and others.

The United States was not alone; European countries, South American countries, Canada, Japan, and many others moved in the same direction, with precedent-setting measures in many labor areas. Mexico set out the most advanced national labor rights and standards in its 1917 Constitution, guaranteeing the right to organize, the right to strike, the eight-hour day, and other basic labor protections.

None of these national legal frameworks is perfectly administered or enforced. Still, they deter a race to the bottom in labor standards inside national borders. Now this brake needs to be applied internationally by the application of *transnational labor law*. Achieving this goal is a challenge because there is no global authority that enjoys the same sovereign power that national governments enjoyed when twentieth-century labor law was created.

III. The Emergence and Limits of Transnational Labor Law

Transnational labor law (TLL) is our term for measures that would do for a global economy what domestic labor law did for the closed national systems of the post–World War II era. We use this term to refer to a package of measures that would operate at various levels from the local to the global, involve the private as well as the public sectors, deploy a range of instruments from hard law to soft guidelines and principles, use new tools to foster a "race to the top," and provide funding where needed. Such a complex amalgam is the only way that the functions performed by twentieth-century labor law within closed national economic spaces can be performed in the complex transnational space of the present.

Transnational Labor Law, thus understood, would include:

Trade rules permitting individual countries to use trade sanctions to deter production under substandard working conditions as measured by international standards

Trade rules granting positive incentives to countries that excel at meeting international fair labor standards

Regional or global labor standards setting forth obligations and mechanisms to assess compliance, whether such standards are enforceable or just aspirational

Programs to augment social protection schemes for people adversely affected by trade

New tools that could encourage a race to the top

Programs to strengthen domestic labor codes in countries with weak systems

Public-private codes of conduct providing for voluntary restraint.

In recent years, advocates of linking workers' rights and trade have made some breakthroughs in creating instruments and mechanisms giving shape to TLL. Experience with the still largely embryonic TLL regime shows mixed results and limited impact. However, some progress has been made. Take as an example the transnational effort to get labor standards considered by the WTO. At the insistence of trade union and environmental advocates, the Clinton administration called for the creation of a WTO labor working group that would merely put the issue on the agenda for discussion. This modest effort was part of the dynamic—

along with 30,000 protesters and a police riot—that broke up the 1999 WTO ministerial meeting in Seattle. Free trade advocates and WTO supporters saw Seattle as a disaster, but for the anti-globalization movement it was a dramatic victory that changed the direction of the international economy.

The "battle in Seattle" appeared to at least stall what globalization critics see as a neoliberal express train bringing "Washington Consensus" policies (market opening, privatization, cuts in public services and public employment, super rights and protections for investors and patent-holders, etc.) to every country, whether or not countries want to adopt these policies and whether or not the policies are good for them. In this new context, the Clinton administration went on to negotiate what some labor rights advocates see as a model labor chapter in the U.S.-Jordan Free Trade Agreement, including it in the main body of the pact (not a "side deal," as in the NAFTA labor accord) and making violations of workers' rights redressable through trade disciplines as with any other violations.

Pursuant to a congressional mandate in 2002's Trade Promotion Authority (TPA) legislation, the United States now demands labor clauses in all trade agreements. Following the TPA labor requirement, bilateral trade agreements with Chile, Singapore, Morocco, and Australia and the regional U.S.-Central American Free Trade Agreement (CAFTA) contain clauses requiring countries (including the United States, it should be clear) to "strive to ensure" compliance with international labor standards and to "effectively enforce" domestic labor laws. However, only the latter obligation on effective application of domestic law is subject to dispute resolution and potential enforcement through trade measures, and countries retain the sovereign power to set labor standards wherever they choose, even below international norms. The "strive to ensure" provision is hortatory, not enforceable. This is a move in the right direction, but it is only a half-step, and it is too soon to know how effective these measures will be.[9]

IV. The World Trade Organization and the "Social Clause"

While the United States has started to include labor rights in bilateral trade agreements, efforts to get the WTO to enforce international labor standards have been unsuccessful. Labor advocates have long sought an amendment that would explicitly authorize the use of trade sanctions to bar imports from countries that failed to implement core labor standards. However, the WTO has resisted pressures for such a so-called social clause.

While most advocates of a social clause have pressed for a treaty amendment, some have argued that the current treaty provides a textual basis that would authorize WTO sanctions in cases involving gross violations of labor rights. And they suggest that the landmark Shrimp-Turtle case provides a precedent for such an interpretation. In that case, the WTO Appellate Body upheld a U.S. law prohibiting imports of shrimp from countries that did not protect turtles in the shrimp-harvesting process. The Appellate Body said that the U.S. measure fit the Article XX exception allowing a nontariff trade barrier for conservation of exhaustible natural resources.[10]

Some believe that the same logic applies to trade measures based on failure to protect workers' fundamental rights in the workplace. Article XX explicitly allows countries to take protectionist measures against imports made by prison labor. Robert Howse and Makau Mutua make a powerful argument that other Article XX exceptions covering "public morals" and "protection of human . . . life or health" should allow trade measures for violations of workers' rights:

> Trade law itself should be interpreted and evolved in a manner consistent with the hierarchy of norms in international law generally, where many basic human rights have the status of custom, general principles, or *erga omnes* obligations, which would normally prevail over specific provisions of a trade treaty, assuming an actual conflict. When properly interpreted and applied, the trade regime recognizes that human values related to human rights are fundamental and prior to free trade itself, which is merely an instrument of basic human values. The primacy of human rights over trade liberalization is consistent with the trade regime on its own terms.[11]

However, Howse and Mutua concede, "The institutions that are the official guardians of trade law pose formidable barriers to the proper and full realization of this insight."[12]

Resisting any move along these lines, the WTO has so far refused to countenance even a working group on labor, a concession earlier made to environmental concerns. The WTO purported to say its final "no" on trade-labor linkage in the 1996 Singapore Ministerial Declaration, which stated:

We renew our commitment to the observance of internationally recognized core labour standards. The International Labour Organization (ILO) is the competent body to set and deal with these standards, and we affirm our support for its work in promoting them. We believe that economic growth and development fostered by increased trade and further trade liberalization contribute to the promotion of these standards. We reject the use of labour standards for protectionist purposes, and agree that the comparative advantage of countries, particularly low-wage developing countries, must in no way be put into question. In this regard, we note that the WTO and ILO Secretariats will continue their existing collaboration.[13]

V. Labor Rights in Domestic Trade Statutes

Under the Generalized System of Preferences (GSP), WTO law allows countries to provide preferential tariffs for developing countries and condition them in various ways. The United States and the European Union have programs that condition their GSP concessions on adherence to basic labor standards, among other conditions.[14]

Congress first inserted a labor rights clause in the 1984 GSP renewal statute conditioning a developing country's favorable tariff treatment on whether it was "taking steps to afford internationally recognized worker rights."[15] The GSP labor rights provision defined such rights as:

1) the right of association;
2) the right to organize and bargain collectively;
3) a prohibition on the use of any form of forced or compulsory labor;
4) a minimum age for the employment of children; and
5) acceptable conditions of work with respect to minimum wages, hours of work, and occupational safety and health.[16]

Trade laws adopted after the 1984 GSP renewal contain similar labor-linked requirements for developing country benefits.

While the United States has used these laws to put pressure on some egregious violators, it has not employed them in an evenhanded manner and has been accused of manipulating the law to achieve unrelated political purposes. Thus the law was applied to cut off GSP benefits to the

Pinochet and Stroessner dictatorships, while equally abusive governments like those of Indonesia under Suharto and Guatemala under a series of murderous military juntas did not face similar sanctions.[17]

Although the unilateral adoption and application of labor rights provisions by the United States in trade laws has had some effect in some cases, the way it has been used provoked widespread criticism from international law experts and from developing country leaders. Human rights lawyer Philip Alston argues:

> As international trade becomes even more important in a post-Cold War world with its many additional would-be market economies, and as protectionist pressures increase in the United States and other developed market economies, the more attractive punitive or retaliatory trade measures become. This is especially true if they can be justified not solely by reference to economic considerations but also on human rights grounds. While measures in response to "market dumping" are a form of economic self-defense, measures to combat "social dumping" can be defended in largely altruistic or humanitarian terms. . . . It is difficult to escape the conclusion that the United States is, in reality, imposing its own, conveniently flexible and even elastic, standards upon other states. It is unlikely that the United States would look kindly upon such an approach if it were targeted in a similar fashion.[18]

Some developing country leaders condemned linking labor rights and trade in the GSP as being imperialist and protectionist. The Prime Minister of Malaysia expressed the argument thus:

> Some of the countries of the South have tried to pull themselves up literally by their own bootstraps. But the moment they appear to succeed, the carpet is pulled out from underneath their feet. GSP privileges are withdrawn and their records of human rights, democracy, etc are scrutinized in order to obstruct their progress. . . . Unemployment in the developed countries is not due to workers in developing countries working hard to compensate for their lack of other competitive advantage, but rather to the profligate ways of the developed nations with their high wages and unemployment benefits. Regrettably, powerful trading nations threaten through unilateral actions to undermine the carefully negotiated agreements. The attempts to link human rights and labor to trade are major threats that would dim the hope of a free environment for trade.[19]

These critiques of the use of GSP to encourage compliance with international labor standards have not stopped the use of this instrument by the European Union and the United States. However, a recent decision by the WTO Appellate Body may affect the way such tools can be used in the future. The Appellate Body ruled that GSP preferences like those offered by the European Union must be based on objective and transparent criteria and applied in such a way that identical treatment is offered to all similarly situated developing countries. Although the WTO only ruled on the special treatment given countries that combat drug traffic, the decision could affect the way the European Union manages its program of special benefits for countries that incorporate international labor standards in national law, requiring that care be taken to be sure that all countries that meet the standards receive equal benefits.[20]

A. Section 301 and China

In 1988, Congress added a labor rights amendment to Section 301 of the Trade Act, using the five-part GSP definition to make systematic workers' rights violations by *any* trading partner an unfair trade practice against which the United States could retaliate with economic sanctions. The labor rights clause lay dormant for fifteen years because potential complainants were daunted by evidentiary requirements to show that foreign labor practices placed a "burden or obstruction" on U.S. commerce.

Labor rights advocates made first use of the Section 301 labor rights clause in a complaint against China submitted by the AFL-CIO in March 2004. The China 301 submission, which comprised 108 pages with 345 footnotes, set forth chilling accounts of workers' rights violations connected to products exported to the United States. The complaint documented the effects of these exports on production by U.S. companies and on jobs and wages of U.S. workers, addressing the "burden or obstruction" element required for a 301 complaint. Violations laid out in the complaint included tight government control of the official trade union organization, the All China Confederation of Trade Unions (ACFTU), and the smashing of workers' independent organizing efforts through arrest and imprisonment of leaders and activists. The complaint also pointed to widespread use of child labor, horrendous health and safety conditions, and a quasi-apartheid system that discriminates against migrant peasant workers in urban factory zones.

The China 301 complaint posed squarely the tension between assertions of human rights and labor rights in trade relations and assertions that a labor-trade linkage is a pretext for protectionism. What the AFL-CIO really intended, said critics of its 301 petition, was to gain higher tariffs on imports from China to preserve jobs in the United States and stick consumers with higher prices in the process. The AFL-CIO just as strenuously argued that its goal was to advance workers' rights in China, to "level the playing field" not by tariffs and higher prices but by halting violations of workers' rights. If the Chinese government continued abusing workers' rights, the resulting tariff hikes should be laid to it, not to labor rights advocates in the United States.

The Bush administration refused to take up the petition for review, dismissing it as an exercise in "economic isolationism." Instead, officials argued, it would use the pending designation of China as a "market economy," a still-unrealized status, as leverage to push for labor reforms. Designation as a market economy rather than a state-run economy carries benefits such as lower penalties in antidumping cases. It is hard to take the administration's argument seriously as there is no evidence that the United States has raised any labor-related issues in talks with China regarding its "market economy" status.[21]

B. NAFTA and the NAALC

Upon taking office in 1993, Bill Clinton insisted on and got labor and environmental side accords to NAFTA. The labor side agreement, known as the North American Agreement on Labor Cooperation (NAALC), brings a social dimension in the form of defined "labor principles" and a mechanism for filing complaints and obtaining reports, public hearings, and recommendations. The NAALC, however, is an oversight system, not an enforcement system, and is limited in scope and effectiveness.

In an unusual procedural feature of the NAALC, complaints of workers' rights violations in a country must be filed with a review body in one of the *other* two countries, not the country where the alleged violations occurred. Negotiators did not want to establish parallel domestic bodies under the NAALC that would "compete" with their domestic law enforcement agencies and possibly arrive at conflicting conclusions about a case. Instead, they agreed to subject themselves to reviews and reports by each other on their enforcement of national labor laws related to the NAALC's labor principles.[22]

Some thirty complaints have been filed under the NAALC alleging violations of workers' rights by companies in all three countries and accompanying "failure to effectively enforce" domestic labor laws by the relevant government.[23] These complaints have not resulted in remedies. The NAALC is a mostly "soft law" system giving rise to investigations, public hearings, reports, recommendations, and the like, not binding orders to reinstate workers fired for organizing or to fix health and safety problems. Enforcement is left to domestic authorities.

The NAFTA labor agreement does contain a "hard" edge in the form of fines against a government that fails to effectively enforce domestic labor laws on minimum wages, child labor, and occupational health and safety, and even trade sanctions against offending firms or sectors. However, these provisions have never been used, and none of the three governments has so far demonstrated a willingness to invoke them.

The NAALC has been criticized from various viewpoints. Labor advocates often call it toothless, although some employers have found it worrisome. One U.S. employer federation argued, "Unions on both sides of the border are abusing the NAFTA process in an effort to expand their power. . . . NAFTA's labor side agreement is an open invitation for specific labor disputes to be raised into an international question and could open the door to a host of costly and frivolous complaints against U.S. employers." A Mexican critic said, "The original goals of the NAALC are becoming adulterated by the perspective which U.S. unions are imposing on it . . . to focus attention on Mexico, which is considered an unfair competitor vis à vis the attraction of regional investment."[24]

While the NAALC's role as a direct enforcement tool is limited, it has generated new forms of cross-border collaboration among trade unions and NGOs in the three countries. The agreement provides an accessible complaint mechanism with no standing requirements. It lets "any person"—and these have included trade unions, human rights groups, community organizations, NGOs, even student groups undertaking a NAALC complaint for course credit—file a complaint alleging workers' rights violations in any of the three countries. This contrasts with the labor chapter of the U.S.-Jordan Free Trade Agreement, seen by many as a stronger trade-labor provision, but which requires complaints to be initiated by one government against the other, an unlikely event given the usual niceties of international diplomacy.

Activists in the three NAFTA countries have taken advantage of the NAALC and its procedures to launch organizing and publicity campaigns that sometimes resulted in improvements for workers. Thus, the NAALC provides some transnational labor protection, but more by indirection and creative maneuvering by labor advocates than by "hard" application of TLL.[25]

C. Labor Rights in the European Union

Unlike NAFTA, whose tools are largely of the "soft law" variety, the European Union has the capacity both to establish "soft" principles and guidelines and to create "hard" labor standards that are binding upon the Union's Member States.[26] Within the area of its legislative competence, the European Union can issue Directives, which require Member States to change their national labor codes to conform to E.U. standards. And a state that fails to conform can be sanctioned by sizable fines.

The European Union has used these powers to establish standards in areas like health and safety, parental leave, consultative employee "works councils," and employment discrimination. But the E.U. system falls far short of a binding, uniform regional labor code. The Union's legislative competence in the labor area is quite circumscribed and E.U. treaties specifically *exclude* collective bargaining, union organizing, and the right to strike from the E.U.'s legislative authority.

In addition to its limited legislative powers, the European Union has several "soft law" mechanisms that can be used to improve labor conditions. These include the *Charter of Fundamental Rights of the European Union* adopted at a summit meeting in Nice in December 2000. This Charter itself is not directly justiciable, but it can be cited by courts as support for interpretations of national and E.U. law. The Charter has now been incorporated into the new E.U. Treaty Establishing a Constitution for Europe, but the Treaty has not been ratified and the precise effect of incorporation of its workers' rights provisions has yet to be determined.[27]

Finally, in addition to Directives and the Charter, the European Union has other tools that can be used to improve the condition of workers in the Member States. These include funding through the European Social Fund and structured coordination through the Open Method of Coordination (OMC). The OMC process includes the European Employment Strategy (EES), which deals with problems of employment and unemployment and seeks to reform labor markets.[28] Other OMCs deal with areas like social exclusion, health, and pensions.

The OMC and the Structural Funds have been used jointly to promote voluntary moves toward improved labor conditions in E.U. Member

States. This innovative approach toward facilitating a "race to the top" employs nonbinding guidelines, quantitative indicators, exchange of best practices, peer review, and multilateral surveillance to encourage Member States to make reforms. It has been used to create new policies that increase employment, combat discrimination, and develop labor market policies that would allow Europe to combine job flexibility with adequate security for its workforce.

In this system, E.U. Member States agree on reform measures, set targets for improvement, and report periodically on their progress toward these goals. Numerous statistical indicators and "league tables," which show who are performing and who are lagging, measure progress toward agreed-upon goals. Member States are accountable to each other and the European Commission. They review each other's progress and exchange best practices. Structural funds are available to support some reform measures. Negotiated guidelines, annual plans, and measured accountability, along with some financial support for selected measures, encourage Member States to make reforms.

The OMC is a relatively new system and evidence of its effectiveness is limited. A recent assessment, based on new empirical work in several countries and drawing on a wider range of studies, concludes that the OMC has changed the way many countries view the employment problem, helped spur government reorganization at the Member State level, facilitated transfer of ideas between countries, and contributed to the enactment of some reform measures. Yet, at the same time, the researchers caution that the system has many weaknesses and has not realized its full potential.[29]

Compared with NAFTA, the European Union has gone a long way toward creating a working body of transnational labor principles, laws, and programs. It has created standards in areas where it has competence and strongly encouraged voluntary action by Member States where it does not. Taken together with the national labor codes of most of the Member States, the result is a relatively strong protective web.

Of course, there are gaps in the system. The European Union cannot supplement national codes in key areas where it has no competence. Even when it does act, Member States have ways to resist E.U. action.[30] And the whole structure depends in large measure on the continued vitality of the national labor law regimes that preceded the creation of the Single Market.

While these regimes are quite strong, they are subject to various pressures that could weaken their effectiveness. These include political pressure for lower standards as well as potential challenges to national laws under the European Union's guarantee of freedom of movement.

While there are many lessons for Transnational Labor Law to be derived from the E.U. experience, the system cannot simply be copied in other regions nor transposed to the global level. The European Union's experience builds on some of the strongest systems of social protection and labor standards in the world. It operates in countries that despite many differences have substantial institutional similarities, shared cultures, and common values. It is embedded in a process of regional political integration that goes well beyond anything being tried elsewhere, complete with a European commission, parliament, and court; a single currency, even a new Constitution (though its constitutional effect is yet to be tested). It offers suggestions to be studied and adapted, not models to be copied.

D. The International Labor Organization

The International Labor Organization has adopted 185 standards called "conventions," but they are only binding on countries that ratify them and enact them into domestic law, and are only enforceable through domestic legal proceedings. The ILO also maintains a technical assistance program meant to help poorer countries strengthen domestic labor codes and enforcement capacity, but its scope and funds are limited.

Rejecting calls to make economic sanctions part of its oversight procedures on workers' rights violations, the ILO instead adopted a promotional *Declaration on Fundamental Principles and Rights at Work* in 1998. The Declaration sets out four "core" labor standards covering freedom of association, nondiscrimination, and prohibitions on forced labor and child labor. However, the Declaration explicitly adds that "labor standards should not be used for protectionist trade purposes, and that nothing in this Declaration and its follow-up shall be invoked or otherwise used for such purposes; in addition, the comparative advantage of any country should in no way be called into question by this Declaration and its follow-up."

Thus, the Declaration is merely hortatory, not enforceable. Indeed, employer delegates to the ILO insisted on and won their demands that the declaration be "on," not "of," fundamental principles and rights, and that they be rights "at work," not "of workers," to avoid giving any impression that the Declaration established new or stronger labor rights. Another potential problem in the ILO's focus on four "core" standards is that other labor rights and labor standards such as health and safety, migrant worker protections, workers' compensation for injury, wage and hour laws, and other important matters move to second-class status; in this regard the NAALC's inclusion of these issues is an important positive feature.

Despite these limitations, the ILO has done a great deal of work in defining labor standards, overseeing their application (in a supervisory rather than enforcement capacity), and providing technical assistance to countries with fragile labor enforcement regimes. By itself, it can do little to offset national resistance when governments choose to attract investment through weak enforcement or nonenforcement of labor laws or by outright suppression of organizing and bargaining by workers. But the ILO retains a strong moral authority and a parallel authoritativeness in its treatment of international labor standards, especially through the advisory rulings of its Committee on Freedom of Association. The ILO has far to go to counterweigh the WTO, but its efforts, when linked to other aspects of a transnational regime, could play a useful role.

E. Codes of Conduct

Corporate codes of conduct are a form of private TLL by which multinational companies set out standards for treatment of workers in their own subsidiaries or supplier firms, and "enforce" the standards through private monitoring and reporting. In some cases, violations can lead to loss of supplier contracts or discipline against a company's own employee-managers. A first generation of corporate codes was largely self-promulgated and promoted by individual firms such as Nike, Reebok, and Levi Strauss & Co. But because of the obvious fox-and-henhouse problem, company-generated codes have given way to what are called "stakeholder" codes negotiated among producers, retailers, unions, consumer organizations, human rights groups, sustainable development advocates, and others.

Some of the most prominent "stakeholder" codes are the European-based Ethical Trading Initiative (ETI)[31] and Clean Clothes Campaign (CCC),[32] and the U.S.-based Fair Labor Association (FLA),[33] Worker Rights Consortium (WRC),[34] and the Social Accountability 8000 (SA8000) plan of Social Accountability International (SAI).[35] These organizations work with companies and unions to identify and promote good practices in the implementation of codes of conduct, including monitoring and independent verification.

Codes of conduct are at best a limited and partial solution to the problems addressed in this essay. Codes of conduct may be helpful for workers in brand-name companies facing image damage by exposés of labor rights abuses in their own and supplier factories. The widely heralded KukDong case in Mexico is an example, where the FLA and WRC combined with Nike and Reebok to ensure the survival of an independent union that supplanted a union installed earlier by management of this Korean-owned firm in collusion with government officials and corrupt union leaders.[36] But this is a limited field that hardly reaches most global assembly-line workers. Moreover, reliance on privately fashioned codes of conduct and monitoring systems creates a danger of undermining trade union organizing, domestic public approaches, and effective labor law enforcement. Many employers would rather deal with scattered, resource-stretched NGOs monitoring codes of conduct than with strong workplace-based trade unions or tough government labor law enforcement.[37]

F. Trade Adjustment Assistance: Compensating "Losers"

Analysts on all sides agree that global commercial flows create winners and losers among companies, investors, and workers in countries and economic sectors involved in trade. One policy approach is to "compensate the losers" through enhanced unemployment insurance benefits and job retraining assistance for workers who lose their jobs due to shifting trade flows. Trade adjustment assistance is available in some countries. Here is how one prominent free trade advocate justified such a policy in the United States:

> Congressional passage of TPA [Trade Promotion Authority] in the summer of 2002 was a major step forward. The TPA legislation dramatically expands the Trade Adjustment Assistance [TAA] program to sharply increase worker eligibility and financing for both safety-net provisions and retraining, and it starts providing partial coverage for losses of wages and health insurance by trade-dislocated workers. These reforms, championed by Senate Democrats, could begin to allay the fears of globalization. And if implemented effectively, they could begin shifting public attitudes within the United States in a more supportive direction.[38]

TAA benefits include free testing, counseling and job placement services, tuition payment for retraining, job search assistance, relocation expenses, and extended weekly unemployment benefits. Workers' eligibility for these special benefits turns on causality: whether imports from trading partners under liberalized trade arrangements like lower tariffs spurred by the WTO or under NAFTA "contributed importantly" to their job loss, as distinct from more general causes like shifts in customer or consumer preference, new technology, or other nontrade-related factors.

Trade adjustment assistance in the United States has fallen far short of its announced goals. Only a portion of potentially eligible workers receive TAA benefits, and the U.S. Court of International Trade, the judicial body charged with overseeing application of the TAA program, has roundly criticized the Labor Department for failing to grant benefits in accordance with the law.[39] For TAA to be an important part of an effective transnational regime, it would have to be more effective and more universally available.

VI. Taking Stock

Our survey shows that those who seek to create an effective regime of transnational labor law have been at work on a wide variety of fronts. Measures have been pushed at domestic, regional, and global levels, and in the private as well as the public sector. Transnational labor advocates have been able to mount some successful campaigns, at times by employing diverse legal tools.[40] It is clear, however, that all these efforts have had limited effects. Their individual impact is often limited. And they have not been woven into an integrated "regime" with real capacity to offset the negative effects of globalization.

The efforts to date to create a transnational labor regime pale in comparison with the work and energy that has gone into creating the conditions for freer economic exchange, conditions that have left many workers among the losers in the new global economy. The volume of cross-border labor solidarity actions, creative and inspiring as they may be, is puny compared with hundreds of cross-border business transactions occurring every day in the normal course of international trade and investment. Trade law provides a foundation for most of these transactions. But as we have seen, much of the "transnational" labor law that is now on the books is either dependent on implementation that has not always materialized, or is "soft" in the sense that it does not create binding obligations or have enforcement machinery behind it.

The European Union's highly developed system does offer some lessons for other regions and the global economy. The European Union has created a multilevel structure with a "floor" in some areas and developed mechanisms to stimulate a race to the top in others. It has a complex mix of hard and soft measures and is trying to weave regional and national efforts together to meet common aims. But even this system is of limited scope and effectiveness. Its success depends to no small degree on the prior existence and continued strength of Europe's traditionally strong national law regimes and the fact that it is embedded in a process of political integration among countries with shared values.

Similarly, some positive lessons can be drawn from experience under the NAALC. The scope of labor rights and standards in its eleven "labor principles" extends far beyond the ILO's four-part "core" definition. Its open complaint procedure generates new forms of cross-border labor solidarity and creative campaigning by advocates. It contains at least the principle of "hard" economic sanctions for systematic violations of some workers' rights. But apart from a small number of isolated gains in some cases, the NAALC has not led to broad-scale improvements for workers in North America.

A. A House Divided

One reason for the slow progress toward a transnational labor regime and labor law is that labor advocates in the North and South are often divided. The national labor laws of the twentieth century emerged because domestic labor movements agreed on the measures they needed and fought for them in national politics. In theory such solidarity exists at the global level. Thus, the International Confederation of Free Trade Unions (ICFTU) maintains a public position of North-South unity in favor of a "social clause" in trade agreements backing up labor standards with trade sanctions against violators.[41] But in day-to-day struggles such solidarity is not always present. Thus, many workers still may see TLL as a zero-sum game where any protection for workers in the North will harm workers in the South and efforts by groups in the North to raise labor standards in the South are disguised forms of protectionism.[42]

Some survey research suggests that, at least among trade union representatives, the North-South divide may not be so pronounced. A survey of union delegates at international labor congresses found equal and overwhelming support among trade unionists from both developed and developing countries for a labor-rights trade linkage based on ILO core labor standards. Even more interesting, there was no statistically significant difference in their support for trade sanctions to enforce labor standards. Of course, the group surveyed comprised exclusively trade union activists already attuned to and involved in international labor work, so results cannot be taken to reflect trade union members' or workers' views generally in their countries. Nonetheless, these results indicate that advocates might bridge a North-South gap on labor rights and labor standards.[43]

B. A Race to the Top?

There is perhaps a win-win solution, but it could come about only if there were an effective transnational labor law regime that generated an "upward harmonization" dynamic in the North and South. Because we lack a complete vision of how such a regime might be constructed, labor in the South has opposed some efforts to use trade law and policy to build it. This undermines labor solidarity and makes it hard to mobilize support for the kind of measures that might lead to a win-win solution.

The result is a vicious circle: lack of a vision of what an effective regime might be undermines labor solidarity, and lack of North-South labor solidarity deters efforts to push through elements of a TLL. Breaking the vicious circle will require a new vision and new approaches. Sanctions are important, but only as part of a larger package. Trade and labor standards must be linked to concern for the broad challenges facing workers in the global economy.

Labor rights advocates must address not only immediate problems of jobs and wages in export- and import-related employment, but also the wider problems faced by developing countries. Some analysts call for a "grand bargain" that incorporates strong, enforceable labor rights and labor standards into international trade disciplines, but only as part of a far-reaching program that includes enhanced adjustment assistance for affected workers, greatly increased development aid, debt relief, controls on currency manipulation and "hot money" investment flows, market access for agricultural and labor intensive products, and other measures to help poorer countries.[44]

Partial efforts may not be sufficient, but perhaps they can serve as building blocks. Soft as well as hard law could be used with some effect. It may be possible to learn from the European Union's Open Method of Coordination to create soft law systems that would encourage a "race to the top." Such systems could use standards drawn from the ILO and the International Covenant on Economic, Social and Cultural Rights.[45] In addition, just as the European Union provides funding transfers to poorer new entrants to the Union to help them meet higher social standards, so such funding might be made available through international development agencies for countries that seek to meet international labor standards.

VII. Conclusion

This essay has surveyed some first, partial steps to offset the inequality that has come in the wake of globalization. However, much more would have to be done to realize fully the promise of a transnational labor law that would not only articulate global standards but also provide means for enforcement. Possibly the WTO and the ILO could, jointly, create such a system.[46] The WTO might incorporate labor rights and labor standards into its trade disciplines, but base any trade-related sanctions on conclusive findings by the ILO. The latter would be far preferable to unilateral measures presently employed by the United States and a patchwork of regional regimes with different labor standards.

We are a long way from any such arrangement, or from any other approach to creating a global system of labor standards with effective enforcement. Indeed, there is no consensus that empowering the WTO in labor matters is a desirable step.[47] Extensive further debate will be needed before agreement is reached on the best way to combine universal standards and effective enforcement. In the meantime, labor rights advocates North and South should work together in the arenas already created, and outlined here, to continue an experience-building process that can inform the ultimate construction of a global regime of transnational labor law. We have not offered a full vision of such a regime but hope we have at least shown that one is needed and that some elements of a truly effective system already exist.

NOTES

1. *See* Laura L. Wright, *Trade Promotion Authority: Fast Track for the Twenty-First Century?* 12 WM. & MARY BILL RTS. J. 979 (2004).

2. 19 U.S.C.A. § 3802 (b)(11)(A) (West 2004).

3. *See* SANDRA POLASKI, CARNEGIE ENDOWMENT FOR INT'L PEACE, CAMBODIA BLAZES A NEW PATH TO ECONOMIC GROWTH AND JOB CREATION (2004), at http://www.carnegieendowment.org/files/cp51polaskifinal2.pdf.

4. *See* Danna Harman, *Hemispheric Trade Zone Stumbles*, CHRISTIAN SCI. MONITOR, Nov. 23, 2004, at 4; *Industry Groups All But Abandon Hopes for Successful FTAA*, INSIDE U.S. TRADE, Dec. 3, 2004, at 3.

5. *See, e.g.*, Carter Dougherty, *Jobless Germans Face a New Round of Benefit Cuts*, N.Y. TIMES, Dec. 30, 2004, at W1; Lawrence J. Speer, *France Modifies 35-Hour Week by Permitting More "Overtime Hours,"* BNA DAILY LAB. REP., Dec. 23, 2004, at A-6.

6. *See, e.g.*, Wolfgang Streek & Anke Hassel, *The Crumbling Pillars of Social Partnership*, 26 WEST EUR. POL. 101 (Oct. 1, 2003).

7. *See, e.g.*, AM. CTR. FOR INT'L LABOR SOLIDARITY, JUSTICE FOR ALL: THE STRUGGLE FOR WORKER RIGHTS IN CHINA (2004), *available at* http://www.solidaritycenter.org; AM. CTR. FOR INT'L LABOR SOLIDARITY, JUSTICE FOR ALL: THE STRUGGLE FOR WORKER RIGHTS IN MEXICO (2003), *available at* http://www.solidaritycenter.org.

8. For a global survey, see SARAH PERMAN ET AL., INT'L CONFEDERATION OF FREE TRADE UNIONS, BEHIND THE BRAND NAMES: WORKING CONDITIONS AND LABOUR RIGHTS IN EXPORT PROCESSING ZONES (Dec. 2004), *at* http://www.icftu.org/www/PDF/EPZreportE.pdf.

9. *See* SANDRA POLASKI, CARNEGIE ENDOWMENT FOR INT'L PEACE, TRADE AND LABOR STANDARDS: A STRATEGY FOR DEVELOPING COUNTRIES (2003), *at* http://www.ceip.org/files/pdf/polaski_trade_english.pdf; *see also* HUMAN RIGHTS WATCH, DELIBERATE INDIFFERENCE: EL SALVADOR'S FAILURE TO PROTECT WORKERS' RIGHTS (2003), *available at* http://hrw.org/reports/2003/elsalvador1203/elsalvador1203.pdf.

10. *See* Robert Howse, *The Appellate Body Ruling in the Shrimp/Turtle Case: A New Legal Baseline for the Trade and Environment Debate*, 27 COLUM. J. ENVTL. L. 491 (2002). The Appellate Body found further that the U.S. law was discriminatorily applied, softening the impact of its ruling but not vitiating the basic finding that "process" can be taken into account.

11. ROBERT HOWSE & MAKAU MUTUA, PROTECTING HUMAN RIGHTS IN A GLOBAL ECONOMY: CHALLENGES FOR THE WORLD TRADE ORGANIZATION (Int'l Ctr. for Human Rights & Democracy Policy Paper, 2000), *available at* http://www.ichrdd.ca/frame00.html.

12. *Id.*

13. *See* http://www.wto.org/english/thewto_e/whatis_e/tif_e/bey5_e.htm (WTO website).

14. But note that U.S. law does not include nondiscrimination, an ILO core standard, among the requirements, while "wages, hours, and health and safety," which are not part of the ILO core, are included. 19 U.S.C.A. § 2462(b)(2)(G) (West 2002). The E.U. formulation is based on the ILO core standards.

15. 19 U.S.C.A. § 2462(b)(2)(G) (West 2002).

16. 19 U.S.C.A. § 2467(4)(A-E) (West 2002).

17. *See* Lance Compa & Jeffrey S. Vogt, *Labor Rights in the Generalized System of Preferences*, 22 COMP. LAB. L. & POL'Y J. 199 (2001).

18. *See* Philip Alston, *Labor Rights Provisions in U.S. Trade Law: "Aggressive Unilateralism?" in* HUMAN RIGHTS, LABOR RIGHTS, AND INTERNATIONAL TRADE (Lance A. Compa & Stephen F. Diamond eds., 2003).

19. *See* Dr. Mahathir Mohamad of Malaysia, Address at the 50th Session of the UN General Assembly (Sept. 29, 1995).

20. *See European Communities—Conditions for the Granting of Tariff Preferences to Developing Countries*, WT/DS246/AB/R; (04-1556); AB-2004-1.

21. *See* Elizabeth Becker, *Bush Rejects Labor's Call to Punish China*, N.Y. TIMES, Apr. 29, 2004, at C4.

22. The NAALC labor principles are: (1) freedom of association and protection of the right to organize, (2) the right to bargain collectively, (3) the right to strike, (4) prohibition against forced labor, (5) child labor protections, (6) minimum wage, hours of work and other labor standards, (7) nondiscrimination, (8) equal pay for equal work, (9) occupational safety and health, (10) workers' compensation, and (11) migrant worker protection.

23. *See* website of the Secretariat of the North American Commission on Labor Cooperation, http://www.naalc.org.

24. *See* Public Comments, *Review of the North American Agreement on Labor Cooperation 1994–1997, at* http://www.naalc.org/english/review.shtml.

25. For an extensive review of NAALC cases and cross-border alliances around them, see Lance Compa, *NAFTA's Labor Side Agreement and International Labor Solidarity, in* PLACE, SPACE AND THE NEW LABOUR INTERNATIONALISMS (Peter Waterman & Jane Wills eds., 2001). For a discussion of how systems like the NAALC can be used by transnational coalitions of labor rights advocates, *see* David Trubek et al., *Transnationalism in the Regulation of Labor Relations: International Regimes and Transnational Advocacy Networks*, 25 LAW & SOC. INQUIRY 1187 (2000).

26. *See* Edward Mazey, *Grieving through the NAALC and the Social Charter: A Comparative Analysis of Their Procedural Effectiveness*, 10 MICH. ST. U.-DCL J. INT'L L. 239 (2001).

27. *See* Manfred Weiss, *The Social Dimension as Part of the Constitutional Framework, in* EUROPEAN INTEGRATION AS A SOCIAL EXPERIMENT IN A GLOBALIZED WORLD (Reiner Hoffmann et al. eds., 2003); Edward Rothstein, *Europe's Constitution: All Hail the Bureaucracy*, N.Y. TIMES, July 5, 2003, at B9; *Special Report: Your Darkest Fears Addressed, Your Hardest Questions Answered—Europe's Constitution*, ECONOMIST, June 21, 2003 (U.S. edition).

28. For an overview, see David Trubek & James Mosher, *New Governance, Employment Policy, and the European Social Model, in* GOVERNING WORK AND

WELFARE IN A NEW ECONOMY: EUROPEAN AND AMERICAN EXPERIMENTS (Jonathan Zeitlin & David M. Trubek eds., 2003).

29. Jonathan Zeitlin, *The Open Method of Coordination in Action: Theoretical Promise, Empirical Realities, Reform Strategy, in* THE OPEN METHOD OF COORDI-NATION IN ACTION: THE EUROPEAN EMPLOYMENT AND SOCIAL INCLUSION STRATEGIES (Jonathan Zeitlin et al. eds, forthcoming 2005).

30. *See France and EU in Legal Tussle over Women's Night Work,* EUROPEAN INDUS. RELATIONS OBSERVATORY, *at* http://www.eiro.eurofound.eu.int/1999/05/Feature/FR9905183F.html.

31. *See* http://www.ethicaltrade.org.

32. *See* http://www.cleanclothes.org.

33. *See* http://www.fairlabor.org/html/monitoring.html.

34. *See* http://www.workersrights.org.

35. *See* http://www.sa-intl.org.

36. *See* Jeff Hermanson, Global Corporations, Global Campaigns: The Struggle for Justice at Kukdong International in Mexico (Apr. 2004) (paper presented to workshop on transnational contention at Cornell University, *available at* http://falcon.arts.cornell.edu/sgt2/PSCP/documents/Jeff%20Hermanson.pdf).

37. For extended discussion on this point, see Lance Compa, *Trade Unions, NGOs, and Corporate Codes of Conduct,* 14 DEV. IN PRAC. 210 (Feb. 2004).

38. *See* C. Fred Bergsten, *Liberalization in Retreat,* FOREIGN AFF., Nov. 1, 2002, at 86.

39. *See* Michael R. Triplett, *Trade Court's Critique of Labor Department Places Spotlight on Handling of TAA Claims,* BNA DAILY LAB. REP., Mar. 30, 2004, at C-1.

40. *See, e.g.,* Trubek et al., *supra* note 25.

41. *See* the *Trade and Labor Standards* page at the website of the ICFTU, http://www.icftu.org.

42. *See* Martin Khor, *The World Trade Organization, Labour Standards and Trade Protectionism,* THIRD WORLD RESURGENCE (May 1994).

43. *See* GERARD GRIFFIN ET AL., TRADE UNIONS AND THE SOCIAL CLAUSE: A NORTH-SOUTH UNION DIVIDE? (Nat'l Key Ctr. in Indus. Relations, Monash Univ., Working Paper No. 81, 2002), *available at* http://www.buseco.monash.edu.au/depts/mgt/research/working_paper/nkcir_working_paper/nkir_workingpaper_81.pdf.

44. *See, e.g.,* Jeff Faux, *The Global Alternative,* AM. PROSPECT, July 2, 2001; *see also Alternatives for the Americas,* the comprehensive trade and investment pro-gram of the Hemispheric Social Alliance, *at* http://www.art-us.org/HSA.html. On currency fluctuation and financial flows, see *The Casino Economy: the Anatomy of Global Control, available at* http://www.ifg.org/analysis/imf/IMFteach-in.html; *see also* JOSEPH E. STIGLITZ, GLOBALIZATION AND ITS DISCONTENTS (2002).

45. *See* Maria Green, *What We Talk About When We Are Talking About Indica-tors: Current Approaches to Human Rights Measurement,* 23 HUM. RTS. Q. 1062 (2001). For discussion of how OMC-like processes might be adapted for other

regions and the global level, see David M. Trubek, Social Rights in a Global Economy (2002) (paper presented at the Catholic Univ. of Porto Alegre, Brazil, on file with author).

46. *See, e.g.*, Daniel S. Ehrenberg, *From Intention to Action: An ILO-GATT/WTO Enforcement Regime for International Labor Rights, in* HUMAN RIGHTS, LABOR RIGHTS, AND INTERNATIONAL TRADE (Lance Compa & Stephen F. Diamond eds., 2003).

47. Indeed, some critics of corporate-driven globalization would prefer to "shrink or sink" the WTO, not give it expanded new powers in the labor area that might be subjugated to commercial goals. *See, e.g.*, LORI WALLACH & PATRICK WOODALL, WHOSE TRADE ORGANIZATION? (2d ed. 2004).

12

Law at the Workplace
The Decline of Collective Bargaining

Julius G. Getman

This chapter exposes the ways in which changes in American labor law have affected the balance of power between workers and employers by impeding the organization of unions, diminishing protections for prounion workers, and increasing deference to managerial prerogative.

I. A Brief History of Collective Bargaining

The National Labor Relations Act of 1935[1] was intended to create a system of industrial democracy to replace the master-servant relationship with a more egalitarian relationship between employers and their employees. In most key industries it worked—for a while. Unions in the automotive, steel, paper, transportation, textiles, and construction industries not only negotiated the ground rules under which employees worked, they also played a key role in defining and enforcing the collective agreements in which these rights were set forth.

Through collective bargaining, backed by the right to strike, unions had by the 1960s gained for the first time in American history a widespread system of power sharing at the workplace.[2] The strike weapon gave employers an incentive to negotiate agreements acceptable to their employees. Wherever negotiated, collective bargaining agreements replaced unilateral employer decisions with provisions covering almost all aspects of employer-employee relations—wages, hours, overtime, discipline, job categories, as well as layoffs and promotion. They also routinely contained procedures for resolving disputes about their application. Any employer action affecting working conditions could be challenged through a grievance filed by the employees affected, or by the union. Most grievances were resolved by negotiation between union and company officials. Typically grievance negotiations began with union stewards and company supervisors and, if not settled, worked their way up the ladder, ending in discussions between national union staff members and high-level management officials. Almost all collective agreements specified that if the grievance negotiation system failed to produce a settlement, the union could submit the case to a neutral arbitrator mutually selected by the parties. Each party agreed in the collective agreement to accept the arbitrator's decision as final.[3]

Collective bargaining changed traditional class-based relationships at every stage of the process. Face-to-face negotiation gave union officers a new and significant status while a collective bargaining agreement changed the status of workers generally. No longer could workers be discharged at the whim of their employers. No longer could employers ignore seniority in job assignments and promotion. And no longer could workers be assigned menial tasks or required to work overtime. Because the grievance process was time-consuming and potentially disruptive, it was in an employer's interest to avoid unnecessary grievances and to resolve quickly those that arose. The desire to minimize and settle grievances gave management an incentive to maintain good relations with union stewards and local union officers. Thus, the successful operation of a unionized enterprise generally required management officials to work effectively with their union counterparts. Union officials thereby acquired a mediating-role, sometimes functioning as the employee's representative to management and sometimes as management's representative to the workers. This entire system was developed by the parties themselves through collective bargaining without significant help from the Labor Board, the courts, the Department of Labor, or the law. It worked because unions were strong and their right to strike robust, and because employees, like management, wanted to avoid strikes.

In 1955, Dean Harry Shulman of the Yale Law School, who also served as permanent arbitrator under the collective bargaining agreement between the United Auto Workers Union and Ford Motor Company, delivered a Holmes Lecture at Harvard Law School[4] describing the relation between labor arbitration, productivity, and industrial relations in a large manufacturing enterprise. He observed that the system of collective bar-

gaining fundamentally changed the nature of the employment relationship and explained the strength of the system as a direct result of private
ordering. The limited nature of the arbitrator's jurisdiction and his role as
the servant of the parties enabled him to supply answers to difficult questions of interpretation that the contending parties would accept:

> He is not a public tribunal imposed upon the parties by superior authority.
> He is . . . part of a system of self-government created by and confined to the
> parties. He serves their pleasure only, to administer the rule of law estab-
> lished by their collective agreement. They are entitled to demand that, at
> least on balance, his performance be satisfactory to them, and they can
> readily dispense with him if it is not.[5]

Because it was the parties' own system, Shulman urged the courts to leave
it alone, noting:

> When it works fairly well, it does not need the sanction of the law of con-
> tracts or the law of arbitration. It is only when the system breaks down
> completely that the courts' aid in these respects is invoked. But the courts
> cannot, by occasional sporadic decision, restore the parties' continuing rela-
> tionship; and their intervention in such cases may seriously affect the going
> systems of self-government. When their autonomous system breaks down,
> might not the parties better be left to the usual methods for adjustment of
> labor disputes rather than to court actions on the contract or on the arbi-
> tration award? I suggest that the law stay out—but, mind you, not the
> lawyers.[6]

Nothing demonstrates the class-altering potential of collective bargaining better than the grievance/arbitration system described by Shulman—a
process for resolving disputes that is jointly established, administered, and
paid for by unions and employers.

The National Labor Relations Act's role in establishing this new and
more egalitarian and democratic system of industrial relations was understood to be crucial, but limited. The commitment to private ordering and
worker choice meant that the Act would neither require unionization nor
play a substantive role in the bargaining process. Yet, its effectiveness was
critical because the new system was based on the strength of the collective
bargaining process, which itself depended on the strength of the union.
The Act established the National Labor Relations Board (hereinafter the

Board), whose primary task was to protect the choice of workers to unionize. Once that choice was exercised, the parties were free to structure their relationship as they chose through free bargaining. Collective bargaining during its early years, and its offspring, grievance arbitration, were widely perceived to be remarkably successful, class-altering, dignity-bestowing processes.

Articles and texts in the mid-1960s trumpeted the success of collective bargaining. And yet today this system of private ordering is in disarray, applying to only a small and steadily shrinking percentage of the private sector workforces. Class distinctions in the workplace are sharpening, as the pay differential between workers and executives reaches and surpasses third world standards.

If the system of collective bargaining worked so well, why does it seem to be disintegrating? The now familiar phenomenon of "outsourcing" depicted in chapter eleven of this book has likely been a cause.[7] But it is also the case that the law enacted to facilitate collective bargaining now fails to do so. Instead the Act has become an impediment to collective workplace management and dispute resolution. The Board members and judges who have had the final say in interpreting the broad general language of the National Labor Relations Act rarely came from the working class, and rarely understood union organizing, collective bargaining, grievance arbitration, or the dynamic of strikes. The result has been a series of court and Board cases that undervalue collective bargaining, make union organizing more difficult, weaken the right to strike, and reflect a basic misunderstanding of the arbitration process.

II. Impediments to Union Organizing: Free Speech at the Workplace

For collective bargaining to flourish, unions must be able to organize successfully. The National Labor Relations Act regulates organizing through two important principles: *free choice* and *exclusive representation*. Exclusive representation is a unique aspect of American labor law established by Section 9(a) of the Act, which states "[r]epresentatives designated or selected for the purpose of collective bargaining by the majority of employees in a unit appropriate for such purposes shall be the exclusive representatives of all the employees in such unit for the purposes of collective bargaining."Pursuant to this principle, a union representing a majority of workers in an "appropriate unit" becomes the bargaining agent for all employees in the unit, including those opposed to the union. Conversely, a union that does not represent a majority is not entitled to bargain on behalf of anyone, including its members.

The principle of free choice is that workers in appropriate units have the right to choose or reject unionization. The Act empowers the Board to determine appropriate units and hold elections to determine whether a majority of workers favors unionization. Much of the Board's work over the years has concerned decisions as to when elections are appropriate and who may vote in them, and administering the elections it orders.

But the Act does not require elections. The Board long ago ruled that once a majority of employees had made their wishes clear, the employer was bound to bargain with the selected union.[8] An employer was entitled to an election only when it had a good faith doubt as to a union's majority status. If this policy had remained in effect, it would have benefited unions who often are in a position to demonstrate majority status soon after an initial organizing drive. But the Court's preference for a formal election process soon took over. The Supreme Court in 1969 held that an employer could refuse recognition whether it knew that the union had achieved majority status or not.[9] Its conclusion that an employer is entitled to an election was supported and announced by judges regarded as liberals not motivated by bias against worker rights. It reflected a belief widely shared among persons of a professional class that an orderly election process following a regulated campaign is preferable to an informal process such as a card check for determining employee choice.

But there is reason to question that belief as applied to employment relationships. The employer has several advantages in a formal campaign that are independent of the merits of its arguments against unionization. The employer has in almost all cases superior access to employees. It knows their addresses and their workstations. It designates their supervisors and controls their time. It can call the employees together whenever it wishes and explain why they should vote against unionization. And employees supporting union organization fear reprisals—a fear that almost always predates the campaign and can generally be strengthened by it. The employer also has the advantage of being able to detect the basis for employee dissatisfaction and to suggest that it will respond positively if the employees vote against unionization. Because the union will already have conducted its campaign and made its arguments by the time any issue reaches the Labor Board, the delay and disruption of an election typically favor the employer.

Theoretically, there are a variety of techniques the Board may use to overcome the employer's inherent campaign advantage. It can hold speedy elections, give unions access to employees, and closely monitor campaign statements and literature to make sure that employers do not improperly seek to use their economic power over employees. But each of these techniques poses problems. Requiring speedy elections is difficult, given ubiquitous management lawyers who are prepared to raise every possible legal issue and objection to the unit, the timing, and the eligibility of voters. For good reason, the Board does not want to be in the position of preventing employers from stating their cases prior to an election. But giving unions equal access to company premises so that they can state their contrary claims presents administrative problems of when, how, and how often. It also requires interference with traditional rights of ownership. And regulating the employer's campaign raises questions of the employer's free speech on the one hand and effectiveness on the other, because the line between legitimate employer argument and coercion is sometimes indiscernible.

The Board and courts reviewing its decisions have opted to attempt regulation of the employer's conduct rather than grant union access to employees. Having favored the employer's property right over the union's right to equal opportunity to express its contentions, they have undertaken to constrain the employer's freedom of expression. This is a curious choice at a time when free speech rights have been extended by the courts in so many other areas such as commercial advertising.[10] But the politics of the workplace is not an area in which the free exchange of ideas has been valued. This evaluation seems to be shared by many members of the professional class who do not perceive the realities or the worth of workplace democracy.

The choice to downplay an employer's right to state antiunion arguments has been manifested at various times both by the Board and by the courts. When a majority of the Board is made up of Democratic appointees, it has regularly found threats of reprisals and promises of benefits in ambiguous statements and in efforts by employers to discover employee attitudes. The Board has held that such conduct violates the unfair labor practices provision of the Act and thus constitutes grounds for setting aside elections in which the union lost.[11]

In the 1960s, the Supreme Court affirmed this approach in two remarkable opinions: *NLRB v. Exchange Parts Company*[12] and *NLRB v. Gissel Packing Company*.[13] The Court, in *Exchange Parts*, held that a grant of employment benefits prior to an election was coercive. In *Gissel*, the employer told its employees that the union was "strike happy" and that a strike would hurt the company economically, perhaps forcing it out of business.[14] The employer argued that its statements amounted to no more than an exercise of its First Amendment rights of free speech. The Court upheld the Board's conclusion that the statements implied a threat of reprisal. The Court reasoned that:

> Any assessment of the precise scope of employer expression, of course, must be made in the context of its labor relations setting. Thus, an employer's rights cannot outweigh the equal rights of the employees to associate freely. . . . And any balancing of those rights must take into account the economic dependence of the employees on their employers, and the necessary tendency of the former, because of that relationship, to pick up intended implications of the latter that might be more readily dismissed by a more disinterested ear.[15]

The Court thus assumed that employees are paying close attention to the campaign, that they perceive threats in vague general statements, and that their choice to unionize can be easily overcome. These assumptions appear to reflect unrealistic expectations of employee voting behavior that are inconsistent with empirical findings.[16]

Even more questionable is the finding that an employer's grants and promises of benefits are unlawful. The Board has never explained why an unconditional grant of benefits during a campaign was unlawful. In *NLRB v. Exchange Parts Co.*, the Supreme Court expressed the principle thus:

> [T]he danger inherent in well-timed increases in benefits is the suggestion of a fist inside the velvet glove—employees are not likely to miss the inference that the source of benefits now conferred is also the source from which future benefits must flow and which may dry up if it is not obliged.[17]

This language supposes that employees did not previously realize that the employer was the source of possible benefits. Even if this were true, why would newly bestowed benefits cause them to vote against the union?

Such assumptions reveal a patronizing and inaccurate view of worker-constituents.

While the Supreme Court has been supportive of the Board's efforts to regulate employer speech and conduct during the campaign, it has rejected rules seeking to equalize access to employee voters. The Court has held that unions are not entitled to respond to employer speeches on company time. Indeed, in *Lechmere v. NLRB*,[18] the Court rejected the Board's conclusion that Section 7 of the Act gave union organizers the right to distribute literature in the Company parking lot. The Court has firmly and regularly concluded that property rights trump the employee's right to hear the case for unionization, thereby reinforcing the employer's advantage by perpetuating the "outsider" status of unions. This means that employees will know the case against unionizing better than the case in favor because those not making the special effort to attend off-premises union rallies will have heard the employer's case more often and more recently than the union's. And it reinforces the union's continuing status as the outsider.

Granting equal union access would mean more election victories for unions,[19] something far more significant than setting aside elections and rerunning them, a technique that almost always leaves the original result in place. Two more union victories would be far more valuable to organized labor than a dozen set-aside elections.[20] Unions need the chance to make their case to the employees far more than they need protection from employer arguments. I have asked many union organizers which approach they would prefer. All announce without hesitation that they would prefer reasonable if not equal access to their constituents to regulation of employer speech.

III. Management Retaliation and the Decline of "Free Choice"

While undermining the effectiveness of union campaigns, courts have also limited the employees' right to "free choice" by acknowledging traditional managerial prerogatives. The "free choice" policy, as described by Justice Frankfurter, is a statutory commitment "to allow employees to freely exercise their right to join unions, [and to] be good bad or indifferent members . . . without imperiling their livelihood."[21] Only when such a "free choice" system is in place can workers' desire for union representation or activity be accurately realized.

The first and most significant rejection of the no-retaliation-for-union-activity policy came in the Supreme Court's 1938 decision in *NLRB v. Mackay Radio*.[22] In *Mackay*, the Court announced that an employer enjoys the unrestricted right under the statute permanently to replace strikers should it so choose. This decision was understandable when issued in 1938. At that time, the Act contained no restrictions on the strike weapon. It was therefore reasonable to assume that the law left the results of industrial conflict to the free play of economic weapons. But in 1947[23] and 1959,[24] Congress imposed sweeping restrictions on the right to strike. Secondary boycotts, appeals to consumers, and strikes for recognition were all outlawed. And standards for evaluating the legality of employer responses to union activity slowly developed. These standards require a balancing of the employer's business needs against the harm done to the right of employees to engage in collective activity. The Court has never undertaken such an analysis of competing values with respect to the hiring of strike replacements. Several scholars have suggested that had such a balancing been undertaken it seems almost certain that the doctrine entitling the hiring of replacement workers would have been eliminated.[25] Such hirings cost the strikers their jobs and usually lead to decertification of the union. And employers are almost always able to continue operations by hiring temporary replacements or by shifting employees around. Yet the Court has shown no inclination to reconsider the issue. The *Mackay* rule is as authoritative today as the day the Court announced it.[26]

The harm to employees implicit in the *Mackay* doctrine was obscured for a time because employers who desired to stabilize their relationships with unions were reluctant to use it. But in recent years, antiunion employers have realized that *Mackay* offers them a technique for taming or ridding themselves of troublesome unions. Starting in the early 1980s, these employers began to use *Mackay* as a weapon in collective bargaining situations by demanding concessions, daring unions to strike, and hiring permanent replacements when they did so. Unions have come to fear the strike, once their most powerful weapon. In the 1980s, a whole series of strikes in the paper industry, in farm machinery, and in newspapers ended disastrously for workers. By the mid 1990s, use of the strike weapon had dropped to an all-time low.[27]

The *Mackay* doctrine is not the Court's only deference to traditional employer property rights at the expense of the policy of free choice. In *Textile Workers v. Darlington Manufacturing Company*,[28] the Court held that an employer who closed down its business to avoid a union did not thereby violate the Act. The Court stated, "[a] proposition that a single businessman cannot choose to go out of business if he wants to would represent . . . a startling innovation." The Court also found that the employer's action was "not the type of discrimination which is prohibited by the Act" because it "yields no . . . future benefit for the employer." It thus concluded that an employer has "the absolute right to terminate his entire business for any reason he pleases." In its concern for a basic employer prerogative, the Court missed the fact that the Board did not order the employer to remain in business but merely ordered the employer to compensate its employees for lost pay. In addition, from the employee's point of view, it did not really matter that the employer was not seeking personal gain and may have been motivated solely by spite and opposition to the exercise of statutory rights. The employees lost their jobs because they joined and voted for a union. And there is no reason why the law should discourage employers from going out of business to punish employees for choosing a union.

The Court's emphasis on the employer's right to close down was extended in the *Darlington* decision to empower an employer to close down one part of a multilocation enterprise. Such action, the Court declared, is an unfair labor practice only if the employer acted for the purpose of intimidating the employees at the secondary location and if it is "realistically foreseeable" that the employees at that location will "fear that such business will be closed down."[29] In several subsequent cases, courts of appeals have permitted employers to terminate a portion of their business immediately after employees voted for union representation. In these cases, the employers explained their decisions in economic terms not based on opposition to unionization. For example, in *NLRB v. Lassing*,[30] the court found that an employer's conduct was not retaliation because "[t]he advent of the Union was a new economic factor which necessarily had to be evaluated by the respondent as part of the overall picture pertaining to costs of operation." The court drew a dubious distinction between actions based on economic considerations and those based on antiunion animus. Employer opposition to unions almost always rests on the belief that unions will cost them money, as often they do. The distinction represents a judicial effort to interpret the National Labor Relations Act so that it does not interfere with employer decision making even when the result is to take away jobs from employees who vote for unionization.

The courts also manifest a related concern for employer decision making when they overturn findings by the Labor Board that an employee was discharged because of union activity and not, as the employer claimed, for some legitimate reason. The National Labor Relations Act does not authorize reviewing courts closely to reevaluate the evidence when reviewing such Board decisions, but they do.[31] They do so because they are reluctant to order the reinstatement of employees whom they find to be unsatisfactory workers even if the employees were fired for union activity and whether or not the court has the authority to make such a finding.

IV. Judicial Deference to Management on the Scope of Bargaining

The NLRA requires an employer to bargain with an incumbent union with respect to "wages, hours, and conditions of employment." These terms are broad. The more generously they are construed, the more say employees have about decisions affecting their welfare. But the courts and the Board have steadily narrowed the scope of collective bargaining, carving out broad areas of decision making in which management is free to refuse collective bargaining.

The Supreme Court's commitment to managerial discretion was most clearly articulated in 1981 in *First National Maintenance Corporation v. NLRB*.[32] It there held that an employer did not have to bargain about a decision to close down part of its operation even though the decision meant the loss of employee jobs. The Court stated that decisions about the scope and direction of the enterprise were presumed to be a matter of managerial discretion since "Congress had no expectation that the elected representative would become an equal partner in the running of the business enterprise in which the union's members are involved."

The Court in that case erroneously proclaimed that the National Labor Relations Act's primary goal was to achieve industrial peace—a peace that was to be achieved by recognizing management's traditional control over basic decisions. It concluded that "the harm likely to be done to an employer's need to operate freely in deciding whether to shut down part of its business purely for economic reasons outweighs the incremental benefit that might be gained through the union's participation in making the decision."[33] It concluded that the economy will work better if management can make key decisions without union involvement. The fear expressed by the Court that unless collective bargaining is limited in scope the union will become "an equal partner in the running of the business" is not correct. Collective bargaining does not give a union a veto over management decisions but merely the right to argue against them or strike against the company, thereby altering the mix of factors influencing those decisions by encouraging some consideration of the impact of management decisions on the lives of workers. An employer is free to implement its bargaining proposals even if the union does not agree. And unions and their members have as much interest as management in making sure that all aspects of a business are profitable. Workers routinely know things about productivity and efficiency that management does not. The collective bargaining process is a valuable way of exchanging ideas about productivity and profitability. It gives management an opportunity to explain why concessions are needed or why new ways of doing things are required.

Moreover, the notion that economic vitality is dependent upon management making key decisions without union involvement is a proposition that the National Labor Relations Act squarely rejects. Explicit in its legislative history is the premise that stable industrial peace requires a system of industrial democracy and the improvement of wages and working conditions. Unsurprisingly, in the aftermath of *First National Maintenance*, the great majority of decisions involving changes in operations have been held to be outside the scope of mandatory bargaining.

V. Arbitration

In 1960, in a series of decisions known to labor lawyers as the Steelworker trilogy,[34] the Supreme Court put the force of law behind arbitration by directing federal courts to enforce promises to arbitrate and arbitral awards, and to infer a promise to arbitrate when a contract is ambiguous. In expressing its support for arbitration, the Court repeatedly cited Dean Shulman's article, even as it rejected his strongly stated conclusion that the Courts should "stay out" of the process.

The policy favoring arbitration has since been expanded.[35] The Board has with increasing frequency used it to refuse to hear claims from employees based on their statutory rights if their disputes could be submitted to arbitration. It has also refused to review arbitral awards for their conformity to the controlling federal law. And the courts have accepted this Board-created policy of deference to arbitration.[36] The Supreme Court has also extended the policy favoring arbitration to nonunion situations in which employees agree as a condition of employment to arbitrate disputes rather than submit them to courts or agencies of the government.[37] The apparent assumption is that arbitration has dominating virtues regardless of context. This assumption is another reflection of the Court's lack of understanding of industrial relations. Shulman was right. The virtues of labor arbitration stem from and are dependent upon its being embedded in a system of collective bargaining. It is an inferior way to find facts or enforce legal rights. When it is required outside of collective bargaining, arbitration is likely to favor employers who are repeat players, to set the terms of the relationship, and to place employees in situations strange to them and familiar to the employer.[38] The consequence of mandatory arbitration is to diminish workers' rights, even to undermine enforcement of federal laws enacted to protect them.

VI. Union Organizing Today

For all these reasons, unions and their supporters have come to see courts, the Board, and the national law as their implacable opponents. The unions most active in organizing low-wage workers in the twenty-first century, the Service Employees International Union (SEIU) and Hotel Employees Restaurant Employees Union (HERE), have largely abandoned law and claims of legal rights in their organizing and in their collective bargaining. They rely instead on the use of raw economic power to force employers to grant recognition based on signed authorization cards. Card check is not in all cases more valuable than the Board's election process, but in many situations it permits unions to use the support of members or allies to offset the campaign advantages of employers. Both SEIU and HERE have had some noteworthy success by relying exclusively on worker activism and loyalty.

HERE and other unions have also developed new bargaining weapons such as the "corporate campaign." Corporate campaigns involve demonstrations, stock holder petitions, civil disobedience, and large-scale publicity attacks on recalcitrant employers. Although the corporate campaign cannot serve as a substitute for the strike, it makes a powerful supplement.

Conclusion

In enacting the National Labor Relations Act in 1936, Congress recognized that the idea of workplace democracy depends on a robust union movement. It is ironic that those whom the Act was designed to protect—those with the least power in the employer-employee relationship—now carry the burden of protecting themselves. We have come full circle so that workers are in about the same position they occupied before the Act—perhaps worse—because today workers must circumvent barriers posed by the very law that was supposed to protect them. If the idea of workplace democracy depends on a robust union movement, its future in America now seems to depend on the adoption by workers of alternative strategies, strategies that avoid recourse to the courts and legal rights and seek attention to the needs of workers by whatever other means may present themselves. That is not the path to happy workplaces, but it is the one to which the Board and the courts have confined them.

Notes

1. National Labor Relations Act of 1935, 29 U.S.C. §§ 151-169.

2. *See* Walter Galenson, *The Historical Role of American Trade Unionism, in* Unions in Transition : Entering the Second Century (Seymour Martin Lipset ed., 1986).

3. *See generally* Julius Getman, *Labor Arbitration and Dispute Resolution*, 88 Yale L. J. 916 (1979).

4. Harry Shulman, *Reason, Contract and Law in Labor Relations*, 68 Harv. L. Rev. 999 (1955).

5. *Id.* at 1016.

6. *Id.* at 1043.

7. *See* David M. Trubek & Lance Compa, *Trade Law, Labor and Global Inequality*, ch. 11 in this collection.

8. Joy Silk Mills, 85 N.L.R.B. 1263 (1949).

9. NLRB v. Gissel Packing Co., 395 U.S. 575 (1969).

10. *See* Lorillard Tobacco Co. v. Reilly, 535 U.S. 525 (2001).

11. The Board, by virtue of its laboratory conditions doctrine, has also claimed the right to set aside elections based on conduct that does not violate the Act (e.g., home visits or calling employees into the company president's office). *See* Julius Getman et al., Labor Management Relations and the Law 56–72 (1999).

12. 375 U.S. 405 (1964).

13. *Gissel*, 395 U.S. 575.

14. *Id.* at 587–89. The *Gissel* case involved an employer who had bargained with a union prior to a long, economically costly strike which nearly put the company out of business. When business activities resumed after the strike had ended, the company began nonunion operations. Years later, the Teamsters conducted an organizing drive and signed up a majority of the employees. Prior to a Board election, the company president conducted a series of talks and meetings in which he discussed the harmful effects of unionization. In the Court's words, the company president "particularly emphasized the results of the long 1952 strike which he claimed 'almost put our company out of business.'" He also emphasized "that the company was still on 'thin ice' financially, that the Union's 'only weapon is to strike,' and that a strike 'could lead to the closing of the plant.'" He warned the employees "to look around Holyoke and see a lot of them out of business."

During the period immediately before the elections, the employer made statements attacking the union as a "strike happy outfit" and stressed the danger to the company from strikes. The union lost the election. The Board concluded that the employer's conduct made a fair election impossible because it "reasonably tended to convey to the employees the belief or impression that selection of the Union . . . could lead . . . to [the closing of the] plant, or to the transfer of the weaving operation, with the resultant loss of jobs to the wire weavers."

15. *Id.* at 617.

16. *See* JULIUS GETMAN ET AL., UNION REPRESENTATION ELECTIONS: LAW AND REALITY (1976); Laura Cooper, *Authorization Cards and Union Representation Election Outcome: An Empirical Assessment of the Assumption Underlying the Supreme Court's* Gissel *Decision*, 79 Nw. U. L. REV. 87 (1984).

17. 375 U.S. at 409.

18. 502 U.S. 527 (1992).

19. *See* GETMAN ET AL., *supra* note 17.

20. While the Board has the power to issue bargaining orders, it rarely does so. When it does, the case is likely to be appealed and the bargaining order set aside. There are very few cases in which bargaining orders have been upheld and even fewer in which a bargaining order led to the establishment of a long-term bargaining relationship.

21. Radio Officers' Union v. NLRB, 347 U.S. 17 (1954).

22. NLRB v. Mackay Radio Tel. Co., 304 U.S. 333 (1938).

23. 61 Stat. 136 (1947).

24. 73 Stat. 519 (1959).

25. Julius G. Getman & Thomas C. Kohler, *The Story of NLRB v. Mackay Radio & Telegraph Co.: The High Cost of Solidarity, in* LABOR LAW STORIES (Laura J. Cooper & Catherine L. Fisk eds., 2005)

26. JULIUS GETMAN, THE BETRAYAL OF LOCAL 14 (1998).

27. *See* Steve Greenhouse, *Strikes Decrease to a 50 Year Low*, N.Y. TIMES, Jan. 29,

1996; Julius Getman & F. Ray Marshall, *The Continuing Assault on the Right to Strike*, 79 TEX. L. REV. 703 (2001). This article also points out other unfair limitations on the strike weapon.

28. 380 U.S. 263 (1965).

29. *Id.* at 275–76.

30. 284 F.2d 781 (6th Cir. 1960).

31. *See* E. G. Mueller Brass Co. v. NLRB, 544 F.2d 815 (5th Cir. 1977).

32. 452 U.S. 666 (1981).

33. *Id.* at 678–79.

34. United Steelworkers v. Am. Mfg. Co., 363 U.S. 564 (1966); USWA v. Warrior Gulf, 363 U.S. 547 (1960); USWA v. Enterprise Wheel & Car Co., 363 U.S. 593 (1966).

35. *See* GETMAN ET AL., LABOR MANAGEMENT RELATIONS AND THE LAW, *supra* note 12, at 193–207.

36. *See generally* ROBERT GORMAN & MATTHEW FINKIN, BASIC TEXT ON LABOR LAW (2004).

37. *See* LAURA COOPER ET AL., ADR IN THE WORKPLACE 546–62 (2000).

38. *See* Stephen J. Ware, *Arbitration and Unconscionability*, 31 WAKE FOREST L. REV. 1001 (1996).

13

Consumers and the American Contract System
A Polemic

Richard E. Speidel

The central question in this book is whether legal reforms in recent decades have emboldened those with economic power (in the United States) to use it more freely, with diminished regard for the interests of those with less? In the area of contract law, it is possible to identify a number of trends that tilt the balance of power in the markets for consumer goods and services from public to private hands and create greater incentives for abuse. Unfortunately, when presented with difficult cases, the contract system has trouble dealing with these abuses.

In 1995 I sketched out the relationships among contract practice, contract law, and contract theory.[1] This effort required a description of the role that contract played in our complex, market-based economy—an economy increasingly linked by electronic commerce with interdependent international markets. The essence of my account was that contract law responds to the human behavior of promising or agreeing to obtain certain objectives—the exchange of resources, indemnification against risk, dispute settlement, and the creation and maintenance of business frameworks and relationships. There is a remarkable amount of freedom to contract or not. Contractual agreements, in the United States at least, are infrequently prohibited and rarely compelled by government. When disputes arise under these agreements that cannot be resolved by the parties, they are usually resolved by courts but increasingly now by mediation and arbitration. It is in the judicial process, however, that the law of contract is most effectively applied.

The contract system, including agreements and law, supports market exchanges by providing rules of liability and remedy. It also permits those with resources to satisfy wants and needs through agreements with others. But for those with fewer resources or less capacity to play the contract game, the system is not very helpful. True, contracts are one method by which income is distributed in our society, but they do not insure that the overall distribution is fair or that any person will have enough resources to survive in the market. Moreover, the contract system says nothing about welfare and social insurance claims that individuals may have—claims that do not depend upon a traditional contractual relationship. Thus, the contract system permits exchange agreements and provides corrective remedies for particular transactions when things go wrong. But it does not guarantee any particular quality of distributive justice[2] and has nothing to say about the entitlement (social justice) structure. Nevertheless, in a society like ours where there is a significant gap between rich and poor and political pressure to cut back on welfare services and to privatize social insurance,[3] the need for an accessible and effective contract system is critical.

I. The Consent Dilemma

Individual consumers—those who buy for personal, family, or household purposes—vary in resources, intelligence, and capacity in using contract to achieve the "American Dream." There are commonalities, however. There must be an income stream, usually through employment, and the consumer must agree to pay to satisfy needs and wants, usually to business organizations. Under current economic conditions, this effort involves a struggle for many American families. Based on 2003 census figures, the median household income is $43,318. On the income side, there has recently been a higher rate of long-term unemployment and a slower wage growth. On the expense side, the costs of health care, housing, and energy have soared. No one should be surprised that individuals have become increasingly in debt to cover the expenses of life. For example, the amount of household debt has risen 10 percent per year since 2001 and the average American carries a credit card debt balance of $9,205.[4]

What do these macro considerations have to do with contract? Consider the world in which the "average" consumer lives. Contract depends upon consent by the parties to the proposed exchange. Consent is the underpinning of the so-called bargain theory of contract[5] and the cluster of values associated with freedom of contract. When consent to a bargain is made by individuals and organizations, the assumption is that the bargain should be enforced on the terms to which the parties have consented. Avoidance of a bargain objectively assented to requires proof of conduct by one party that impairs the process by which the bargain was made, such as fraud or duress by one party, serious mistakes by one or both, or proof that the terms of the bargain were unreasonably one-sided or against public policy. The burden of proof, however, is on the consumer.

The problem of drawing a line between bargains that should be enforced and those that should not is exacerbated by the prevalence of standard form contracting in this country and around the world.[6] Granting that there may be cost savings through standardization,[7] how does one decide when objective consent to a standard form prepared by one party to its advantage and offered on a take-it-or-leave-it basis should be enforced? What standards determine whether a party who has apparently consented to a bargain with "fine print" should be protected from those terms? And what should be made of the compelling evidence that individuals simply do not read the "fine print" even though the contents are disclosed?[8] If the focus is on the negotiated terms of the deal and not the boilerplate, then how can one factor in this prevalent behavior? In this world of adhesion contracts, the "average" consumer is required (as a condition to contracting) to assent to non-negotiable, one-sided terms that are neither read nor understood.

Drawing the line between freedom to and freedom from contract[9] has traditionally been the job of courts, whether the source of law is case law, a code, or state or federal regulatory legislation. In disputes over consumer contracts, the availability of courts for a prompt and relatively inexpensive decision on these questions is essential to the health of the contract system. If the courts are not available because of cost or other factors, what little influence contract law has on contract behavior is quickly dissipated.[10] Up to a point, I applaud the development of mediation systems and the increased use of arbitration to resolve disputes involving individuals and organizations. But mediation produces an agreed settlement without a decision and arbitration produces a decision that is confidential and not subject to judicial review.[11] In a system where common law methodology is interspersed with private law codification and regulatory legislation of various sorts on the state and federal level, the firm, sure hand of the courts is needed. More importantly, relatively easy access to the courts for the protection of individual rights is crucial for all consumers.

We all use the contract system in various forms and contexts,[12] and in most cases we are satisfied. However, for those with less capacity to contract (individuals and small businesses),[13] the contract system with its consent requirements and standard forms dictated by one party may not be a happy place. For those people who depend upon contract, the opportunity to enforce rights to which they are entitled and obtain protection from abuse is critical. If the contract system is unbalanced and if access to courts is restricted by costs and other factors, these rights and defenses are left to competition in the market or, in the final analysis, to the goodwill of the larger corporations who tend to dominate the markets for employment, health care, insurance, goods and services, and credit.[14]

II. The Response of Contract Doctrine

Since the 1980s, despite changes in domestic and international markets, little has changed in the content of American contract doctrine as developed by courts, codified by the Uniform Commercial Code, or restated by the American Law Institute. The response of contract doctrine to the standard form dilemma has been to preserve the consent requirement and the bargain theory. While courts and commentators have recognized the advantages and disadvantages of standard form contracting, no comprehensive approach for drawing the appropriate lines has been developed in the United States.[15]

On the other hand, there have been sea changes in the nature and content of the competing academic theories, both positive and normative, about contract law over the same period. At great risk of oversimplification, the insights that dominated in the mid-twentieth century, insights gleaned in evaluation of actual as opposed to theoretical conditions, have been displaced by concepts derived from economic analysis,[16] rights theory,[17] and formalism.[18] The cumulative effect of this trilogy eschews paternalism, emphasizes rules over standards, minimizes the role of the courts and government in the market, and, by leaving more disputes for private settlement, reduces the importance of contract law. These developments, among other things, put a premium on the development of efficient "default" rules and ignore Karl N. Llewellyn's notion that standard form terms should be treated differently than negotiated terms.[19]

At the same time, the consumer protection movement of the 1960s and 1970s has been blunted and fragmented. The promise of uniform, comprehensive state consumer protection law has not been realized.[20] The more radical Critical Legal Studies movement became the rage for a while[21] and then quietly imploded, leaving fragments of ideas that are largely irrelevant to contract doctrine. Finally, the occasional claim that contract law, represented by the bargain theory, would be "swallowed up" by tort, represented by promissory estoppel, has not panned out.[22] In fact, the bargain theory, with its dependence on consent, is alive and well and fits nicely with the trilogy's underlying concepts of efficiency, judicial restraint, and formalism.

How has contemporary contract doctrine dealt with the effect of objective assent to standard terms contained in a bargain? Do individuals still have a "duty" to read and understand an agreement with standards terms? Let's look at three contract doctrines that have emerged over the last fifty years, namely, unconscionability, good faith, and promissory estoppel. Each has the potential to reign in abuses by stronger parties. Put differently, to the extent that the bargain theory supports bargains made by the stronger parties, our three doctrines offer the potential for some controls or alternatives. How successful have these controls or alternatives been in protecting weaker parties from abuse?

A. Unconscionability

The principle that a court will not enforce an unconscionable contract or clause was first announced in the 1960s for sales contracts in Section 2-302 of the Uniform Commercial Code[23] and was restated in 1980 in Section 208 of the Restatement, Second, of Contracts. Unconscionability is an extension of the traditional grounds for nullifying a contract, such as fraud, mistake, and duress. The primary purpose is to protect parties who objectively consented to writings that contained standard form terms that were not read or understood or, if understood, terms over which they could not bargain. In these "take it or leave it" deals, the standard terms are highly favorable to the drafting party but not so shockingly one-sided as to be per se against public policy.

To establish the defense, the courts require a party to prove both procedural (unfair surprise or oppression) and substantive (an unreasonably favorable term) unconscionability. The assumption is that if there is no procedural unconscionability, consent to a one-sided standard term that is not against public policy will be enforced. This requires the courts to examine the quality of consent in settings where most people either do not read the forms or do not try to understand what is going on,[24] and in which many could not understand if they tried, given their limited ability to read English. Since very few standard terms are per se against public policy, if there is no unfair surprise (because the consenting party had access to information or had a choice to "leave it"), the reasonableness of these terms is for all practical purposes beyond the scope of judicial review.

Unless there is a state consumer protection statute empowering administrative regulation of contract terms (not likely), the job of finding unconscionability is left to the courts. This is expensive and fact-specific litigation. There is no "bright line" rule with which to work. Except for episodic battles, such as the current fight against alleged unconscionable agreements to arbitrate,[25] the presence of the doctrine of unconscionability as administered by courts probably has little impact on how stronger parties draft contracts. More importantly, the defense does not work if there is no procedural unconscionability, that is, no unfair surprise or oppression. Thus, if one-sided (even "shocking") terms are disclosed by conspicuous print, if they are clearly drafted, and if a contracting party has an opportunity to review and reject them, the terms in all probability are not unconscionable.[26]

B. Good Faith

Another control device is the duty of good faith, which is imposed by law on the performance and enforcement of every contract.[27] The duty can be employed throughout the life of a bargain to protect one party against dishonest and unfair behavior by the other, behavior that is almost but not quite a breach of contract. Bad-faith breaches can result in remedies tailored to the type of misconduct, including in egregious cases punitive damages. Under an expansive duty, the parties should be expected to act in good faith in the negotiation and performance of the contract, the negotiation of modifications and adjustments, and the enforcement after breach.[28]

The American model of good faith, however, is more restricted. The duty does not apply to precontract negotiations and there is no duty to negotiate in good faith over a proposed adjustment to deal with changed circumstances.[29] Moreover, there is no independent duty of good faith that exists apart from the obligations created by the contract.[30] Rather, good faith limits the choices given to a party by the contract itself, such as determining requirements, conditions of satisfaction, or decisions made in enforcing the contract after breach. For example, in a contract where the parties have agreed to a termination clause, good faith is satisfied if the terminating party follows or exercises the choices given by the clause regardless of the reasons or motives for the termination.[31] Similarly, the option of one party to breach or perform the contract is not hedged by the good-faith duty. A deliberate and opportunistic breach—a bad-faith breach—of contract (other than in insurance contracts) is remedied by conventional contract remedies without the additional sanction of punitive damages.[32] As a result, the limited good-faith duty vibrates in tune with the terms of the contract and if those terms favor one party over the other, the vibration supports that imbalance.[33]

C. Promissory Estoppel

In brief, the unconscionability doctrine focuses on consent rather than the substance of standard terms. The duty of good faith insures that those standard terms, if not unconscionable, are performed honestly and fairly. Neither doctrine responds directly to the consent dilemma. Are there any other protective devices worth noting?

The doctrine of promissory estoppel, which was first announced in Section 90 of the Restatement, First, of Contracts, protects those who reasonably rely on the promises of others. In theory, the doctrine protects induced rather than bargained-for reliance—it operates outside the scope of the bargain theory. The goal is particularized justice in the form of flexible remedies in situations where the bargain theory does not apply or has failed to work. Thus, promissory estoppel might be invoked to enforce a gift promise, promises made in precontract negotiations, a firm offer, or a modification without consideration, or to avoid the statute of frauds.[34] The doctrine might also work to provide additional protection for promises not otherwise enforceable, made and relied on within an apparent bargain.[35] It was the potential scope of this doctrine that led Grant Gilmore to suggest that contract, as represented by the bargain theory, was dead and to predict that it would be swallowed by promissory estoppel.[36]

The problem with promissory estoppel is that there must be a promise, express or implied, that induces reliance.[37] Even then, current Section 90 is hedged with conditions and gives the courts discretion in the interest of justice in both imposing liability and exacting remedies.[38] More importantly, in cases of conflict the bargain theory trumps the reliance theory. As one court put it:

> Promissory estoppel is meant for cases in which a promise, not being supported by consideration, would be unenforceable under conventional principles of contract law. When there is an express contract governing the relationship out of which the promise emerged, and no issue of consideration, there is no gap in the remedial system for promissory estoppel to fill. . . . To allow it to be invoked becomes in those circumstances gratuitous duplication or, worse, circumvention of carefully designed rules of contract law.[39]

As should now be clear, those "carefully designed rules of contract law" tend to favor those parties with sufficient power to offer and then administer the adhesion contract. As we shall now see, Article 2 of the UCC perpetuates this bias.

III. Products Liability and the Economic Loss Doctrine

A. Warranty Claims under the Uniform Commercial Code

Among the many contracts made by American consumers are those for the purchase and lease of goods and the licensing of software. These contracts and the security agreements entered to secure extensions of credit contain many standard terms drafted by sellers, lessors, licensors, and secured parties which, to no one's surprise, favor those drafters. Thus, a typical consumer contract for the purchase of a "big ticket" item on credit might contain clauses disclaiming implied warranties, limiting remedies for breach of warranty to recovery of the price, prescribing shorter times for giving notice, and providing strong remedies if the consumer defaults in payment. These sales of goods are governed by Article 2 of the Uniform Commercial Code which permits large retailers, manufacturers, and other such, if you will, "strong sellers" to shift by contract a significant part of the risk of product failure to the consumer buyer.[40]

Sales contracts and terms under Article 2, of course, must be conscionable and performance or enforcement of the contract must be in good faith. But as discussed above, these controls are limited. Moreover, neither the original nor the recently revised text of Article 2 distinguishes between standard form and negotiated terms, and all efforts to include such a distinction were rejected in the process to revise Article 2.[41] Thus, under Article 2 all buyers of goods, whether merchants, corporations, or consumers, are subject to the same rules and standards.

To illustrate Article 2's strong seller bias, assume that a consumer has purchased goods that are determined to be unmerchantable. The goods were made by a manufacturer and purchased from a retailer. What pitfalls confront the consumer buyer under Article 2?

First, it is easy for the retail seller to disclaim all implied warranties. The inclusion of certain magic words in conspicuous type will do the job: if the disclaimer is in writing, the seller must say in conspicuous type that the warranties of merchantability or fitness are disclaimed.[42] The assumption is that ordinary consumers will understand from these magic words that they assume the risk that the goods may be unfit for ordinary purposes. Although revised UCC 2-316(2) requires clearer language to disclaim implied warranties in consumer contracts, the revision does not invalidate implied warranty disclaimers altogether.[43]

Second, Article 2 permits sellers to limit the remedies available to a buyer upon breach of warranty. For example, the exclusive remedy may be limited to repair or replacement of defective parts or workmanship for a stated period of time,[44] coupled with an explicit exclusion of all liability for consequential damages.[45] The clauses are drafted to insure that even if the limited remedy of repair or replacement fails in its essential purpose, the clause excluding consequential damage liability is still enforceable.[46]

Third, the buyer must notify the retail seller within a reasonable time of any breach "or be barred from any remedy."[47] Revised UCC 2-607(3)(a) softens this by stating that the remedy is barred "only to the extent that the seller is prejudiced by the failure" to give notice. Nevertheless, prompt notice is still required at the peril of losing any claim for breach.

Fourth, under Article 2 there must be privity of contract for a buyer to enforce a breach of an implied warranty claim. Thus, if the goods made by a manufacturer are unmerchantable, the buyer's claim must be against the retailer. The manufacturer is insulated from direct responsibility to the ultimate consumer. There are, of course, exceptions to this, but they depend upon the application of other state or federal law.[48] It is possible, however, that a manufacturer will make an enforceable express warranty to the consumer, either through the retailer or directly by advertising or by making representations about a product to the ultimate consumer.[49] Finally, the four-year statute of limitations generally begins to run from the time when nonconforming goods are tendered, not when the nonconformity is discovered.[50]

My conclusion from this is that Article 2 favors strong sellers where consumer product claims are involved and that the recently approved revisions to Article 2 did little if anything to correct that imbalance. Thus, consumer protection in this area depends upon the Magnuson-Moss Warranty Act[51] and state "lemon laws" and other consumer legislation—protection that is limited and which varies from state to state.[52]

B. The Economic Loss Doctrine

One possible escape from these "intricacies of the law of sales" is in tort, where the balance favors the individual who is injured in person or property by a defective product. Under the strict tort liability regime, the plaintiff may sue a manufacturer or distributor of a defective product without regard to privity of contract. Moreover, disclaimers of liability and limitations of remedy are generally unenforceable, notice is not required, and the statute of limitations begins to run on discovery of the defect rather than at the time of tender.[53]

This escape, however, is blocked by the court-created "economic loss" rule, which holds that if an allegedly defective or nonconforming product causes only economic loss (and not harm to person or injury to property other than the goods themselves) tort law is not available. Thus, if the nonconformity causes only lost profits or reliance expenditures or is limited to damage to the goods themselves, the applicable law is the UCC— the law of contractual warranty—not the law of torts.[54] As the New York Court of Appeals put it:

> Tort recovery in strict products liability and negligence against a manufacturer should not be available to a downstream purchaser where the claimed losses flow from damage to the property that is the subject of the contract. Transforming manufacturers into insurers with the empty promise that they can guarantee perpetual and total public safety, by making them liable in tort for all commercial setbacks and adversities is not prudent or sound tort public policy. In such instances, no directly related or commensurate public interest is served or protected by holding manufacturers liable. Tort law should not be bent so far out of its traditional progressive path and disci-

pline by allowing tort lawsuits where the claims at issue are, fundamentally and in all relevant respects, essentially contractual, product-failure controversies. Tort law is not the answer for this loss of commercial bargain.[55]

One can doubt the soundness of any bright-line rule that turns on the nature of the loss caused rather than the type of risks created when a product is manufactured and sold. This doubt is exacerbated when recovery for economic loss depends upon Article 2 of the UCC, that comprehensive scheme for allocating economic losses by contract. As we have seen, that comprehensive scheme favors the seller almost as much as the tort regime favors the injured person. The UCC scheme is designed to permit the risk of economic loss to be placed on the ultimate consumer. Unless express warranties are made by the manufacturer to the ultimate consumer, that buyer is required to deal with its seller, the retailer, and the limitation clauses almost certainly included in the contract. If that seller is insolvent or out of business, the real risk is that the manufacturer of the product will be insulated from liability. When push comes to shove, this is the result sanctioned by Article 2's "carefully designed rules of contract law."

IV. Conclusion

Have legal changes in recent decades contributed to an increase in and abuse of market power by strong organizations over individual consumers? When the content of contract doctrine alone is considered, the answer is "no." American contract doctrine has not changed significantly in the last fifty years. The bargain theory, with its consent requirement, and the countervailing doctrines of unconscionability, good faith, and promissory estoppel have remained relatively constant and have been applied in a restrained manner by the courts. Furthermore, there is little evidence that strong economic interests have promoted or engineered doctrinal changes in basic contract law or in Articles 2 or 2A of the UCC to suit their own agendas. But does this mean that the thesis of abuse is a nonstarter?

Not necessarily. There are subtle changes in and around contract doctrine that cumulatively suggest that strong parties have achieved greater power in the consumer market and with it the increased opportunity for abuse.

First, the use of standard forms by stronger parties has clearly increased, both in direct dealings and through the Internet.[56] The "take it or leave it" method of contracting is ubiquitous. Recent studies have emphasized the "bounded rationality" of the average consumer (they do not read even when they can) and have suggested that the incentives are high for sellers and others to include terms highly favorable to themselves, terms that are outside what the ordinary consumer would consider to be "salient."[57]

Second, our legal system has not adequately responded to the question of when the terms of an "adhesion contract" are unreasonable. For example, the unconscionability doctrine is preoccupied with the consent problem rather than the substance of the terms and the duty of good faith asks simply whether the conscionable terms of the bargain (the ones dictated by the strong party) have been performed or enforced honestly and fairly. The rejection in this context of the applicability of duties akin to those in the tort system, duties not necessarily tied to the issue of consent, has one level of impact on the strength of the consumer's position. This position is further weakened by the economic loss doctrine, which closes the door to tort where a nonconforming product causes no injury to person and property and requires the employment of the proseller contract risk allocation system of UCC Article 2. Moreover, promissory estoppel and theories of promissory fraud require that the stronger party actually make a promise that is not within the scope of the bargain theory. Finally, it is an open question whether there is sufficient direct regulation on either the state or federal level to detect and remedy actual abuse. What seems clear is that the rise of the consumer protection movement in the 1970s stalled somewhere in the 1980s and has struggled to maintain an effective presence ever since.

Third, the cost to individual consumers (not involved in a class action) to protect their "freedom from contract" rights in court is too high to insure a consistent application of any protective doctrine. And when litigation occurs, it is against a party who can afford it and who has drafted the standard terms under attack.[58] Although there are advantages to arbitration as an alternative, arbitration clauses have increasingly become part of the standard terms offered by strong parties on a take-it-or-leave-it basis.[59] The risk of this is that claims against the stronger party, statutory or otherwise, are decided by arbitrators rather than judges and decisions are generally insulated from judicial review.[60] Put succinctly, if assertions of contract rights and defenses increasingly take place "beyond the shadow" of the law and that law, in any event, is biased in favor of the stronger party, who or what will protect the interests of the individual?

Fourth, in contract law, the problem is not that interest groups representing strong sellers, lessors, and licensors, have captured the law revision processes and dictated the terms of revision. Rather, the reality is that these interest groups, whether involved in the National Conference of Commissioners on Uniform States Laws ("NCCUSL") or the American Law Institute ("ALI"), can assert pressure to preserve doctrines that serve their interests and block proposed revisions that do not.[61] There is no effective countervailing power in these private law-making processes—the consumer protection lobby is virtually nonexistent—and the vast majority of law teachers in the areas of contract and commercial law appear to be mesmerized by the siren call of the trilogy of efficiency, rights theory, and formalism.

In 1970, I argued that applying the consent theory in consumer contracts with standard terms was not workable. It was not realistic to require individuals to have the information and choice needed to protect themselves against one-sided terms or the parties that drafted them. Rather, I argued that even if the consumer had objectively assented to standard terms, the burden should shift the drafting party to prove that the term was reasonable. Put differently, in the so-called adhesion contract, a standard term objectively assented to by a consumer is presumptively not enforceable unless the drafter establishes that, in context, it was a reasonable allocation of risks and responsibilities.[62] This would shift the presumption in litigation where standard form terms were involved.

Thirty-five years later my view of this matter, aided by the research on "bounded rationality," has not changed. In fact, California courts have held that procedural unconscionability is presumptively present when "a party in a position of unequal bargaining power is presented with an offending clause without the opportunity for meaningful negotiation." In these cases, the court's attention shifts to whether the terms in the writing are so "one-sided as to shock the conscience."[63] In short, the California courts have concluded that the consent theory does not work in consumer adhesion contracts and that some judicial review of the allegedly offending clause is required.[64]

This is, of course, a helpful but relatively minor contribution. It is one thing to protect an individual consumer's freedom from contract in court and quite another to rely on litigation to correct power imbalances. A more effective strategy might be to carry the reversed presumption into law-making processes other than courts. It would change the stakes in the public choice game in that business interests would be required to explain and justify their contract practices rather than benefit from the presumption that what they do is fair and reasonable unless someone shows otherwise. It would also better engage the legal system in the difficult process of restructuring markets in advance of transactions and developing regulations that adjust distributive outcomes.[65]

In the final analysis, however, the problem is less what should be done to correct power imbalances in consumer markets and more whether anything can be done. The line between law and politics in the arena of consumer protection is difficult if not impossible to draw. The recent history of the revision of Article 2 suggests that any efforts before private "law-making processes," such as NCCUSL or the ALI, to shift significantly the proseller bias in American contract law would be rejected. What does this say about the theme of this book? Simply that any attempt to engage in direct regulation of or to require a justification for standard form terms is an anathema to American business and will be resisted on all fronts. This, in effect, leaves indirect regulation to the uncertain forces of market competition and the goodwill of business and creates incentives for abuses of power, whether provable or not, that will never be redressed by the courts.

In Enron we trust?

NOTES

1. Richard E. Speidel, *Afterword: The Shifting Domain of Contract*, 90 Nw. U. L. Rev. 254 (1995).

2. As Judge Posner put it: "Since the law of contracts cannot compel the making of contracts on terms favorable to one party, but can only refuse to enforce contracts with unfavorable terms, it is not an institution well designed to rectify inequalities in wealth." Amoco Oil Co. v. Ashcroft, 791 F.2d 519, 522 (7th Cir. 1986).

3. On the gap between rich and poor, see ROBERT B. REICH, REASON: WHY LIBERALS WILL WIN THE BATTLE FOR AMERICA 103–45 (2004).

4. *See* Martin Kasindorf, *Kerry: Credit, Loan Rules Are Unfair to Middle Class*, USA TODAY, Aug. 27, 2004, at 4A.

5. In essence, the "bargain theory" posits that a "manifestation of mutual assent to the exchange and a consideration" equals a contract. RESTATEMENT (SECOND) OF CONTRACTS § 17(1) (1980).

6. Oblix, Inc. v. Winiecki, 374 F.3d 488, 491 (7th Cir. 2004) (Easterbrook, J.) ("[s]tandard form agreements are a fact of life").

7. According to Judge Frank Easterbrook, "few consumer contracts are negotiated one clause at a time. Forms reduce transactions costs and benefit consumers because, in competition, reductions in the cost of doing business show up as lower prices." Carbajal v. H & R Block Tax Servs., Inc., 372 F.3d 903, 906 (7th Cir. 2004).

8. *See generally* Russell Korobkin, *Bounded Rationality, Standard Form Contracts, and Unconscionability*, 70 U. CHI. L. REV. 1203 (2003), who argues that because of an individual's limited powers of cognition, there will be "non-salient" aspects of objectively assented to standard terms. It is these nonsalient features that are most likely to foster abuse.

9. *See* Symposium, *Freedom from Contract*, 2004 WIS. L. REV. 261–820 (2004).

10. *See* Edward L. Rubin, *The Nonjudicial Life of Contract Behavior: Beyond the Shadow of the Law*, 90 Nw. U. L. REV. 107, 109 (1995).

11. For a typical statement of this limitation, see *Baxter Int'l, Inc. v. Abbott Laboratories*, 315 F.3d 829, 831–32 (7th Cir. 2003). The effect of increased arbitration on the development and application of common law principles is discussed by Charles L. Knapp, *Taking Contracts Private: The Quiet Revolution in Contract Law*, 71 FORDHAM L. REV. 761 (2002).

12. Consider the wide list of contracts made by individuals where standard form terms will be found: (1) sale or lease of personal property or interests in realty, (2) personal and professional services, (3) employment, (4) insurance, (5) investment services, including retirement, (6) construction, (7) health care, (8) banking and financial services, including credit transactions, and (9) utilities.

13. For an excellent study of small business contracting, see Blake D. Morant, *The Quest for Bargains in an Age of Contractual Formalism: Strategic Initiatives for Small Businesses*, 7 J. SMALL & EMERGING BUS. L. 233 (2003).

14. The counterargument is that in many cases consumers with information and choice can reject proposed standard terms and shop for a better deal. Internet shopping opportunities may increase these choices. Some economists believe that "shopping behavior by a relatively small proportion of consumers is sufficient to create a competitive market" for terms. *See* Edward Rubin, *Why Law Schools Do Not Teach Contracts and What Socioeconomics Can Do about It*, 41 SAN DIEGO L. REV. 55, 70 (2004) (discussing the issue). In addition, the overall impact of federal and state consumer protection legislation and enforcement on business practices is arguably more effective than judicial decisions or arbitral awards. Whether consumers do shop for terms and the impact of competition and regulatory legislation on firm behavior are empirical questions for which there are no clear answers.

15. For a survey of other approaches, see James R. Maxeiner, *Standard-Terms Contracting in the Global Electronic Age: European Alternatives*, 28 YALE J. INT'L L. 109 (2003); Michael J. Bonnell, *Policing the International Commercial Contract against Unfairness under the Unidroit Principles*, 3 TUL. J. INT'L & COMP. L. 73 (1995).

16. For a helpful collection of articles, see *Festschrift to the Work of Charles J. Goetz and Robert E. Scott*, 6 VA. J. 12–121 (2003); *see also* LOUIS KAPLOW & STEVEN SHAVELL, CONTRACTING (2004).

17. *See* Randy Barnett, *A Consent Theory of Contract*, 86 COLUM. L. REV. 269 (1986); Philip Bridwell, Comment, *The Philosophical Dimensions of the Doctrine of Unconscionability*, 70 U. CHI. L. REV. 1513 (2003).

18. *See generally* Jay M. Feinman, *Un-Making Law: The Classical Revival in the Common Law*, 28 SEATTLE U. L. REV. 1 (2004); Robert E. Scott, *The Case for Formalism in Relational Contracts*, 94 NW. U. L. REV. 847 (2000); Morant, *Quest, supra* note 13, at 261–67.

19. KARL N. LLEWELLYN, THE COMMON LAW TRADITION: DECIDING APPEALS 370–71 (1960).

20. There is, of course, a lot of consumer protection legislation on the state and federal books. *See* ABA, SECTION OF ANTITRUST LAW, CONSUMER PROTECTION HANDBOOK (2004) (collecting and analyzing statutes, regulations, and cases). The question, as always, is the overall effectiveness of this legislation.

21. *See* ROBERTO M. UNGER, THE CRITICAL LEGAL STUDIES MOVEMENT (1986); Jay Feinman, *Critical Approaches to Contract Law*, 30 UCLA L. REV. 829 (1983).

22. GRANT GILMORE, THE DEATH OF CONTRACT 72 (1974).

23. For a recent update, see Carol B. Swanson, *Unconscionable Quandary: UCC Article 2 and the Unconscionability Doctrine*, 31 N.M. L. REV. 359 (2001). The "unconscionability" doctrine is also found in U.C.C. 2A-108 (leases of goods) but in no other Article of the U.C.C.

24. *See* Robert Hillman & Jeffrey J. Rachlinski, *Standard-Form Contracting in the Electronic Age*, 77 N.Y.U. L. REV. 429 (2002); *see also* Russell Korobkin, *Bounded Rationality, Standard Form Contracts, and Unconscionability*, 70 U. CHI. L. REV. 1203 (2003).

25. *See* Jeffrey W. Stempel, *Arbitration, Unconscionability, and Equilibrium: The Return of Unconscionability Analysis as a Counterweight to Arbitration Formalism*, 19 OHIO ST. J. ON DISP. RESOL. 757 (2004); Susan Randall, *Judicial Attitudes toward Arbitration and the Resurgence of Unconscionability*, 52 BUFF. L. REV. 185 (2004).

26. For example, if there was no procedural unconscionability (consumer understood term and could "leave it"), the term would not be substantively conscionable unless it was per se against public policy.

27. One source of the "duty" of good faith is U.C.C. § 1-203. Revised U.C.C. § 1-304 (2004). Except for Article 5 of the U.C.C., "good faith . . . means honesty in fact and the observance of reasonable commercial standards of fair dealing." Revised U.C.C. § 1-201(20). Another source is the common law, restated as Section 205 of the Restatement (Second) of Contracts (1981).

28. This describes the model of good faith developed in the Unidroit Principles of International Commercial Contracts. *See* Richard E. Speidel, *The Characteristics and Challenges of Relational Contracts*, 94 NW. U. L. REV. 823, 840–43 (2000).

29. Although the duty to negotiate in good faith is not imposed, an agreement to negotiate will be enforced. *See* Copeland v. Baskin Robbins, U.S.A., 117 Cal.Rptr.2d 875 (Cal. App. 2002).

30. *See* Commentary No. 10 of the Permanent Editorial Board of the Uniform Commercial Code (1994), *preserved in* Comment 1 to Revised U.C.C. § 1-304; *see also* Northern Nat. Gas Co. v. Conoco, Inc., 986 S.W.2d 603, 606 (Tex. 1998).

31. *See* United Airlines, Inc. v. Good Taste, Inc., 982 P.2d 1259 (Alaska 1999); Sons of Thunder, Inc. v. Borden, Inc., 690 A.2d 575 (N.J. 1997).

32. For example, New York does not recognize a "separate cause of action" for breach of the implied duty of good faith and fair dealing where a breach of contract on the same facts is pled. Harris v. Provident Life & Accident Ins. Co., 310 F.3d 73, 60, n. 3 (2d Cir. 2002); *but see* William S. Dodge, *The Case for Punitive Damages in Contracts*, 48 DUKE L.J. 629 (1999) (claiming that certain bad-faith breaches deserve the imposition of punitive damages).

33. According to Dennis Patterson, this restricted view of good faith gives private parties, more particularly those who draft terms and require others to assent to them, control over the duty. Dennis Patterson, *A Fable from the Seventh Circuit: Frank Easterbrook on Good Faith*, 76 IOWA L. REV. 503 (1991).

34. *See* Juliet P. Kostritsky, *The Rise and Fall of Promissory Estoppel or Is Promissory Estoppel Really as Unsuccessful as Scholars Say It Is: A New Look at the Data*, 37 WAKE FOREST L. REV. 531 (2002); Charles L. Knapp, *Rescuing Reliance: The Perils of Promissory Estoppel*, 49 HASTINGS L. J. 1191 (1998).

35. *See, e.g.*, Cohen v. Cowles Media Co., 479 N.W.2d 387 (Minn. 1992) (promise to maintain confidentiality in exchange for disclosure of information enforced on reliance rather than bargain theory).

36. *See supra* note 21.

37. If a promise is made with the present intent not to perform, a claim for promissory fraud may be stated. *See* EDWARD J. MURPHY ET AL., STUDIES IN CONTRACT LAW 519–23 (6th ed. 2003).

38. *See* Jason Scott Johnson, *Investment, Information, and Promissory Liability*, 152 U. PA. L. REV. 1923, 1930–36 (2004) (exploring limitations in the context of pre-contractual liability).

39. All-Tech Telecom, Inc. v. Amway Corp., 174 F.3d 862, 869 (7th Cir. 1999) (Posner, J.).

40. Thus, the implied warranty of merchantability, U.C.C. 2-314, can be disclaimed, U.C.C. 2-316(2), and the usual buyer's remedies available for breach, *see* UCC 2-711, can be limited or excluded, *see* UCC 2-719.

41. *See* Michael M. Greenfield and Linda J. Rusch, *Limits on Standard Form Contracting in Revised Article 2*, 32 UCC L. J. 115 (1999); *see also* Linda J. Rusch, *Is the Saga of the Uniform Commercial Code Article 2 Revisions Over? A Brief Look at What NCCUSL Finally Approved*, 6 DEL. L. REV. 41 (2003).

42. U.C.C. § 2-316(2).

43. *See* Revised U.C.C. 2-316(2); Revised U.C.C. § 1-201(b)(31). Disclaimers of express warranties are not permitted under UCC 2-316(1), but express warranties made during negotiations may be excluded from the bargain by the parol evidence rule, U.C.C. § 2-202.

44. U.C.C. § 2-719(2).

45. Such excluder clauses are enforceable unless unconscionable. U.C.C. § 2-719(3).

46. U.C.C. § 2-719(2).

47. U.C.C. § 2-607(3)(a).

48. For example, states enacting Alternative C to U.C.C. § 2-318 may permit direct actions by consumers against manufacturers for unmerchantable goods. Similarly, privity of contract is not required when asserting express warranty claims made by manufacturers and suppliers to consumers under the Magnuson-Moss Warranty-Federal Trade Commission Improvement Act, 15 U.S.C.A. §§ 2301-2312.

49. Revised U.C.C. § 2-313A and § 2-313B.

50. U.C.C. § 2-725(1) & (2).

51. 15 U.S.C.A. §§ 2301-2312. Other federal regulation includes FTC Regulations-Door-to-Door Sales, 16 C.F.R. § 429, and Preservation of Consumers' Claims and Defenses, 16 C.F.R. § 433.

52. Although federal regulation through the FTC has achieved results in specific areas, the success of most state and local consumer protection laws is in doubt. The statutes, usually designed to regulate unfair and deceptive practices, are relatively new with few cases interpreting them. Moreover, "not only do states vary greatly in their enforcement aggressiveness, but consumer protection cases are less likely than many others to be litigated through trial." ABA, SECTION OF ANTITRUST LAW, CONSUMER PROTECTION HANDBOOK 1, 67 (2004).

53. *See* RICHARD E. SPEIDEL & LINDA J. RUSCH, COMMERCIAL TRANSACTIONS: SALES, LEASES, AND LICENSES 612–16 (2d ed. 2004).

54. *See, e.g., Jimenez v. Superior Court of San Diego County*, 58 P.3d 450, 483 (Cal. 2002) (applying tort law where the defective product (windows) caused damage to other property).

55. Bocre Leasing Corp. v. Gen. Motors Corp., 645 N.E.2d 1195, 1199 (N.Y. 1995).

56. *See* Christina L. Kunz, et al., *Browse-Wrap Agreements: Validation of Implied Assent in Electronic Form Agreements*, 59 BUS. LAW. 279 (2003); *Click-Through Agreements: Strategies for Avoiding Disputes on Validity of Assent*, 57 BUS. LAW. 401 (2001).

57. *See generally* Korobkin, *supra* note 8; Symposium, *Empirical Legal Realism: A New Social Scientific Assessment of Law and Human Behavior*, 97 NW. U. L. REV. 1079–392 (2003).

58. *See* Symposium, *Access to Justice: Does It Exist in Civil Cases?* 17 GEO. J. LEGAL ETHICS 455, 457–63 (2003) (comments of Dennis Archer); *see also* Stewart

Macaulay, *Freedom from Contract: Solutions in Search of a Problem?* 2004 WIS. L. REV. 777, 778–88 (discussing the "vanishing" contracts trial).

59. For example, the courts have held that predispute, mandatory arbitration agreements to arbitrate Title VII claims are enforceable. *See* Mahon v. Staff Line, Inc., 100 Fed. Appx. 37 (2d Cir. 2004); *see also* Carbajal v. H & R Block Tax Servs., Inc., 372 F.3d 903, 906 (7th Cir. 2004).

60. It is difficult to state the arbitration problem in a nutshell. For an excellent group of articles assessing so-called "Mandatory Arbitration," see Symposium, *Mandatory Arbitration*, 67 LAW & CONTEMP. PROBS. 1–336 (2004).

61. *See* Richard E. Speidel, *Revising UCC Article 2: A View from the Trenches*, 52 HASTINGS L.J. 607 (2001).

62. Richard E. Speidel, *Unconscionability, Assent, and Consumer Protection*, 31 U. PITT. L. REV. 359 (1970); *see also* Larry Lawrence, *Toward a More Efficient and Just Economy: An Argument for Limited Enforcement of Consumer Promises*, 48 OHIO ST. L.J. 815 (1987).

63. Ferguson v. Countrywide Credit Indus., Inc., 298 F.3d 778, 788 (9th Cir. 2002) (holding arbitration clause was unconscionable). Other courts have rejected this approach. *See* Carter v. Countrywide Credit Indus., Inc., 362 F.3d 294 (5th Cir. 2004) (no rebuttable presumption under Texas law).

64. Recently, Professor Omri Ben-Shahar argued that liability without consent should be imposed in some commercial contracts where bargaining actually takes place. Omri Ben-Shahar, *Contracts without Consent: A New Basis for Contractual Liability*, 152 U. PA. L. REV. 1829 (2004). Professor Mann disagrees. *See* Ronald J. Mann, *Contracts—Only with Consent*, 152 U. PA. L. REV. 1873 (2004).

65. *See* HUGH COLLINS, REGULATING CONTRACTS 222, 254–55, 285–86, 301–02 (1999) (setting forth essential elements of effective regulation).

14

Congress and the Credit Industry
More Bad News for Families

Elizabeth Warren

Every fifteen seconds in this country, someone declares bankruptcy. That is every fifteen seconds, twenty-four hours a day, 365 days a year.[1] In 2006, more people will end up bankrupt than will suffer a heart attack. More adults will file for bankruptcy than will be diagnosed with cancer. More people will file for bankruptcy than will graduate from college. And, in an era when traditionalists decry the demise of the institution of marriage, more Americans will file petitions for bankruptcy than for divorce.[2] Heart attacks. Cancer. College. Divorce. These are milestones in the lives of nearly every American family. And yet, we will soon have more friends and colleagues who have gone through bankruptcy than any one of these other life events.

Bankruptcy is not the only indication that millions of Americans are in financial trouble. In the past twenty-five years, home mortgage foreclosures have increased more than threefold. Credit card default rates are up. Even as Federal Reserve Chairman Alan Greenspan declares that American families will enjoy "continuing prosperity,"[3] one in five families says it is taking on more debt because the family simply "cannot pay [its] bills."[4] Economists estimate that for every family in bankruptcy, seven more should file for bankruptcy, if only they were more knowledgeable.[5]

Bankruptcy can be an upside-down world. Contracts, leases, rent-to-own arrangements, and dozens of other agreements that are otherwise legally enforceable can be discharged in bankruptcy. If a debtor is willing to hand over everything she owns and publicly declare herself a financial failure, she can get some relief from creditors who otherwise could enforce their legal rights by garnishing her paycheck, seizing her assets, or simply calling and sending collection agents to her home all day, every day. The terms of bankruptcy are complex—the debtor can keep certain property, but even in bankruptcy the debtor must pay certain debts such as child support, taxes, and student loans. In effect, the law operates as a safety valve, a place where a debtor takes refuge when catastrophes or ignorance have left her mired in debts she cannot possibly repay. Bankruptcy is the softening edge of lawful, but often unforgiving, enforcement of contract law.

Most of the debt discharged in bankruptcy is consumer debt—credit cards, payday loans, and some auto financing when the loan balance is far greater than the value of the car.[6] Most of the families that carry such debt—and that end up in bankruptcy—are middle-class, working families. They are people who have gone to college, gotten decent jobs and bought homes, and now they are in desperate financial trouble.[7] As a group, neither the chronically poor nor the well-to-do ordinarily run up large amounts of such debts, nor are the rich and the poor likely to file for bankruptcy to try to straighten out their financial affairs. Instead, bankruptcy—and the need for bankruptcy—is generally a middle-class, working family story. As this chapter explains, recent changes in the credit industry and proposed changes in the bankruptcy laws paint a grim future for these families.

I. The Changing Face of Creditors

Consumer debt has been part of the American economy since colonial times, when merchants kept "book debt" for their customers.[8] But the identity of creditors has evolved over time. A generation ago, individual retailers and small drugstores extended credit to their customers and bore the losses when those customers defaulted. Today, consumer credit is dominated by huge risk pools. Local retailers have now been joined by physicians, dentists, and hospitals in scaling back their own extensions of credit and accepting national credit cards for immediate payment. More than 190 million Americans now carry credit cards, and they are toting an average of 7.6 cards per person.[9] When an individual cannot pay, the card issuer—not the retailer or physician—bears the loss.

In one generation, the credit card industry itself has undergone substantial consolidation. Today, just ten credit card banks hold more than 90 percent of all credit card debt.[10] Credit card issuers in turn offload much of their debt in securitized investment pools. The consequence is that much of the risk of customer default is borne by sophisticated investors who buy the stock of the card issuers or participate directly in the debt pools.

The dramatic shift in risk bearing has occurred at a time when the consumer financial service industry has been quietly deregulated. As changes in federal law in the late 1970s and early 1980s preempted states from regulating most consumer credit, a new product was born: sub-prime debt. Sub-prime lenders extend credit to people with poor credit records, charging interest rates and servicing fees that are much higher than those charged to prime customers. Sub-prime lending has also infiltrated the prime credit market, as credit issuers reserve the unilateral right to change interest terms and fee assessments long after customers have borrowed the money. Today, even customers with spotless credit can be hit with interest rates of 20, 30 and 40 percent if a credit card company decides to change the terms on outstanding debt. The companies impose fees so that anyone who falls a little behind suddenly discovers that she is way behind. Not surprisingly, rates are particularly likely to climb when some other event, such as a job loss, medical problem, or divorce has upset the family budget.

This new industry is extraordinarily profitable, with income generated from late fees and overlimit fees now its fastest-growing segment.[11] Sub-prime lenders make their profits from the extremely large spread, that is, the difference between the low cost of funds to the investors and the high rates the company can charge. Even with high defaults and debts written off, credit card companies are reaping record profits.[12]

Thus the conflict between borrower and lender arises, and bankruptcy becomes the battleground. Bankruptcy protection is a zero-sum contest between working families in financial trouble and huge pools of investors represented by sub-prime loan servicing companies. The degree of protection available to families directly affects the collection rights of the creditors. If families get very little bankruptcy protection, then large, investor-run credit pools can continue to collect for as long as they find it profitable to do so. Without bankruptcy protection, high interest rates and additional fees will mean that some families will literally never escape from their debts because they can never earn enough to pay off the debts in full; compounding interest and late fees mean that they will pay on their debts until they die.[13] By contrast, if bankruptcy is a viable option, then families caught in debt traps have choices: they can forfeit some of their assets, discharge much of their unpaid credit card and other consumer debt, and stabilize themselves financially.

In the contest between big pools of investors and even bigger pools of families who face uncertain futures, bankruptcy reflects a long struggle between those who have little and those who have the most. The news from the frontlines is not good for families.

II. Why Bankruptcy?

For middle-class families in financial trouble, bankruptcy is America's only safety net. Overwhelmed by debts, a family can head to the bankruptcy courts, offer to give up everything except a few exempt assets, and declare itself flat broke and unable to continue. If the debtor has been honest and if there are insufficient resources for repayment, the court will grant a discharge of some debts. Even in bankruptcy, the obligation to pay child support and alimony, taxes, and student loans continues no matter what. And if the bankrupt family wants to keep its home or car, it must continue those payments as well.

Bankruptcy relief is limited, but the system offers debtors a chance to shed impossible mountains of credit card debt, payday loans, and medical bills. A family in trouble has a chance to start over, a chance to use its future income to pay the mortgage and utilities, to buy food and clothing, without the endless compounding interest and fees and the constant threat of garnishment.

Bankruptcy is also a place of refuge for businesses. In this regard, bankruptcy is an American success story. Entrepreneurs whose businesses are failing may head to the bankruptcy courts to deal with the personal liability associated with bank loans and trade debt that, despite corporate form, is traditionally backed up with the owner's personal guarantee. Huge companies may file for bankruptcy when markets collapse or when the company itself is mired in scandal. Businesses that might have been liquidated or that laid off thousands of workers have regained their footing and prospered. Texaco and Toys-R-Us are the visible examples of postbankrupt companies that have prospered, but their ranks are swelled by thousands of smaller companies that manage to survive a rough patch and right themselves financially. Even when businesses are liquidated, bankruptcy can add value by creating an efficient, organized proceeding that assures that the remaining assets are distributed according to law, and not according to which creditor knew someone on the inside. Companies may reorganize their balance sheets, restructure their business operations, or liquidate all their assets through the bankruptcy system.

For working families, bankruptcy operates as insurance. Families borrow from credit card companies, run up bills at hospitals, commit to mortgages, and borrow to buy cars. Most repay. Even now, more than 95 percent of all credit card debt is current, with families paying in full or making minimum monthly payments on time when the company sends its bills.[14] Mortgage debt has even higher rates of automatic repayment.[15] But if the wage earner loses his job, if someone is too sick to go to work, if a child is diagnosed with a terrible illness, or if Mom and Dad split up, typical middle-class families can quickly find themselves owing a mountain of debt that they can never repay. Without bankruptcy, they would be trapped forever—always subject to a credit card company's wage garnishment, always at risk that a hospital might put a lien against their homes, always concerned that repossession of their car could leave them unable to get to work.

Bankruptcy eliminates some debt and protects debtors from creditors that might be willing to hound the debtor forever. At the same time, bankruptcy increases incentives for troubled workers to continue to earn and to remain a part of the producing economy rather than giving up and sliding onto the welfare rolls. And bankruptcy gives debtors a chance to work out a payment plan with the mortgage company or the car lender, discharging other debts so they can concentrate their efforts on making the payments that keep a roof over their heads or ensure that the car they need to get to work remains in the driveway.

Eventually virtually every social and economic problem in the United States threads its way through the bankruptcy courts. For families, bankruptcy is the place to deal with lost jobs, erratic incomes, inadequate health insurance, no disability insurance, and the financial impact of divorce. The bankruptcy courts deal indirectly with the fallout from stagnant wages and a part-time or "consulting" workforce, with the high cost of housing and day care that chews through a parent's take-home pay. Even families who never declare bankruptcy use the system when they get into financial trouble: every negotiation with a credit card company or mortgage lender takes place in the shadow of the possibility that the debtor will turn to bankruptcy.

III. The Changing Creditor Response

Creditors have always supported laws that helped them enforce their rights and resisted those that gave more protection to debtors. The basic push-and-pull between debtor and creditor remains the same. In decades past, however, creditors knew that a substantial amount of the general unsecured debt listed in bankruptcy was uncollectible in any event. More than half had been written off before the bankruptcy filing, a cost of doing business on credit. While creditors always wanted the opportunity to continue to try to collect, their resistance to consumer protection legislation was somewhat moderated by the reality that their debtors could not pay anyway, bankruptcy or no bankruptcy.

But creditor practices have changed in the past two decades. With the advent of computers packed with personal data, a new element has been introduced into the debtor-creditor dynamic—the persistent caller. It is now cost-effective to have minimum-wage workers located in a call center in Tulsa, Oklahoma, or Bombay, India, calling people who are delinquent on their bills. The script flashes on the computer screen, modified to identify where the person works, the names of the children, when the person gets paid, how much the take-home pay will be, what to ask for today, and whether to threaten court action or offer more credit as an inducement for payment. Collection calls go on all day and all evening, with a peak period in the afternoon as children arrive home from school and are left to deal with bill collectors until Mom or Dad gets home. Calls go forward on Christmas, Thanksgiving, Easter, and the Fourth of July. One of the primary reasons given by families for filing bankruptcy is to "stop the calls."

The growth of this new form of debt collection has been accompanied by a transformation in credit-pricing practices. A generation ago, a lender thought hard before setting an interest rate that reflected the risk that a customer could not pay. If the customer got into trouble, the payments stayed pretty much the same, and the customer had a chance to dig out of the hole. Today, when someone starts to stumble, the cost of the already-outstanding credit surges and the odds of ever getting caught up disappear. Those who stumble find themselves needing to run faster and faster—thrown hard to the ground if they cannot make it. Consider the following illustrative case. A national credit card company filed a routine claim in bankruptcy court for payment from one of its bankrupt customers. The court, in a highly unusual move, asked the company, Capital One, to explain just how much of its claim for payment was for what the person actually charged and how much was for interest and fees.[16] The numbers were astonishing. For every dollar that Capital One claimed the customer had borrowed, the company now wanted the dollar back plus two more for fees and interest.

What makes these numbers more amazing is that most people in cases like this will have already made payments for months, some for years. For example, in another published opinion, a bankruptcy court traced the payment history of Josephine McCarthy.[17] Two years before filing, she owed Providian, another national credit card company, $2,223. Over the ensuing twenty-four months, she made payments of $2,008. With various fees and interest charges, after all her payments, Providian said she still owed $2,607. Without bankruptcy, Ms. McCarthy would keep making her regular payment of $83.66 a month, and she would still owe Providian money on the day she died—all on a bill of $2,223.

Individual families behind on credit card bills or payday loans become small, lifetime annuities for the companies. Default rates of interest, late fees, overlimit fees, and bounced check fees mean that once someone falls, the charges keep adding up faster than they can ever be paid off. And cheap nationwide collection capacity keeps someone on the telephone, urging, entreating, or just plain scaring debtors "just to pay something."

Today even "bad debt" is valuable. Big credit card issuers collect on their outstanding debts, and then accounts that are ninety days or more past due are bundled together and auctioned off to investors. Why would someone buy bad debts? To work over the debts more aggressively, to stay after them, to fire up the folks in calling centers to get $50, $80, and $100 payments month after month after month.

The only legal way to stop this practice is bankruptcy. The person who protests, "I don't have anything, stop calling me," can accomplish nothing. But a bankruptcy petition stops the calls cold. An automatic stay on all collection actions falls into place, and the phone calls must cease. In nearly all cases, this form of debt will be discharged. Any company that calls after that is in violation of federal law.

It is little wonder that the big banks that have trillions in credit card debt and that collect on the debts owed to them or sell those delinquent debts to collection specialists want to change the bankruptcy laws. If they can keep even a fraction of those 1.6 million households that file for bankruptcy each year away from the bankruptcy courts, they can preserve those accounts for lifetime collection. And if they can deny bankruptcy to more of those households that would otherwise file, their profits will go up even faster.

IV. The Bankruptcy Battleground

The 1978 Bankruptcy Code modernized a section of the law that had not been significantly revised since the Great Depression. Creating a workable consumer bankruptcy system in response in part to the growing burden of household debt was one of the stated objectives.

The ink was barely dry on the new law when the credit industry began complaining that bankruptcy had become "too easy." By 1984, the industry was able to get a dozen or so amendments passed to make it harder for consumers to discharge debts. At the same time, however, a few proconsumer amendments were added, in part to preserve the balance of the bankruptcy bill. For example, in 1986 an amendment to help hard-pressed family farmers was added with strong bipartisan support. The credit industry nonetheless kept pressing for more changes. Credit card debt was up, profits were up, but bankruptcy filings were up as well. The idea of keeping families out of bankruptcy so that creditors could continue to collect from them forever was beginning to take hold.

Howard Metzenbaum, the proconsumer senator from Ohio, fought off the industry with a compromise. Just before he retired, he agreed to a few procreditor amendments, but held off the other items on the industry wish list with a promise of a blue-ribbon commission to be appointed to make recommendations for further change. The National Bankruptcy Review Commission, coming out of the 1994 amendments, was to be appointed by Congress (four members), the White House (three members), and the Chief Justice of the Supreme Court (two members). The Commission's chairman, Congressman Mike Synar, appointed me to be the Senior Adviser to the Commission with the explanation that I should do the research, organize the hearings, and write the final report. He died just as the Commission got underway, and Brady Williamson, an attorney from Madison, Wisconsin, stepped in to run the Commission.

Credit industry lobbying was intense. Literally dozens of lobbyists showed up for every Commission meeting. They brought their own witnesses, issued their own reports, and ultimately drafted their own proposed laws. They lobbied Commission members individually and collectively, and they churned out media packages describing what they claimed was the need for bankruptcy "reform" and purporting to show how ordinary families declaring bankruptcy were "cheating" the system. In a now-infamous series of advertisements, the industry advanced the specious claim that bankruptcy costs every bill-paying family in America $400. It has been discredited, but the nonsensical allegation is nonetheless repeated today.[18]

As the Commission's work advanced, divisions among commissioners on the issue of consumer bankruptcy became sharper. Ultimately, the Commission took a middle path, recommending some procreditor reforms and some prodebtor reforms. When it was clear that the Commission would not give them everything they wanted, the credit industry wasted no time. It persuaded a friendly congressman to introduce the industry's version of a bill to amend the bankruptcy laws in September 1997—just a few days before the Commission issued its eleven hundred-page report to Congress on October 1, 1997.

The battle lines were drawn. There would be no compromise bill, no bipartisan adjustment to the bankruptcy laws as there had been in the past. The credit industry wanted its version of consumer bankruptcy, and it believed that it could easily get enough support in Congress to push it through.

V. The Issue of Class

The Commission's recommendations were far from proconsumer. The report made a number of recommendations that would have imposed significant restrictions on consumer debtors. One of the most important proposals would have hit hard at the richest debtors. Those with multimillion dollar homes in Texas and Florida, for example, would have lost their state-granted homestead protections if they declared bankruptcy. The Commission Report also focused on creditor abuses, recommending that creditors not be permitted to prowl the bankruptcy courts trying to persuade people to agree to repay the debts they were about to discharge. Not surprisingly, the credit industry loudly derided the Commission Report, dismissing it as "dead on arrival" in Congress. The industry ignored the Commission's efforts at a balanced bill that would curtail certain abuses on both sides, and instead insisted on its own bankruptcy bill.

The bankruptcy laws have long had a "millionaires' loophole." With adequate planning and substantial help from their lawyers, the troubled rich can sock away assets in million-dollar homes, offshore trusts, and other obscure devices, putting these assets out of the reach of their creditors. The devices are well-known among lawyers who work in the field, and the credit industry bill was carefully crafted. Instead of targeting these practices, the credit industry bill focused like a laser beam on middle-class families. So, for example, under the industry proposal a millionaire who was a longtime Florida resident could keep that beachfront home, and a business executive in Delaware could put millions in an asset protection trust.[19] But a single person earning $22,000 a year would be denied access to Chapter 7 and forced into a five-year repayment plan for debt relief. An out-of-work debtor bringing home $600 a month in unemployment benefits would not be forced to pay any more in bankruptcy, but he would nonetheless be put to the task of filling out a sheaf of detailed new forms and reports—or, more accurately, paying a lawyer to take care of the increased paperwork burden. A recently divorced woman who did not have access to her joint tax returns for the past two years would automatically be denied access to bankruptcy. The bill was hundreds of pages long, with complex and technical amendments designed to have big cumulative effects on consumer bankruptcy. Through dozens of changes, the bill would drive up the costs for debtors, reduce the costs for creditors, reduce the protection for debtors, and increase the odds that a debtor would trip up somewhere in the system and get tossed out altogether.

Increasing costs by a few hundred dollars and making the consumer system more complex would have no effect on big businesses. Nor would it affect the rich, who have ample resources both to hire counsel to exploit every possible loophole in a complex statute and to engage in careful pre-bankruptcy planning to protect their assets. The impact of such changes would fall exclusively on the ordinary families that turn to the bankruptcy system when they are head over heels in debt and cannot possibly pay. These changes would affect those who lose their jobs, those who get sick, and those whose families break apart. Some number of these families would never file for bankruptcy, and some more of them would file but be dismissed from the system without ever getting a discharge from their debts. In other words, it would mean that more people would remain in the bad debt pool, available for more phone calls from Tulsa or Bombay, and paying $80 here and $90 there until they die.

VI. Just in Case Someone Didn't Catch the Point

The bankruptcy debates pit the investor class against families, but just in case anyone missed the point, there is another dimension to the class conflict—the Chapter 11 changes.[20]

Businesses of any size can declare Chapter 11 and reorganize their debts. The system that has been host most recently to Enron, Worldcom, United Airlines, Adelphia, and TWA, is also home to family enterprises hoping to save their businesses. In fact, while the big cases soak up all the newsprint, it is small businesses—those with $2 million or less in debts—that comprise more than two-thirds of the Chapter 11 cases.[21] These businesses are a mix of sole proprietorships, partnerships, and corporate entities in which the owner/operator usually had to give a personal guaranty of the business debts.

Perhaps stung by the charge that the credit industry bill was nothing more than a giveaway to the credit card companies, the proposed bankruptcy legislation was rewritten to separate "big" Chapter 11s (those with more than $2 million in debts) from "small" Chapter 11s (those with less than $2 million in debts). New laws were proposed to make Chapter 11 much tougher and much more expensive—but only for the little guys. New deadlines would force a quick liquidation of companies in Chapter 11, but the deadlines would not apply to any company that owed more than $2 million. New forms, new limitations on business operations, and greater trustee supervision would make Chapter 11 less hospitable—but only for small businesses. For the Enrons and Worldcoms all would be business-as-usual.

The Chapter 11 provisions in the credit industry bill are almost certainly the first time that Congress has deliberately and by name singled out small businesses for worse treatment than big businesses. There may have been laws that had the effect of favoring big over small, but no law made its intent so clear. And, as a side note, the bill was not opposed by the small business lobby in Washington and never went to the Small Business Committee for study. The bankruptcy option, a critical backstop for entrepreneurs who risk everything and for little companies vulnerable to the slightest changes in the markets, was on the chopping block with virtually no opposition. At the same time, access to bankruptcy for the big companies remained safe.

VII. Many Battles in a War

The credit industry first introduced its own bill in the legislative hopper in the fall of 1997 through a cooperative congressman who was the recipient of substantial donations. In 1998, the House of Representatives adopted the bill, but in a cliff-hanger vote, the Senate balked. In 2000, the bill passed both the House and the Senate, only to earn distinction as President Clinton's last veto before leaving office. In 2002, a lame-duck Congress came back to tidy up a few matters, including the industry's bill. This time the bill failed in the House. In 2003 and 2004, the House passed the bill again, but the Senate did not move. Finally, luck ran out for families and small businesses in trouble. In the spring of 2005, the Senate and House both passed the bill, which was quickly signed into law.

In its many incarnations in the House and Senate, the industry's bill acquired a number of odd pieces, perhaps none quite so strange as the abortion provision. A small number of abortion protestors had big judgments against them for violating the federal laws on access to women's health clinics. They immediately declared that they would seek refuge in bankruptcy. This prompted Senator Schumer to offer an amendment to the bankruptcy bill to assure that their debts could not be dischargeable. The provisions passed the Senate in 2002, but the House balked. When the House passed the bill without the amendments in 2003 and 2004, the Senate balked. But in 2005, the supporters of the bill fought off the Schumer Amendment, so the Senate produced a bill acceptable to a majority in the House.

VIII. The Battle outside Congress

An unspoken but very real class conflict has played out in the congressional debates over bankruptcy. The credit industry tried to brush aside the obvious fact that its bill squeezed middle-class families in order to pump up credit card company investor profits. They claimed that costs of bankruptcy are borne by other consumers and that the card companies are mere conduits in the reallocation of money from families who pay to families who do not pay.[22] There was undoubtedly a time when that view of credit accurately described lending practices. Yet, in a world in which the customers who pay promptly are derided as "deadbeats" by the industry because they produce little revenue for the credit card companies and when the most profitable customers are those who are in financial trouble and paying extraordinarily high fees and interest, this claim is hard to sustain.

Indeed, some customers have paid so much on their credit card accounts before they finally tumble into bankruptcy that they might better be thought of as having prepaid for their own bankruptcies. The only loss imposed on the credit card company is the loss of the expectation that the company could collect interest on these old debts forever.

Over the past decade, returns to investors on credit card debt have outstripped every other form of lending—even taking into consideration all bad debt and bankruptcy losses.[23] A multibillion dollar wealth transfer has, in fact, taken place, but not the one the credit card industry claims. Families that have lost jobs, families that have no health insurance, and families that have split apart following divorce or death of a spouse have paid billions to investors. They are not costing the system money; they are a major profit center. And just to clarify the class-driven point, it is worth noting that across the United States, half of all families have not one dollar of savings put aside for their retirements and 73 percent of all families have not one dollar in the stock market.[24] It is a fair assumption that paying dearly for consumer credit has not created a wealth transfer within the middle class, but rather a transfer from working families to stock-owning, upper-income families.

There has also been a profound asymmetry in the battle over bankruptcy laws. The creditors are well-funded and experienced. They can make savvy decisions about how much they would profit from reducing the bankruptcy filing rate by a few percentage points. There is no organized group to oppose them. Families headed for trouble have little access to Congress or little reason to push for fairness in bankruptcy laws—until the moment they find themselves on the steps to the bankruptcy courthouse. Consumer bankruptcy lawyers are better financed than their clients, but they have little left over for Washington campaigning. A few public interest groups have gotten involved, but there is no group for which bankruptcy is the first—or even the tenth—priority. It is little wonder that U.S. Senator Russell Feingold once described the bankruptcy bill as "the poster child for campaign finance reform."

Bankruptcy laws may seem a little obscure. They are complex in the extreme, and the diversity of users—from the neighbor who lost a job to the multibillion dollar corporation—makes it hard to get a firm fix on how the system operates. But make no mistake: the efforts to amend the bankruptcy rules were an attack on the middle class. The campaign has been well-funded and ferociously pursued, even as more families face the risks of job losses, no health insurance, and a mounting pile of debts.

There is nothing subtle about the struggle over the bankruptcy laws. No one denies that the money, organization, and influence are all on one side. Many think that this combination of benefits meant that the outcome was foretold.

Notes

1. I thank Brady Williamson both for his extraordinary leadership of the National Bankruptcy Review Commission and for his help with this chapter.

2. In 2002, 2 million people filed for bankruptcy (including both husbands and wives who filed jointly). By comparison, 1.1 million Americans had a first or a recurrent coronary attack. AM. HEART ASS'N, TARGETING THE FACTS: OUR QUICK GUIDE TO HEART DISEASE, STROKE AND RISKS (2002), *available at* http://www.americanheart.org/downloadable/heart/1014993119046targetfact.pdf (last visited Feb. 14, 2003). Approximately 1,284,900 new cancer cases were diagnosed. AM. CANCER SOC'Y, CANCER FACTS AND FIGURES 2002, *available at* http://www.cancer.org/downloads/STT/CancerFacts&Figures2002TM.pdf (last visited Feb. 14, 2003). In 2001, American universities and colleges awarded 1.2 million bachelor's degrees. NAT'L CTR. FOR EDUC. STATISTICS, U.S. DEP'T OF EDUC., TABLE 247, EARNED DEGREES CONFERRED BY DEGREE-GRANTING INSTITUTIONS, BY LEVEL OF DEGREE AND SEX OF STUDENT: 1869–70 to 2010–11 (August 2001), *available at* http://nces.ed.gov/pubs2002/digest2001/tables/dt247.asp (last visited Feb. 14, 2003). In 2000, there were 1.1 million divorces in the United States, compared with 1.5 million bankruptcy filings. Calculated from CTRS. FOR DISEASE CONTROL AND PREVENTION, BIRTHS, MARRIAGES, DIVORCES, AND DEATHS: PROVISIONAL DATA FOR 2001, 50 NATIONAL VITAL STATISTICS REPORT (Sept. 11, 2002). Bankruptcy data from Administrative Office of the United States Courts, including unpublished data on joint filings.

3. FED. RESERVE BD., SEMIANNUAL REPORT TO THE CONGRESS (July 20, 2004) (testimony of Alan Greenspan).

4. Calculations from ALLEN GROMMET, CAMBRIDGE CONSUMER CREDIT INDEX (Mar. 5, 2004), *available at* www.CambridgeConsumerIndex.com. Of those surveyed, 41 percent were taking on more debt. Of those, 51 percent were taking on more debt they were confident they could repay, while 49 percent said they had no other option because they could not pay their bills.

5. Michelle J. White, *Why It Pays to File for Bankruptcy: A Critical Look at the Incentives under U.S. Personal Bankruptcy Law and a Proposal for Change*, 65 U. CHI. L. REV. 685 (1998).

6. While some families have large medical debts when they file for bankruptcy, a substantial amount of medical costs will already have been translated into consumer debt. Credit cards, payday loans, and second mortgages may have been used to pay doctors and hospitals, but by the time of the bankruptcy filing, these debts are listed in the files as straightforward consumer debts. Melissa Jacoby et al., *Rethinking the Debates over Health Care Financing: Evidence from the Bankruptcy Courts*, 76 N.Y.U. L. Rev. 375, 383 (2001).

7. Elizabeth Warren, *Financial Collapse and Class Status: Who Goes Bankrupt?* 41 Osgoode Hall L.J. 115 (2003).

8. Bruce H. Mann, Neighbors and Strangers: Law and Community in Early Connecticut 14 (1987).

9. http://www.cardweb.com/cardlearn/faqs/2003/november/24.xcml (last visited Aug. 2, 2004).

10. At the end of 2003, holdings were ranked by receivables as follows:

1. JPMorganChase/Bank One 19.3 percent

2. Citigroup 17.3 percent

3. MBNA 12.9 percent

4. American Express 11.1 percent

5. Bank of America/Fleet 8.3 percent

6. Capital One 7.5 percent

7. Discover 7.2 percent

8. HSBC 2.7 percent

9. Providian 2.5 percent

10. Wells Fargo 1.9 percent

All the Rest 9.3 percent

Nilson Report, Issue 803 (Jan. 2004), *available at* http://www.nilsonreport.com/issues/2004/803.htm.

11. Christine Dugas, *Credit Card Fees Become Cash Cow*, USA Today, July 13, 2004, at A1.

12. At Citibank, a company with mixed product lines, their credit cards have the highest returns among the various product lines, with the possible exception of private banking. Citigroup, Risk Capital and Capital Allocation 17 (Mar. 29, 2004), *available at* http://www.citigroup.com/citigroup/fin/data/p040329.pdf (last visited August 11, 2004). For 2003, Capital One, MBNA, and American Express enjoyed a Net Interest Margin on Average Earning Assets of 9.65 percent, 8.39 percent, and 9.21 percent respectively. This compares rather favorably to the average return of 3.66 percent for the top fifty banks and thrifts. Company Reports, SNL DataSource, KBW Research (2004).

13. Typical families filing for bankruptcy owe more than a year's worth of income in credit card and other consumer debt. Christine Dugas, *Middle Class Barely Treads Water*, USA Today, Sept. 15, 2003, available at http://www.usatoday

.com/money/perfi/general/2003-09-14-middle-cover_x.htm (citing 2001 study by Harvard University's Consumer Bankruptcy Project).

14. In 2004, the American Bankers Association reported that about 4.43 percent of credit card accounts were in default. *Credit Card Delinquencies Set Record High*, 14 CONSUMER BANKR. NEWS 1 (Apr. 16, 2004).

15. In 2003, for example, about 0.38 percent of mortgages were in foreclosure. That is considerably higher than the 0.13 percent in foreclosure in 1979, but still much lower than the delinquency rate of 4.43 percent on credit card accounts. MORTGAGE BANKERS ASS'N, MORTGAGE FORECLOSURE DATA (2004).

16. In re Blair, No. 02-11400 (Bankr. W.D.N.C.) (Feb. 10, 2004).

17. In re Mitchell, No. 04-10493 (Bankr. E.D. Va.) (July 14, 2004).

18. For a more in-depth discussion of the industry charges and its pseudoresearch, see Elizabeth Warren, *The Market for Data: The Changing Role of the Social Sciences in Changing the Law*, 2002 WIS. L. REV. 1.

19. *See* Ed Flynn & Gordon Bermant, *Bankruptcy by the Numbers: Lifestyles of the Rich and Bankrupt*, 19 AM. BANKR. INST. J. 22 (2000), *available at* http://www .justice.gov/ust/press/articles/abi800.htm.

20. For a business, Chapter 7 essentially means liquidation. Chapter 11, however, gives the business a chance to fight on if it can confirm a plan of reorganization to make some payments in the future and discharge some of its debts.

21. Elizabeth Warren & Jay Westbrook, *Financial Characteristics of Businesses in Bankruptcy*, 73 AM. BANKR. L.J. 499 (1999) (66 percent of cases had less than $1 million in debts).

22. *See* Warren, *supra* note 18; Elizabeth Warren, *The Phantom $400*, 13 J. BANKR. L. & PRACT. 77 (2004).

23. For details, see *supra* note 12.

24. Percentage of All Families:

Families holding no assets in retirement accounts	47.8
Families holding no assets in stocks	78.7
Families holding no assets in mutual funds	82.3

FED. RESERVE BD., 2001 SURVEY OF CONSUMER FINANCE (Table 5.E, Public data, Family holdings of financial assets, by selected characteristics of families and type of assets, 1989, 1992, 1995, 1998 and 2001 surveys), *available at* http://www.fed-eralreserve.gov/pubs/oss/oss2/2001/scf2001home.html#summary.

15

The Misfortunes of the Family Farm

Paul Y. K. Castle

The United States is a nation of abundance. We walk into a chain grocery store expecting to find—and, indeed, almost feeling that it is our right to find—aisles and aisles of shelf and refrigerator space filled and stacked with meats, fresh produce, dairy products, seafood, cereals, bread, pasta, wines, cheeses, candy, cooking oils, and health foods. Truly, there is no end to this list. And we expect these food products to be available in large quantities, at modest prices, and in the best condition imaginable, regardless of their growing season or their place of origin. That is our way of life.

Few know the social cost of this abundance. There are those who prefer to shop at Whole Foods stores because they are concerned about the unknown effects of genetically modified food products, dairy and beef cattle injected with growth hormones, chickens raised on antibiotics and animal by-products, and the like. Some are appalled at the cruelty to animals involved in industrialized meat production and for that reason boycott consumption of meats altogether.

However, most appear to be unaware of another unfortunate feature of American agriculture in the last quarter century. A great many American family farmers, caught in a whirlpool of pressures and demands for which they were largely unprepared, have found themselves quickly going out of business or being reduced to one anomalous link in a food-production chain otherwise consisting of the world's most powerful and concentrated companies. Responsibility for the rapid demise of the American family farmer, once an icon for independent, reliable, and courageous citizenry, rests not only with agribusiness firms maximizing profits, but with the federal and state judiciaries who have shaped the law to reshape the rights of small farmers to the advantage of these megafirms.

I. Then and Now

Until the mid-twentieth century, traditional farms were operated by families owning them in fee simple and making a living off their own land. The farms were operated in a highly *diversified* and highly *integrated* manner. As noted by one commentator, a half dozen standard field crops, two or three cash crops, some wasteland in pasture, a half dozen or more cows, a team of horses, a hundred chickens, some pigs, an orchard, a garden, a woodlot, swamp, pond—all of those and more were packed into the eighty-acre family farm. On such farms, each element was tied to the others. The farmer "hauled the hay that fed the cows that fertilized the fields that grew the grain that thickened the milk that fattened the pigs that supplied the bacon that fed the family that hauled the hay."[1]

This mode of agriculture—rooted in tradition, diversified, hand and horse powered, extremely labor intensive, not particularly efficient, but relatively self-sufficient—was, in important ways, a system of small hedges against total failure. "[T]he potatoes might be blighted one year, but the bean crop could be depended upon; milk prices might drop, but egg prices would hold; if not, [farmers] could sell some chickens, feed the grain to the cows, and sell cream."[2] The rhythms and variables of small-time mixed farming were precisely geared to all major demands of the system—feeding the family, cash flow, insurance against hard times, predictability, and paying off the mortgage on the farm itself steadily over the course of three decades or less.

On a family farm, projects and commitments, as well as the objects with which the farmer worked—such as flocks, fields, and tools—had a scale that was manageable. Every farmer knew his own land intimately, understanding its strengths and weaknesses. To a very large extent, the produce of that land was on his family's dinner table. And every farmer knew his neighbors, and worked with them. In harvesttime, neighbors exchanged work, each lending a hand to the other. On the whole, farm families found themselves in a harmony of many and diverse elements, with farm, family, work, crops, animals, neighbors, community, ecosystem, woodlots, gardens, worship, leisure—all coalescing to shape community life.[3]

However, the heroic days of the self-sufficient farm with its varied crops and animals are long gone as pressures of industrialization have increased, making traditional modes of farming economically unviable. A great many small farmers, suddenly finding themselves unfit—and, indeed, almost irrelevant—in the face of a radically altered rural dynamic, have chosen to leave the countryside in search of an uncertain future in urban settings. For example, 1990 census data show that Iowa's farm population declined by 34 percent during the 1980s with nearly 135,000 people deserting the farmland. Similar or steeper drops were recorded in Illinois, Minnesota, and Missouri. In 1993, only 9 percent of the Iowa population was classified as rural while 61 percent was urban.[4]

Industrialized agriculture is everything that traditional mixed farming was not: specialized, consolidated, vertically integrated, contracted out, and globally intertwined. Most farmers today—unlike the traditional farmer who lived by the creed of crop diversification—specialize in just one crop, aiming to maximize efficiency in its production and marketing. In such a setting, each farmer indirectly competes, for markets and efficiency, with every other farmer raising the same commodity. This naturally gives rise to a process where large farms, wholesalers, or processors absorb their smaller neighbors or competitors because such consolidations result in economies of scale. Indicating the extent of market consolidations presently under way, in mid-2003 81 percent of all beef consumed in the United States was processed by four firms: Tyson-IBP, ConAgra Beef, Cargill, and Farmland National. In broilers, sales by the four largest processors made up 50 percent of the total. In hogs, the top six processors slaughtered three-quarters of the nation's entire herd, up from one-third in 1989.

Large agribusiness firms tend to be vertically integrated. A vertically integrated corporation—with, for example, the harvester, the wholesaler, the processor, and the distributor all under one owner—not only exercises control over a large portion of the food production-distribution chain, but also tends to bargain with any market participant not part of its system from a position of superior strength. Small farmers, in particular hog and poultry farmers, raise their products under a production contract with a huge integrator or processor. Production contracts provide the only means of assuring the farmers a fixed market and price for their products. But, for reasons explained herein, many farmers under production contracts soon realize that they have made a pact with the devil.

Not only are American farmers in direct competition with one another, they are also competing with producers from other countries. Market changes in another part of the globe can have an immediate impact on prices and profitability in the U.S. agricultural markets. In an industry driven by ever-rising production efficiency, it has been American consumers who come out on top. In the year 2000, on average Americans spent about 10 percent of their income on food. In 1950, they spent 30 percent. In 1990, farmers received 21 cents out of every dollar spent on agriculture. Today, they get a nickel, with the difference being absorbed by seed, chemical, fertilizer, equipment, and processing companies.[5] In a contest shaped by market structure and technology, giant agribusiness corporations are the winners.

The full costs of industrialized agriculture extend beyond the experiences of the farmer. Billions of dollars of taxpayers' money are paid out each year to industrial agriculture in the form of direct farm crop subsidies. Also, large-scale, technology-driven, factory farming has wreaked havoc on the landscape and the environment through fertilizer runoffs polluting rivers and groundwater, through haphazardly applied pesticides, and through huge fields that lack breaks against erosion. Many of the elements belonging to this widening circle of unmeasured and hidden problems that arise from the new mode of farming affect the American people in a multitude of ways in their health, safety, insurance costs, and pocketbook, thus presenting important policy challenges to those responsible on the state and federal level.

A legal dimension of this development arises from industrialized agriculture's practice of imposing production contracts that squeeze the small farmer while simultaneously leaving her without legal recourse to redress wrongs suffered. This use of standard form contracts between parties of unequal bargaining power is also addressed elsewhere in this volume and is not a uniquely agricultural problem.

II. The Plight of Contract Farmers

Consider the plight of chicken growers working under production contracts. The use of such contracts is not limited to poultry or hog farming, but is becoming common practice for many commodities, including many fruits and vegetables. The poultry industry, however, is a leader in this field, and therefore provides a useful illustration of agribusiness's abuse of power.

Until the 1930s, farmers raised chickens and shipped them to urban centers where vendors sold the birds live or with only the blood and feathers removed. Today, corporate poultry processors control almost all aspects of poultry production, from raising, slaughtering, and cleaning the birds, to packaging and distributing the final product, ready to cook, to grocery stores and supermarkets throughout the country.[6] As of 1999, the five largest companies—Tyson Foods, Gold Kist, Perdue Farms, Pilgrim's Pride, and ConAgra—controlled more than half the business in the industry and processed more than 226 million pounds of poultry each week.

These processors are known as integrators because they own the birds, control the farming techniques used to raised them, process the birds, and put the final product on the market. Typically, integrators do not buy products from independent farmers, but instead contract with farmers for the labor and services necessary to raise the livestock they, the integrators, own. Some estimates suggest that 99 percent of the poultry in America is produced by integrators and that 86 percent of the total value of poultry production results from such a contractual arrangement. In a production contract between integrator and farmer, the company agrees to provide the farmer with day-old chicks and adequate feed, medicine, and management direction to keep the birds alive and growing during the six weeks before they are ready to be shipped to the slaughterhouse. The farmer, or grower, agrees to provide the land, buildings, equipment, utilities, and her time and effort in feeding and caring for the birds.

In order to enter the business, a contract farmer must first build chicken houses, generally at least two at about $128,000 apiece.[7] The hopeful grower is required to make this investment before he or she signs a contract to grow poultry for an integrator. The federal government plays a facilitating role in the financing of contract farming ventures by guaranteeing up to 90 percent of the value of certain loans made to farmers. Government guarantees lower the risks to lenders and make it easier for farmers to obtain loans necessary for building expensive poultry houses— the bottom line being that in the event of foreclosure on a loan, taxpayers will help make up 90 percent of the difference between the amount the bank is owed and what it can recoup when the collateralized property— the farmer's family farm, in most cases—is auctioned off.

In contrast to the significant investments that growers must make to receive a production contract, the typical contract has the duration of one flock, which is about seven weeks.[8] The result is that, once the promissory note for the loans has been signed, growers must, on an ongoing basis, live with the fear that their integrator may, at any point, decide not to renew their contract, leaving them with no income to repay the loans. If a grower mortgaged her farm to secure a loan for a chicken house, as is frequently done, the farm would be subject to foreclosure.[9]

A grower's first big loan is unlikely to be his last, because most production contracts require that the grower make any improvements deemed necessary by the integrator at the grower's expense. As a practical matter, a grower is generally told by the integrator's representative that his contract will not be renewed unless he complies with the improvement requests; it is not uncommon for the required improvements to cost from $5,000 to $30,000. Integrators sometimes require farmers to install unproven new equipment, as in the case of one integrator's requirement that chicken houses be equipped with expensive cooling systems even though loss of birds due to heat had never been a problem. Nevertheless, most growers cannot refuse to make such added investments because they have mortgaged their farms to build the chicken houses. Refusing to make requested improvements will mean loss of the production contract, which in turn means loss of the income to service the debts, which in turn means foreclosure on the farm. Instead of losing the farm, growers frequently take jobs in town to fund the improvements, thus giving rise to the sad irony that they subsidize the poultry business rather than derive income from it.[10]

Growers get paid through a ranking system. All growers who received baby chicks on the same day are ranked based on the weight and feed conversion efficiency (FCE) of the birds they raised. The net effect of the ranking system is that growers must compete for their shares in a pool of money predetermined by the integrators. In this artificial economy conjured up by poultry integrators, half or more of the growers must receive below-average pay, even if they are vigilant and efficient. If a grower ends up at or near the bottom of the pecking order twice or more, her contract is unlikely to be renewed.

While integrators may defend the system as a quintessentially American way of life—where whoever does best earns the most money—growers point out that key variables of success—that is, factors that largely determine the birds' weight and FCE—are exclusively within the integrators' control. A farmer may, by accident or by design, get a weak flock while her neighbor may receive a strong one. According to an integrator representative's deposition statement, sick chicks were intentionally placed with certain growers to set them up to fail.[11] Feed deliveries, too, create plenty of room for mistrust, as they are weighed at the feed mill and not at the grower's farm. Another factor is that each delay, at the farm and at the factory, in weighing the birds can cost the grower poundage. Finally, some integrators are known to have cheated at the scales. In *Braswell v. ConAgra, Inc.*,[12] a class of growers proved that ConAgra had deliberately undervalued the weight of the finished birds by using false weights. Similarly, one former employee of Cargill admitted in deposition that Cargill's employees had used a forklift to prevent the full weight of trucks loaded with chickens from resting on the scales.

Here is the bottom line. In the 1950s there were more than a thousand companies competing to offer production contracts to chicken growers. Today there are fewer than fifty, with just a handful carrying the most clout. The stock of Tyson Foods Inc., the largest of the poultry integrators, is worth nearly two hundred times what it was twenty-five years ago. On the other hand, a new poultry farmer today can expect a net income of $8,160 per year—about half the poverty level for a family of four—until the fifteen-year loan he took to get into the business is paid off. The cause is no mystery. Gold Kist, a major integrator, for example, currently pays its growers five cents per pound. A 1999 Purdue University survey of one thousand chicken farmers showed that half of them had a total farm debt of more than $100,000.[13]

Unsurprisingly, there is much anecdotal evidence that a fair number of poultry-growing ventures end up in foreclosure. It is difficult to say how many because the government does not track foreclosures and integrators are seldom forthcoming about how many of their contract growers did not make it.

Then, why do so many farmers sign on to grow poultry for integrators? Most companies boast of waiting lists of people wanting to become growers and of existing farmers wanting to add capacity by building more chicken houses. Several factors may explain this state of affairs. First, integrators tend to recruit growers in economically depressed regions, where farmers are more likely to be eager for the promised income of production contracts and less likely to be wary of integrators' bargaining advantage. For example, in 1998 integrators began recruiting heavily from among tobacco farmers in Kentucky, as the future market for their tobacco crop was becoming increasingly bleak.

Second, in their recruitment drives, integrators use cheery promotional ads ("Invest in part-time work for full-time pay," "This is the best job I've ever had, and I've had some good jobs," etc.) and optimistic income projections that highlight gross, not net, pay. A recent Perdue newspaper ad suggested a possible minimum annual gross income of more than $26,500, one "you can't get from crops or livestock."[14] Another integrator is said to hand out to potential growers a glossy pamphlet, entitled Partners in Profit, containing sample income projections, which are, unbeknownst to the farmers, sometimes based on bonuses awarded for being a "top performer."

Third, growers sign on with integrators because they are lured by the specter of income stability. In theory, because contract growers are guaranteed a fixed price for the commodity grown, they do not bear the risk of price fluctuations, as do farmers who compete on the open market. However, few growers getting into the business are aware that under unfavorable market conditions integrators are likely to terminate contracts with growers.[15]

III. A Judiciary out of Step with Agricultural Realities

While there are a number of statutory remedies available for growers— such as those provided for in the Packers and Stockyards Act ("PSA") and the Agricultural Fairness Practices Act ("AFPA")—these remedies are not sufficiently comprehensive to address all the growers' concerns. Crucially, although the PSA prohibits termination of contracts without economic justification, the Act offers no assistance to growers who make huge capital investments as a condition of winning short-term contracts only to find themselves unable to secure the contract renewals necessary to repay the loans.[16] The job of enforcing legitimate claims for fraud and breach of contract that are not covered by statute devolves on federal and state courts. However, the judiciary, as much as any other government body, has been out of step with the realities on the ground in rural America. I offer four illustrations.

In *Starling v. Valmac Industries*,[17] the Starlings, at the prompting of Valmac, applied in 1970 for a $17,500 loan to build new chicken houses. This loan was to be secured by a mortgage on their forty-acre family farm. The lender, obviously concerned about Starling's ability to repay the loan, inquired whether his business relationship with Valmac would last for the life of the loan. When contacted, a Valmac representative represented to the Starlings and the lending agency that as long as the Starlings continued to perform satisfactorily, "there was no reason to believe that Valmac would not continue to supply them with chicks."[18] Although the Valmac representative did not bind his company to continuing its business relationship with the Starlings over any particular length of time, the Starlings and the lending agency were led to count on continued delivery of chicks by Valmac to the Starlings for a substantial duration of time over the life of the loan. Within five years of making this representation, however, Valmac terminated its business relationship with the Starlings, citing the long distance between the processing facility and the Starlings' farm as the reason.

The court dismissed the plaintiff's breach of contract claim, holding that the relationship between the parties was governed exclusively by their written contract. Under that contract, the court concluded that Valmac had an unqualified right not to renew contractual relations with the Starlings. Importantly, the court invoked the parol evidence rule to exclude evidence of the parties' oral agreement, even though it acknowledged the widely accepted inapplicability of that rule "where the promissory representations were made fraudulently for the purpose of inducing the party sought to be charged to enter into the contract."[19] But the court found no fraud on Valmac's part in inducing the Starlings to enter the contract. It explained that should the oral representations be deemed admissible, the Starlings would still not have a cause of action because they at most had "a reasonable expectation" that "other things being equal they could expect to continue to receive chicks for the foreseeable business future."[20] This expectation, according to the court, did not amount to a contract right, and the Starlings had no reason to think that it did.[21]

A similar result was reached in *Hinkle v. Cargill, Inc.*[22] In this case, the Hinkles initially balked at obtaining the $240,000 loan necessary to finance construction of cage-type chicken houses with a sixty-thousand chicken capacity, because the income estimates made by a Cargill representative, Griffin, did not seem sufficiently large to allow repayment of the loan in seven years as required by the bank. According to Mr. Hinkle, within a few weeks he was contacted and asked by Griffin to consider the option of obtaining a construction loan with a longer term for repayment. Griffin allegedly represented to Hinkle that if the Hinkles constructed the proposed chicken houses and served as satisfactory egg producers for Cargill, then Cargill would supply chickens for these chicken houses for the whole duration of the long-term loan, which was, in this case, twenty years.

When they were then offered a one-year written contract by Cargill, the Hinkles asked Griffin about the potential effect of the contract's merger clause on Griffin's oral representation that Cargill would continue to supply chickens until the construction loan was repaid. Griffin allegedly told the Hinkles that the written contract was a "working contract" covering the particular flock and that Cargill's commitment to provide chickens for the entire duration of the loan would stand, regardless of the contract. Cargill eventually sold its operations to another poultry company, which discontinued its relationship with the Hinkles.

The Hinkle court dismissed both the Hinkles' breach of contract claim and their fraud claim. The reasoning was that unless the Hinkles could show that Cargill acted with intent to defraud, not only the fraud claim but also the breach of contract claim must be set aside, because the latter claim, based on an oral agreement, was subject to the Statute of Frauds. Not surprisingly, the Hinkles were deemed to have produced insufficient evidence to show intent to defraud on Cargill's part. In the court's view, even though Cargill failed to provide the Hinkles with chickens as its agent had promised, this did not prove that Cargill never intended to supply chickens for twenty years as promised. Therefore, there was no fraud.

The court in *Smith v. Central Soya, Inc.*[23] reached a similar conclusion in dealing with oral representations made by an industry representative. In this case, the Smiths were allegedly promised by agents of Central Soya that Central Soya "would continue putting chickens in the houses" and that the Smiths "would have an income for twenty years on the poultry houses."[24] Relying on these representations, the Smiths invested considerable sums in constructing four chicken houses. However, each written contract offered them by Central Soya was for one year only, and Mr. Smith admitted that he had not asked Central Soya to put the twenty-year term into their contracts. As it turned out, Central Soya's operations were sold to another company after some time, and the new company soon thereafter ceased supplying chickens for the Smiths' chicken houses. The Smiths' suit never proceeded beyond the pleading stage because the court concluded that neither their breach of contract claim nor their fraud claim stated a cause of action. In disposing of the breach of contract claim arising from Central Soya's oral representations, the court found that the merger clause in the parties' contracts created a rebuttable presumption that the writings were a "complete and exclusive statement of the contract terms."[25]

The Smiths failed to rebut that presumption because insufficient evidence was offered to establish "the existence of fraud, bad faith, unconscionability, negligent omission or mistake in fact."[26] That the merger clause was offered to the Smiths on a non-negotiable basis as part of a preprinted form contract did not persuade the court that it was unfair. The Smiths "did not have to enter into the contracts,"[27] the court opined. Nor did the court think that there was any evidence that the Smiths were under economic duress or occupied an inferior bargaining position. That the Smiths had already made huge investments in the chicken houses by the time they were asked to sign the written contract drafted by Central Soya was a fact that did not count for much in the court's estimation.

The evidence of oral representations by Central Soya's agents that their company would supply chickens for the Smiths' chicken houses for twenty years was excluded qua inadmissible parol evidence. And with respect to the fraud claim, the Smiths had "alleged a promissory representation by Central Soya of its intent to supply chickens *in the future*,"[28] but a breach of such a promise would not give rise to an action for fraud unless the promisor—Central Soya, in this case—had no intent to carry out the promise when made.

These cases illustrate a pattern that seems to pervade judicial decisions dealing with poultry farming cases. Oral terms, even though negotiated by the parties and duly relied upon by growers, are disregarded in favor of written instruments drafted by integrators whose agents exploit the misplaced trust of farmers inexperienced in making deals. If courts were to give effect to oral agreements between integrators and growers, then growers' contractual rights would rightly be protected and the effects of the parties' unequal bargaining power would be mitigated to some extent.

A seemingly contrasting case is *Braswell v. ConAgra, Inc.*[29] In *Braswell*, a class of 268 farmers raising poultry for ConAgra sued for fraud and breach of contract, alleging that ConAgra intentionally misweighed chickens over an eight-year period. The growers eventually prevailed after a jury trial, and they obtained an award of $4.55 million in compensatory damages and $9.1 million in punitive damages. Crucially, the growers in *Braswell* based their breach of contract claim on ConAgra's written promise that the farmers were going to be paid based on the weight of the chickens raised. The court found that ConAgra's failure properly to weigh the chickens constituted a breach of that promise. In a similar vein, the growers' fraudulent misrepresentation claim was tied to a provision of their production contract stating that ConAgra would provide the farmers with an accurate report of the birds' weight. The court found that ConAgra employees' conduct in misweighing the birds and representing to the farmers that the weights were accurate, when coupled with the farmers' reliance on the weights to their detriment, created a cause of action for fraud.

Braswell was certainly good news to farmers, as it offers hope to those who are able to ground their claims on specific provisions of written contracts. However, on a deeper level, the result reached in *Braswell* does not depart from the pattern of adjudication emerging from the cases reviewed earlier. In *Braswell*, as in the other cases, the written contract between the parties—not the oral agreements between them—was the basis for the enforcement of rights. ConAgra transgressed even the self-imposed limits on predatory conduct written into their production contracts.

The law being administered in these examples rests on a lack of understanding that the written contract between an integrator and a grower is not a contract negotiated by two commercial enterprises. Commercial enterprises assisted by legal counsel will, and should, take the time and care to negotiate each item of their contractual agreements, with attention to niceties and pitfalls of the law. However, the typical grower is not usually in a position to dot the i's and cross the t's. By the time a grower is asked to sign a production contract drafted by an integrator, the grower has already obtained a loan in the amount of $250,000 or more to finance the project, using the family farm as collateral. Typically, growers are not represented by counsel. Buried in debt, they lack bargaining power. In such a situation, Samuel Williston himself might not try to negotiate before signing the contract.

It is also pertinent that the poultry industry is dominated by just a handful of major players nationwide, with one integrator or at most two operating in a region. Consequently, the existing imbalance of bargaining power between a grower and an integrator is magnified to an even greater degree, because a grower whose contract has been terminated by one integrator will, almost certainly, not be able to secure a contract with any other integrator. Naturally, bearing down on the grower is the weight of the inescapable Aristotelian syllogism that losing the contract means losing the income to repay the loan and losing the income to repay the loan means losing the family farm. For these reasons, cases such as *Braswell* offer scant comfort. Integrators can run their serfdoms as they wish if they remain strictly within the bounds of written contracts whose terms they largely control.

It bears notice that the legal principles used by the courts in these four cases would not have applied if the contracts had involved foreign integrators. In transactions governed by the Vienna Convention on the International Sale of Goods, there is no parol evidence rule justifying the exclusion of testimony about oral agreements. Extending international law to these cases would reverse the adverse result in three of them.

IV. Mandatory Arbitration

Poultry integrators have taken an additional step to redefine their relationships with growers by requiring growers to consent to predispute arbitration clauses included in production contracts. Predispute arbitration clauses offered in this non-negotiable fashion are bad news for growers. Proceeding in a forum in which their procedural rights are reduced diminishes the likelihood that growers will be able to enforce any contractual or other substantive rights they might have.[30] Critically, much of a poultry grower's case is generally built on information obtained in discovery.[31] Yet, arbitral forums often limit discovery rights. In addition, arbitrating a claim can be more costly than a judicial proceeding, again making it more difficult for cash-strapped farmers to obtain relief.

For integrators, however, it makes sense to impose mandatory predispute arbitration clauses on growers. Unconscionable though it may be to insert disadvantageous predispute arbitration clauses into the preprinted production contracts offered to growers on a take-it-or-leave-it basis, courts will give effect to these clauses so long as they are part of a written instrument. There are currently two cases pending in the Mississippi State Supreme Court in which the main issue is whether a mandatory arbitration clause included in a poultry production contract should be given effect.[32] It remains to be seen how the court is going to decide the issue. Given the preemptive effect lately assigned to the Federal Arbitration Act, the Mississippi court can invalidate the mandatory arbitration clauses only by holding that the contracts are unconscionable as a matter of Mississippi law.

The recent moves by poultry integrators to insert mandatory arbitration clauses are but one example of the ways in which agribusiness corporations can stay ahead of small farmers. Another example comes from recent developments in tobacco farming. Until recently, most tobacco farmers owned and raised their crop based on federal quotas and looked to auction houses as the main market for their commodity. Over the years, however, the six industry giants (Phillip Morris, R. J. Reynolds, American Brands, Lorillard, Liggett, and Brown & Williamson) have engaged in multiple practices making auction houses economically nonviable. Many auction houses have closed. Without auction houses to serve as an alternative market for their crop, tobacco farmers will have no more bargaining power with tobacco companies than do poultry growers with poultry integrators.[33]

V. Conclusion

The poultry industry persists in calling poultry growers "independent contractors." This designation, however, does the growers no good; it merely removes them from the coverage of the National Labor Relations Act. Poultry growers are not independent contractors in any practical sense. They are, in practical terms, low-paid employees who are required to mortgage their farms as a condition of working at all. Seen this way, what befalls many poultry farmers is not simply the failure of a commercial relationship, but a regression to feudalism.

NOTES

1. RONALD JAGER, EIGHTY ACRES: ELEGY FOR A FAMILY FARM 14 (1990).

2. *Id.* at 13–14.

3. RONALD JAGER, THE FATE OF FAMILY FARMING: VARIATIONS ON AN AMERICAN IDEA 27 (2004).

4. Neil D. Hamilton, *Feeding Our Future: Six Philosophical Issues Shaping Agricultural Law*, 72 NEB. L. REV. 210, 217 (1993).

5. Jedediah Purdy, *The New Culture of Rural America*, AM. PROSPECT ONLINE (Dec. 20, 1999), *available at* http://www.prospect.org/print/V11/3/purdy-j.html.

6. Edward P. Lord, *Fairness for Modern Farmers: Reconsidering the Need for Legislation Governing Production Contracts*, 33 WAKE FOREST L. REV. 1125, 1125 (1998).

7. Dan Fesperman & Kate Shatzkin, *The Plucking of the American Chicken Farmer*, BALTIMORE SUN, Feb. 28–Mar. 2, 1999 (three-part series on the chicken industry).

8. The contracts for egg farmers are generally longer (twelve months) because egg layer houses are more expensive than broiler houses.

9. Lord, *supra* note 6, at 1125, 1132.

10. Randi Ilyse Roth, *Redressing Unfairness in the New Agricultural Labor Arrangements: An Overview of Litigation Seeking Remedies for Contract Poultry Growers*, 25 U. MEM. L. REV. 1207, 1211–12 (1995).

11. *Id.* at 1207, 1212.

12. 936 F.2d 1169 (11th Cir. 1991).

13. Monte Mitchell, *Some You Lose: Raising Poultry for the Big Boys Can Quite Suddenly Turn into a Losing Proposition*, Cheap Smokes! June 20, 2004, *available at* http://www.rafiusa.org/programs/CONTRACTAG/NC_WSJ_poultrycontracts_part1.

14. Fesperman and Shatzkin, *supra* note 7.

15. Lord, *supra* note 6, at 1125, 1129.

16. Lord, *supra* note 6, at 1125, 1142.

17. 589 F.2d 382 (8th Cir. 1979).

18. *Id.* at 385.

19. *Id.* at 386.

20. *Id.* at 387.

21. *Id.* The court also dismissed the plaintiff's fraud claim without discussion, holding that there was no evidence that would justify submission of the issue to a jury.

22. 613 So.2d 1216 (Ala. 1992).

23. 604 F. Supp. 518 (E.D.N.C. 1985).

24. *Id.* at 522.

25. *Id.* at 526.

26. *Id.*

27. *Id.* at 527.

28. *Id.* at 530 (emphasis added).

29. 936 F.2d 1169 (11th Cir. 1991).

30. The procedural rights that may be lost in arbitration are "the rights to (1) a convenient forum, (2) trial by jury, (3) a public hearing, (4) an impartial judge, (5) a judge who is accountable to a higher court for his or her adherence to the governing law, (6) exemplary or treble damages, if provided by controlling law, (7) provisional remedies such as preliminary injunctions or attachments, (8) the traditional American rule with respect to the taxation of attorneys' fees, (9) the right to conduct a private investigation of possible wrong doing and gain access to the information of an adversary through the use of modern discovery rules, and (10) the right to participate in class action." Paul D. Carrington, *Unconscionable Lawyers*, 19 Ga. St. U. L. Rev. 361, 362 (2002).

31. Roth, *supra* note 10, at 1207, 1230.

32. *See* Kenney Austin v. Sanderson Farms, Inc., No. 02-0225; Tanya Ballard v. Sanderson Farms, Inc., No. 2000-0246.

33. I am indebted to Keith Parrish, a tobacco farmer in Harnett County, North Carolina, for this account.

16

Health Law and the Broken Promise of Equity

M. Gregg Bloche and Lawrence O. Gostin

On its surface, American health law is committed to equality. It takes a dim view of efforts to lower standards of medical care on economic grounds, promises poor people access to mainstream care through public programs, and bars racially disparate treatment by caregivers. Likewise, public health regulation purports to address populationwide risk with a blind eye toward socioeconomic status. Indeed, many in public health seek reductions in socioeconomic disparities. But, just as the poor have always been with us, so has the divergence between what health law says and what it does about social and economic inequity. Over the past generation, this gap has widened. In this chapter, we point to evidence of this growing divergence and then try to explain it.

Americans, we will argue, still view health and medical care as "different"—as things that, unlike ownership of cars or clothing, should not be by-products of prevailing distributions of wealth. This conviction has pushed courts and legislators to reject overt efforts to tie health services to status and wealth. Yet the law has relaxed its limits on the tacit translation of status and wealth into advantages in medical care and health.

A confluence of factors explains this change. American culture more openly tolerates the expression and enjoyment of wealth and privilege, and it is more inclined to treat people's disparate life circumstances as a matter of personal responsibility. Meanwhile, voters have become more skeptical of the government's ability to ameliorate the harshest consequences of economic and social disadvantage. Polarizing debates about faith and race have supplanted discussions of economic fairness in political campaigns and the public sphere more generally. Political liberalism, we believe, has been complicit in these trends. Its shift in emphasis, over the past forty years, from issues of economic fairness to questions of cultural expression and personal license has cost disadvantaged Americans dearly, in health and other spheres.

I. Medical Care

For a generation, market-oriented scholars of health care law have urged courts and legislatures to treat medical care and insurance coverage as things to be distributed, like cars and clothing, based on ability and willingness to pay. Egalitarians winced at the prospect of multiple, legally recognized tiers of medical quality, while market enthusiasts celebrated this prospect as an expansion of personal choice. For market enthusiasts, the premise of a single, physician-ordained standard of care was a product of the medical profession's monopolistic control over health care's cost-quality tradeoffs. For health care egalitarians, this premise (however fictional) set needed limits on the extent of wealth-driven variation in care.

A. Medical Malpractice

To the dismay of market purists, courts have so far declined to endorse openly the idea of multiple tiers of health care quality and price. In medical malpractice cases, courts have rejected proposals to permit clinical standards of care to vary by contract, and they have refused to apply lower standards to HMO physicians or other lower-cost providers. To be sure, some judges have allowed rural and community-based providers to plead resource constraints as a defense when plaintiffs allege negligent failure to supply specialized, technology-intensive services. Other courts have tacitly tolerated wealth-related differences in care by invoking such doctrines as the "respectable minority" rule or requiring that medical experts come from similar locales. But judges have refused to recognize multiple economic tiers of care as a basis for determining tort liability.

Socioeconomic status, nonetheless, is a major determinant of the strength of the deterrence signal sent by medical tort law. Wealthier Americans are more likely to file medical malpractice suits, and their higher incomes translate into larger economic damage awards. Higher anticipated awards empower plaintiffs to retain superior attorneys, who can in turn tap into stronger networks of potential experts. To the extent that clinical caregivers respond to these differential incentives, they are more likely to provide higher-intensity service (including costly, state-of-the-art tests and treatments) to their wealthier patients.

B. Insurance Coverage and Medical Necessity

Courts also have resisted health insurers' efforts to construe "medical necessity" provisions with varying degrees of frugality for different tiers of coverage. Even when health plan contract language defines "medical necessity" in cost-conscious terms, judges generally look to professional standards of care as the metric of medical need (and of insurers' duty to provide coverage). When, in 2002, the U.S. Supreme Court upheld laws in more than forty states empowering patients to obtain independent review of coverage denials,[1] the Justices characterized assessment of "medical necessity" as a matter of professional opinion, not contractual interpretation. Formally, at least, the law treats medical need, and thus health plans' duty to provide coverage, as a matter to be determined without regard for resource differences among plans. When insurers' contracts with subscribers set "medical necessity" as the standard for coverage, as virtually all these contracts do, courts base coverage obligations on clinical standards that do not vary by economic tier.

In practice, though, patients' ability to pay has a large impact on legal enforcement of coverage obligations. For the 150 million or more Americans who obtain health insurance through the workplace, the ability to pay out-of-pocket for tests and treatments when health plans deny coverage makes it easier to challenge these denials. In more than forty states, patients able to pay out-of-pocket can demand independent review of coverage denials after they receive (and pay for) treatment. For these patients, reversal of coverage denials yields coverage after-the-fact, in the form of a reimbursement check. But patients who cannot self-pay must obtain independent review—and prevail—as a precondition for getting treatment, unless providers are willing to take the risk of nonpayment.[2] To seek independent review at a moment of medical urgency requires knowledge of this option, the presence of mind to pursue it, and access to lawyers or other advocates. Also helpful are financial resources and help from well-informed friends and family members. For patients who do not seek independent review and who cannot self-pay, denial of coverage is tantamount to denial of care, unless providers are willing to risk nonpayment. Independent review, in short, operates as a more potent enforcement tool for health plan subscribers who can afford to pay out-of-pocket while coverage is in dispute.

During the early 2000s, the threat of liability functioned as a deterrent against questionable coverage denials. Patients who could not self-pay and who therefore went without care could sue in tort for wrongful coverage denial and hope to prevail. Taking cues from Supreme Court rulings that seemed to relax federal employee benefits law's preemption of state remedies against health plans, courts allowed such suits to go forward, ignoring several early 1990s holdings to the contrary.[3] But in June 2004, the Supreme Court held that federal employee benefits law preempts state tort actions against health plans for negligent coverage refusals.[4] The Justices thereby immunized employment-based plans against liability for coverage denial, leaving independent review as a beneficiary's only remedy when these plans withhold coverage.[5]

C. Public Programs

Formal equality in the bestowing of benefits is a feature of the law governing standards of care in public programs. The legislation that created Medicaid promises its impoverished beneficiaries access to mainstream, medically necessary care, as does the federal Medicare program for elderly and disabled Americans. Other federal and state programs, such as the Indian Health Service and the Children's Health Insurance Program, make similar commitments. Along similar lines, Title VI of the Federal Civil Rights Act bars health care institutions from engaging in practices that have racially disparate effects, absent clinical justification.[6]

These formal commitments to equity are belied by budgetary and other policy choices that sustain inequality. Neither the states nor the federal government have funded Medicaid at levels necessary to put its beneficiaries on equal footing with privately insured patients when seeking acute or preventative care from doctors and hospitals. As a consequence, Medicaid patients have been largely consigned to a separate system of hospital and community-based outpatient clinics, staffed by doctors who do not treat large numbers of privately insured Americans.[7] Such clinics are often short on support staff and other resources, and economic constraints (or aggressive managers) often put pressure on their physicians to see large numbers of patients in short periods of time. The upshot has often been weaker doctor-patient relationships, poorer prevention-oriented care, poorer patient compliance with tests and treatments, and a higher risk of failure to diagnose serious illness. Medicaid has done better at gaining access for its beneficiaries to acute inpatient care. Its inpatient payment rates have approached and sometimes exceeded those negotiated between hospitals and private insurers. But in some states, draconian limits on numbers of covered inpatient days (or other units of care) per year have left beneficiaries uninsured for care covered by even the most restrictive private plans.

Medicaid's financing scheme virtually ensures the program's inability to keep pace with privately purchased coverage and care. Medicaid's dependence on general tax revenues (at both the state and federal level) guarantees a growing mismatch between available funds and the perpetually rising costs of mainstream medical care. State legislatures and governors (and voters) have proven unwilling to raise taxes to keep pace with medical costs. As a consequence, Medicaid absorbs growing shares of state budgets, squeezing out spending on public education and other programs. Not surprisingly, states have reacted by cutting back on what Medicaid has to offer. Many have moved to tightly-managed care (without the patient protections available in the private marketplace) and have retreated from their efforts in the 1990s (most notably in Tennessee) to extend Medicaid's benefits to larger numbers of poor Americans. Also of note are the cuts that states refrain from making. Medicaid coverage for long-term nursing home care (a benefit middle-class Americans rely upon) has so far escaped the constraints imposed on Medicaid's acute and prevention-oriented services for the poor.

Medicaid's statutory design deliberately puts states in the driver's seat: each state decides what benefits to offer, and the federal government's contribution to a state's Medicaid program follows (via a formula) from this decision. But this could soon change. To limit entitlement spending, some propose that the federal contribution be recast as an outright grant to each state, then fixed annually in a fashion that would impose austerity on Medicaid. Absent similar health care in the private sphere, this approach would inevitably widen the gap between care provided to Medicaid recipients and private patients. So long as people's generosity as taxpayers fails to keep pace with their willingness to pay (in the marketplace) for coverage and care for themselves, the quality chasm between Medicaid and privately purchased care will expand.

Ongoing state and federal efforts to move Medicaid patients into tightly managed health plans underscore this point. In 1998, the federal government stopped requiring that Medicaid HMOs draw at least 25 percent of their subscribers from the private marketplace. By compelling Medicaid HMOs to attract private subscribers, the 25 percent rule limited these health plans' freedom to skimp on quality and constrain patient choice. Elimination of this rule allowed states (and health plans) to develop separate, Medicaid-only managed care systems with diminished levels of care, patient protection, and choice between treatments and providers. This has made Medicaid managed care highly attractive to states. The dismal logic of mismatch between rising medical costs and taxpayer willingness to bear them ensures a growing gap between Medicaid managed care and private coverage.

Medicare, by contrast, benefits politically—and thus financially—from the connection Americans see between their payments into the system and the benefits they anticipate. Medicare, like Social Security before it, was sold to Americans as a social insurance plan, not a welfare program. As many have noted, this has insulated it from the stigma and skepticism that attach to safety net programs for the poor. In practice, the link between "premium" payments and expected benefits involves some virtual reality. Payments to Medicare "count," for budgetary purposes, like general tax revenues. The separate "trust fund" into which they go is an accounting fiction, since this fund is entirely "invested" in federal debt instruments. The availability of this fund to cover future benefits thus depends on future political will to pay this debt, either through follow-on borrowing or federal taxes. But this bit of virtual reality has been enough to sustain public support for Medicare as an insurance scheme, not a welfare program. This has translated into taxpayer willingness to pay into the program at rates that keep pace with rising medical spending. Not only have Americans proven willing to make rising FICA payments (for Medicare "Part A" hospital benefits), but they have tolerated use of a rising share of general revenues to subsidize Medicare's outpatient coverage. And as proposals for federal Medicaid cuts loom, Medicare is poised to tap into general revenues to support prescription drug coverage.

But even Medicare's promise of socioeconomic equity is now in jeopardy. Efforts to transform the Medicare entitlement into a voucher for the purchase of private coverage have been gaining strength since the late 1990s. During the run-up to congressional passage of the prescription drug benefit, the Bush administration abandoned its effort to use prescription drug coverage as a lever to coax Medicare beneficiaries into private health plans. But market-oriented Republicans keep winning national elections, and the long-term, "Ownership Society" vision for Medicare calls for a fixed subsidy to beneficiaries for the selection of a private plan.

In the short run, this approach will not contain medical costs. To have a chance at political success, a Medicare voucher scheme would need to be sufficiently generous to support care equal to that now accessible through the Medicare program. But transition to a voucher strategy would give Congress and the president a powerful tool, over the long haul, to cap the program's costs—Congress could simply limit the voucher to meet its budget objectives. Should the voucher fail to keep pace with rising medical costs, beneficiaries would need to ante up more and more of their personal resources[8] to maintain access to mainstream care. "Bare-bones" health plans might or might not arise to serve beneficiaries without the wealth needed to supplement the voucher.[9] If such plans do emerge, they will relegate their subscribers to a lower tier of health care quality and clinical choice, breaching Medicare's promise of equity. Should such plans fail to emerge, Americans eligible for Medicare but unable to pay to supplement the voucher could find themselves among the uninsured.

D. The "Consumer-Directed" Medical Marketplace

Among the employee benefits managers and consultants who drive change in the medical marketplace, the shifting of costs to consumers has become the next new thing. Higher copayments, deductibles, and employee contributions toward health plan premiums are supposed to motivate medical care consumers to make more considered cost-benefit trade-offs and smarter choices from among clinical alternatives. Better "decision tools"— data concerning the performance of doctors, hospitals, and health plans and web-based software designed to help users make comparative assessments—are supposed to improve the quality of consumer decision making (and, in turn, to increase market pressure on caregivers and insurers to deliver quality and value). Congressional Republicans and the Bush administration are intent on catalyzing these developments by changing the tax laws to encourage high-deductible, "catastrophic" coverage in combination with medical savings accounts.

This trend could achieve a measure of cost control by rewarding employees for choosing more frugal coverage and by making them into more skeptical shoppers for small-ticket outpatient care. But it will do little to control the big-ticket, inpatient spending (typically covered by "catastrophic" plans) that is mainly responsible for rising medical costs. It will, moreover, catalyze the stratification of levels of care according to family wealth.

It is well established that soaring medical costs are driven, in the main, by technology-intensive tests and treatments provided to hospital patients, often at or near the end of life. High-deductible health plans do not deter provision of this care, which can cost tens or hundreds of thousands of dollars. Their deductibles—typically a few thousand dollars—are exhausted during the first few days of a hospital stay (if they have not already been exhausted by the patient's preadmission work-up). Absent other coverage limitations, high deductible plans are no more able than conventional insurance to rein in such spending. On the other hand, high deductibles discourage those without substantial wealth from obtaining outpatient diagnostic work-ups that might lead to costly (and well-insured) hospital treatment. They thus deter inpatient spending indirectly—disproportionately so for the least well-off—creating a cross-subsidy from the worst-off to the wealthy within medical risk pools.

High deductibles and copayments, moreover, are blunt instruments for deterring outpatient spending. It has long been known that these mechanisms discourage people from obtaining prevention-oriented outpatient treatment for asymptomatic problems (e.g., high blood pressure) that carry large, long-term health risks and high costs.[10] Such treatment delivers high value—the cost-benefit case for it is compelling—and should be a high priority in an economically rational health system. Absent coverage for this treatment, the well-off are more likely to obtain it than the worst-off. Changing the tax laws to allow Americans to save and spend pretax dollars for such care does not ameliorate this inequity; it makes it worse, since this tax benefit is worth the most to the well-off.

Likewise, the shifting of insurance premium costs from employers to workers will contribute to the socioeconomic stratification of employment-based coverage. In theory, from a labor economics perspective, whether firms or workers pay for health insurance does not matter: either way, medical coverage is part of each worker's compensation package, and every dollar put toward health insurance is unavailable for salary or other benefits. But higher employee contributions that vary substantially among health plans will tend to sort wealthier workers into more pricey (and more generous) plans. Higher employee contributions give workers more say about their total compensation packages, but this input comes at a social cost: distribution of medical coverage more closely approximates the distribution of income and wealth.

II. Public Health

Before the antibiotic revolution, government action to address looming threats to the health of the population was widely perceived as an urgent priority. Infectious disease epidemics were, by far, the country's most murderous natural disasters, and public preparedness efforts included large investments in sanitation and sewage treatment, draining of swamps, vaccination, and other preventative measures. Failure to control epidemics put entire populations at risk: the poor were often the worst affected, but outbreaks of infection did not confine themselves by class. Not only did the coming of antibiotics bring about a dramatic drop-off in morbidity and premature mortality from infectious disease, it also diminished Americans' understanding of illness as a public problem. Antibiotics made infection a private matter, something to be treated by doctors for a fee. Support for state and federal measures to protect *public* health dropped off even as government made growing financial commitments to biomedical research and health insurance coverage.[11]

This made sense for infectious diseases that antibiotics could decisively treat. But the rise of drug-resistant strains, the slowness of progress toward cures for viral illnesses, and the emergence of new and devastating infections made America's retreat from public health premature. These twenty-first-century infectious disease problems disproportionately afflict the poor, at a time of minimalist commitment of public resources toward prevention. HIV/AIDS and tuberculosis that is resistant to multiple drugs are high-profile examples.

The growing American propensity to think of health as a private matter has had an even larger impact outside the realm of infectious disease. Cardiovascular disease, many cancers, diabetes, asthma, and obesity are among the conditions amenable to populationwide preventative measures. Yet public officials (and taxpayers) have been disinclined in recent years to back such measures. Support for educational efforts (to promote such things as smoking cessation and healthier eating) and environmental cleanup has been tepid. Legislators, regulators, and judges have been reluctant to employ law in a robust fashion to discourage marketing and consumption of tobacco products and high-risk foods. Because heart disease, cancer, diabetes, asthma, and other illnesses mediated by environmental and lifestyle factors affect the poor disproportionately,[12] the privatization of health in American culture, politics, and law has had highly regressive distributive effects.

A. The Ties between Health and Socioeconomic Status

Epidemiological studies consistently show a strong correlation between socioeconomic status (SES) and measures of morbidity, mortality, and ability to function.[13] SES is a complex phenomenon, related to income, wealth, education, and occupation. Researchers commonly characterize the relationship between SES and health as a "gradient" because of the continuous nature of the association: populationwide health status improves as one moves from the lowest through the middle levels of SES. This empirical finding persists across time and cultures,[14] though there is controversy over whether the upward gradient continues through the highest levels of SES.[15]

Some researchers go further, concluding that the overall extent of economic inequality in a given population correlates with (and adversely affects) populationwide health.[16] That is, they say, societies with wide gaps between rich and poor tend to have worse health status than societies with smaller gaps, after controlling for per capita income. These researchers hypothesize that societies with higher degrees of inequality provide less social support and cohesion, making life more stressful, pathogenic, and short. Drawing upon this line of argument, some ethics commentators contend that "social justice is good for our health."[17]

Other researchers cast doubt on this line of reasoning, while acknowledging that raising the incomes of the least advantaged will improve their health and thereby increase societywide health. The authors of a recent metaanalysis argue:

> Overall, there seems to be little support for the idea that income inequality is a major, generalizable determinant of population health differences within or between rich countries. Income inequality may, however, directly influence some health outcomes, such as homicide in the United States, but even that is somewhat mixed. Despite little support for a direct effect of income inequality on health per se, reducing income inequality by raising the incomes of the most disadvantaged will improve their health, help reduce health inequalities, and generally improve population health.[18]

Opponents of redistributive policies challenge this last claim, arguing that such policies punish personal accomplishment and thereby discourage economic growth. Pointing to the correlation between populationwide health and nations' per capita income, they say redistribution *reduces* populationwide health over the long run by suppressing the growth of per capita income. Even if redistribution were to reduce inequality in health status, it is ill-advised, they argue, since diminished inequality would come at the cost of a net drop in overall health at the population level.[19] Redistribution of private wealth, they contend, is a political matter, outside the appropriate scope of the public health enterprise.[20] Richard Epstein, for example, distinguishes between the "old" public health, focused mainly on infectious disease, and the "new" public health, aimed more broadly at the social and economic determinants of health.[21]

We doubt the existence of an ironclad, adverse relationship between redistributive policies, economic prosperity, and health status. As many commentators, most notably Amartya Sen, have observed, redistributive programs that take the form of investment in education, health promotion, and vital economic infrastructure (e.g., transportation and communications essential for business) spur long-term economic development.[22] In so doing, they improve measures of social welfare, including indicators of health status. Sen and others point to a variety of international examples, including the correlation between public spending on health and education and rapid economic development in East Asia in recent decades. Does "pure" redistribution—cutting checks to the poor from tax proceeds taken from the wealthy—undermine health status by slowing growth? Perhaps (though this has not been proven), but this possibility is a red herring, given what we know about the potential of some forms of public spending to catalyze economic growth.

B. Public Health and Equity: The Distorting Effect of Biosecurity Programs

There is wide agreement on the general aims of the public health enterprise—to achieve the largest possible positive impact on population health with every dollar spent and to distribute the benefits of public health services equitably. Within this broad framework, there is room for debate—about cost-benefit trade-offs and about the comparative value of alternative strategies and objectives. But it is beyond dispute that the post-9/11 preoccupation with bioterror is pushing public health policy in cost-ineffective directions that magnify inequality. The new focus on bioterror is drawing resources away from programs that target common health threats. It is channeling money and effort toward hazards that are lower-risk and interventions that are lower-yield.

Public health funds are, or at least should be, directed toward the most common causes of morbidity and premature mortality, in order to afford the greatest benefits to the most people. Although many traditional public health programs have not been fully evaluated, some are known to be highly cost-effective. Immunization programs are one example. Traditional public health programs also typically benefit those least likely to be able to help themselves, since many of the illnesses and risks they address disproportionately affect those with the lowest SES.

What are the most prevalent causes of ill-health and how might resource allocation be most effective and fair? The lifestyle decisions at the root of much chronic disease include smoking, overeating, and sedentary habits. Lifestyle also plays a large role in infectious disease, including HIV/AIDS, other sexually transmitted diseases (STDs), tuberculosis, and influenza. And childhood diseases such as measles, mumps, and chicken-pox are no longer common, but would be absent immunization programs. One might expect, therefore, that most public health resources would be channeled toward lifestyle change, vaccination programs, and other high-impact health-promotion efforts.

The unprecedented spending on biosecurity that followed the 9/11 attacks and the release of anthrax via the U.S. Postal Service weeks later was expected by many to enhance public health preparedness. "Dual use" public health infrastructure, commentators said, would protect Americans from bioterror attack while strengthening the nation's ability to detect and respond to epidemic disease. But "dual use" programs failed to materialize. Even after the influx of bioterrorism funds, the public health infrastructure was still in disarray.[23] Public health watchdogs noted that most states lacked a well-trained workforce, electronic information and communications systems, rapid disease surveillance, sufficient laboratory capacity, and response capability.[24] Not only has the ramping-up of biosecurity funding failed to strengthen the public health infrastructure, but the emphasis on biosecurity has come at the expense of traditional public health services directed at the most common causes of ill-health.

The reasons for this are multifaceted. First, the federal government has issued specific legal and political instructions to *avoid* "dual uses" of biosecurity funding. Oversight mechanisms were put in place to ensure that federal money cannot be used to improve ongoing public health programs.[25] Second, money for biosecurity has been taken from preexisting public health programs. Many such programs have been downsized or eliminated.[26] Third, preoccupation with bioterror diverts the attention of public health agency leaders and staff from their core disease-control mission.

All this might be defensible were the risk of biological attack so great as to support such trade-offs on cost-benefit grounds. But fear of bioterror (and the Strangelovian scenarios this fear has spawned) far exceeds known risks. The likelihood of a terror network or rogue state being able to stage a biological attack capable of killing many is remote and speculative.[27] Meanwhile, millions of Americans die each year from preventable causes—illnesses that ensue from unhealthy lifestyles, poverty and its social sequelae, the physical environment, and failure to bring available knowledge to bear to prevent and control infectious disease. Policy makers' preoccupation with biosecurity has weakened public health agencies' efforts to sustain the most cost-effective programs directed toward common diseases. Smoking cessation, obesity control, and prevention and treatment of HIV/AIDS, tuberculosis, STDs, and common childhood infectious conditions have been set back. Vital services such as disease surveillance, laboratory diagnosis, health education, and immunization also have been curtailed.

The failed smallpox vaccination campaign offers an apt illustration of biosecurity policy's perverse effects. In the wake of the 9/11 attacks, the Bush administration initiated an attempt to immunize five hundred thousand health care workers. Federal and state public health agencies were given this responsibility and told to treat it as a high priority. Yet the suspected risk of a smallpox attack was exceedingly low, and the suspicion, it turns out, was based on inaccurate intelligence.[28] The risks of smallpox immunization, on the other hand, were substantial: one per thousand people vaccinated develop serious, non–life threatening adverse effects, and fourteen to fifty-two people per million people vaccinated experienced potentially life-threatening reactions.[29] Personnel, funding, and political attention were diverted from ongoing programs to address a disease that had been eradicated decades ago. The program, moreover, never achieved its goals because most health care workers declined to be vaccinated. Out of the targeted half million workers, the program immunized barely forty thousand,[30] a fortunate failure, given the unfavorable balance of benefit and risk.

Not only has biosecurity policy been cost-ineffective, but it has been especially harmful to the disadvantaged. Public services for common infectious diseases (e.g., HIV/AIDS, tuberculosis, and STDs) and common chronic diseases (associated with smoking, diet, and sedentary lifestyles) benefit poor people, African Americans, Latinos, and other underserved populations in disproportionate numbers. Diversion of resources from these services to support high-cost campaigns against remote and speculative bioterror threats thus disproportionately harms the disadvantaged. America's post-9/11 venture into biosecurity has, in short, brought new inefficiencies and unfairness to public health policy.

C. Population-Based Health Policy

Rising medical spending contributes enormously to inequity and inefficiency in the health sphere. Through the second half of the twentieth century, American medical costs rose at more than double the overall rate of inflation. The mismatch between this spending and our nationwide health need is huge. Medical care has much less of an impact on populationwide health than do behavioral and environmental factors.[31] Technology-intensive interventions near the end of life generate most of American medical spending, yet they yield minimal gains in longevity and quality of life. Meanwhile, American health policy gives short shrift to control of common health risks that lead to premature mortality.[32] The unsurprising result is that the health status of Americans is poor when compared to other countries at similar levels of economic development. Among the thirty member states of the Organisation for Economic Co-operation and Development, the United States ranks twenty-third in infant mortality (7.1 deaths per 1,000 live births) and eighteenth for life expectancy at birth (76.7 years for men and women, combined).[33]

At the federal and state levels, soaring medical spending is crowding out investment in population-based health improvement strategies that would make the largest difference in the lives of the least well-off. State and local public health agencies are in disarray.[34] These agencies lack the capacity to perform essential public health services at levels that match the constantly evolving threats to Americans' health.[35] Despite recent improvements, the Centers for Disease Control and Prevention (CDC) has concluded that the public health infrastructure "is still structurally weak in nearly every area."[36] This infrastructure remains mostly a state responsibility; large-scale federal assistance is not on the political horizon. Soaring

Medicaid spending and voter resistance to higher taxes have made state budgetary pressures much worse in recent years, forestalling new initiatives aimed at such problems as obesity, smoking, sedentary lifestyles, and resurgent and emerging infectious diseases. Beyond this, budget crises in many states are putting existing capabilities at serious risk.[37] Not only are current funding levels inadequate; uncertainty about future commitments and rigid, "stove-pipe" program rules often discourage evidence-based planning, policies, and programs.

III. Summing Up: Equity and the Future of Health Law

American health law has broken its promise of equity. Courts and legislators increasingly treat illness and access to medical care as matters of personal responsibility. Health law and policy tolerate disparate life circumstances—inherited and acquired differences in wealth and privilege—to a greater degree today than a generation ago. In the health care sphere, an outer shell of equity survives. Courts have not, so far, embraced the proposition that clinical standards of care in medical malpractice and coverage disputes should vary based on patients' ability to pay. Medicare and Medicaid, meanwhile, still promise access to mainstream care. But the law's real-world performance increasingly belies these commitments to equity. Courts, regulators, and legislatures have become more permissive in practice toward variations in care associated with socioeconomic position. Likewise, public health policy is increasingly responsive to the needs and concerns of the well-off at the expense of the worst-off. The American propensity to treat health as a private matter, policy makers' tepid responses to lifestyle and environmental factors that undermine health, and the priority given to bioterror preparedness at the expense of other programs are pushing populationwide health policy in a reverse Robin Hood direction.

For many American progressives, the main reason for this trend is clear: corporate interests have growing influence over political and regulatory processes—and over the composition of the courts. We do not doubt this influence. Health plans have become large players in Washington and many state capitals. Major employers (and their powerful trade associations) have made medical cost issues a high legislative and legal priority. The managed care industry, supported by employer groups, has blocked "Patients' Bill of Rights" legislation in Congress and weakened bills passed in many states. Manufacturing firms and utilities have staved off robust environmental clean-up requirements, and food manufacturers and others have resisted efforts to revamp the American diet. Political leaders are limiting access to tort remedies ranging from class action product safety litigation to lawsuits against firearm manufacturers and fast food suppliers.

Yet we doubt that corporate influence is the main force behind the trend away from equity in health law and policy. Larger cultural change, we think, is playing a decisive role. Political liberals as well as conservatives today put heightened emphasis on personal choice in many spheres of life. By comparison with New Deal liberals and the populists of a century ago, progressives have, since the 1960s, put less emphasis on economic equity and more stress on individual liberties in the public and intimate spheres. The bioethics movement—and its impact upon the law—has both reflected and reinforced this trend.[38] Mainstream bioethics has emphasized individual autonomy and, for the most part, taken individuals' resource constraints as a given.[39] There is thus a congeniality between traditional, laissez-faire conservatives' resistance to government restrictions and bioethics (and other post-1960s) progressives' commitment to individual choice.

In pushing the bounds of personal freedom, progressives in the health sphere (and beyond) did not mean to abandon the traditional liberal commitment to the socioeconomically disadvantaged. But the priority they put on personal choice undercut this commitment. Not only did post-1960s progressives put less emphasis on social justice concerns, but their defense of liberty and diversity in sexual and other intimate matters drew fire from traditionalist Americans inclined toward an agenda that put economic fairness first. Conservatives solicitous of economic privilege seized this chance, allying themselves with working-class Americans hostile to the new, intimate liberties. The irony of a working class conjoined to the wealthy on such matters—and angry enough about personal license to disregard its economic interests—helped to deliver seven of the last ten presidential elections to Republican candidates, transforming domestic policy, the courts, and health law.

Another irony, dating to the 1960s, has undercut the ability of health law and policy to pursue equity. Cynicism about government and politics, on the rise since America's debacle in Vietnam, engenders great skepticism toward proposed public solutions to the health problems of the disadvantaged. Republicans have been far ahead of Democrats in realizing this. In a 1993 memo, Republican political strategist William Kristol urged his party to make the defeat of President Clinton's health plan a high priority.[40] Kristol's prescient rationale was that if the Clinton plan prevailed, Americans would be more inclined to see government as able to deliver in matters of social and economic security—and thus more inclined toward the Democrats in the domestic policy realm. Failure of the Clinton plan, on the other hand, would encourage attitudes of skepticism and self-reliance, attitudes favoring Republicans in national elections and undercutting public support for large domestic programs.

Americans have become more inclined toward self-reliance in recent decades—and less confident in their government's ability to provide economic security. This increased self-reliance is, in part, a product of past public policy success. Better-educated people who own their homes, follow their IRAs and 401(k) funds, and otherwise enjoy prosperity are more likely than their Depression-era forebears to believe in their ability to fend for themselves. If American health policy and law are to do better than they have recently in matters of socioeconomic equity, they will need to acknowledge and build on this basic cultural change.

In the health care realm, pursuit of universal coverage through strategies that emphasize individual responsibility is more likely to gain political traction than are single-payer plans or employer mandates. Schemes that aggregate buying power and provide subsidies for low-wage workers and the poor, but that make the purchase of coverage a personal obligation,[41] stand a decent chance of success in the current cultural climate. Public health law and policy as well will need to take greater account of the American cultural shift toward self-reliance in order to take strides toward equity. To some, this may sound like a contradiction, but it need not be. Tax policy can and should encourage subscription to health plans that promote prevention-oriented services, through tiered cost-sharing schemes and other means. Efforts to target unhealthy behaviors—smoking, consumption of saturated fats, alcohol abuse, and the like—should emphasize informative and inspiring public education campaigns, not legal prohibition and punishment.[42] Environmental policies that create market incentives to avert or clean up dangerous conditions in disadvantaged locales are more likely than command-and-control proposals to win acceptance. Educational programs, tax incentives, and other initiatives aimed at creating opportunities for the least well-off are more likely than wealth transfer schemes to win support—and thereby to make inroads against the disparities in health status that arise from economic inequality.

Short of a catastrophe orders of magnitude larger than the events of 9/11, a national shift toward greater reliance on public provision and regulatory action in health matters is unlikely, at least in the near term. For all concerned about the broken promise of equity in health and medical care, dismay and frustration are understandable reactions. But the current political and legal climate offers opportunities worth seizing. Progressives should take care not to permit their disappointments to block their lines of sight toward present possibilities.

Notes

1. *See* Rush Prudential HMO, Inc. v. Moran, 536 U.S. 355 (2002).

2. The Emergency Medical Treatment and Active Labor Act (EMTALA), 42 U.S.C.S. § 1395dd, as well as statutes and common law in many states, require hospitals to take this risk when patients who cannot pay present with emergency conditions.

3. M. Gregg Bloche & David M. Studdert, *A Quiet Revolution: Law as an Agent of Health System Change*, 23 Health Aff. 29–42 (2004).

4. Aetna Health Inc. v. Davila, 124 S. Ct. 2488 (2004).

5. M. Gregg Bloche, *Back to the 90s—The Supreme Court Immunizes Managed Care*, 351 New Eng. J. Med. 1277 (2004).

6. Sara Rosenbaum & Joel Teitelbaum, *Civil Rights Enforcement in the Modern Healthcare System: Reinvigorating the Role of the Federal Government in the Aftermath of* Alexander v. Sandoval, 3 Yale J. Health Pol'y L. & Ethics 215 (2003).

7. These physicians are often house officers (physicians-in-training at hospital-based residency programs) or doctors who have completed their training with weaker credentials than most physicians who treat private patients.

8. Depending on program design at both the legislative and health plan levels, beneficiaries' growing financial burden could take the form of rising personal contributions to health plan premiums or of higher copayments, deductibles, and other out-of-pocket obligations.

9. Statutory and regulatory prerequisites (e.g., minimum standards for coverage, quality of care, and clinical choice) for participation by private plans in the Medicare program could prevent the emergence of such low-cost plans.

10. Willard G. Manning et al., Health Insurance and the Demand for Medical Care: Evidence from a Randomized Experiment (Rand, 1988); *see also* Joseph Newhouse, Free for All? Lessons from the Rand Health Insurance Experiment (1993).

11. Lawrence O. Gostin, Public Health Law: Power, Duty, Restraint (2000).

12. *See* INSTITUTE OF MEDICINE, UNEQUAL TREATMENT: CONFRONTING RACIAL AND ETHNIC DISPARITIES IN HEALTH CARE (2003).

13. *See* A MORTALITY STUDY OF 1.3 MILLION PERSONS BY DEMOGRAPHIC, SOCIAL, AND ECONOMIC FACTORS: 1979–1985 FOLLOW-UP, NAT'L INST. OF HEALTH (Eugene Rogot et al. eds., 1992).

14. M. G. Marmot et al., *Health Inequalities among British Civil Servants: The Whitehall II Study*, 337 LANCET 1387–93 (1991); D. ACHESON, INDEPENDENT INQUIRY INTO INEQUALITIES IN HEALTH (1998); EVELYN M. KITAGAWA & PHILLIP M. HAUSER, DIFFERENTIAL MORTALITY IN THE UNITED STATES: A STUDY OF SOCIO-ECONOMIC EPIDEMIOLOGY (1973).

15. *See* Lawrence O. Gostin & M. Gregg Bloche, *The Politics of Public Health: A Reply to Richard Epstein*, 46 PERSP. IN BIOLOGY AND MED. S160–S175 (2003).

16. RICHARD G. WILKINSON, UNHEALTHY SOCIETIES: THE AFFLICTIONS OF INEQUALITY (1996).

17. N. Daniels et al., *Justice Is Good for Our Health*, 25 BOSTON REV. 6–15 (2000); D. E. Beauchamp, *Public Health as Social Justice*, 13 INQUIRY 3–14 (1976).

18. John Lynch et al., *Is Income Inequality a Determinant of Population Health? Part 1: A Systematic Review*, 82 MILBANK Q. 5 (2004).

19. Critics of the public health case for redistributive policies also note that the explanatory variables for the relationship between SES and health are not entirely understood. Some deny the existence of a causal relationship between SES and health, suggesting instead that people who are ill tend not to attain high SES. The SES gradient probably does involve multiple pathways. Mitchell D. Wong et al., *Contribution of Major Diseases to Disparities in Mortality*, NEW ENGLAND J. MED., Nov. 14, 2002, at 1585–92 (2002); N. E. Adler and K. Newman, *Socioeconomic Disparities in Health: Pathways and Policies*, 21 HEALTH AFF. 60–76 (2002). These include material disadvantage (e.g., access to food, shelter, and health care), toxic physical environments (e.g., poor conditions at home, work, and community); psychosocial stressors (e.g., financial or occupational insecurity and lack of control); and social contexts that influence risk behaviors (e.g., smoking, physical inactivity, diet, and alcohol consumption). Finding the exact pathways or causal relationships presents many challenges; these lie beyond our scope here. But we believe the available data support the conclusion that SES is, in the main, a cause, not a consequence, of health status.

20. Mark Hall, *The Scope and Limits of Public Health Law*, 46 PERSP. IN BIOLOGY & MED. S199–S209 (2003); Richard A. Epstein, *Let the Shoemaker Stick to His Last: A Defense of the "Old" Public Health*, 46 PERSP. IN BIOLOGY & MED. S138–S159 (2003).

21. *Id.* For our critique of Epstein's case for the narrowing of public health's political and legal agenda, see Lawrence O. Gostin & M. Gregg Bloche, *The Politics of Public Health: A Reply to Richard Epstein*, 46 PERSP. IN BIOLOGY & MED. S160–S175 (2003).

22. Amartya Sen, Development as Freedom (1999).

23. Institute of Medicine, The Future of the Public's Health in the 21st Century (2002).

24. Trust for America's Health, Ready or Not? The Public's Health in the Age of Bioterrorism 51 (2004), *available at* http://healthyamericans.org/reports/bioterror04/.

25. Megan McHugh et al., *How Prepared Are Americans for Public Health Emergencies? Twelve Communities Weigh In*, 23 Health Aff. 201–09 (2004).

26. *A Case of Neglect: Costs of Complacency*, Governing (2004), *available at* http://governing.com/gpp/2004/public.htm.

27. M. Gregg Bloche, *Rogue Science*, 91 Geo. L.J. 1257–75 (2003).

28. Much of the smallpox vaccination campaign was predicated on intelligence that rogue nations, such as Iraq, were in possession of the smallpox virus. Yet, systematic efforts failed to discover a stockpile, or a capacity to produce, pathogens for use in bioterrorism.

29. http://www.bt.cdc.gov/agent/smallpox/vaccination/reactions-vacc-public.asp.

30. Institute of Medicine, The Smallpox Vaccination Program: Public Health in an Age of Terrorism 33 (2005) (prepublication form on file with National Academies Press).

31. J. M. McGinnis & W. H. Foege, *Actual Causes of Death in the United States*, 270 J. Am. Med. Ass'n 2207–12 (1993).

32. The vast majority of U.S. health spending, more than 95 percent, is directed toward personal health care and biomedical research; only 1–2 percent of health spending is directed toward prevention. J. Bouford & P. R. Lee, Health Policies for the 21st Century: Challenges and Recommendations for the U.S. Department of Health and Human Services (2001); K. W. Eilbert et al., Public Health Foundation, Measuring Expenditures for Essential Public Health Services (1996).

33. Organisation for Economic Co-Operation and Development, *National Accounts of OECD Countries*, vol. I, 1989–2000, main aggregates (Organisation for Economic Co-Operation and Development, 2002); Organisation for Economic Co-Operation and Development, *OECD Health Data 2002* (News Release: Organisation for Economic Co-Operation and Development, 24 June 2002); U.E. Reinhardt et al., *Trends: Cross-National Comparisons of Health Systems Using OECD Data, 1999*, 21 Health Aff. 168–91 (2000).

34. Institute of Medicine, The Future of the Public's Health in the 21st Century (2002).

35. Institute of Medicine, Improving Health in the Community: A Role for Performance Monitoring (1997); Institute of Medicine, Using Performance Monitoring to Improve Community Health: Exploring the Issues (1996); Institute of Medicine, Healthy Communities: New Partnerships for the Future of Public Health (1996).

36. DEPARTMENT OF HEALTH AND HUMAN SERVICES (U.S.), PUBLIC HEALTH'S INFRASTRUCTURE: A STATUS REPORT (Prepared for the Appropriations Committee of the United States Senate, 2001).

37. Lawrence K. Altman & Anahad O'Connor, *Threats and Responses: The Bioterror Threat; Health Officials Fear Local Impact of Smallpox Plan*, N.Y. TIMES, Jan. 5, 2003, at 1.

38. Lawrence O. Gostin, *Health of the People: The Highest Law?* 32 J. LAW MED. & ETHICS 509–15 (2004); M. Gregg Bloche, *Medical Ethics in the Courts*, in ETHICAL DIMENSIONS OF HEALTH POLICY 133 (M. Danis, C. Clancy, & L. Churchill eds., 2002); M. Gregg Bloche, *Clinical Counseling and the Problem of Autonomy-Negating Influence, in* HIV, AIDS, AND CHILDBEARING: PUBLIC POLICY, PRIVATE LIVES 257 (R. Faden & N. Kass eds., 1996).

39. To be sure, some bioethics commentary considers health-related social justice matters, including the case for universal insurance coverage and the question of fairness in health care rationing. *See, e.g.,* NORMAN DANIELS, JUST HEALTH CARE (1985); PAUL T. MENZEL, STRONG MEDICINE: THE ETHICAL RATIONING OF HEALTH CARE (1990). But the most influential bioethics text has long given patient autonomy special emphasis, BEAUCHAMP & CHILDRESS, PRINCIPLES OF BIOMEDICAL ETHICS (2001), and the approach to informed consent taken in this and other leading bioethics sources treats patient choice as autonomous, with little regard for the economic pressures felt by the patient.

40. Adam Clymer, *Debate on Health Care May Depend on "Crisis,"* N.Y. TIMES, Jan. 17, 1994, at A5.

41. *See, e.g.,* MICHAEL CALABRESE & LAURIE RUBINER, UNIVERSAL COVERAGE, UNIVERSAL RESPONSIBILITY: A ROADMAP TO MAKE COVERAGE AFFORDABLE FOR ALL AMERICANS (New Am. Found., Working Paper No. 1, 2004).

42. M. Gregg Bloche, *Obesity and the Struggle within Ourselves*, 93 GEO. L.J. 1335 (2005).

17

The Elusive Goal of Equal Educational Opportunity

Gerald Torres

About seven years ago, I began a small-scale educational reform project looking at models for improving K-12 education in poor schools.[1] I began the project with three assumptions: (1) that there were existing models of academic excellence in poor schools in Texas and I had to try and capture the common elements of those programs; (2) that the legislature would not allocate additional funding to improve public education despite the state's constitutional mandate to provide for the education of all children; and (3) that race would continue to be a factor in determining how educational opportunities were provided.

Living in a southern state, I understood that these assumptions were closely related. What became evident was that while race historically played a role in the maldistribution of educational resources, this distribution not only affected the life chances of people of color, but those of many whites as well. Notwithstanding this fact, my conversations with experts, parents, teachers, and activists about the problem of underfunding of primary and secondary education were almost always colored by race. Some of this can be explained as the residue of Jim Crow rules (in Texas there was Juan Crow, as well). Some of it is attributable to an intergroup racial management that took concrete form in residential and occupational segregation that is largely experienced as natural. And some of it can only be understood in terms of intragroup class management that "naturally" took on a racial cast.[2] The result of this naturalized inequality has been radically unequal funding of K-12 education. Before the celebrated *Edgewood* case started Texas down the road toward greater equality in funding, the richest districts spent over seven times the amount per student as the poorest district.[3]

One effect of this unequal provision of primary and secondary public education appears in the inequitable distribution of elite postsecondary education. This effect is compounded by the now ingrained idea that access to elite *public* postsecondary education is a natural entitlement for students from the better supported primary and secondary schools, but not for graduates of poor schools. It is this unequal access to higher education that provides the focus of this essay.

I. Who Goes to College?

The belief in class mobility is one of the central tenets of the American creed. A corollary to this belief is that education is the principal vehicle of individual advancement. As the United States has moved away from a manufacturing economy, higher education has become increasingly critical to a person's success. So, who is going to college?

The good news is that women and racial and ethnic minorities are participating in higher education in greater numbers than ever before. According to the June 2002 Postsecondary Student Population Report, 15.3 million students were enrolled in two- or four-year colleges and universities. As might be expected, the makeup of this group is primarily White. Approximately 69 percent of the student population is White, 15 percent is Black, 10 percent is Hispanic, and 7 percent is Asian.

What the admissions numbers obscure is that there is on college campuses even less socioeconomic diversity than racial or ethnic diversity. Among the pool of potential students, which is all high school graduates, it is much more likely that students from higher-income families will actually enroll in college, regardless of race. Those students who come from families with annual incomes of $75,000 or more are almost twice as likely to attend college as those from families with annual incomes of less than $25,000. When one considers all income groups, Whites from the upper-income cohort appear to be more likely to go to college directly from high school and to graduate in four years.[4]

Because admission to elite or selective colleges is tied to performance on standardized admission tests like the SAT or the ACT, the impact of wealth on performance on those tests is a crucial variable. Wealth provides access to tutoring and other support and therefore increases the odds of doing well. Perhaps more important is the link between income and the likelihood that a high school student will even take either of those tests. In 2001–02, there were 2,568,956 public high school diplomas issued. Yet, in that same period, only 1,276,320 students took the SAT and 1,069,772 took the ACT.[5] Failure to sit for either the SAT or the ACT guarantees that a student will not be admitted to a selective college.[6] This possibly class-linked impact is hidden when the population of currently enrolled college students is taken as the baseline for measuring socioeconomic diversity. The better, although much harder, question to ask is what percentage of *all potentially eligible* students is enrolled in postsecondary schools? When one considers the number of students who are made ineligible by failing to sit for the appropriate examinations, the universe of possible students becomes much larger than the 15 million students who are currently enrolled.

This universe expands further when one factors in students who fail to graduate from high school or who complete high school in nontraditional ways. For example, in 2000-01 there were 8,097,610 seventeen- and eighteen-year-olds in the United States.[7] Because most students graduate from high school at seventeen or eighteen, this age group ought to reflect the pool of potential college students over a two-year period. If all graduated, that would be a little more than 4 million a year. But in order to be eligible for postsecondary education, one has to get out of high school. So, what does that number look like?

About 2.5 million students received high school diplomas in the fifty states and in the District of Columbia during the 2000–01 school year and following summer, and another 42,452 received other high school completion credentials (other than a diploma or a GED), such as certificates of attendance, or their equivalent. With this in mind, the proper term to encompass all of these students is high school "*completers*," not "graduates."

Unfortunately, information on national high school completer rates from the fifty states, while available, is at best scant and at worst unreliable. Some states grant only diplomas and high school equivalency certificates and do not recognize other types of high school completion. Many states neither compile nor report their high school completer numbers by socioeconomic status or by race or ethnicity, even if they do compile them at all. The overall reported numbers are little more than expanded sample data enlarged to reflect the entire population. As a result, the sampling errors are so large that the statistics are not very reliable or comparable among the states. Nonetheless, with these disclaimers in mind, in 2000 there were about 2,756,000 high school completers,[8] and 1,745,000 students enrolled in college.[9] In 2001, there were 2,545,000 high school completers, and 1,569,000 students enrolled in college.[10]

Thus, for 2000 and 2001 combined, there were just over 5 million potential high school completers, but only three out of five in fact did complete. And, as noted earlier, in 2001, 1,276,320 students took the SAT and 1,069,772 took the ACT. So less than half of those who graduated were eligible to enroll at selective colleges. Of course, we do not know the extent to which socioeconomic class led to these disparities. However, it is not unreasonable to assume that class variables played a key role.

Because this scant enrollment data collapses information on public institutions with private institutions, selective with nonselective colleges, two- with four-year institutions, as well as failing to distinguish academic and vocational tracks within community colleges, it really obscures the multiple functions of postsecondary education and the distribution of the most valuable postsecondary academic assets. Without a fine-grained analysis of each subcategory of postsecondary institutions (including, unfortunately, federal, state, and local correctional institutions), it is virtually impossible to say with any precision which segments of which socioeconomic classes are occupying which seats. Nonetheless, income data on students who enter selective four-year colleges upon graduation from high school suggest that the distribution of that prime economic and educational asset continues to be, as Anthony Carnevale termed it in a remark to the author, "a gift from the poor to the rich."

Examination of age distributions across various institutions also sheds light on the ways in which class pressures affect students' abilities to take advantage of educational opportunity efficiently. In short, more members of ethnic and racial minorities and women are among the cohort of older students. There are many possible explanations for this, but the two leading hypotheses are that the overrepresentation of students from minority groups and women stems from their overrepresentation among lower-income students. Because they need to work while attending school, they take longer to graduate. In contrast, upper-income whites are more likely to start school and finish before they are twenty-four. The other hypothesis is that students from ethnic and racial minorities are less likely to enter college directly from high school. Long-term longitudinal studies have not yet sorted out a single explanation, so it is probable that a mixture of explanations (though all tied to class position) will be at the heart of the matter. When understood in terms of opportunity costs, lost time is an additional class-based consequence that largely goes unnoticed.

The importance of educational opportunity in the mythology of a classless society cannot be overstated, especially where education is seen as a path that any able person willing to work hard can pursue—a path that allows individuals to slip the bonds of birth that have historically defined and, to a greater extent than we like to admit, continue to rigidly circumscribe a person's life chances. Since there is an income bonus that comes with graduation from an elite college, the impact of wealth on access to these schools should not be underestimated.[11]

II. Who Gets the Money?

According to *New York Times* reporter Greg Winter, the federal government "typically gives the wealthiest private universities, which often serve the smallest percentage of low-income students, significantly more financial aid than their struggling counterparts with much greater share of poor students."[12] For example, the median college received an extra 7 cents for every Pell dollar one of its students received in the 2000–01 academic year (and they could each get up to $4,000). In contrast, Harvard received 98 cents. MIT received $1.09. And Princeton got $1.42.

Of course, these disparities might simply be explained by reference to the relative costs of the programs provided by these schools. It would make sense that the more expensive schools would get the bigger share of federal aid in order to reduce cost barriers and to enable more poor students to attend. However, it is not at all clear that varying costs sufficiently account for the difference. As Heather McDonnell, director of financial aid at Sarah Lawrence College explained, though Sarah Lawrence costs as much as federal aid winners in the Ivy League, in one category her college received only a sixth as much money as the least expensive Ivy League schools. Winter notes, "Ivy League colleges were given five to eight times the median to pay their students in work-study jobs; that is money [that institutions received] directly, to be spent on behalf of needy students; they received five to twenty times the median amount of grant money to look after everyday needs of their poor students."[13] From the perspective of all colleges, the disparities are staggering. "For each of its aid applicants, the median college got $87.67 to help pay wages for work-study jobs. Yale got $592.75. Duke got $600.28. Columbia got $677.93. But nearly one hundred other colleges got less than $20."[14] Need levels or the abundance of poor students at these schools cannot explain this cascade effect. The more elite the school, the larger seems the subsidy given by the poor to the rich.

How did this happen? When it was designing the system of federal aid to higher education, Congress turned to experts, in part to produce the best thinking in the area and in part to insulate legislators from any direct responsibility for hard decisions. Financing disparities resulted in the 1970s when regional panels of educational experts, not formulas, determined how much money colleges would receive. "Because each university had to make its own case for the money, those with long histories and a certain financial savoir-faire tended to do particularly well."[15] In fact, notwithstanding their indirect conflicts of interest, the panels were sometimes composed of the administrators of the colleges and universities that would be receiving the federal aid.

Because this approach to decision making yielded something close to self-dealing, in the 1980s congressional overseers were forced to act. To correct inequalities in aid distribution, Congress replaced the regional panels approach with a "fair share" formula. However, the formula only applied to new monies that Congress added to the federal aid program and therefore effectively fixed existing disparities in place. In other words, notwithstanding Congress's good intentions, the fair share formula merely reinforced the structural inequality produced by the regional panels. By "guaranteeing that no college would receive less than it was already getting," the reform did not directly address the real flaw with the distribution; federal monies were not going to the neediest students, they were going to the most politically astute or well-connected colleges. And so this problem continues today.

Despite the continuing efforts of some legislators and education activists to reform the financial aid formula, structural inequality remains a feature of federal aid to higher education. If Congress had appropriated substantial additional money into the system, then locking in the 1970s preferences might not have institutionalized such a continuing deleterious effect. Yet Congress has added little new money and indeed some money has left the system. Thus, continued reliance on the formula leaves "little money available for two- and four-year public colleges that now enroll greater proportions of financially needy students."[16] In other words, federal monies aid the richest schools to the detriment of those schools that are actually enrolling the greatest number of poor students—the very students who are depending upon education to be a class escalator.

The locking in of historic disparities not only continues to funnel the bulk of federal money to the institutions serving the fewest poor students, it also has failed to reflect the changing geography of higher education. "Enrollments in Arizona, Texas, Georgia and other states have more than doubled in the last thirty years, while the cluster of Northeastern states that once seemed to anchor higher education have not grown nearly so fast."[17] Those schools receiving the bonus represented by the preformula distribution are not the ones bearing the brunt of national population shifts and growth patterns. Although elite schools draw from the nation as a whole, it is local schools that carry the burden of providing access to higher education for the bulk of poor students.

Because of the country's changing demographics, as well as the locking in of aid shares, "[m]any student-aid experts agree that the programs no longer serve the country's neediest students very well."[18] If aid to the most elite schools were eliminated, however, the effect could be a total exclusion of the poor. A two-tier system would result: one for the poor, one for the rich. It seems clear, then, that a complete withdrawal of aid to elite schools is no solution. Rather, federal aid should be tied to the job schools do in educating poor students. Even if no new dollars are committed to the system, reducing the disparities is imperative if we want to maintain even the pretense of equal educational opportunity. Given that private colleges typically spend more on their programs than public universities do, perhaps there is some justification for their receiving more money. But ten times more than the median? Or twenty?

Because existing disparities were born in politics, any discussion of reducing them will also be political and influenced by the respective clout of affected schools.[19] Moreover, to the extent that aid-disparate allocations have been naturalized into the budgeting process, these allocations become more difficult to change without a perceived crisis that could appear to threaten the entire system. Without a champion willing to bear the political costs of reshuffling accounts to benefit the economically disadvantaged, there is little hope—because there is so little political incentive—that the money will be redistributed to those who need it most.

Even those schools that ought to support a redistribution of these funds have incentives to resist a wholesale change to a need-based funding system. An analysis by the American Council on Education (ACE) using fiscal year 2002 data found that "public four-year institutions could lose 3.3 percent of their Work-Study dollars, 4.3 percent of their funds for Perkins Loans, and 5.9 percent of their supplemental-grants funds if Congress phased out a portion of the formula that distributes student aid based on historical allocations."[20] Among the hardest hit by the formula change would be the nation's historically black institutions.[21]

What would happen if the existing system were dismantled in favor of a formula based on serving poor students and their families? "[T]he financial aid officer's association has a pretty good idea of who would be the big beneficiaries: community colleges and perhaps most surprisingly, for-profit universities."[22] Although these institutions enroll high percentages of low-income students, they were not players in the national higher education scene when federal money was initially being apportioned.[23] And without new money, reallocation is a zero-sum game. If these schools were to get a larger share of the higher education aid dollar, the current winners would have to lose. Perhaps for this reason, many would prefer to define "equity" in terms of fairness to current recipients. Rodney Oto, Carleton College's associate dean of admissions and director of student financial services, says that he "understands the concerns of aid administrators at community colleges. The formula was designed years ago, and the student populations have changed." He believes that "the best way for Congress to spread the campus-based aid money more widely is for it to provide larger annual appropriations for these programs."[24]

None of us should be holding our breath waiting for larger annual appropriations. In early 2005 President Bush, apparently aware of the firestorm ignited by his education department's proposals, proposed changes that would increase the total amount available for individual Pell Grants.[25] Some have suggested that the White House needed a response to the claims that over 90,000 students would have been cut out of the Pell Grant program. Whether the new Bush proposal will actually remedy the harms inherent in his education department's plan is uncertain because the details of the new plan have not been released. This much seems to be clear: the budgeting of the Pell Grant program will be changed to eliminate the deficit it has been running over the past several years. Instead of being limited to the amount allocated in the budget while simultaneously being obligated to give aid to all who are eligible, the Bush proposal calls for the program to receive the amount of money that it spends. This would, in effect, convert the program to an entitlement program. This is precisely the idea most vociferously resisted by Republicans in Congress.

Congressional Republicans are also likely to resist the Bush proposal because it includes a $500 increase in the maximum Pell Grant award. At the time of this writing in 2005, it remains to be seen whether the Bush proposal is a temporary plan, a public relations initiative, or a real effort at reform. But unless the reform also includes a shift of money among the various institutional beneficiaries, it will not remedy the structural defects in federal financial assistance. Opposition to meaningful reform has been foreseen because the Senate committee in charge of higher education is largely composed of lawmakers from New England who are expected to protect the interests of established institutions of higher learning in their states.[26]

III. Government Intervention and Who Goes to College

The 2004 national budget did not increase the Pell Grant level from its current maximum of $4,050.[27] However, in a Scrooge-like gift two days before Christmas 2004, the Department of Education announced that it would change the formula parents, students, and families use in calculating their actual costs for attending school. Because the new formula changes the amount of state and local tax payments applicants will be able to claim, it changes the apparent amount of money they have available for school and modifies eligibility. According to the *Chronicle of Higher Education*, the new formula will reduce the Pell Grant program by $300 million and prevent up to ninety thousand students nationwide from receiving financial assistance.[28]

This effect was predicted by education experts in 2003. According to a commentator in the *Chronicle of Higher Education*, "the department lowered the amount it forgives families for the state and local taxes they pay, making families *appear* to have more money available to pay college costs than they really do."[29] If parents or students could pay their tuition with "apparent" dollars, these changes would make no difference. Unfortunately, most schools require payment in a currency with greater solidity.

The new formula will affect all federal aid programs that consider family contributions in determining eligibility. The American Council on Education has estimated the magnitude of the loss as affecting over 1.3 million students across various loan programs,[30] including the Stafford Loan and college work-study programs.[31] In addition, because of the new eligibility calculations, students who are disqualified from Pell Grants will also appear to be wealthy enough to be disqualified from state and direct school aid.[32] Brian Fitzgerald, staff director of the Advisory Committee on Student Financial Assistance, a panel that advises Congress on student aid issues, notes "[t]he real concern here is that the change will have a significant trickle-down effect because many states and colleges use the federal formula when awarding need-based aid."[33]

The Department of Education insists that the new formula will not greatly affect poorer students. In fact, the department maintains that by changing the formula Congress will be able to raise the maximum Pell Grant for those most in need. Of course, this would only be true if the formula change results in more money to be distributed, an outcome no one sees as likely.

On my own campus, the University of Texas, the student newspaper was quick to respond when the initial cuts were proposed. It noted that the new Pell Grant formula would have exactly the trickle-down effects predicted by opponents of the change. "In addition to the 6,600 UT Pell Grant recipients, the revision would have impacted all students who are still dependent on their parents. The revision would have decreased the amount of tax credit parents receive toward their estimated family contribution by a percentage point, which would mean less financial aid."[34] The principal problem with the proposed changes is that the formula does not really take into account what is happening with state and local taxes. As Senator Corzine from New Jersey has observed, "[t]he changes proposed by the Department of Education would give American families less credit for paying taxes when those taxes are going up and provide less financial aid to students when tuition costs are skyrocketing."[35]

Not only do the proposed changes to the Pell Grant program threaten by their own terms to eliminate a number of students from federal assistance, but the change in the formula calculations does not take into account the real expenses facing students and their families. Rising educational costs have increased financial pressures on students and have reduced the affordability of college for poor and working-class students. This is true whether the analysis focuses on those payments made directly to the students or to the schools.

A quick look at the run-up in tuition cost illustrates part of the problem. From 1976 to 2002 average tuition rose from $924.00 to $6,067 (in constant dollars).[36] When room and board are included, the change is even more dramatic: from $2,647 to $14,907. These figures are for all universities and thus collapse any differences that might exist between public and private schools (as well as differences between two- and four-year institutions). They nonetheless reflect the overall magnitude of the change. (For publics alone the change from 1964 to 2002 was from $1,051 to $10,660, whereas for privates alone the change over that same time period was from $2,202 to $31,052). While these numbers must be adjusted for inflation, there is some evidence that these costs have exceeded changes in the wages of working families. Another interesting trend in higher education has been a run-up in the real salaries of full-time tenured faculty and a decline in the salaries of nontenured teaching faculty. Some might conclude that the beneficiaries of federal aid to education were not the targeted impecunious students, but faculties and administrators.

IV. A New GI Bill?

Recently, Professor Lani Guinier argued that the democratic mission and broader public goals of higher education are in danger of being lost.[37] The increasing public acceptance of locked-in inequality[38] reflects resistance to the costs of changing from one regime to another. We see this in the conflict over federal financial aid programs. We are also witnessing a growing ideological commitment to the idea of individualized "contest" mobility as an answer to the problem of class disadvantage. The idea of class mobility remains a central tenet of the American Dream, and is explicitly embraced in the Bush administration's vision of an "ownership society."[39] Despite the ideological appeal of the narrative of individualized advancement, our history tells a different story. Certainly the emergence of striking individual talent is not to be discounted, but the conditions under which such talents are able to blossom are the real story. See, for example, the rhetoric advancing the nomination of Clarence Thomas to the Supreme Court and, more recently, of Alberto Gonzales to the office of U.S. Attorney General.

Importantly, the middle class in this country did not simply develop as a natural and inevitable consequence of the working of the capitalist economy. Rather, it resulted from active and effective management of the economy in an attempt to reduce the most pernicious effects of the politics of Social Darwinists.[40] The Homestead Act, the Reclamation Act, and the Mining Act of 1879, just to choose three examples, each created opportunities to transfer public resources to individuals in the interest not only of wealth creation and economic growth, but of greater social cohesion as well. The land-grant college system does the same for education. Fundamental to all these initiatives is a belief that public resources should be used in a way that strengthens the capacity of all members of the polity to participate in the more gratifying aspects of American social life. Though their aims were seldom achieved, most education Acts were crafted in this belief. As Professor Guinier puts it:

> The mission statements of selective public universities feature three common concerns: building students' knowledge, advancing existing knowledge, and producing a cadre of future citizens and leaders who are both willing and able to serve the public good. These purposes date back to the founding of the American republic. Benjamin Franklin, for example, argued that colleges should teach citizens about practical subjects. Thomas Jefferson believed that public higher education should "develop both leaders and the citizens capable of monitoring them." When Jefferson founded the first public university, the University of Virginia, in 1819, he had explicitly democratic principles in mind, including the education of citizens and officials, and the training of public leaders. *A commitment to education as a vehicle for the advancement of individual opportunity and broader democratic values was also true of the land grant colleges, which obtained public land in exchange for explicit commitments to public service.* This broad commitment to public service also characterizes the present-day mission statements of many elite private institutions, which use the language of "service" to anchor their educational purpose. *Thus, the historical guiding principle of both public and private universities has been to educate people who would then better serve society as workers, citizens, and leaders.*[41]

What is critical about both the education and resource Acts is not just the idealism or ideology underlying them, but the way in which they changed the nature of opportunity in the social conditions of the day. What these Acts share is what, in the context of education, Professor Guinier calls "structural mobility." Instead of valuing competitive individualism as the high road to opportunity, structural mobility takes as its starting point what Professor Guinier and I have in another context called "linked fate."[42] What has apparently declined in importance for some powerful policy makers is the idea that what constitutes effective public policy ought not to be measured by anecdotes of individual success, but by the extent to which individual success is a function of a successful and cohesive community. "In a world of structural mobility, individuals are given access to educational opportunities not because they win a 'contest' or because they have been hand-picked by elites, but because the relevant stakeholders have come together to make a set of public-minded choices."[43]

There is a readily available model for this kind of structural mobility in education.[44] Yet there are also cautionary lessons to be taken from its evolution. The example to be considered here was inspired by the 15 million Americans who were called from their roles in a depressed economy to perform military service in a war effort that commanded universal approval. On June 22, 1944, President Franklin D. Roosevelt signed the Servicemen's Readjustment Act of 1944, which became known as the GI Bill of Rights. The Bill was to assist servicemen and women returning from World War II to adjust to civilian life and allow them an opportunity to go to college.[45] The GI Bill covered tuition, fees, and books as well as a monthly stipend of $75 (equivalent to $450 today).[46] In return for their service, GIs could count on the rest of us to assist them in their reentry into "normal" life. Roosevelt's GI Bill served as a model for subsequent education programs, including the Korean War bill and the Vietnam bill. In 1985, Representative G. V. "Sonny" Montgomery introduced a provision to provide "all three-year enlistees a post-service educational stipend of $300 a month for thirty-six months of college."[47] To be eligible, service members are required to contribute $100 per month for one year.

For qualified service members who have served more than three years of active duty, total benefits for this program are currently $35,460, which must be spent within ten years of service.[48] However, the monthly benefits only cover about half of a given semester's tuition and fees. For example, a full-time student with tuition of at least $5,800 per semester is allowed to receive only $985 a month (which is the maximum allowed for any one person). This leaves the former soldier/current student to find a different source for the remainder. In addition, a full-time student with tuition of $3,000 per semester is allowed to receive approximately $500 per month, accounting for only half of a semester's tuition. Thus we have a decline in financial commitment to veterans combined with an increase in costs associated with attending college. And all this is occurring in a very different social context. As Dennis B. Douglass, Deputy Director for Education Services at the Department of Veteran Affairs, puts it, "[w]hile the veteran of the 1940's was going to school to get ahead of the curve, the veteran of today is doing it just because he's trying to keep pace."[49]

The armed services traditionally have relied on high school graduates who do not intend to enroll in colleges or universities to make up the bulk of their enlistees.[50] Yet, because more high school graduates are attending colleges and universities, the armed services have had increased difficulty in recruiting skilled men and women. The limitations on funding mean that the Armed Services are no longer able to provide incentives sufficient to sway would-be college students into enlisting. "The discrepancy between the growth of tuition costs and GI Bill benefits has created concern among policymakers about the adequacy of the benefit for veterans and its ability to attract recruits."[51] In its current state, the Bill's financial incentives are insufficient to keep would-be recruits from seeking alternative funds that would not require that they put in years of service. Because more recruits are attending college (despite increased costs) and the GI Bill has not been able to match the increased pace, officials believe that educational benefits must be increased in order to compete.

A proposal for change to the GI Bill includes increasing the financial rewards for those who choose to enlist in the military rather than immediately enrolling in a university. Known as the "Principi Report," the proposal recommends that GI Bill benefits should cover "most" of the costs of postsecondary education.[52] Given the state of the budget and current domestic priorities, it is unlikely that the Report's recommendations will be adopted because the total cost of the proposals is expected to be higher than the current cost of the program.

Even though we have failed to continue to embrace completely the promises of the original GI Bill, the idea that motivated it was sound: not just to reward those who served, but to recognize the public content of higher education and its relationship to building a democratic polity. Would it be wise then to extend the idea of the GI Bill into other government financial aid programs? We might first need to understand how GI Bill benefits diminished to the point of being less advantageous than simply applying for loans. For the kind of structural mobility we are advocating to be realistically supported, the current GI Bill has to increase benefits. What the history of the original bill suggests is that when the benefits of the Bill are more on par with the benefits of applying for aid and taking out loans, some people are willing to choose the former over the latter. A more effective Bill would act to increase the general population's education level, offering at least a partial return to the general good from the ill of targeting those who are not likely to attend college, and enlisting them in military service. The reader may question whether it is prudent to link educational reform to willingness to perform military service, especially in ventures more questionable than World War II, but until we address the inadequacies of the current GI Bill, and the tendency of legislatures to reduce funding to initiatives the public assumes are continuing to function correctly, it seems premature to speculate about what other linkages would be preferable.

Conclusion

Class remains an important determinant in whether potential students have an equal opportunity to attend any college, let alone the most selective institutions. Poor students continue to be at a disadvantage in competition for financial aid because of the way funds are allocated among institutions of higher education. Currently, Ivy League and four-year institutions continue to receive the most financial aid. However, under recent proposals, changes may occur that will shift resources to two-year and for-profit institutions, where more low-income and needy students are actually enrolled. We can expect the debate over these proposals to be fierce because many schools will see the changes as a zero-sum game.

Much of the debate on proposed changes to federal aid relies on the old argument that shifting resources from Ivy League and four-year institutions could lead to damaging results in terms of the capacity of those institutions to continue providing high-quality education. Surely that cannot be the case. And if it is, consider the strength of an argument, based on simple fairness, for making the change. (A "beggar thy neighbor" argument should have no place in determining where the money goes.) Need levels ought to be the main factor in determining funding to student aid programs. Nonetheless, lest we ghettoize students from disadvantaged backgrounds, a balance must be struck between providing more funds where most low-income and needy students are attending college and continuing to provide funds to elite institutions that are willing to provide education to low-income and need-based students.

While the GI Bill originally inspired individuals to enlist in the military and provided substantial education benefits thereafter, today it is in need of changes that will allow it to meet current education costs for those who serve the public in this way. The Bill did reflect a commitment to provide structural mobility and rejected individualistic contest mobility as the basis for schools to meet their public obligations. Should these policies be embraced again, history suggests that the number of people receiving education benefits will increase, providing our country with a more educated society with social solidarity as its foundation, rather than the class position of a student's parents.

NOTES

1. The author would like to thank Professor Tamara R. Piety for her comments and help.

2. *See* NEIL FOLEY, THE WHITE SCOURGE, MEXICANS, BLACKS AND POOR WHITES IN TEXAS COTTON CULTURE (1997) (chronicling the evolution of intragroup class management in Texas).

3. Edgewood Indep. Sch. Dist. v. Kirby, 777 S.W. 2d 391, 392 (Tex. 1989).

4. JEFFREY J. KUENZI & JAMES STEDMAN, CONG. RES. SERV., THE POSTSECONDARY EDUCATION STUDENT POPULATION 13 (Feb. 9, 2005).

5. In 1988, there were upward of 300,000 students who demonstrated a capacity to score well on the SAT, but who did not sit for the test. NAT'L CENTER EDUC. STUD., NATIONAL EDUCATIONAL LONGITUDINAL STUDY OF 1988 (1988); BETH A. YOUNG, NAT'L CENTER EDUC. STUD., PUBLIC SCHOOL STUDENT, STAFF, AND GRADUATE COUNTS BY STATE: SCHOOL YEAR 2001–2002, *available at* http://nces.ed .gov/pubs2003/snf_report03/table_06.asp; BETH A. YOUNG, NAT'L CENTER EDUC. STUD., STATE NONFISCAL SURVEY OF PUBLIC ELEMENTARY/SECONDARY EDUCATION: SCHOOL YEAR 2001–02, *available at* http://nces.ed.gov/ccd/stNfis.asp.; THE COLLEGE BOARD, 2001 COLLEGE-BOUND SENIORS: A PROFILE OF SAT PROGRAM TEST TAKERS, *available at* http://www.collegeboard.com/sat/cbsenior/yr2001/pdf/ NATL.pdf; ACT National Normative Data for High School Profile Report for Graduating Class of 2001 (unpublished data on file with author).

6. This is not true in Texas, where any high school graduate who finishes in the top 10 percent of his or her class is automatically eligible for admission to either of the two flagship public universities.

7. U.S. Census Bureau, *available at* http://census.gov (see Detailed Tables P12A–P12I; Data Set: Census 2000 Summary File 1 (SF 1) 100-Percent Data, QT-P2; Data Set: Census 2000 Summary File 1 (SF 1) 100-Percent Data, and PCT12–PCT12O; Data Set: Census 2000 Summary File 1 (SF 1) 100-Percent Data).

8. This figure includes individuals ages sixteen to twenty-four who graduated from high school or completed a GED during the preceding twelve months. *See* DIGEST OF EDUC. STATISTICS, CH. 3. POSTSECONDARY EDUC., tbls. 183–184 (2001).

9. *Id.* This figure includes individuals who enrolled in college as of October of each year who were aged sixteen to twenty-four and who graduated from high school during the preceding twelve months.

10. *Id.*

11. There is a 20 percent wage premium that accompanies graduation from elite

colleges. ANTHONY CARNEVALE & STEPHEN ROSE, SOCIO-ECONOMIC STATUS, RACE/ETHNICITY AND SELECTIVE COLLEGE ADMISSIONS 19 (2003).

12. Greg Winter, *Rich Colleges Receiving Richest Share of U.S. Aid*, N.Y. TIMES, Nov. 9, 2003, at A1.

13. *Id.*

14. *Id.*

15. *Id.*

16. Stephen Burd, *Unfair Advantage?* CHRON. HIGHER EDUC., Aug. 15, 2003, at A21.

17. *Id.*

18. Winter, *supra* note 12.

19. *Id.*

20. Kelly Field, *Top Public Universities Said to Lose in Aid Plan*, CHRON. HIGHER EDUC., June 4, 2004, at A1.

21. *Proposed Change in the Formula for Campus-Based Aid: Winners and Losers*, CHRON. HIGHER EDUC., June 4, 2004, at A16–18.

22. Winter, *supra* note 12, at 22.

23. *Id.*

24. Burd, *supra* note 16, at A21.

25. Stephen Burd, *President Bush Calls for Increase in Pell Grants*, CHRON. HIGHER EDUC., Jan. 28, 2005, at 25.

26. Stephen Burd, *House Republicans Challenge New England Senator on Shaping Aid Policy*, CHRON. HIGHER EDUC., Feb. 15, 2002, at A14.

27. Stacy Waite, *Congress Finally Passes 2004 Budget*, BADGER HERALD, Jan. 26, 2004, *available at* http://www.badgerherald.com/news/2004/01/26/congress_finally_pas.php.

28. Stephen Burd, *Changes in Federal Formula Means Thousands May Lose Student Aid*, CHRON. HIGHER EDUC., Jan. 7, 2005, at A1.

29. *84,000 Students Could Lose Pell Grants under New Formula, Education Department Estimates*, CHRON. HIGHER EDUC., Aug. 1, 2003, at A19 (emphasis added).

30. Stephen Burd, *Changes in Federal Formula Means Thousands May Lose Student Aid*, CHRON. HIGHER EDUC., Jan. 7, 2005, at A1.

31. Delaney Hall, *Students May Not Receive Aid under New Formula*, DAILY TEXAN, June 23, 2003, *available at* www.dailytexanonline.com.

32. Burd, *supra* note 30, at A1, A34.

33. *Id.*

34. A. J. Bauer, *Measure Could Save Aid for Some*, DAILY TEXAN, Sept. 16, 2003, *available at* www.dailytexanonline.com/news/2003/09/16/topstories.

35. *Id.*

36. National Center for Education Statistics, *available at* www.nces.ed.gov. (accessed Mar. 18, 2005).

37. Lani Guinier, Comment, *Admissions Rituals as Political Acts: Guardians at the Gates of Our Democratic Ideals*, 117 HARV. L. REV. 113 (2003).

38. Daria Roithmayr, *Locked in Inequality: The Persistence of Discrimination*, 9 MICH. J. RACE & L. 31 (2003).

39. David E. Rosenbaum, *Bush to Return to "Ownership Society" Theme in Push for Social Security Changes*, N.Y. TIMES, Jan. 16, 2005, at A17.

40. *See* William E. Forbath, *Caste, Class, and Equal Citizenship*, 98 MICH. L. REV. 1 (1999) (arguing that there is a constitutional tradition that sees the injuries of class as antithetical to the democratic underpinnings of our national tradition).

41. Guinier, *supra* note 37, at 126–27 (emphasis added).

42. LANI GUINIER & GERALD TORRES, THE MINER'S CANARY: ENLISTING RACE, RESISTING POWER, TRANSFORMING DEMOCRACY (2002).

43. Guinier, *supra* note 37, at 161.

44. The Texas Ten Percent Plan is another example of structural mobility. *See supra* note 6.

45. Given that many more men than women served in the armed forces, the legislation has mostly helped men. *See* LIZABETH COHEN, A CONSUMER'S REPUBLIC 138 (2003).

46. PETER SHAPIRO, A HISTORY OF NATIONAL SERVICE IN AMERICA, CENTER FOR POL. LEADERSHIP & PARTICIPATION, *available at* http://www.academy.umd.edu/publications/National Service/education_natservice.htm.

47. *Id.*; *see also* Greg Winter, *From Combat to Campus on the G.I. Bill*, N.Y. TIMES (Education Supplement), Jan. 16, 2005, at A4.

48. *Education: Solving the GI Bill Mystery, available at* http://www.military.com/Education/ Content/O, 13302,Education_GIMystery,00.html; *see also* Winter, *supra* note 47, at A4.

49. Winter, *supra* note 47, at A4.

50. MONTGOMERY G.I. BILL, RAND RESEARCH, 2000, *available at* http://www.rand.org/publications/RB/RB7538/.

51. *Id.*

52. Winter, *supra* note 47, at A4.

18

The Rise and Fall (and Rise Again?) of Accident Law

A Continuing Saga

Jeffrey O'Connell and John Linehan

Accidents are ubiquitous in the modern industrialized world, challenging advanced societies to construct remedial solutions—a task that requires the evaluation of priorities in distributing burdens and benefits from personal injuries. In the United States, the growth of accident costs over time has changed both tort law and insurance. Although of independent origin and development, these two areas became self-consciously fashioned along interdependent lines. A growing appreciation of their functional relationship inspired progressive reformers to construct legislative plans capable of promoting victim compensation, starting most impressively with workers' compensation plans early in the twentieth century. Inspired by such early successes, the fledging enterprise liability movement gained considerable momentum by midcentury in promoting the general expansion of tort liability. By the early 1970s, the rise of strict products liability, and legislation in automobile no-fault insurance, marked the apex of the movement to elevate victim compensation as the chief priority of accident law.

Our law defining the rights of accident victims purports to be more concerned than it was in 1970 with the protection of workers and consumers exposed to risk. But that is largely a mirage. In recent decades, the continuing inadequacies of our accident law, especially, but by no means limited to, unmet costs of health care and lost wages of the seriously injured, have become ever more apparent. Organized special interest groups equipped with enormous resources have wielded dominant influence in the policy debate over personal injury compensation reform. But the opposing partisanship of trial lawyers on the one side and insurance companies and their corporate and professional insureds on the other has frustrated reform as both sides have sought to further their respective narrow agendas.

This phenomenon has not only deflated constructive approaches to reform, but has led to reaction against what pro-plaintiff advances have been made.[1] Enterprise liability and the movement to align tort and insurance in order to achieve better victim compensation has been stalled and personal injury compensation in the United States remains appallingly deficient for most accident victims, especially for the seriously injured. Ensuing crises have merely refueled the contentious and confused battle over accident law as various parties vie to advance their individual positions. By delineating the tumultuous history of American accident law, this chapter offers insight into the deep flaws of today's system, despite its boasts of well serving the public and accident victims, and comments on what can be done to rectify things.

I. A Brief History of Accident Law

The law of torts long remained theoretically murky and undeveloped from its English origins. Tort law's immaturity is explained by the fact that accident costs in the preindustrial world did not reach levels that required systematic societal address and serious scholarly attention. The identity of tort law was often considered through analogy to its more ancient sibling, criminal law.[2] Tort law was seen as grounded in vengeance and to be used to punish individuals deemed responsible for civil wrongs.

With his seminal publication in 1881 of *The Common Law*, Oliver Wendell Holmes was among the first to pursue a theoretical independence for tort law. Holmes grasped the policy implications of viewing accident law in a functional manner, as a means to promote broader societal goals. This perspective sprang from the intuitive notion that "even a dog distinguishes between being stumbled over and being kicked."[3] He argued that the tendency of his contemporaries to import the moralizing tone of criminal law into the realm of tort failed to respect the fact that accidents are—by definition—unintentional. Holmes further argued that a negligence regime should balance victim compensation and deterrence of unsafe behavior. Holmes's approach thus expanded the theoretical analysis of tort to include a utilitarian weighing of the economic costs and benefits of injurious conduct. But thereupon Holmes made a crucial mistake; he erroneously predicted that as courts continually dealt with determinations of negligence, findings thereof would become routinized and efficient, and thereby less case-specific. But that, as Kenneth Abraham has lucidly demonstrated, never happened, and likely never will.[4] Attempts to establish negligence, in all its frustrating particularity, continue to plague our judicial system with no discernible letup, contrary to Holmes's overly optimistic prediction.

As noted in chapter 1 of this book, the rise of the negligence regime in the latter half of the nineteenth century coincided with the emergence of the modern industrial world. Morton Horwitz and others have argued that judges purposefully employed an instrumental approach in their application of liability rules in order to facilitate the rise of heavy industry and to promote economic growth.[5] Under their theory, courts refashioned existing tort doctrine in order to subsidize industrialization, mirroring common law changes in property and contract law. Notably, producers of goods and services were insulated from potential liability by the "unholy trinity" of affirmative defenses: contributory negligence, assumption of risk, and the fellow-servant rule. These developments combined to simultaneously elaborate tort doctrine and contract its overall scope of liability. Judges, Horwitz argued, reasoned against the background policy judgment that liability for injury victims must not present an unmanageable obstacle for industrial expansion.

Despite the protective effect of the emerging common law, the risk of liability was becoming an increasing concern for enterprising ventures in the modernizing economy. In the search for a more efficient means to manage risk, business interests increasingly relied upon insurance mechanisms, which allowed parties to distribute their risks efficiently. First developed to protect against losses resulting from fires and marine calamities, the scope of insurance grew exponentially, spawning a huge service industry of its own. Coverage was eventually provided across nearly every category of potential loss, as individuals increasingly began to obtain personal life insurance to cover even death. Crucial to business interests in the long term was the development of insurance coverage for liability due to negligence, leading to today's system of third-party liability insurance. While favorable to business, this form of insurance reduced the retributive sanction of civil liability, and therefore conflicted with the underlying moral justification of tort law. It was therefore criticized for emasculating tort law's underlying morality and its deterrent effects. Nevertheless, such insurance was favored on the grounds that it protected companies from undue costs and unpredictability while further facilitating compensation for the injured.

Industrial growth, the spread of insurance coverage, and the rise of modern technology were especially potent agents of change in the workplace environment, where that "unholy trinity" of defenses served as a stubborn barrier against worker recompense for job-related injuries. Seeking a viable solution for this emerging crisis, progressives sought a means by which insurance and tort law could be jointly manipulated for beneficial results. Working in the midst of labor unrest, legislators relied upon recent scholarship as a basis for achieving reform. They succeeded in passing a compromise solution that made employers strictly liable for compensating worker injuries, but limited that compensation to lower, predetermined levels with no payment for pain and suffering. Victims were also barred further recourse to litigation.

Workers' compensation laws served as a milestone in the evolution of accident compensation. Such reforms enacted in the Progressive era manifested the confluence of insurance, tort law, and public policy. The true merit of the legislation lay in its ability to further victim compensation without unduly burdening employers. Employers recognized that these laws were efficient, as they eliminated the delays and transaction costs derived from expensive litigation over fault. The laws also acted as deterrents. Industry-specific and experience-rated premiums were established, giving employers an incentive to maintain safe workplaces. In addition, the moral hazard on the workers' side was addressed by lessening the accessibility of overcompensation through tort. As a result, implementation of these reforms led to an enormous reduction in industrial accidents,[6] as well as a dramatic and more equitable increase in victim compensation through prompt and guaranteed payouts. Workers' compensation expanded liability for employers, but did so to a predictable and limited extent, and was therefore manageable.

An important consequence of the workers' compensation movement was that it spurred appreciation of the synergistic relationship between tort law and insurance—a result with far-reaching theoretical implication. The success of these reforms for workers militated against the antiquated and more punitive underpinnings of accident law and in favor of a functional conception of tort and insurance as a combined tool for achieving public policy objectives. With newfound emphasis upon compensation, observers had formulated the paternalistic contention that employers could more easily and effectively insure their workers than workers could insure themselves. Thereupon, eminent scholars like Leon Green and Fleming James pioneered what became known as the enterprise liability movement, which aimed to change radically the nation's personal injury system by extending the workers' compensation model to other types of accidents.[7] Their purpose was to facilitate compensation, but in a manner that would distribute accident costs to the social entities most capable of absorbing them, namely, business enterprises.

With the growing momentum of enterprise liability, tort law began to develop outside a theoretical vacuum, as insurance considerations played an increasing role in liability rule allocation. With compensation as a goal, reformers struggled to deemphasize fault as a basis for liability and encouraged a transition from negligence to strict liability, especially in cases involving defendants with superior cost-absorbing capacities. In the landmark 1944 case, *Escola v. Coca Cola Bottling Co.*,[8] Justice Roger Traynor's famous concurring opinion signaled increasing judicial acceptance of enterprise liability. Justice Traynor claimed that in the context of mass production, defendants should be held to a form of strict liability rather than negligence due to the fact that manufacturers could more easily obtain insurance, spread their losses, and more efficiently curtail accident costs. In addition, Traynor observed that under the previous negligence standard, injured consumers were faced with unfair obstacles in proving liability, and that mass producers were consequently insufficiently deterred. Traynor's opinion was increasingly cited by courts during the 1960s and 1970s, spreading the application of strict liability in product liability cases.

At midcentury, the landscape for personal injury compensation was increasingly shaped by instrumental judges who were motivated by cost-spreading considerations in formulating tort doctrine. Beyond products liability and the statutory introduction of comparative negligence, lawmakers and judges expanded the scope of duty in negligence law, broadened both vicarious liability and contribution among joint tortfeasors, established less stringent standards for finding causation, and expanded other areas of liability and damages. The aggregate effect of these changes was the eventual transformation of accident law along pro-plaintiff lines by favoring a third-party insurance system that greatly expanded defendants' exposure to liability. Tort law, expansively developed doctrinally and theoretically, had a widely recognized influence on social policy.

Some scholars, including the senior author of this essay, sought additional revolutionary reform in accident compensation through the promotion of more ambitious no-fault plans by legislation. This movement was especially ambitious in that it aimed past mere pro-plaintiff modifications in tort to challenge explicitly the fault-based premise that underlay the litigation system. The goal of applying the no-fault model outside the employment context was first championed by Fleming James and others in the early and mid-twentieth century. However, there were enormous barriers to transporting true no-fault plans to litigation-prevalent fields such as products liability and medical malpractice where it is almost impossible to predetermine the insured event. Under workers' compensation, the inquiry is limited to the simple question of whether the injury occurred on the job, but no such convenient test existed or exists in malpractice and products liability.

But these complications were absent in the context of automobiles, which had long become the leading cause of accidental injury and death in the United States. Automobile coverage was amenable to no-fault reform, for just as in the employment context, the insured event could be readily defined in that compensation could be guaranteed to any victim injured in an accident "arising out of the ownership, maintenance or use of a motor vehicle," regardless of anyone's fault. Following the 1965 publication of *Basic Protection for the Traffic Victim*,[9] a series of no-fault automobile laws were enacted in various states.

II. Accident Law Today

The no-fault automobile movement coincided, as indicated above, with the rise of strict products liability in the early 1970s and represented the high point of enterprise liability and the promotion of compensatory goals in accident law. However, political barriers and growing special interest influence soon coalesced to stall any momentum. Although twenty-six U.S. jurisdictions passed some form of no-fault automobile legislation, few plans were anywhere near a "pure" form of no-fault. Most measures were qualified either by thresholds allowing for tort claims above a minimal level of injury, or by add-on plans permitting a no-fault beneficiary to bring a tort suit and only requiring the deduction of no-fault benefits from any tort award.[10] In recent years no-fault schemes have met increasing resistance and even rebuke, with a few states repealing their plans.[11] Existing proposals for choice no-fault automobile measures, which allow motorists the option of forgoing tort claims in return for no-fault benefits, were set back in 1999 when a federal bill failed to pass either the House or the Senate.[12]

Outside the category of auto accidents, efforts to implement more substantive no-fault reform gained even less traction. Despite the theoretical expansion of strict products liability during the 1960s, frustrating litigation in this category has remained prevalent, having merely shifted from the question of defendants' faulty conduct to the question of defendants' faulty (i.e., defective) product. In medical malpractice, because of the difficulty of defining the insured event, no-fault reform largely went nowhere. Even when no-fault legislation was passed, it typically contained measures that were narrowly drawn and accident-specific, as in the case of plans for victims of nuclear accidents, black lung disease, childhood vaccines, birth-related injuries, and more recently with the September 11th Victim Compensation Fund of 2001.[13]

Concurrent with such barriers to broad-based, no-fault reforms, organized interest groups have become hostile to progressive change. The opposing pincers of the defense interests and the plaintiffs' bar have been very effective in ensuring that the success of workers' compensation not be widely expanded.

Plaintiffs' lawyers have mustered the most strident opposition—after all they profit enormously from the bloated excess of the current system, and stand to lose the most if tort law is substantially changed. They continue to uphold the efficacy of the third-party system, and blame current deficiencies on oligopolistic pricing practices and industrywide mismanagement by insurance companies. They argue that premiums would be more effectively reduced through systematic restructuring of the nation's insurance markets and more rigorous regulation of rates.

Trial lawyers have also defended their interests through the "remoralization" of fault, by emphasizing defendant culpability and the desirability of retribution through litigation.[14] Focusing on dramatic stories of real and imagined instances of egregious defendant misconduct, they attempt to confine the public's concentration to a primary goal of punishing wrongdoing ("sending a message"). Reversing the relatively amoral mandate of enterprise liability, moralistic connotations increasingly overwhelm notions of loss spreading and wider compensation, reverting to an antiquated view of tort law. Moreover, today's "remoralization" of fault is deceptive in light of the fact that third-party insurance largely deflects the direct blow in any retributive sanction. As a result, the fallout of tort litigation often rains on the relatively innocent through the form of increased insurance premiums. The public thus bears a greater share of the ultimate burden through increased prices for goods and services, and even on occasion, through economic stagnation and, it is argued, marketplace abandonment. But the trial bar encourages this remoralization by promoting the expansion of a quasi-criminal approach to civil litigation. Of course punitive damages are justified in response to egregious defendant misconduct. But personal injury lawyers now routinely seek such damages quite without regard to whether the facts would justify them.[15] Note too that compared to commercial disputes, punitive damages are rarely in fact awarded in personal injury cases, including those arising from the delivery of medical services or manufactured products.

The tragic result of this retributive stance for personal injury cases is that it undermines the fuller compensatory goal that guided the enterprise liability movement. Viewing fault through the always subjective and debatable moral lens only amplifies the uncertain effects of an already arbitrary system that leaves much to the whim of litigation's indeterminacy and chance. Too often inculpable defendants are held liable and undeserving claimants overcompensated—or culpable defendants exonerated and deserving claimants left stranded.

Not only does inequity exist across the bar between plaintiffs and defendants, but among different types of plaintiffs as well. The tort system consistently favors those with greater resources to withstand the law's delays while poorer plaintiffs remain burdened by those delays and are therefore more likely to accept lower settlements in order to receive at least some measure of desperately needed early compensation. As a result, what remains is a situation in which individuals of the same class of injury can receive vastly different levels of compensation unrelated to need. Such arbitrary variation would seem the very definition of inequity. Although supposedly speaking for the interests of victims, the trial bar's retributivist prescriptions ultimately hamstring efforts to distribute compensation sensibly.

Obstinately opposed to lessening litigation, advocates on the Left too often promote unilateral expansion in first-party coverage (i.e., health and disability insurance) as an additional means to compensate injury.[16] Some observers argue that broader first-party coverage, including, for example, a system of universal health care, would decrease society's dependency upon tort litigation for compensation. But existing data undercuts this hopeful prediction. In fact, increases in first-party insurance mean ever more sub-sidization of tort claims as accident victims are afforded greater short-term isolation from financial need.[17] With greater first-party insurance proceeds and lawyers hired on a contingent fee, victims are able to buy more time and leverage in their attempts to tap third-party insurance to obtain pain and suffering damages. In addition, because pain and suffer-ing awards are often based on a rough multiple of medical bills, claimants have an incentive to pad medical expenses paid by first-party health insur-ance. Any expansion of first-party insurance without any corresponding constraint in tort law has the adverse effect of increasing inefficiency while entrenching erratic victim compensation. Effective reform must appreci-ate the interrelated nature of insurance and tort law, and target correlative, structural modifications in both. Finally, the goal of universal health care in the United States is not only highly chimerical, but even if achieved, will surely not simultaneously cover universal wage losses, a remaining defi-ciency for which tort claims must provide the remedy. And wage loss in America is covered much less than health care by either private or social insurance[18] and, in cases of serious injuries, dwarfs the costs of health care.[19]

Compensatory goals are even more directly subordinated by a growing countermovement inspired by the Right, which perceives the flaws in the current personal injury system as solely rooted in the distinctly pro-plain-tiff trend in tort law since the rise of enterprise liability. Backed by insur-ance companies and defense interests, this movement has waged a "tort reform" crusade in response to the recurring insurance crises of recent decades, supposedly precipitated by unrestrained juries awarding inflated damages to plaintiffs. These groups argue that the expansion and liberal-ization of tort doctrine has destabilized the system and elevated insurance premiums. Their main substantive reforms, which include the curtailment of joint and several liability and the collateral source rule, as well as limits on awards for pain and suffering, punitive damages and attorneys' contin-gency fees, make it harder for claimants to be paid or restrict payments when they are made. These reform proposals, by definition, frustrate com-pensatory goals. This stems from a myopic and asymmetrical focus upon the goals of reducing liability premiums and provider costs and a simulta-neous disregard for proper victim compensation. The facts are that nearly 45 million Americans are without any health insurance, not to speak of the many more lacking significant disability insurance.[20] While little can be expected to change soon in that regard at least in the foreseeable future, tort liability could be structured to sensibly fill the gaps much better than it now does. Thus even if those gaps far exceed payments available from tort liability insurance, the latter does entail billions of dollars that can be far better used than now in serious cases of crying need. The conservative legislative agenda, on the other hand, with its goals of simply limiting defendant liability, places an even greater burden upon victims, whose continued state of undercompensation is, after all, a crisis in its own right.

III. The Possibilities of Neo-No Fault

Today's political battles over accident law and tort reform reveal the enormous power that opposing interest groups wield in the war of finger-pointing and mudslinging. It is accident victims themselves who remain the losing party. The opposing prescriptions of the Left and the Right are alike in that they ultimately fail to address existing deficiencies in victim compensation. Under the traditional litigation system—whether contracted or expanded—precious money, time, and resources are inefficiently expended in seemingly ceaseless adversarial battles.

But there are alternatives. For example, motivated by the practical shortcomings of traditional no-fault models, the senior author of this article has developed an "early offers," or "neo no-fault," statutory regime to reform today's defective system.[21] Neo no-fault resembles its no-fault progenitor in that it aims to compensate accident victims for economic loss promptly on a periodic basis without the hassle, unpredictability, and inefficiency of full-fledged tort claims. The advantage of this proposal over traditional no-fault laws is that it eschews the need to predetermine the insured event—a nearly impossible task, as pointed out above, in the contexts of medical malpractice and products liability. Moreover, it retains an effective element of the tort system as a means to provide defendants and plaintiffs with choices and to incorporate a deterrent device aimed at promoting incentives for safety.

As envisioned, the mechanics of a neo no-fault statute are relatively streamlined. Upon the filing of a personal injury claim, a defendant has 180 days to decide whether or not to offer plaintiffs periodic payment of their net economic losses as they accrue. Net economic losses are defined as all unpaid medical expenses, including rehabilitation, plus unpaid wage loss, and a reasonable but reduced attorney's fee. Upon receiving an early offer, the claimant is then barred from pursuing a normal tort claim for both economic and noneconomic losses under traditional common law principles. But a claimant may reject the offer and still pursue full tort recovery on conditions that (1) the standard of misconduct is raised, allowing tort liability only where "wanton misconduct" is proven; and (2) the standard of proof is also raised, requiring proof of such misconduct beyond a reasonable doubt or at least by clear and convincing evidence.

Under this system whereas defendants are not required to make early offers, there are clear incentives for them to do so. These early payments are reduced from typical tort payouts since they deduct all collateral payments and reduce both plaintiff and defendant attorneys' fees by ensuring a quick resolution of the case. Even more significantly, upon tendering payment for net economic losses, the defendant earns immunization from the threat of having to pay full tort damages including noneconomic payments, except in the very exceptional cases of gross misconduct—which deserve criminal-like sanctions. When defendants determine that such an early offer would still not be economically advantageous, then normal tort procedures prevail. Therefore, the neo no-fault scheme is at best a huge benefit for defendants, and at the very least, no worse than the current system.

Plaintiffs would also find their options under neo no-fault to be advantageous. With mounting unreimbursed medical expenses and lost wages, a prompt and assured level of compensation for such essential losses, undiminished by high contingency fees, would be very appealing to injury victims—especially those with serious losses, who ought to be the prime concern of any insurance system. Therefore, as in the case of workers' compensation, victims would not be disadvantaged as a class. Nevertheless, in more exceptional cases of grave defendant misconduct, a victim would still have recourse through tort to recover for pain and suffering damages and even to impose the retributive and deterrent effect of punitive damages. While victims would have to surrender their unmodified, common law tort rights upon acceptance of an early offer, in the vast majority of arguably deserving cases they should welcome the prompt recompense of economic damages as an attractive quid pro quo.

Neo no-fault would be a compromise solution that addressed victim compensation in a manner analogous to workers' compensation, without unfairly burdening providers of goods and services. The balanced nature of this proposal is apparent in that it effectively combines tort law and insurance in order to promote important policy objectives. Such reform would provide for enormous gains in systematic efficiency by circumventing, in the great majority of present cases, extensive disputes over fault and the value of noneconomic damages with their attendant uncertainty, delay, and transaction costs.[22] Nor would the advantages of neo no-fault cause a sacrifice of deterrence, because neo no-fault requires prompt payment of net economic loss to avoid tort liability and retains tort's potent weapon of noneconomic damages as a coiled threat for serious misconduct. In the twenty-first century, can such a scheme as neo no-fault attract support despite the opposition of both the trial bar and those stridently demanding one-sided "tort reforms"?

Throughout much of the twentieth century, the enterprise liability movement relied on the factors of insurability and cost-spreading capabilities as a foundation for the expansion of tort liability. Nevertheless, even its original proponents, especially Fleming James, viewed such expansion as merely a temporary means to encourage plaintiff recovery, and viewed the tort system as inherently inimical to satisfactory compensation. Enterprise liability reforms in tort law were viewed as a form of scaffolding that would eventually lead to a broader system of social insurance. But herein James, like Holmes, made a crucial mistake. He failed to anticipate that if tort law based on fault were greatly expanded, then lawyers and even insurers, with a huge investment in its expensive cumbersomeness, would rise to oppose the fundamental alterations James had overoptimistically predicted.

IV. Conclusion

We live at a critical time in the history of personal injury law in the United States. Accident costs are rising, insurance coverage is incomplete, and victim welfare continues to be grossly inadequate. Nevertheless, there is a history rich with lessons and examples that illuminate an effective path for reform. Since Oliver Wendell Holmes, scholars have espoused functional considerations in tort law as applied to personal injury over and above moral judgments and emotional reactions, in order to fairly and systematically deal with problems related to accidents. The workers' compensation movement serves as a powerful example of how tort law and insurance could be modified in a creative manner to address the problem of accidents. But the subsequent history of accident law has been more influenced by popular hysteria and knee-jerk reactions than by sophisticated and deliberate social policy rationales. Special interest groups are able to divert the public debate from the complexity of the reality, to the simplicity of their messages, fortified by emotive power from their often outlier data. This takes the dialogue over liability rule allocation back to the moralizing tone that prevailed long before tort law, backed by insurance, came of age. Reason must be reinvested in the debate in order to reinstall hope for balanced reform. The history of early-twentieth-century accident law showed that some sensible progress is possible. When will the twenty-first century see this hope come to fruition?

NOTES

1. On the expansion of claimants' rights, see 1 AMERICAN LAW INST., REPORTERS' STUDY ON ENTERPRISE RESPONSIBILITY FOR PERSONAL INJURY 59–66, 80–103 (1991); JOHN G. FLEMING, THE AMERICAN TORT PROCESS 32–67 (1998); Patrick S. Atiyah, *American Tort Law in Crisis*, 7 OXFORD J. LEG. STUD. 279, 293–301 (1987). On legislative attempts to roll back or curb such expansion, see JEFFREY O'CONNELL & C. BRIAN KELLY, THE BLAME GAME: INJURIES, INSURANCE, AND INJUSTICE 107–08 (1987).

2. MARK C. RAHDERT, COVERING ACCIDENT COSTS 11 (1995).

3. OLIVER WENDELL HOLMES, THE COMMON LAW 3 (1881).

4. Kenneth S. Abraham, *The Trouble with Negligence*, 54 VAND. L. REV. 1187, 1223 (2001); *see also* Jeffrey O'Connell & Andrew S. Boutros, *Treating Medical Malpractice Claims under a Variant of the Business Judgment Rule*, 77 NOTRE DAME L. REV. 373, 405–06 (2002).

5. *See generally* MORTON HORWITZ, THE TRANSFORMATION OF AMERICAN LAW, 1780–1860 (1977); *but see* Gary T. Schwartz, *Tort Law and the Economy in Nineteenth-Century America: A Reinterpretation*, 90 YALE L.J. 1717, 1720 (1981) (challenging Horwitz's subsidization thesis).

6. *See* JOHN FABIAN WITT, THE ACCIDENTAL REPUBLIC: CRIPPLED WORKINGMEN, DESTITUTE WIDOWS, AND THE REMAKING OF AMERICAN LAW 187 (2004).

7. *See generally* George L. Priest, *The Invention of Enterprise Liability: A Critical History of the Intellectual Foundations of Modern Tort Law*, 14 J. LEGAL STUD. 461, 472 (1985).

8. 150 P.2d 436 (Cal. 1944) (Traynor, J., concurring).

9. ROBERT KEETON & JEFFREY O'CONNELL, BASIC PROTECTION FOR THE TRAFFIC VICTIM: A BLUEPRINT FOR REFORMING AUTOMOBILE INSURANCE (1965).

10. *See* PETER A. BELL & JEFFREY O'CONNELL, ACCIDENTAL JUSTICE: THE DILEMMAS OF TORT LAW 211 (1997).

11. *See* Gary T. Schwartz, *Auto No-Fault and First-Party Insurance: Advantages and Problems*, 73 S. CAL. L. REV. 611 (2000).

12. *See* S. 837, 106th Cong. (1999). This bill failed despite initial bipartisan support and a study by the Congressional Joint Economic Committee that predicted savings of as much as 32 percent of auto insurance premiums nationally, or $45 billion a year. *See* Mitch McConnell, Daniel Patrick Moynihan, & Joseph Lieberman, *Auto Insurance: A Better Way*, WALL ST. J., Sept. 22, 1997, at A22. The bill was reintroduced on October 7, 2004 by Senators John Cornyn, Mitch McConnell, and John McCain. *See* Auto Choice Reform Act of 2004, S. 2931, 108th Cong. (2004).

13. Also known as the "9/11 Fund," this program was enacted as part of the Air Transportation Safety and System Stabilization Act (ATSSA), Pub. L. No. 107–42, 401–09, 115 Stat. 230, 237–41 (2001) (codified at 49 U.S.C.A. 40101 note (West Supp. 2004)). The program provided compensation to injury victims and victim family members who waived their rights to sue the airlines industry. *See* Julie Goldscheid, *Crime Victim Compensation in a Post 9/11 World*, 79 TUL. L. REV. 167, 170–71 (2004).

14. Anthony J. Sebok, *The Fall and Rise of Blame in American Tort Law*, 68 BROOK. L. REV. 1031, 1044–46 (2003) (highlighting "the present attraction of punishment to progressive torts scholars and activists"); *see generally* Jeffrey O'Connell & Joseph R. Baldwin, *(In)Juries, (In)Justice, and (Il)legal Blame: Tort Law as Melodrama—Or Is It Farce?* 50 UCLA L. REV. 425 (2002) (criticizing the ever-increasing moralizing emphasis of contemporary personal injury law).

15. *See* David G. Owen, PRODUCTS LIABILITY LAW § 18.6 n.12 (2005).

16. WILLIAM HALTOM & MICHAEL MCCANN, DISTORTING THE LAW: POLITICS, MEDIA, AND THE LITIGATION CRISIS 289 (2004) (urging legislation mandating adequate health care coverage, unemployment benefits, and related social services. But at the same time, these scholars decry legal reforms that would curb tort rights and thereby reduce access to legal remedies. *Id.* at 293.)

17. *See* Jeffrey O'Connell, *Blending Reform of Tort Liability and Health Insurance: A Necessary Mix*, 79 CORNELL L. REV. 1303, 1305 (1994).

18. *See* 1 AMERICAN LAW INST., REPORTERS' STUDY ON ENTERPRISE RESPONSIBILITY FOR PERSONAL INJURY 59 (1991).

19. *See* JEFFREY O'CONNELL, ENDING INSULT TO INJURY: NO-FAULT INSURANCE FOR PRODUCTS AND SERVICES 75 (1975).

20. The number of health uninsured reached 15.6 percent of the American population in 2003, up from 15.2 percent in 2002. Associated Press, *Ranks of Poverty and Uninsured Rose in 2003, Census Reports*, N.Y. TIMES, Aug. 26, 2004, at A1.

21. The "early offers" idea was originally set forth in Jeffrey O'Connell, *Offers That Can't Be Refused: Foreclosure of Personal Injury Claims by Defendants' Prompt Tender of Claimant's Net Economic Losses*, 77 NW. U. L. REV. 589 (1982). For the application of this idea to medical malpractice cases, see Henson Moore & Jeffrey O'Connell, *Foreclosing Medical Malpractice Claims by Prompt Tender of Economic Loss*, 44 LA. L. REV. 1267 (1984). For the terms of a federal bill, which also serves as

a model for state legislation, applying the early offers plan to medical malpractice claims, see S. 1960, 131 CONG. REC. 36 (1985) (presenting and discussing the proposed Medical Offer and Recovery Act).

22. Indeed, one experienced malpractice defense attorney predicted that under neo no-fault he would advise making the offer in as much as 80 percent of the cases in his firm's portfolio. Interview with William Ginsburg, Esq., in Durham, N.C. (Apr. 1986).

19

Welfare Reform and Deform

Joel F. Handler and Danielle Sarah Seiden

The great dividing line in U.S. welfare policy is between the "deserving poor" and the "undeserving poor." The former are excused from the paid labor force; the latter are not. As the labels—"deserving" and "undeserving"—imply, this division has always presented deeply contested views of race, gender, and moral behavior. This chapter will trace policy changes in welfare reform since the beginning of the twentieth century. We will concentrate on the cash assistance program for single mothers and their children—formerly Aid to Families with Dependent Children (AFDC), and now Temporary Assistance for Needy Families (TANF). Although not the largest welfare program in the United States, TANF is the most contested and it is what most Americans mean by "welfare."

I. Welfare before 1996

Welfare for mothers first appeared in the United States in the second decade of the twentieth century in state programs favored by Progressives. Initially enacted under the rubric Aid to Dependent Children (ADC), these programs were popularly known as "Mothers' Pensions," and later acquired the name Aid to Families with Dependent Children (AFDC). The beneficiaries were "fit and proper" mothers, a term most often taken to apply to white widows. Single mothers who were divorced, deserted, never married, or of color were seldom deemed to qualify. Funds were limited and were distributed at the discretion of state and local administrators.[1]

In the Social Security Act of 1935,[2] the New Deal supplied federal grants-in-aid to cover half the cost of state programs to assist mothers. An unstated purpose at that time was to pump some cash into a beleaguered national economy. A few federal standards were enacted, but primary responsibility for administration remained with state and local governments. Local authorities might in some communities have a small source of added funding derived from state or local appropriations for "general relief."

Dramatic changes came in the late 1950s and 1960s. Over the next three decades, the ADC/AFDC rolls went from 2 million to about 13 million, in part due to the War on Poverty, the legal rights revolution, and the massive migration of African Americans from the South to urban cities in the North. Expenditures rose from about $500 million to about $23 billion.[3] In streamed those who had been previously excluded: African Americans, women who were divorced, separated, or deserted, and an increasing number of mothers who had never married—in short, the "undeserving poor." Welfare was then in crisis. Eligibility was tightened; benefits were cut. Nevertheless, costs and numbers rose steadily and the program appeared out of control. Political and popular concern focused with increasing alarm on the large number of African American single mothers, on out-of-wedlock births, and on the specter of generational dependency.

To address these concerns, many states developed their own work programs, and in 1967, the federal government introduced a mandatory work program—the Work Incentive Program (WIN). Egalitarian critics of a work requirement contended that it was unjust to impose a requirement on poor mothers to which mothers not on welfare were not subject. But the prevailing view was that in light of rising costs and the risks of dependency, poor mothers should be sent to work when feasible.

By 1980, there was growing agreement that AFDC mothers should be expected to earn what they could. President Reagan coined the term "welfare queen" to dramatize his perception of the risk that the undeserving poor were increasingly dependent on handouts from federal taxpayers. Pertinent too was the fact that social norms had changed so that a majority of nonwelfare mothers were working. It was therefore deemed reasonable to expect welfare mothers to work. In addition, it was widely perceived that families are better off materially and socially if their adults are gainfully employed and not forever dependent.[4]

The claimed rehabilitative benefits from paid labor illustrate a fundamental characteristic of welfare policy. Although that policy is often described in seemingly objective terms—labor markets, wage rates, incentives, earnings, and so forth—these terms are heavily laden with subjective meaning. Determinations about who the poor are, why they are poor, and whether and under what conditions they should be helped involve social judgments. Importantly, these judgments are both consciously and sub-consciously influenced by people's beliefs about work, family, and gender, as well as their attitudes toward race and ethnicity. Consequently, the resulting stigma associated with the "undeserving" poor is much broader than a mere failure to become gainfully employed would suggest. Rather, the term "welfare" has become in many minds a code word evoking the stereotypical image of a young, inner-city, African American woman, who is most likely a substance abuser, who allegedly has no qualms about pro-ducing children in order to stay on welfare, and who (because she is a bad mother) will breed a criminal class or perpetuate intergenerational welfare dependency.

II. The 1996 Welfare Reform and the "Work First" Strategy

It was the Personal Responsibility and Work Opportunity Reconcilia-tion Act of 1996 (PRWORA) that replaced Aid to Families with Depen-dent Children (AFDC) with Temporary Assistance for Needy Families (TANF).[5] Through the use of block grants based on prior caseloads, TANF increases state discretion. Its main features, however, are stiff work re-quirements and enforced time limits. There are two sets of time limits. First, recipients cannot receive welfare for more than two years at any given time. Second, there is a cumulative lifetime limit of five years (with exceptions for no more than 20 percent of the caseload). States have the option of imposing shorter time limits, which many have. In the six years following PRWORA's enactment, states were required to move an in-creasing percentage of welfare recipients into the workforce, starting with 25 percent of the adults in single-parent families in 1997 and increas-ing to 50 percent by 2002. The Act also requires states to reduce grant amounts for recipients who refuse to participate in "work or work activi-ties." These welfare-to-work requirements are enforced by funding cuts in block grants.

In addition to work requirements, PRWORA includes a variety of pro-visions dealing with "family values." For example, PRWORA prohibits the use of federal funds for minor parents under eighteen years of age who are neither in school (or participating in other specified educational activi-ties) nor living in an adult-supervised setting. States are required to reduce a family's grant by 25 percent if the mother fails to cooperate (without good cause) with efforts to establish paternity. States may eliminate cash assistance to families altogether or provide any mix of cash or in-kind benefits they choose. They can deny aid to all teenaged parents or other selected groups, deny aid to children born to parents receiving aid, or deny aid to legal immigrants. States may choose to deny cash assistance for life to persons convicted of a drug-related felony (which in many states can consist of possession of a small amount of marijuana). PRWORA authorized states to provide new residents with benefits equal to the amount offered in their former state of residence for up to one year, but this provision was subsequently declared unconstitutional.[6] The 1996 legislation also modifies other programs that bear on the well-being and work efforts of welfare recipients, including Medicaid, food stamps, and other nutritional programs, as well as programs directed at child support or child care.

PRWORA also directly limits support for immigrants. With some exceptions, immigrants entering the United States after August 22, 1996 are not eligible for most welfare benefits, including TANF, until they have been here for at least five years. The five-year ban applies after they become citizens. This includes "qualified" aliens—permanent residents, refugees, admitted asylum seekers, as well as some others. So-called "non-qualified" aliens are only eligible for emergency assistance (especially Medicaid).[7] The 1996 legislation also requires that most legal immigrants have sponsors with incomes over 125 percent of the poverty line. This income is deemed available when calculating welfare eligibility, usually resulting in disqualification. In addition, sponsors are liable for the costs of any welfare. Not surprisingly, the use of welfare by noncitizens has declined even more than by citizens, including U.S.-born children whose parents are immigrants. On the other hand, the use of Medicaid and the State Children's Health Insurance Program (SCHIPS) has remained stable. Still, the percentage of children of legal immigrants who lack health insurance is higher than children of citizens.[8] Again, unsurprisingly, there is more hardship for them, including rising food insecurity.[9]

Prior to TANF, over forty states had pending or approved variances from the AFDC program that enabled them to impose diverse work requirements enforced by some form of time limits. Welfare reformers used the reported experience of these states to justify the current welfare-to-work approach, known as the "work first" strategy. The premise underlying the work requirement (as well as the family values provisions of TANF) is that welfare encourages dependency. Instead of seeking to improve themselves and to become self-sufficient, some critics believe welfare recipients produce children to qualify for and stay on welfare, which then becomes a way of life from generation to generation. Welfare recipients are thus seen to threaten both the two-parent family and the Protestant work ethic. Tough work requirements, enforced by time limits, are therefore deemed necessary not only to reduce welfare costs, but, more importantly, to replace the entitlement status and permissiveness of the past system with the values of responsibility and self-sufficiency. This is supposed to benefit not only parents utilizing welfare, but also to provide positive socialization for their children. In essence, the "work first" strategy tells recipients: get a job, any job, stick with it, and you will emerge from poverty.

Pursuant to waivers, many states began implementing welfare-to-work programs between 1993 and 1995. By 1995 these state reforms had begun taking effect and welfare rolls fell sharply.[10] AFDC/TANF cases, nationwide, declined from their peak of 5 million families in March 1994, to 4.4 million when TANF was enacted in 1996, to 2.8 million in December 1998.[11] A critical question is the extent to which the decline in the rolls has been the result of these reforms.

III. The Low-Wage Labor Market

The success of a "work first" policy is highly dependent on the availability of jobs that unskilled mothers can fill. Yet, welfare recipients do not fare particularly well in the competition for low-skilled jobs. Employers of low-skilled workers are looking for high school diplomas, work experience, and social skills ("soft skills").[12] Welfare recipients often lack these things, particularly high school diplomas and work experience. In addition, employers often hire through networks, and, in general, prefer workers with similar ethnic backgrounds. This often places African Americans and other racial minorities at the end of the queue. Finally, and perhaps most significantly, welfare recipients are often handicapped because they are parents, especially mothers, of small children and bear all the responsibilities good parenting entails. Not only are there the usual child care problems, but children get sick; there may be school or preschool issues; and there is the difficulty of adjusting to shift work and overtime hours. Due in part to these concerns, research on women in the low-wage labor market shows that many job applicants do not disclose that they have small children.

The "work first" reform requires mothers of children as young as three months old to enter the paid labor force. This means that if a welfare recipient finds a job, she/he also has to compete in the child care market. Yet there is a crisis in child care for low-wage workers. Millions of infants, children, and adolescents are at high risk of having their health and overall development compromised because of mediocre child care. Child care centers are at capacity, and even when there are vacancies the price is usually too high for welfare recipients to manage. Most welfare recipients thus use unregulated relative or family day care (informal care). Indeed, a substantial portion of the working poor—perhaps as many as half—rely on family members.[13] Informal caregiving can be of high quality if the caregiver is a close relative or friend or has some other kind of close attachment to the child. If, however, this attachment is not present, then there is a strong risk of poor care. Even with informal care, costs are high and availability varies depending on the age of the children and whether the parent's work hours are fixed or variable.[14]

New reforms proposed by the Bush administration will increase the demand on child care even further by requiring even greater workforce participation. Under these reforms, work requirements are to be increased by 5 percent per year until they reach 70 percent and welfare recipients will be required to work a full forty-hour workweek. Since child care spending will remain unchanged despite the increased workweek, child care slots are likely to become even scarcer. Little apparent concern has been given to how single mothers are supposed to manage one or two jobs and take their children to child care and/or school, often without adequate transportation. As long as families are not on welfare, it is assumed that all is as it should be.

The problem of health care is also crucial. Poor health in either a parent or a child affects the parent's ability to work.[15] Because of poorer health, low-income families need to use more health care services than high-income families. Yet low-income families have greater difficulty getting health insurance and health care. Although TANF recipients qualify for Medicaid, they are not automatically enrolled in the program. Even when they are enrolled, recipients can only receive Medicaid benefits up to one year after they exit from welfare. There has been a sharp decline in Medicaid rolls for reasons that are not clear. (The same drop is occurring in food stamp enrollment.) It could be that aid workers are not advising recipients of their eligibility or are discouraging them from applying. Former recipients may also mistakenly think that they are ineligible. In the meantime, fewer low-wage employers are providing health insurance, especially for family members, and access to health care for low-wage working mothers is thus becoming increasingly more difficult. Some observers take the position that the uninsured can get necessary care from doctors and hospitals. In fact, the health status of the uninsured is considerably worse than the insured. Unsurprisingly, women remaining on welfare as compared to working and nonworking leavers have better overall access to health care, including health insurance and a regular health care provider.[16]

In addition, the "work first" strategy imposes considerable transportation demands on both welfare recipients and welfare leavers. Welfare recipients and leavers must conduct job searches, get to and from jobs that may have irregular hours, drop off and pick up children from child care and school, carry out household responsibilities, and attend to other business such as medical appointments. Yet welfare reformers rarely mention transportation as a significant barrier. Surveys have nonetheless shown that as welfare recipients become employed, their travel patterns and problems come to resemble those of other low-wage workers.[17]

One of the biggest problems is that large numbers of low-wage workers, especially minorities, live in communities that are spatially isolated from job opportunities.[18] In other words, jobs are not readily accessible to inner-city residents.[19] In Los Angeles, for example, black job seekers have to cover more geographical area than whites or Latinos.[20] Where public transportation is available and reliable, it helps. Difficulties remain, however, when welfare recipients have to travel to unfamiliar areas in order to fill a quota of job applications, while at the same time trying to manage other life demands. Not only is commuting time by public transportation far longer than by private car, but often public transportation is not designed to serve inner-city workers working suburban jobs. Inner-city commuters often have to make two or three time-consuming transfers and frequently suburban workplaces are not close to transit stops. For example, in Los Angeles, a one-way trip from the central city to the predominantly white suburban San Fernando Valley is approximately two and a half hours and requires three bus transfers. In Atlanta, only about a third of low-skilled jobs in white suburbs are within a quarter mile of a public transit stop.[21] When one factors in the need to drop off and pick up children from child care and school, it becomes clear why welfare administrators often mention transportation as an important barrier to moving recipients off welfare.[22]

Second, adequate recognition has been given to those who need support in order to work. At least until the current recession, thirty-two states provided postemployment support. During the 1990s, over 20 million new jobs were created in the United States. Until the current recession (2001), unemployment was approximately 4 percent and for a long time there seemed to be no sign of inflation. Moreover, over the past decade, there has been a tremendous increase in labor market participation of less-skilled women. Despite the economic expansion and the rise in productivity between 1973 and 1993, the household income of the poorest fifth declined. Wages began to rise among less-skilled workers after the mid-1990s. This slowed the growth of wage inequality, but the wage growth of the past few years has not made up for the large declines in the 1980s and early 1990s. Real wages in 1999 were below their 1979 levels for those with the lowest levels of education.[23] For a while, the inequality in women's wages narrowed, more because of an increase in the hours worked *and* the significant decline in male earnings than because of the increase in female wages.[24] The decline in real wages for the less skilled, less educated workers was especially pronounced for adults aged twenty-four to thirty-five with a high school diploma or less. Female dropouts earned only 58 percent of what male dropouts earned.[25]

In recent decades, jobs have became increasingly contingent or short-term, and without benefits. Very few of the poor work full time, at least at one job. In 1998, only 13 percent of the poor were fully employed.[26] Reemployed workers usually suffer a decline in wages. Employment instability continues to be a major problem for less-skilled and disadvantaged workers. They experience frequent and long spells of unemployment.[27] Low wages and unemployment are most severe for young workers, minorities, single-parent families, and those who lack a high school diploma.[28]

Given the state of the low-wage labor market, a significant number of welfare recipients will not be able to leave welfare permanently via work. How many will actually be cut off—whether under the two-year or the five-year time limits—depends in part on the size of the rolls. For the first time in U.S. history, welfare rolls have been declining. Whether they continue to decline, to stabilize, or to increase depends on two factors—the severity of employment deficits for those who remain on the rolls and the economy. Before the current economic slowdown, the decline in the rolls had been slowing, which is not surprising since those who were left faced more employment barriers.[29] By 2004, employment was rising, but welfare rolls were not declining. It could be that the improved economy is not affecting the job market for some welfare recipients.

The consequences for children are grave. Of the 1.6 million children on TANF rolls in California, approximately 36 percent are long-time recipients.[30] Projecting this ratio to the national population, it would appear that the combined effects of welfare cutoffs will affect 1,158,000 children. What will happen to these children? Long-term parents will have the greatest difficulty finding and keeping a job. Day care will be a significant problem. Whether working or not, acute poverty will increase for these families. Because such poverty is the single most important predictor of poor outcomes for children, the future looks bleak.

The gravity of the situation becomes even more apparent when one considers the potential impact of welfare cutoffs on the foster care system. Existing state foster care systems are in crisis. To date, the number of children in foster care has not increased significantly due to welfare reform because the more stringent cutoffs have yet to set in.[31] However, if only a fraction of the children subject to the welfare cuts enter the foster care system, costs will skyrocket.[32] The consequences for children in foster care are likely to be severe. Foster children have higher rates of both acute and chronic medical and mental health problems, higher rates of growth problems, and three times the national average for asthma. Infants and toddlers are more likely to manifest developmental problems such as motor, language, cognitive, and self-help concerns. These children are already at high risk of failing to become successful, productive adults. The odds will now be increased.[33]

IV. The Decline in Welfare Rolls: What Happens to Those Left Out?

A. Causes of Decline

If employment is so uncertain for unskilled mothers, then what accounts for the steep decline in welfare rolls and poverty rates of female-headed households?[34] Although most economists agree that the macroeconomy is responsible, they differ as to the relative importance of welfare reform. Estimates of the effects of welfare reform range from "trivial" to 30 to 40 percent. A major difficulty is determining what is meant by "welfare reform." For many people, "welfare reform" means that recipients are obtaining jobs through welfare services. If this was the causal factor leading to lower welfare rolls, it would suggest that the "work first" strategy was working. Closer scrutiny, however, reveals that there are a number of variables influencing the lower numbers.

First, there has been a significant increase in benefits to working families which are not considered part of "welfare reform." Indeed, over the past twenty years, benefits to working families have increased from about $5 billion to over $50 billion. Most of that increase is attributable to the Earned Income Tax Credit (EITC),[35] which some economists view as the single most important factor in the decline of the welfare rolls and of poverty rates.

Second, diversion plays a significant role. Diversion occurs when a welfare department refuses to accept an application. "Recent empirical work indicates that as much as one-half of the recent decline in [welfare] caseloads is attributable to declining rates of entry."[36]

Finally, sanctions have contributed substantially to decreasing rolls. One report estimates that 15 percent of the decline in the welfare rolls was due to welfare reform, but half of this was because of sanctions.[37] If recipients are not leaving welfare because they are gainfully employed, but rather because of statutorily permitted punitive measures, then perhaps welfare reform is not helping poor families very much at all. Because of the significance of this observation, evidence in support of this conclusion merits closer examination.

B. The Impact of Sanctions

Welfare reform dramatically expanded the range of circumstances in which a family could have its welfare benefits reduced or canceled. Federal law requires at least a partial benefit reduction for families who do not satisfy work and child support requirements. In addition, sanctions can affect food stamp benefits for the entire family and Medicaid coverage for sanctioned adults. States may impose more stringent penalties and may expand the penalties to other parts of the program.

Sanctions have become a central characteristic of most state TANF programs,[38] and sanction rates are quite high. One study found that one-quarter to one-half of families subject to work requirements were sanctioned over a twelve- to twenty-four-month period. Many sanctions are imposed because of missed appointments and deadlines. A large percentage of recipients, however, comply with welfare regulations. These individuals may nonetheless find themselves subject to sanctions because of bureaucratic errors. For example, if a computer fails to record a required appointment, the recipient is automatically sanctioned.[39] Additional rules regarding age eligibility, paternity requirements, and limits on additional children born to current recipients can also result in welfare terminations. Importantly, welfare recipients are often unaware of exemptions from program requirements and are reluctant to oppose or to appeal sanctions.[40]

1. WHO GETS SANCTIONED?

A number of state studies have shown that sanctioned recipients have limited educational training.[41] In Tennessee, 60 percent of sanctioned families lacked a high school diploma or a GED compared to 40 percent who left welfare for work; 34 percent of the sanctioned families did not understand what they were required to do. In South Carolina, 36 percent of high school dropouts were sanctioned as compared to 22 percent of high school graduates. Studies in Arizona and Minnesota report more than half of the families receiving full sanctions had a parent with less than a high school education. Sanctioned families are also disproportionately hard to employ and have more limited work experience. In Maryland, for example, 41 percent of sanctioned families had no employment history, compared to 31 percent who left welfare for other reasons.

In addition to the above, sanctioned families have longer histories of being on welfare. In South Carolina, 38 percent of long-term recipients as compared to 21 percent of short-term recipients were sanctioned. Many sanctioned families also experienced personal or family challenges (such as chemical dependency, physical and mental health problems, and domestic violence) at a higher rate than other recipients. Transportation difficulties and heightened child care problems resulting from families with three or more children may also increase the likelihood of sanctions.

2. WHAT HAPPENS TO WELFARE LEAVERS?

Some states are beginning to track what happens to sanctioned families. Most can be said to be coping, but at what level? The most thorough study of sanctions to date, Delaware's "A Better Chance" program, found that in an eighteen-month period, 60 percent of the recipients had been sanctioned, and of these, 45 percent had their cases closed. Those who were sanctioned had more children, lacked transportation or access to public transportation, and lacked an understanding of program requirements. The average payment loss was a 60 percent reduction in the grant. These clients were less equipped to offset the lost income through earnings due to less work experience, longer welfare dependence, and lower levels of education. Less than a third (32 percent) eventually cured their sanctions; 45 percent remained noncompliant until their cases were closed, and 23 percent left the rolls before the sanctions progressed to case closure.

The available evidence indicates that more than a third of the leavers are not working. Fourteen percent rely on the earnings of a spouse or partner. Of the remaining 25 percent, more than a quarter report that they are disabled, sick, or otherwise unable to work. Others explain their unemployed state by pointing to, among other things, family responsibilities, a lack of access to employment, the absence of work supports, and transitions between jobs. Of those not disabled, 69 percent report that they are looking for work. Only a small percentage receive unemployment benefits. Less than half were using food stamps and Medicaid. Almost three-quarters of all former recipients report receiving no private help in the first three months after leaving welfare. Former recipients report cutting down or skipping meals because of lack of money (33 percent), worrying about lack of money for food (57 percent), running out of food at the end of the month (about 50 percent), inability to pay rent, mortgage, or utility bills (39 percent), and having to move in with others because of lack of money (7 percent).[42] Significantly, a rise in no-parent families was recently reported because many poor inner-city mothers could no longer cope with the low-wage labor market and take care of their children. Rather than leave them with an abusive father or stepfather, these mothers placed their children with a grandmother or other relative.[43]

As noted above, many former welfare recipients are not getting food stamps or Medicaid even though they are eligible for these programs. Families who are no longer eligible or who are deterred from cash assistance through TANF may also think that they are no longer eligible for other programs or may not be informed of the existence of these programs. From 1995 to 1997, the poorest 20 percent of families who left welfare lost an average of $577 a year primarily because wages did not make up for lost benefits. The next 20 percent, with incomes between 75 percent and 112 percent of the poverty line, had an average increase in earnings of $900 and an average EITC of $400. These gains, however, were offset by the loss of means-tested benefits (the average loss was $1,460 per family).

The decline in means-tested assistance was particularly severe for poor children. The reduction in means-tested benefits is one of the reasons why poverty has not decreased as fast as welfare caseloads.[44]

In light of the above, it is not surprising that most recipients and leavers cycle in and out of the labor market. But they return to welfare rather than Unemployment Insurance. A reason is that in most states they do not qualify for Unemployment Insurance. Some do not satisfy the minimum hours and earnings requirements given the instability of their jobs. Many fail to satisfy the "nonmonetary eligibility" conditions,[45] which require (1) that work separations result from no fault of the worker (i.e., misconduct or a voluntary separation); and (2) that workers seek and be willing to accept available work. (In many states, "available work" means full-time work regardless of how many weekly hours the applicant worked in his or her last job.) Interestingly, most job separations are not because of job loss (which accounts for only about 25 to 40 percent of unemployment). Women are much more likely than men to have "voluntary" reasons for leaving a job (i.e., quitting because of child care and other family responsibilities and transportation difficulties).[46] For these women, welfare is their unemployment compensation. In the past, when jobs disappeared or child care broke down, former recipients would return to welfare. Now, with the time limits, this option will no longer be available.

V. The Future

If the past is any guide, one would not predict dramatic improvements in welfare. Throughout history, welfare policy has been largely symbolic. Myths and stereotypes gain prominence; drastic reforms are enacted; but policy at the field level is usually decoupled from political administrations. There are many reasons, but usually the policies as enacted are too draconian or, more importantly, too costly. More often than not, states and local governments bear the increased costs. Serious welfare-to-work programs—including community-service jobs—are more expensive than traditional programs, as are other alternatives such as shelter and foster care.

The present situation, however, is different from the past. Four kinds of change have been occurring. One is the continued gradual erosion of benefits. There has been a 45 percent decline in federal expenditures since 1970. The second is the dramatic decline in the rolls. Whereas in the past those who remained on the rolls were further stigmatized, now that "welfare as we know it has ended," there seems to be more support for the working poor (e.g., the EITC, child care). Third, there has been a vast increase in *privatization*. In most states, many parts of welfare services are contracted out and contractors are given incentives to come up with "positive results"—that is, a decline in the rolls. Fourth is the financial incentive to cut the rolls. Under AFDC, states would lose the federal share of each terminated case; now, under the block grant formula, states make money for each case off the rolls. Finally, there is the uncertainty of the economy. Whether and how much an improved job market might help former recipients is unknown.

A. Improving the Job Market

Since the great majority of welfare recipients are presently working, have recently worked, are trying to work, and will eventually leave welfare via work, the most obvious reforms would involve improving the low-wage labor market so that more jobs, with increased earnings and benefits, are available. Improving existing jobs decreases the need for welfare. To achieve this goal, a number of measures must be taken, including job creation when unemployment is high or when unemployment begins to rise and jobs become less available,[47] continued support of the EITC,[48] reformation of unemployment and disability insurance, and modest raises in the minimum wage.[49]

B. Child Care

Adequate, reliable child care is essential if poor parents are to be able to support their families with work outside the home. One viable strategy for overcoming child care availability problems is the expansion of public sector programs like pre-kindergarten, kindergarten, and Head Start, which are not usually considered child care. All-day kindergarten is spreading, and there is support for providing free pre-kindergarten for four-year olds. Professor Barbara Bergmann says that by expanding these programs as well as before- and after-school care, the four- and five-year olds of working parents would be covered. Even with the problems many public schools are facing, the quality of care would be far higher than in a great many current settings.[50] Bergmann notes that present appropriations cover only about 12 percent of eligible children. She proposes additional funding to cover all eligible children, which would perhaps cost an additional $15 billion. A sliding eligibility scale would cost about $50 billion. Professor David Blau offers an alternative approach. Blau suggests the following three-step proposal: (1) a means-tested child allowance for up to two children in the form of a refundable tax credit; (2) subsidization of the cost of accreditation; and (3) additional outreach for high-quality care and means-tested vouchers for upto two children depending on the quality of care. Blau estimates the net cost of his proposals to be about $95 billion.[51] Either way, parents would not be forced into cheap, unlicensed day care, and infants and children would have a better start in life. Whether any of these proposals or others like them can or will be funded is uncertain.

C. Health Care

Families should not be made worse off by losing health insurance and food stamps when they leave welfare for work or be forced to return to welfare to obtain such assistance.[52] Welfare policy should be sensitized to varying degrees of employability. Some of the problems with health care can be ameliorated by information, education, immunization, prenatal care, and the like. Forms can be simplified. Office hours can be expanded. Other problems, however, are more intractable (e.g., time and wages lost, transportation, and child care difficulties). A major problem is financing. Medicaid is now seriously inadequate, covering fewer than half of those below the poverty line.[53] Another basic problem with Medicaid is its eligibility cutoff—one dollar above the limit and a family loses coverage, which, of course, creates a strong disincentive to increase one's earnings or to leave welfare. Other outstanding problems include variations in coverage and services among the states, lack of coverage of the working poor and adults who do not have dependent children, low reimbursement rates for providers, and the inability to combine Medicaid with private insurance.[54]

D. Transportation

One way to improve access to suburban jobs would be to attack residential and employer discrimination. Another would be to subsidize commuting with van pools, improved public transportation, and cars. Employment problems are eased considerably when low-income workers have cars, especially in areas where public transportation is not well developed. Yet welfare policies still restrict recipients in their ability to own a car.[55]

E. The More Difficult Cases

We have not adequately noticed the recipients with multiple barriers to employment (e.g., low skills, cognitive limitations, health problems, language barriers, addictions, and domestic violence). These recipients may need sustained and expensive assistance. Some are probably unlikely ever to become fully self-sufficient. Others may be able to do part-time, low-wage work. A distinction has not been drawn between those who can reasonably be expected to work and those who cannot. TANF should apply to those who can reasonably be expected to work, and Supplemental Security Income (SSI) should apply, on a nonlimited time basis, to those who cannot.[56]

In addition, adequate recognition is not given to those who need support in order to be able to work. Thirty-two states do provide postemployment support that includes transportation aid, the purchase of work clothing or tools, and payment of work-related fees. A few states offer short-term cash payments to help cover work expenses or emergencies. So far, there is little information as to how many welfare recipients are involved in these programs, but the numbers seem small.[57] In addition, education and job training should fulfill some work requirements, but they generally do not.

Finally, little is done to inform marginally employable workers of work opportunities or of possible sources of support. There should be community-based, employment-related organizations to provide information, postemployment support, monitoring, and advocacy services for the working poor. Although most employment is obtained through informal networks, many welfare recipients lack these connections. In addition, recipients need information concerning the EITC, health benefits, the availability and quality of day care, and related programs such as disability and unemployment insurance. Community-based agencies could be encouraged to provide this information, monitor health and child care services, and provide counseling and advocacy services for low-income working mothers.[58]

Notes

1. Winifred Bell, Aid to Dependent Children (1965).
2. Pub. L. No. 74-271, 49 Stat. 620.

3. JOEL HANDLER & YEHESKEL HASENFELD, THE MORAL CONSTRUCTION OF POVERTY (1991).

4. DAVID ELLWOOD, POOR SUPPORT: POVERTY IN THE AMERICAN FAMILY (1988); IRWIN GARFINKEL & SARA McLANAHAN, SINGLE MOTHERS AND THEIR CHILDREN: A NEW AMERICAN DILEMMA (1986).

5. PUB. L. NO. 104-193, 110 Stat. 2105; Shapiro v. Thompson, 394 U.S. 618 (1969).

6. Saenz v. Roe, 526 U.S. 489 (1999).

7. Michael Fix & Ron Haskins, *Welfare Benefits for Non-Citizens*, Brookings Institution Policy Brief 15, at 2 (Feb. 2002), *available at* http://www.brookings.edu/es/research/projects/wrb/publications/pb/pb15.htm.

8. *Id.* at 2–3.

9. Wendy Zimmerman & Karen Tumlin, *Patchwork Policies: State Assistance for Immigrants under Welfare Reform*, Urban Institute—Assessing the New Federalism: Occasional Paper No. 24 (Apr. 1, 1999), *available at* http://www.urban.org/url.cfm?ID=309007.

10. WENDELL PRIMUS ET AL., THE INITIAL IMPACTS OF WELFARE REFORM ON THE INCOMES OF SINGLE-MOTHER FAMILIES (1999).

11. MARK GREENBERG, BEYOND WELFARE: NEW OPPORTUNITIES TO USE TANF TO HELP LOW-INCOME WORKING FAMILIES (1999).

12. HARRY HOLZER, WHAT EMPLOYERS WANT: JOB PROSPECTS FOR LESS-EDUCATED WORKERS 30 (1996).

13. Barbara Wolfe & Deborah Vandell, *Child Care for Low-Income Working Families*, 22 FOCUS 106, 110 (2002).

14. Lucie White, *Quality Child Care for Low-Income Families: Despair, Impasse, Improvisation, in* HARD LABOR: WOMEN AND WORK IN THE POST-WELFARE ERA 116 (Joel Handler & Lucie White eds., 1999).

15. Jack Hadley, *Sicker and Poorer: The Consequences of Being Uninsured*, Report of Kaiser Commission on Medicaid and the Uninsured 6, 8–9 (2002), *available at* http://www.kff.org/uninsured/20020510-index.cfm.

16. GREG DUNCAN & P. LINDSAY CHASE-LANSDALE, FOR BETTER AND FOR WORSE: WELFARE REFORM AND THE WELL-BEING OF CHILDREN AND FAMILIES 28 (2001).

17. Paul Ong & Douglas Houston, Travel Patterns and Welfare to Work, Los Angeles, CA (2002) (unpublished manuscript, *available at* http://www.uctc.net/papers/603.pdf).

18. Michael Stoll, *Search, Discrimination, and the Travel to Work, in* PRISMATIC METROPOLIS: INEQUALITY IN LOS ANGELES 417 (Lawrence Bobo et al. eds., 2000).

19. Michael Stoll et al., *Within Cities and Suburbs: Racial Residential Concentration and the Spatial Distribution of Employment Opportunities across Sub-Metropolitan Areas*, 19 J. POL'Y ANALYSIS & MGMT. 207 (2000).

20. Stoll, *supra* note 18.

21. Stoll et al., *supra* note 19, at 217.

22. Ong & Houston, *supra* note 17, at 1.

23. Rebecca M. Blank & Lucie Schmidt, *Work, Wages, and Welfare, in* THE NEW WORLD OF WELFARE 70–102 (Rebecca M. Blank & Ron Haskins eds., 2001).

24. LAWRENCE MISHEL ET AL., THE STATE OF WORKING AMERICA 1998–99, at 134–35 (2000).

25. Bruce Katz & Katherine Allen, *Help Wanted: Connecting Inner-City Job Seekers with Suburban Jobs*, 17 BROOKINGS REV. 31–35 (1999).

26. Paul Osterman, *Organizing the U.S. Labor Market: National Problems, Community Strategies, in* GOVERNING WORK AND WELFARE IN THE NEW ECONOMY 240–65 (Jonathan Zeitlin & David Trubek eds., 2003).

27. Katz & Allen, *supra* note 25.

28. Gary Burtless, *Growing American Inequality: Sources and Remedies*, 17 BROOKINGS REV. 31–35 (1999).

29. Melissa Healy, *Welfare Rolls Fall to Half of '96 Numbers*, L.A. TIMES, Aug. 23, 2000, at A12.

30. Data prepared by the Western Center on Law and Poverty 1996 (on file with author).

31. Somini Sengupta, *No Rise in Child Abuse Seen in Welfare Shift*, N.Y. TIMES, Aug. 10, 2000, at A1.

32. Jennifer Wolch & Heidi Sommer, *Los Angeles in an Era of Welfare Reform: Implications for Poor People and Community Well-Being*, The Southern California Inter-University Consortium on Homelessness and Poverty (April 1997), available at http://www.usc.edu/dept/geography/SC2/sc2/pdf/welfare.pdf.

33. Jennifer Wolch, *America's New Urban Policy: Welfare Reform and the Fate of American Cities*, 64 J. AM. PLAN. ASS'N 8 (1998).

34. The poverty rate for female-headed households fell from 36.5 percent in 1996 to 30.3 percent in 1999, and child poverty has declined from over 20 percent to less than 17 percent. Poverty in the United States: 1999, Table B-1. STATISTICAL ABSTRACT OF THE UNITED STATES: 2001. Table 680.

35. The EITC is the largest cash transfer program for low-income parents in the United States. A growing number of studies of the EITC have produced evidence regarding its positive effects. During 1998, EITC was responsible for lifting more families out of poverty than all other means-tested programs combined.

36. JEFFREY GROGGER ET AL., CONSEQUENCES OF WELFARE REFORM: A RESEARCH SYNTHESIS XXV (2002).

37. *Id.*

38. Jan Kaplan, *The Use of Sanctions Under TANF, in* 3 Issue Notes (Welfare Information Network, April 1999), *available at* http://www.financeprojectinfo.org/publications/sanctionissuenote.htm; LaDonna Pavetti & Dan Bloom, *State Sanctions and Time Limits, in* THE NEW WORLD OF WELFARE, *supra* note 23, at 245–69.

39. Matthew Diller, *The Revolution in Welfare Administration: Rules, Discretion, and Entrepreneurial Government*, 75 N.Y.U. L. REV. (2000).

40. Yeheskel Hasenfeld et al., Characteristics of Sanctioned and Non-Sanctioned Single-Parent CAL WORKS Recipients; Preliminary Findings from the First Wave Survey in Four Counties: Alameda, Fresno, Kern, and San Diego, Los Angeles, CA 11–12 (2001).

41. *Id. at* 11–14.

42. Pamela Loprest, Families Who Left Welfare: Who Are They and How Are They Doing? (Urban Institute, Washington, D.C., Discussion Paper No. 99-02, 1999).

43. Nina Bernstein, *Side Effect of Welfare Law: The No-Parent Family*, N.Y. TIMES, July 29, 2002, at A1.

44. Mark Greenberg & Michael Laracy, Welfare Reform: Next Steps Offer New Opportunities: A Role for Philanthropy in Preparing for the Reauthorization of TANF in 2002, at 1–30 (2000), *available at* http://www.nfg.org/publications/welfare.htm.

45. Cynthia Gustafson & Philip Levine, *Less-Skilled Workers, Welfare Reform, and the Unemployment Insurance System* (Nat'l Bureau of Econ. Research, Working Paper No. 6489, 1998); White, *supra* note 14.

46. Gustafson & Levine, *supra* note 45, at 3.

47. Philip Harvey, *Liberal Strategies for Combating Joblessness in the Twentieth Century*, 33 J. ECON. ISSUES 497–504 (1999).

48. PRIMUS ET AL., *supra* note 10.

49. Ed Lazere, New Findings from Oregon Suggest Minimum Wage Increases Can Boost Wages for Welfare Recipients Moving to Work (1998), *available at* http://www.cbpp.org/529ormw.htm.

50. Barbara Bergmann, *Decent Child Care at Decent Wages*, 12 AM. PROSPECT A8 (2001).

51. David Blau, *Rethinking U.S. Child Care Policy*, 18 SCI. & TECH. 66–72 (2001).

52. Robert Greenstein & Jocelyn Guyer, *Supporting Work through Medicaid and Food Stamps, in* THE NEW WORLD OF WELFARE, *supra* note 23, at 335–68.

53. Welfare recipients account for about a quarter of Medicaid enrollees, but the major cost increases in recent years have been for the disabled, the blind, and the aged.

54. Barbara Wolfe & Steven Hill, *The Effects of Health on the Work Effort of Single Mothers*, 30 J. HUM. RESOURCES 42–62 (1995).

55. Paul M. Ong, *Car Ownership and Welfare-to-Work*, 21 J. POL'Y ANALYSIS & MGMT. 255 (2002). In about half the states, a TANF, food stamp, or Medicaid recipient cannot own a car worth more than $4,650.

56. Lynn Karoly et al., *Effects of the 1996 Welfare Reform Changes on the SSI Program, in* THE NEW WORLD OF WELFARE, *supra* note 23, at 482–99.

57. Julie Strawn et al., *Improving Employment Outcomes under TANF*, Pub. No. 01-17, 14–17 Center for Law and Social Policy (Feb. 15, 2001).

58. HANDLER & HASENFELD, *supra* note 3.

The Hierarchy in Criminal Law

Evidence Law to Protect the Civil Defendant, but Not the Accused

Margaret A. Berger

Traditionally, evidence law's function was to provide ground rules for fact-finding at jury trials.[1] Indeed, James Bradley Thayer told us that evidence law was "the child of the jury system,"[2] and many evidentiary rules can best be understood as the means to control illogical or biased inferences by lay fact-finders.[3] So it is perhaps not surprising that interest in evidentiary issues has waned as the number of jury trials continues its downward trend.[4] Evidence scholarship no longer stands at the forefront of legal thought,[5] and evidentiary concerns are no longer perceived as central to law reform.[6] Virtually nothing has happened in the past quarter century with regard to evidence rules that affect civil litigation—except in one area. During the last decade, we have witnessed a fundamental change in the law of evidence bearing on the use of scientific evidence, a change that has realigned the balance in civil litigation between plaintiffs and defendants to favor defendants. No similar realignment has been made in criminal cases.

I. The Trilogy

Starting in 1993 with *Daubert v. Merrill Dow Pharmaceuticals, Inc.*,[7] the Supreme Court issued a trilogy of opinions[8] governing the admissibility of expert testimony in federal courts. In doing so, it created a new role for evidence rules in civil cases. Rather than seeking to improve the jury's functioning, *Daubert* and its progeny provide an infallible shortcut to this goal; they decrease any potential risk of irrational juror behavior by eliminating many trials at which jurors would be the fact-finders. Ironically, evidence law which, in large measure, owed its existence to the system of trial by jury has now become an important tool in disposing of litigation without a trial.

The trilogy has an enormous impact because in our technologically oriented, specialized world, expert testimony is often essential. Before considering in more detail some of the consequences, let us first look briefly at exactly what the Supreme Court did. The first, and still most cited, of the Supreme Court's opinions on the admissibility of expert proof is *Daubert* itself.[9] In *Daubert*, the chief controverted issue was whether Bendectin, an anti–morning sickness pill taken by millions of pregnant women, had caused severe birth defects in the women's offspring. The trial court found plaintiffs' expert testimony insufficient to prove a causal connection, and granted summary judgment. The Supreme Court converted the sufficiency issue into one of admissibility. Rather than scrutinizing plaintiffs' expert testimony for sufficient proof of causation, trial courts were directed to determine whether an expert should be allowed to testify at all. The Court told trial judges they were "gatekeepers" who must screen proffered expertise to ensure that what is admitted is "not only relevant, but reliable."[10]

Relevancy means that the expert's theory has to be tied sufficiently to the facts of the case.[11] In the scientific context at issue in *Daubert*, the Court found that the reliability prong requires trial judges to make sure that a proffered expert opinion is "ground[ed] in the methods and procedures of science."[12] It is no longer enough for a proposed expert to have appropriate or even sterling qualifications (e.g., the right degree or the right experience). The methodology underlying the expert's opinion has to be scientifically valid. The majority opinion noted a number of factors, which although not definitive, operate as markers of the scientific method: hypothesis testing, subjecting studies to peer review and publication, ascertaining known or potential rates of error, adopting standards for controlling a technique, and general acceptance of the methodology in the relevant scientific community.[13]

Defendants immediately realized that *Daubert* furnished them with a new procedural weapon; they could make *in limine* motions, soon known as *Daubert* motions, asking the trial judge to exclude plaintiffs' experts as witnesses. If the motion succeeded in keeping out plaintiffs' expert testimony on a crucial issue like causation, defendants would be entitled to summary judgment because plaintiffs would be unable to prove a material issue in their case.

That is what happened in *Joiner*, the second case in the trilogy, when the district judge found that plaintiff's experts' opinions on causation did not meet *Daubert* standards.[14] The summary judgment grant was reversed by the circuit court which applied a stringent standard of review to the exclusion of plaintiff's experts.[15] The Supreme Court reversed. In so doing, the Court rejected a stringent standard of review and instead adopted an abuse of discretion standard for reviewing *Daubert* rulings. Trial judges were thereby given enormous control over the outcome of a case and considerable immunity from review; decisions barring plaintiff's experts would stand unless "manifestly erroneous."[16] Although grants of summary judgment are reviewed de novo, the exclusion of the expert—the crucial decision that led to the grant in *Joiner*—would evade this strict standard even though the Supreme Court acknowledged that the decision on expert testimony was "outcome determinative."[17]

The Supreme Court also enhanced the trial judge's power to exclude experts by its seeming willingness to accept the *Joiner* district court's approach of evaluating each scientific study on which the plaintiff's experts relied independently of any other, instead of considering them together.[18] Only Justice Stevens objected to this process of looking at the parts rather than the whole.[19] This piecemeal approach makes it easier for a trial judge to reject as unreliable the data on which an expert is relying. Furthermore, as we will see below, the Court's comments about the studies on which the experts sought to rely provide a template for rejecting expertise in toxic tort litigation.

In the final case in the trilogy, *Kumho Tire Co. v. Carmichael*, the Court took certiorari to decide whether *Daubert* applies only to scientific evidence.[20] In *Kumho*, the challenged testimony about alleged manufacturing defects in a tire was furnished by an engineer. The Court unanimously held that the trial court as gatekeeper must screen *all* proffered expert proof to determine whether it meets *Daubert's* two-pronged relevancy-reliability test.[21] It also extended *Joiner's* abuse of discretion standard to all decisions a district court makes in ruling on the admissibility of expert testimony, including the procedures it employs in handling *Daubert* motions.[22] Although nothing in the *Kumho* opinion is inconsistent with *Daubert*, the opinion seems somewhat more flexible by stressing the need to look at reliability in the context of the particular case.[23] *Kumho* is the latest word from the Court on how to decide whether an expert may testify. But the lower courts and commentators clearly cite *Daubert* more than they do *Kumho*.[24]

II. The Trilogy's Effect

We can now consider the trilogy's impact in more detail. First, it should be noted that although the trilogy interpreted the Federal Rules of Evidence and consequently applies only to cases in federal court, it has had enormous influence in state courts as well. Many states have adopted *Daubert*,[25] but even in jurisdictions that have not, the Supreme Court's spotlight on expert testimony has led state judges to reconsider standards for admitting expert proof.[26]

As we have seen, the trilogy provides the trial judge with substantial ammunition to bar experts from testifying. Furthermore, the Supreme Court seems to be telling courts not to hesitate to exercise this power. Even though the abuse of discretion standard theoretically affords considerable leeway to a trial judge who *admits* expert proof, the Supreme Court may be signaling that exclusions are preferable. Each Supreme Court case ended with the exclusion of the plaintiffs' experts and summary judgment for the defendant. And the brief concurring opinion in *Kumho* by Justices Scalia, O'Connor, and Thomas, warning that the abuse of discretion standard "is not discretion to abandon the gate-keeping function or to perform the function inadequately,"[27] may intimate to appellate courts a more pressing need for reversals when trial judges admit rather than exclude expert proof.

Kumho's extension of *Daubert's* standards to all expert witnesses means that plaintiffs are at risk of summary judgment whenever expert proof is required to make out an essential element of their case. Plaintiffs may find themselves out of court regardless of whether the excluded expert is a scientist, engineer, psychologist, or anyone else whose "scientific, technical or other specialized knowledge" will assist the trier of fact.[28] The exclusion of experts crucial to a plaintiff's case provides trial judges who mistrust jurors with a clear path to summary judgment unimpeded by the complex obstacles courts face if they try to abrogate the jury's fact-finding function on grounds such as the complexity exception to the Seventh Amendment,[29] or by reclassifying an issue as one of law rather than of fact.[30] *Joiner's* abuse of discretion standard insulates the district court from the stringent scrutiny its dismissal of plaintiff's case might otherwise receive.

And even when an expert's exclusion does not result in summary judgment, plaintiffs may still find their ability to prevail greatly constrained, as, for instance, when plaintiffs' experts on damages are precluded from testifying.

Now, of course, not all plaintiffs are have-nots, and not all defendants are rich and powerful, but certainly plaintiffs are less likely to be part of the corporate establishment that possesses power, influence, and resources in the United States.[31] The evidence trilogy favors defendants in federal courts because it has made it extremely difficult for some plaintiffs to get past a motion for summary judgment. A by-product of *Daubert* is that it is leading some plaintiffs to litigate in state courts in which they think they will have a better chance of presenting their case to a jury.[32]

A. Access to the Courts

In diversity cases, the trilogy has the potential to re-create the climate that existed in the federal courts in the era of *Swift v. Tyson*.[33] Federal judges were then free to apply the "general law"—a result which Holmes and Brandeis believed clearly favored corporate interests.[34] Bringing the action in state court often failed to protect plaintiffs because corporate defendants were able to remove to a federal forum. Of course, since *Erie Railroad v. Tompkins*[35] a federal court may no longer select the "substantive" law it considers superior. It is, however, free to apply federal "procedural" law. Evidentiary rules, including those interpreting the *Daubert* trilogy, are viewed as satisfying *Hanna v. Plumer*'s "arguably procedural" test.[36] As before, corporate defendants can often remove state-instituted cases to federal court, and indeed did so in each of the three cases that constitute the trilogy. The consequence is that more than sixty years after *Erie*, a federal judge again possesses a potent weapon to effectuate procorporate biases.

Recent studies by the Federal Judicial Center[37] and the RAND Institute for Civil Justice[38] agree that judges are more likely since *Daubert* to engage in pretrial scrutiny of expert testimony in civil cases, and to preclude experts from testifying.[39] The RAND study, published in 2001, also concluded that the rate of exclusion of expert testimony has begun to drop and suggested that this may be due to better testimony being offered, or counsel not pursuing cases in which *Daubert* standards cannot be met.[40] There is an alternative explanation as well. Plaintiffs may be avoiding *Daubert* exclusions by proffering more expert testimony on an issue than formerly, a choice forced on them by the Supreme Court's 2000 opinion in *Weisgram v. Marley*,[41] sometimes referred to as the Supreme Court's fourth case on expert testimony.

In *Weisgram*, the trial court permitted plaintiffs' experts to testify after a *Daubert* challenge, and plaintiffs secured a jury verdict. On appeal, despite the abuse of discretion standard, the appellate court found the plaintiffs' experts should have been excluded. The appellate court therefore reversed the lower court and entered judgment for defendant. In the Supreme Court, the plaintiffs argued that they should have been granted a new trial at which they could produce other experts. The Supreme Court did not review the exclusion of the plaintiffs' experts by the appellate court; it dealt only with plaintiffs' claim to a new trial, which it rejected. The Court explained:

> Since *Daubert*, moreover, parties relying on expert evidence have had notice of the exacting standards of reliability such evidence must meet. . . . It is implausible to suggest, post-*Daubert*, that parties will initially present less than their best expert evidence in the expectation of a second chance should their first try fail.[42]

It is, however, expensive to hire experts. Plaintiffs' lawyers who are faring well in district court, and believe that the abuse of discretion standard will protect them on appeal, may be reluctant to lay out funds for what they view as unnecessary expert testimony. Furthermore, preparing expert reports that comply with Rule 26 of the Federal Rules of Civil Procedure and *Daubert*, and priming experts for depositions (that often play an important role in *Daubert* challenges) and hearings takes considerable time. This process is particularly burdensome for plaintiffs' attorneys who work on a contingency fee basis as they cannot bill for these services. The consequence is that, in addition to increasing transaction costs, *Daubert* may well be affecting access to the courts. Given the huge expense in dollars and time that *Daubert*-driven activities can entail,[43] lawyers are turning down meritorious lawsuits unless the would-be plaintiff stands to recover substantial damages.[44] A person who has suffered genuine harm may be unable to secure any compensation because the anticipated transaction costs make litigation unaffordable.

Daubert is also being invoked by defendants as a weapon to defeat class certification.[45] Defendants claim that plaintiffs cannot satisfy the typicality and commonality requirements of Rule 23(a) of the Federal Rules of Civil

Procedure without expert proof. Then, defendants claim the expert proof fails to meet *Daubert* standards. Some courts have rejected these attempts to interject *Daubert* as forbidden inquiries into a case's merits at the certification stage, but other courts have pursued *Daubert* issues during the class certification process. Even if the court eventually grants certification, an additional hurdle has been placed in plaintiffs' path.

B. Toxic Tort Litigation

We can see how judicial interpretations of *Daubert* adversely impact plaintiffs if we look at toxic tort litigation, the subject that roused the Supreme Court's interest in expert proof in the first place. The trilogy causes considerable problems for plaintiffs, who must prove causation to prevail. Although Justice Blackmun's opinion in *Daubert* acknowledged that there could be legitimate disagreements among scientific experts that would require resolution by a jury, some district judges seem determined to find one, and only one, scientifically valid answer despite the uncertainty that presently surrounds our understanding of mechanisms that cause illness and birth defects.

Some courts, like the *Joiner* district judge who was found not to have abused her discretion, reject epidemiological studies lacking a .05 level of statistical significance, without acknowledging that a lack of statistical significance does not mean a study has no probative value.[46] Some judges ignore statistically significant studies unless the authors found causation, without noting that researchers use a stringent standard of proof far exceeding the more-probable-than-not standard which applies in civil litigation.[47] And some courts evaluate each study on which an expert relies independently of any other even though scientists would combine the available data in drawing inferences about causation.[48] Some trial courts have gone beyond *Joiner*. Although few courts say outright that epidemiologic evidence is essential,[49] many denigrate all other types of evidence, including animal studies, assert that an epidemiologic study cannot prove causation unless the relative risk is greater than 2.0,[50] dismiss differential diagnoses,[51] and spurn adverse reaction reports as mere anecdotal evidence unworthy of serious consideration.[52]

By insisting on a stringent standard of reliability, courts ignore the realities of toxic tort litigation. Would-be plaintiffs who suspect that they have been injured by a defendant's product are unlikely to have information about relevant scientific data. And indeed such data may not exist, or may not be publicly available. Epidemiological studies—favored by many courts as the preeminent, if not the only appropriate, method for proving causation—are expensive and difficult to design and carry out. They are unlikely to be undertaken until a critical mass of litigation has begun,[53] a public health outcry is raised,[54] or a pharmaceutical company wishes to sell its drug to treat something other than the disease for which the drug was approved.[55] Other public regulators of food and the environment regularly rely upon the scientific analysis provided by toxicologists who do not have access to epidemiological data, and who might not be convinced by it even if it were available.

These "gatekeeping" rulings irk some scientists who believe that they reflect an oversimplified view of science and uncertainty that is not in society's best interest: crippling plaintiffs' ability to litigate toxic tort cases means that manufacturers of pharmaceuticals and chemicals receive fewer incentives to guard against unknown risks to public health.[56] Furthermore, by bringing about dismissals via summary judgment when a plaintiff's experts on causation are excluded, the trilogy guarantees that the story of what the defendant did will never be heard in a public courtroom. Even when plaintiffs are unable to prove causation, that does not mean that the defendant's actions were above reproach. Toxic tort litigation raises important policy concerns about risk and regulation that should be the subject of public debate in a democracy. *Daubert* not only closes off a forum for this discussion, but the failure to hold a trial makes it less likely that the media will know what is happening.

C. Criminal Cases

The anti-have-nots attitudes that attend *Daubert* are highlighted if we look at the very different approach courts take to admitting expert testimony in criminal cases.[57] Judges are much less aggressive in applying the exacting standard of reliability that generally prevails in civil litigation to prosecution experts, although analytically it would seem that a higher standard should prevail.[58] Not only does the prosecutor, like the plaintiff, have the burden of proof, but the prosecutor's burden of proof beyond a reasonable doubt greatly exceeds the usual preponderance of evidence standard that applies in civil litigation. And, of course, criminal cases involve life and liberty and not just money, and the forensic evidence being offered by the prosecutor has usually been analyzed in a government laboratory through techniques created in government laboratories.

Despite these differences, prosecution experts are almost never excluded on *Daubert* grounds even when they are expressing conclusions that have never been subjected to any systematic examination.[59] Indigent criminal defendants, after all, are the ultimate have-nots.

III. Conclusion

Evidence law has always had to meet the challenge of achieving justice in situations of less than perfect knowledge, and of devising mechanisms to cope with parties who make needed information unobtainable. But in applying the expert trilogy, courts ignore traditional evidentiary principles, such as burden-shifting when facts are peculiarly within an adversary's knowledge,[60] and fail to accord probative value to admissions by defendants[61] or conduct by defendants that demonstrates consciousness of guilt.[62] Some of this evidence might be admissible were the case to go to trial, but as we have seen, a major impact of the trilogy is the termination of litigation at the pretrial stage. The only evidence law that will play a role in some cases is the *Daubert* trilogy. In less than a decade, restrictive interpretations of what the trilogy requires have trumped long-established doctrine in the field of evidence.

The gatekeeping power given trial judges to decide on the admissibility of expert testimony provides them with a potent new weapon for controlling litigation and taking fact-finding away from jurors. This shift in the way evidence law is applied has altered the balance between plaintiffs and defendants.[63] Plaintiffs are the losers, and consequently it has become more difficult for those who wish to challenge the establishment to do so successfully in a federal court. A mere rule of evidence that is supposedly neutral and transsubstantive is having an enormous effect on litigation outcomes.

NOTES

1. I am grateful to Brooklyn Law School for support I received from a summer research stipend.

2. JAMES BRADLEY THAYER, A PRELIMINARY TREATISE ON EVIDENCE AT THE COMMON LAW 222 (1898).

3. Arguably the most important of the Federal Rules of Evidence is Rule 403, which authorizes a trial judge to exclude relevant evidence if "its probative value is

substantially outweighed by the danger of unfair prejudice, confusion of the issues, or misleading the jury, or by considerations of undue delay, waste of time, or needless presentation of cumulative evidence." FED. R. EVID. 403. Some version of Rule 403 is found in every American jurisdiction.

4. In 1970, 4.3 percent of civil cases were resolved after jury trial; in 2001 1.8 percent of cases went to trial. *See* Hope V. Samborn, *The Vanishing Trial*, 88 A.B.A. J. 24 (2002).

5. Roger C. Park, *Evidence Scholarship, Old and New*, 75 MINN. L. REV. 849, 862 (1991) (noting that no articles on any evidence topic were included in a recent compilation of most-cited law review articles). At a 2002 AALS Conference on Teaching Evidence, Professor Park reiterated that top law reviews rarely publish articles on evidence.

6. Although an Advisory Committee on the Federal Rules of Evidence was reconstituted in 1992, its work has been limited to fine-tuning existing rules.

7. 509 U.S. 579 (1993).

8. The other two cases in the expert testimony trilogy are *General Electric Co. v. Joiner*, 522 U.S. 136 (1997), and *Kumho Tire Co. v. Carmichael*, 526 U.S. 137 (1999).

9. Indeed, *Daubert* has become a cottage industry. There are databases, loose-leaf services, newsletters, and innumerable CLE programs dealing with *Daubert* issues.

10. *Daubert*, 509 U.S. at 589.

11. *Id.* at 591.

12. *Id.* at 590.

13. *Id.* at 593–94.

14. Gen. Elec. Co. v. Joiner, 522 U.S. 136, 140 (1997).

15. Gen. Elec. Co. v. Joiner, 78 F.3d 524, 528–29 (11th Cir. 1996).

16. *Joiner*, 522 U.S. at 141–42 (quoting *Spring Co. v. Edgar*, 99 U.S. 645, 658 (1879)).

17. *Id.* at 143.

18. Plaintiff's experts had relied on a toxicological study and four epidemiological studies. The district court found each wanting. The Supreme Court concluded that the court of appeals had erred in rejecting the district court's determination that the studies were insufficient, "whether individually or in combination," to support [the experts'] conclusions about causation. 522 U.S. at 146–47.

19. *Id.* at 153 (Stevens, J., concurring in part and dissenting in part) ("[I]t would seem that an expert could reasonably have concluded that the study of workers at an Italian capacitor plant, coupled with data from Monsanto's study and other studies, raises an inference that PCBs promote lung cancer."). *Id.* at 153.

20. 526 U.S. at 146.

21. *Id.* at 152.

22. *Id.*

23. *Id.* at 158.

24. According to a Westlaw search on September 29, 2004, *Daubert* has been cited a total of 10,202 times since March 23, 1999, the day *Kumho* was decided. Of these cites, 3,148 appeared in court opinions. In comparison, *Kumho* has been cited a total of 5,413 times: 1,629 times by courts.

25. David E. Bernstein & Jeffrey D. Jackson, *The Daubert Trilogy in the States*, 44 JURIMETRICS J. 351, 354–57 (2004) (finding that nine states have adopted the entire trilogy, and that by the middle of 2003, twenty-seven states had adopted a test that broadly construed is "consistent" with *Daubert*).

26. *Id.* (discussing partial adoptions of the trilogy and other reactions).

27. *Kumho*, 526 U.S. at 158–59.

28. FED. R. EVID. 702. Rule 702 states: "If scientific, technical, or other specialized knowledge will assist the trier of fact to understand the evidence or to determine a fact in issue, a witness qualified as an expert by knowledge, skill, experience, training, or education, may testify thereto in the form of an opinion or otherwise." *Id.*

29. Margaret L. Moses, *What the Jury Must Hear: The Supreme Court's Evolving Seventh Amendment Jurisprudence*, 68 GEO. WASH. L. REV. 183 (2000); Joseph A. Miron, Note, *The Constitutionality of a Complexity Exception to the Seventh Amendment*, 73 CHI.-KENT L. REV. 865 (1990).

30. *Cf.* Arthur R. Miller, *The Pretrial Rush to Judgment: Are the "Litigation Explosion," "Liability Crisis," and Efficiency Cliches Eroding Our Day in Court and Jury Trial Commitments?* 78 N.Y.U. L. REV. 982, 1095–1104 (2003) (discussing at length *In re* Software Toolworks, Inc., 789 F. Supp. 1489 (N.D. Cal. 1992), in which the trial judge sought to avoid jury trial by reclassifying matter of fact as matter of law after she found that evidence on "due diligence" was unreliable because it came from biased experts); Markman v. Westview Instruments, Inc., 517 U.S. 370 (1996) (construction of patent claims by judge, not jury, does not violate the 7th Amendment).

31. Two Australian observers have recently concluded that "recent federal jurisprudence, including Supreme Court jurisprudence, seems to have been shaped, and simultaneously reinforced, by a range of values which appear closely aligned to the perspectives and concerns promoted by politically conservative corporate-sponsored proponents of tort and evidence reform." David Mercer & Gary Edmond, Daubert *and the Exclusionary Ethos: The Convergence of Corporate and Judicial Attitudes towards the Admissibility of Expert Evidence in Tort Litigation*, 26 LAW & POL'Y 231–32 (2004).

32. *See* Ned Miltenberg, *How to Prevail in Daubert Challenges*, 2003 ATLA ANN. CONVENTION REFERENCES MATERIALS 2 (advising plaintiffs' attorneys to "whenever possible stay out of federal court (and state courts that have adopted *Daubert*) and thus avoid *Daubert's* often fatal consequences").

33. 41 U.S. (16 Pet.) 1 (1842).

34. *See* Edward A. Purcell, Jr., *The Story of* Erie: *How Litigants, Lawyers, Judges,*

Politics and Social Change Reshape the Law in CIVIL PROCEDURE STORIES 26–32, 49 (Kevin M. Clermont ed., 2004).

35. 304 U.S. 64 (1938).

36. In *Hanna*, 380 U.S. 460, 472 (1965), the Court explained that in diversity cases federal rules adopted through the rule-making process trump conflicting state rules:

> the constitutional provision for a federal court system (augmented by the Necessary and Proper Clause) carries with it congressional power to make rules governing the practice and pleading in those courts, which in turn includes a power to regulate matters which, though falling within the uncertain area between substance and procedure, are rationally capable of classification as either.

This formulation appears to have convinced federal judges that all decisions about the admissibility of expert proof couched in evidentiary terms can be classified as procedural. *But see* Margaret A. Berger, *Upsetting the Balance between Adverse Interests: The Impact of the Supreme Court's Trilogy on Expert Testimony in Toxic Tort Litigation*, 64 LAW & CONTEMP. PROBS. 289, 308–21 (2001) (arguing that judge-made rules need not apply when they conflict with important state interests).

37. Carol Kafka et al., *Judge and Attorney Experience, Practices and Concerns regarding Expert Testimony in Federal Civil Trials*, 8 PSYCH. PUB. POL'Y & LAW 309 (2002).

38. LLOYD DIXON & BRIAN GILL, RAND INST. FOR CIVIL JUSTICE, CHANGES IN THE STANDARDS FOR ADMITTING EXPERT EVIDENCE IN FEDERAL CIVIL CASES SINCE THE *DAUBERT* DECISION (2001).

39. The extent to which this is true is difficult to substantiate. Serious research on the effects of the trilogy has barely begun, and empirical work is difficult to do. Although cases in which judges exclude the plaintiff's experts and grant summary judgment can generally be found because the trial court must explain its reasoning to avoid being reversed for an "abuse of discretion," many cases in which plaintiffs win a *Daubert* hearing undoubtedly settle without being counted, or go to trial and verdict without an opinion.

40. DIXON & GILL, *supra* note 38, at 62.

41. 528 U.S. 440 (2000).

42. *Id.* at 455. Of course, in contingent fee cases, plaintiffs' lawyers who thought the trial judge would allow their experts to testify might simply have been trying to save money that would come out of their pockets if plaintiffs lost the lawsuit; plaintiffs' counsel can no longer afford this gamble.

43. Aside from the risk of losing a case if experts are excluded on *Daubert* grounds, a lawyer may risk becoming a defendant. Malpractice actions against experts are becoming more frequent and successful as jurisdictions are reviving their rules on expert immunity. *See* Mark Hansen, *Experts Are Liable, Too: Client*

Suits against Friendly Experts Multiplying, Succeeding, 86 A.B.A. J. 17 (2000). Successful suits for the blatant disregard of *Daubert* principles will undoubtedly lead to malpractice actions against attorneys who selected the experts and failed to supervise them properly.

44. One lawyer, quoted in the *New York Times*, explained: "I can no longer afford to spend $300,000 trying a case that is only worth $500,000, and that's ridiculous." Greg Winter, *Jury Awards Soar as Lawsuits Decline on Defective Goods*, N.Y. TIMES, Jan. 30, 2001, at A1 ("To better their prospects under the new rules [about expert testimony], many plaintiffs' lawyers are buttressing their arguments with platoons of experts, and improving their chances of winning by choosing only truly egregious cases involving the most seriously injured parties.").

45. *See* Mandi L. Williams, *The History of* Daubert *and Its Effect on Toxic Tort Class Action Certification*, 22 REV. LITIG. 181 (2003).

46. Sander Greenland, *The Need for Critical Appraisal of Expert Witnesses in Epidemiology and Statistics*, 39 WAKE FOREST L. REV. 291 (2004).

47. Neil B. Cohen, *The Gatekeeping Role in Civil Litigation and the Abdication of Legal Values in Favor of Scientific Values*, 33 SETON HALL L. REV. 943 (2003).

48. Jerome P. Kassirer & Joe S. Cecil, *Inconsistency in Evidentiary Standards for Medical Testimony: Disorder in the Courts*, 288 JAMA 1382, 1383–84 (2002).

49. They also do not say that animal studies never count; instead they usually point out that in the case before them one must extrapolate from animals to humans and that the doses given the animals were much higher. As these distinctions will always exist, it is hard to imagine that an appellate court will ever fault a district judge who concluded that in the case under review the animal studies were not sufficient to prove causation.

50. *See* Sander Greenland & James M. Robbins, *Epidemiology, Justice, and the Probability of Causation*, 40 JURIMETRICS 321 (2000); Sander Greenland, *Relation of Probability of Causation to Relative Risk and Doubling Dose: A Methodologic Error That Has Become a Social Problem*, 89 AM. J. PUB. HEALTH 1166 (1999).

51. Edward J. Imwinkelried, *The Admissibility and Legal Sufficiency of Testimony about Differential Diagnosis (Etiology) of Under-and-Over Estimations*, 56 BAYLOR L. REV. 391 (2004).

52. The extraordinarily high burden that courts place on plaintiffs in satisfying *Daubert* challenges is illustrated in Siharath v. Sandoz Pharms. Corp, 131 F. Supp. 2d 1347, 1370 (N.D. Ga. 2001), *aff'd sub nom.* Sandoz Pharms. Corp., 295 F.3d 1194 (11th Cir. 2002). In explaining under what circumstances it would allow an expert to testify, the court stated:

> This would be a different case if there was at least some support for the causal hypothesis in the peer-reviewed epidemiologic literature, a predictable chemical mechanism, general acceptance in learned treatises and other scientific literature of a causal relationship, a plausible animal model, and dozens of well-documented case reports involving postpartum women with no other risk factors for

stroke. In such a case, the totality of the evidence would be enough to satisfy the demands of *Daubert*.

53. Joseph Sanders, *The Bendectin Litigation: A Case Study in the Life Cycle of Mass Torts*, 43 HASTINGS L.J. 301, 34–47 (1992) (concluding that scientific research into Bendectin became a hot topic after litigation began).

54. The moratorium on breast silicon implants imposed by the Food and Drug Administration in 1992 is what prompted much of the research into the implants' effects.

55. Vioxx, Merck's best-selling arthritis drug, was pulled from the market by Merck only after a study designed to show the drug's effectiveness in preventing the recurrence of colon polyps found an increased risk of heart attacks and strokes. Barry Meier, *For Merck, Defense of a Drug Crumbles at a Difficult Time*, N.Y. TIMES, Oct. 1, 2000, at CI.

56. *See, e.g.*, AM. PUB. HEALTH ASS'N, INTERIM POLICY STATEMENT LB03-1, THREATS TO PUBLIC HEALTH SCIENCE, APPLICATION OF SUPREME COURT DECISIONS, http://www.apha.org/legislative/policy/2003/LB-03-01.pdf.

57. Compare the skepticism expressed by Judge Kozinski on the remand of *Daubert* about scientific studies offered by plaintiffs that were performed in anticipation of litigation. *See* Daubert v. Merrill Dow Pharms., Inc., 43 F.3d 1311, 1317 (9th Cir. 1995) (the court then adds, without further explanation, that as to disciplines like "fingerprint analysis, voice recognition, DNA fingerprinting and a variety of other scientific endeavors . . . the fact that the expert has developed an expertise principally for purposes of litigation will obviously not be a substantial consideration."). *Id.*

58. Richard D. Friedman, *Squeezing* Daubert *Out of the Picture*, 33 SETON HALL L. REV. 1047, 1048 (2003).

59. Courts continue to admit fingerprint evidence (*see, e.g.*, United States v. Llera Plaza, 188 F. Supp. 2d 549 (E.D. Pa. 2002)) even though no studies have been done to determine the reliability of matches, the probabilities associated with matches, or error rates. The lack of data is particularly acute with regard to the partial, latent smudged prints often found at crime scenes. *See* Sandy Zabell, *Fingerprint Evidence*, 13 J.L. & POL'Y 143 (2005); Michael J. Saks, *The Legal and Scientific Evaluation of Forensic Science (Especially Fingerprint Expert Testimony)* , 33 SETON HALL L. REV. 1167 (2003).

60. It is the manufacturer-defendant, not the customer-plaintiff, who has access to information needed to determine causation, or has the means and resources to acquire additional data. *See* Campbell v. United States, 365 U.S. 85, 96 (1961) ("the ordinary rule, based on considerations of fairness, does not place the burden upon a litigant of establishing facts, peculiarly within the knowledge of his adversary").

61. *See, e.g.*, Soldo v. Sandoz Pharm. Corp., 244 F. Supp. 2d 434, 523–24 (W.D. Pa. 2003). Furthermore, at a jury trial a relevant statement by a party-opponent or

its agent is admissible (*see* Fed. R. Evid. 801(d)(2)(A), (C), (D)) and the jurors must decide whether it is against interest and if so how much probative weight it should be accorded. At a *Daubert* hearing, it is the judge who makes this determination. *See, e.g.*, Glastetter v. Novartis Pharm. Corp., 107 F. Supp. 2d 1015, 1036–38 (E.D. Mo. 2000), *aff'd*, 252 F.3d 986 (8th Cir. 2000).

62. For example, consider litigation surrounding certain controversial antidepressant drugs. In 2003, the New York Attorney General brought suit against GlaxoSmithKline claiming it published only one study on the use of Paxil to treat depression in adolescents and children, and that it failed to publish anything about four additional negative clinical trials. Furthermore, the state alleged that by 2002 the pharmaceutical company knew that Paxil was no more effective than a placebo in treating depression and might even provoke suicidal thoughts. *See When Drug Companies Hide Data*, N.Y. TIMES, June 6, 2004, sec. 4, at 12. The outcry over the S.S.R.I. antidepressants led to congressional hearings, suggestions that all drug trials be registered (and the introduction of a bill to that effect), and the F.D.A.'s ordering of a "black box" warning of the risk of suicide for all antidepressants "because the currently available data are not adequate to exclude any single medication from the increased risk of suicidality." Maria Newman, *U.S. Orders New Warnings on Antidepressants Used by Children*, N.Y. TIMES, Oct. 15, 2004. Yet, in Miller v. Pfizer, 356 F.3d 1326 (10th Cir. 2004), the Tenth Circuit affirmed a grant of summary judgment after the trial judge, on *Daubert* grounds, excluded expert testimony stating that the suicide of plaintiff's thirteen-year-old son was caused by his taking Zoloft and that Zoloft causes some adolescents to commit suicide.

63. Margaret A. Berger, *supra* note 36, at 289.

21

America's Misguided War on Drugs

Joseph D. McNamara

We have turned the corner on drug addiction in America.[1]

In 1972, in the waning years of his presidency, Richard Nixon launched what has turned into a sea change in America's drug control efforts by declaring a "drug war." The federal budget for the war was roughly $101 million that year. Thirty-three years later, it is around $20 billion a year.[2] By comparison, the average monthly Social Security retirement check in 1972 was $177.[3] If Social Security benefits had increased at the same rate as drug war spending, today's check would be around $30,000 a month, instead of approximately $900. When state and local costs are added to federal costs, the annual cost of the drug war exceeds $30 billion a year.[4] This astonishing fiscal escalation has been accompanied by stunning increases in arrest and incarceration rates for drug crimes. There are now over 2 million Americans in prison largely because of drug war arrests, and the United States per capita incarceration rate is probably the highest in the free world. Minority groups, the poor, and the uneducated are over-represented among drug inmates.[5] Most of those imprisoned for drug crimes have no record of violence.

This chapter examines the drug war in historical context and from the perspective of a career law enforcement officer. It questions the criminal-ization of drug use and examines the extent to which U.S. drug policy has been and continues to be driven more by class division and racial stereo-type than by any hard evidence of effectiveness.

I. A View from the Trenches

As a young patrolman in New York City, I early developed doubts about the efficacy of trying to control drug use through criminal law. One day in Harlem, my partner and I made a routine arrest of an addict on the top floor landing of an apartment building. Addicts frequented these "shooting galleries" where they could share needles and get off with a "rush." They would remove the cork from a metal bottle cap (bottles had corks in those days), empty a $5 bag of heroin into the cap, add some water and heat the mixture with a candle. Next, they would siphon the fix into a hypodermic needle, or "spike," in street jargon. The addicts would then inject the drug into any vein they could still find. Heroin is an opiate, a depressant, and these were pathetic and often sick individuals. Users rarely resisted arrest. Indeed, cops called the arrests "falling off a log" because they were so easy. After booking an addict, we would simply send the bottle cap to the police lab, which invariably found a residue of heroin. Although the Supreme Court in *Robinson v. California*[6] ruled that being an addict and having the substance in your blood was not a crime, the spike or the residue in the bottle cap, although unusable, constituted possession of an illegal substance and called for a six-month jail term.

Drug arrests, like most police work, are potentially dangerous. Then, as now, the possibility of a needle prick during a search was a nightmare to officers. Because the majority of hard-core addicts have AIDS, Hepatitis B, syphilis, or other diseases, a skin puncture by an infected needle may mean a death sentence for a cop.

That day, in 1961, the addict we arrested was cooperative. He surrendered the needle he had hidden in his belt, where it had been invisible. He pleaded with us, asserting that he was "just a junkie" and that he couldn't "take a bust right now." He promised that if we let him go, he would give us a pusher. To my surprise, my partner agreed with the suggestion, and because he was senior, I reluctantly went along. We put the bottle cap and needle in the glove compartment of our police car and followed the addict. It was broad daylight on a warm summer day, and there were lots of people on Lenox Avenue. We coasted along, never more than five feet from our prisoner. I had my hand on the door handle, ready to bolt after him if he decided to break the agreement. But he was good to his word. He walked down the street, talking to one dealer after another. The third dealer agreed to make a sale. When the two went into a hallway, we charged in and arrested the dealer. The addict "escaped."

It amazed me that in broad daylight, our prisoner had talked to pushers about buying illegal drugs, with a marked police car and two uniformed policemen five feet away. No one had been deterred by our presence. The first two dealers saw no reason to hesitate; they had already sold out their supply. If we had not known what the addict was doing, we would have guessed the men were talking about cars, girlfriends, sports, politics, or other innocent things. Drug dealing and drug use were confidential, con-sensual transactions between willing parties who treasured their secrecy. These parties had cultivated a simple "hide in plain sight" street life all their own.

It was easy for working cops during the 1960s to believe that lenient judges and an inefficient correctional system were to blame for America's continuing drug problem. After all, officers were working hard making drug arrests. But doubts about this conclusion were growing within the police ranks. On this day in Harlem, I began to realize that even with the harshest judges and the strictest penalties, the criminal law could not con-trol what people put into their bloodstreams in private.

II. The Vanishing Declaration of Independence: The Evolution of U.S. Drug Policy

The federal government first outlawed narcotics more than ninety years ago in the Harrison Act of 1914.[7] Protestant missionary societies and other religious groups joined forces with Prohibitionists to have their version of sin codified in a federal penal statute. Racist stereotypes held by Anglocen-tric American elites also influenced antidrug legislation. These elites tar-geted the "strange" religions, languages, and cultures of black, immigrant Irish, German, Italian, Jewish, Asian, Native American, and Hispanic pop-ulations.[8] As the debates surrounding passage of the Harrison Act indi-cate, many believed it was the duty of whites to save these "inferior races." Some of those moving to criminalize drugs also voiced concern about the deleterious consequences of minority drug use for whites, expressing fear that "Negroes" under the influence of drugs would murder whites and that "Chinamen" would seduce white women with drugs.[9]

The Harrison Act represented a gross departure from the federal prac-tice of not interfering with state police powers. Historian David Musto notes that racist arguments convinced Southern representatives, who were reluctant to acknowledge federal power over states' rights, to vote for the Act.[10] Uneasiness regarding the law's constitutionality caused Congress to label the Act a revenue measure.[11] In 1915, however, the U.S. Supreme Court correctly interpreted it as a penal statute,[12] making it the cornerstone of laws leading to the present "war on drugs."

Prominent politicians, like President Theodore Roosevelt, who harbored many racial, ethnic, and class biases, greatly encouraged antidrug groups. Roosevelt, who was known often to serve champagne and other wine at his government social functions, was not an alcohol prohibitionist. Like many others of his social class, he was, however, greatly concerned about consumption of drugs and alcohol by the lower classes. Earlier in his career, as chairman of the New York City Board of Police Commissioners, he had caused an uproar by trying to close beer gardens and taverns on the Sabbath.[13] Commissioner Roosevelt explained that it was quite different for a gentleman and his family to consume a bottle of wine in their "club" than for someone to be in a saloon on Sunday.[14]

Theodore Roosevelt and others supporting antidrug legislation were not only motivated by "moral concerns," but also by a desire to develop America as one of the great world powers. This was most apparent in efforts to ban the opium trade. The hope was that by stopping England, France, Holland, and Spain from compelling China to accept highly profitable opium shipments, the United States would win Chinese goodwill and would be better positioned to compete with the imperial trading nations in opening the vast China market to other goods. All this would be done without the United States resorting to military force as other opium-trading nations had done.[15]

Today, public and police attitudes toward the danger of drugs are still shaped by mistaken prejudices regarding their users. The average white American's image of drug users is of dangerous young men of color who rob to obtain money for drugs, or youthful black female prostitutes who spread disease and deliver crack babies as a result of their enslavement to drugs. These enduring misconceptions form the erroneous foundation of the ill-conceived "war" on drugs. This foundation is unsupported by facts: the overwhelming majority of American drug users have been, and still are, Caucasian. And many, perhaps the majority, are middle class, including many business executives and other professionals who use illegal drugs. Notwithstanding this fact, blacks constitute more than one-third of adults arrested for drug violations even though they are only 15 percent of

America's drug users. Similar distortions in drug arrests and incarcerations apply to Hispanics.[16] The government explains the disparity by contending that lower classes frequent open street markets and are more susceptible to police sweeps than more prosperous citizens. The fact that less affluent minorities are arrested and incarcerated at vastly disproportionate rates for drug offenses contributes to false stereotypes and encourages the escalation of one of the most irrational public policies in U.S. history.

American attitudes are also shaped by ignorance of the actual social impact of the use of illegal drugs. Relatively few of America's estimated 90 million illegal drug users go on to commit nondrug crimes. In fact, the majority of policemen I hired during my eighteen years as police chief in two of the largest cities in America admitted prior use of illegal drugs. They did not commit other crimes and moved beyond their early drug use. As one candidate put it to me, "Of course, I smoked pot. I was in the Army. I went to college." And I can remember, some forty years ago, as a young policeman in Harlem in New York City, gathering with my colleagues in a tavern after work, listening to vigorous complaints about the junkies who made our work so difficult. During our discussions, we drank prodigious amounts of beer, a drug that could be as lethal as heroin, as many of us very well knew. Far more of my fellow policemen died in driving accidents after these drinking sessions than were slain in the line of duty.

There was thus a measure of irony in President Gerald Ford's claim that the high priority his administration placed on the federal drug abuse program would continue until the public was properly protected from the abuse of hard drugs.[17] His comment apparently was not directed at drug abuse within his own household. Fortunately, Betty Ford, the president's wife, recovered from her alcoholism and was never charged with a crime. Not being stigmatized as a criminal enabled Mrs. Ford to establish the Betty Ford Clinic, a treatment facility that has helped many individuals addicted to alcohol. Despite revelations about drug use from Russ Limbaugh, Bill Clinton, Al Gore, John Kerry, Newt Gingrich, and George W. Bush among others, our government continues to paint users as evil and immoral, when in fact they are frequently successful people from across the political spectrum.[18] The aforementioned confessors are lucky that none were tried and convicted under today's draconian laws, for they likely would have spent much of their lives in prison rather than being afforded an opportunity to mature into careers that most of us can admire and envy.

III. A Drug-Free America?

For the first one hundred forty years of our nation's existence, the right to life, liberty, and the pursuit of happiness included the right to consume whatever chemical substance one desired. In fact, Thomas Jefferson criticized France for passing laws regulating diet and drugs, noting that a government that tries to control the food you eat and the medicine that you take will soon try to control how you think. Yet, as pointed out earlier, the idea that pleasure could be derived from sex, gambling, dancing, consumption of alcohol and other drugs struck many powerful groups as sinful and immoral and led to passage of the failed Eighteenth Amendment and other drug legislation.[19] To a great extent, these "moral" concerns about the lower classes still drive drug policy today.

This odd tendency (for an avowedly secular government) to impose the heavy hand of criminal law on "sinful" and "immoral" behavior has caused numerous anomalies. For one thing, it has diverted scarce resources from the pursuit of mala-in-se crimes[20] such as murder, assault, rape, and theft. In those crimes, there are victims and witnesses who can testify against criminals. In contrast, with drug crimes, most addicts and users do not commit criminal acts against third persons.

In addition, law enforcement in this area is fraught with endemic ethical and legal problems. The police operate sizable secret programs. Undercover officers pretend to be criminals and, at times, become criminals. Police drug enforcement relies heavily upon informants who are paid to produce arrests and convictions—either in cash or in reduction of their own sentences for criminal wrongdoing. The line between an informant receiving significant rewards for "reporting" ongoing drug crimes and "orchestrating" such crimes is not easily detectable during legal proceedings. Furthermore, harsh mandatory drug sentences lead many defendants, some of whom are innocent, to plead guilty if they can negotiate a plea bargain with prosecutors to avoid risking draconian mandatory sentences. The unintended consequence of mandatory sentencing is that only the more successful and wealthy drug dealers have information to trade (and assets to be seized) sufficient to induce prosecutors to recommend lesser sentences. The longest incarceration falls upon the impoverished users guilty of minor drug crimes.

Characterizing drug use as sinful or unnatural has also led to questionable class divisions among drug users. Individuals taking Prozac (fluoxetine), Valium (diazepam), or other psychoactive prescription drugs are regarded as patients. Yet the millions who use heroin, cocaine, or marijuana—all of which were medicines prior to being declared illegal—have been, and are still, regarded as dangerous enough to be caged in brutal prisons, frequently under mandatory sentences more characteristic of a totalitarian society than a democracy. State and local police average about 1,600,000 drug arrests a year.[21] Most drug arrests, approximately 650,000 annually, are for marijuana.[22] All except a couple of hundred thousand of total drug arrests are for possession of small amounts of drugs.[23] But the arrests nevertheless frequently trigger long mandatory prison sentences, especially for the "mules" who are the individuals most exposed to the risk of arrest.

Racism, class bias, religious pressure, and an elitist desire to protect the lower classes from the temptation to lead "immoral" lives based upon the mistaken belief that lower-class people are the primary users of "bad" drugs have prevailed over the promises of the Declaration of Independence. Though it may sound far-fetched, Jefferson's fear of government "thought control" has come to fruition in the drug war. The Clinton White House was embarrassed when a journalist disclosed that the government had been secretly paying television entertainment and news programs, magazines, and newspapers to covertly insert into their presentations "politically correct" material on drug use.[24] Today, the government openly spends hundreds of millions of dollars on simplistic antidrug ads such as those televised during the Super Bowl extravaganza. These antidrug ads run alongside commercials pushing beer and drugs to cure erectile dysfunctions and other real or imagined illnesses. The critical questions, of course, are: to whom are these ads directed and what do they say about the real motivation behind the war on drugs?

IV. What Price Glory?

Since 1914, American drug control efforts have ebbed and peaked. Yet, sixteen years after Congress's 1989 proclamation that we would have a drug-free America by 1995 (the United Nations has made an even more grandiose claim for a drug-free world),[25] opium production has doubled in Southeast Asia and cocaine crops have increased by a third in Central and South America.[26] In 1983, there were 54 to 71 tons of cocaine available in the United States.[27] By 1987, there were 322 to 418 tons available.[28]

Today, there are approximately 800 metric tons of cocaine and 4,500 tons of opium available each year.[29]

Periodic government announcements of crises in the use of methamphetamine, ecstasy, and other designer drugs, increasingly being manufactured in Mexico and domestically, are intended to mobilize more public support for the drug war. What the antidrug propaganda really illustrates, however, is the futility of American attempts to reduce world drug production and trafficking. Temporary success in diminishing production may lead to production and smuggling displacement and/or users turning to other equally or more dangerous psychoactive substances. Accordingly, the government is forced to concede that despite interdiction efforts, around 80 to 90 percent of the illegal drugs that arrive in the United States are undetected. Illegal drugs are more potent, cheaper, and about as plentiful as ever in the United States despite massive expansion in drug war efforts. The United States, as well as most of the world, is awash in illegal drugs, the violence of the illegal drug black market, and unprecedented police and political corruption resulting from the extreme black market profits resulting from the criminal prohibition of cheaply produced chemical substances.

Some scholars, bureaucrats, prosecutors, judges, and politicians who can no longer ignore the inevitable failure of past practices and the injustice of long mandatory drug sentences for minor offenders have now proclaimed a new, compassionate solution—not legalization, but rather "coerced abstinence."[30] Coerced abstinence is the practice of continuously drug-testing accused criminals (and eventually, in all probability, many others) by special drug courts. Federal sponsorship and financing of drug courts has expanded in recent years despite reliable data indicating that these courts have not reduced the incidence of drug relapses. Indeed, we have long known that coercion simply does not achieve its intended result. As far back as 1937, one experienced and well-informed observer noted:

> Stringent laws, spectacular police drives, vigorous prosecution, and imprisonment of addicts and peddlers have proved not only useless and enormously expensive as means of correcting this evil, but they are also unjustifiably and unbelievably cruel in their application to the unfortunate drug victims. . . . Drug addiction, like prostitution, and like liquor, is not a police problem; it never has been, and never can be solved by policemen. It is first and last a medical problem, and *if there is a solution* it will be discov-

ered not by policemen, but by scientific and competently trained medical experts whose sole objective will be the reduction and possible eradication of this devastating appetite.[31]

Supporters of drug courts generously financed by the federal government cite anecdotal successes, but there is little reliable empirical evidence that drug courts have done any better than other approaches to solving the drug problem. The federal government's official position is that it is too early to supply empirical proof of success. On the other hand, the harm drug courts have caused is apparent. Many judges, who traditionally functioned as impartial guarantors of due process, have now become shamans taking on the responsibility of judging who is falling under evil spells. Legions of real-life "Judge Judys" are routinely operating with religious fervor, denouncing and incarcerating people not on the basis of what they did, but because certain chemicals are present (or not present) in their urine.

Medical information once thought to be sacrosanct under doctor-patient privacy relations is now reported by medical personnel and used by judges to incarcerate "clients." In drug courts, in the name of therapy, the ancient adversarial relationship between prosecutors and defenders, and the traditional disinterested role of the judge to ensure due process is abandoned. The fact that the "beneficiaries" of this so-called treatment often end up behind bars does not seem to matter since it is for their "own good."

Scholars who know well the difference between correlation and causation have casually disregarded this fundamental distinction of behavioral science by advancing coerced abstinence (drug courts) as something new when, in fact, this policy reflects the same demonization of certain drugs and the same dehumanization of their users that has existed in American culture for over a century. To be sure, it is true that many individuals convicted of crime do have a history of previous use of illegal drugs. But criminal populations also have histories of illegitimacy, illiteracy, extreme poverty, lack of health care, child abuse, failure in school, smoking, gambling, unhealthy diets, poor employment, and a host of other variables. Drug use as the sole explanation for criminal behavior is no more persuasive than any of these other characteristics would be. If we outlawed these other behaviors, we would make criminals of most citizens. If that seems foolish, then must we not ask whether it is not similarly foolish to criminalize certain drug use simply because we believe it might lead to other kinds of criminal behavior?

America's drug war has always trifled with science in seeking to answer this question and to justify current policy. But experts know that past behavior, including the use of certain chemicals, cannot be used to predict the future behavior of a particular individual with sufficient accuracy to justify imprisonment. The assumption that the presence alone of a particular chemical in a person's bloodstream is cause for incarceration, because it preordains future nondrug crimes, replaces the fundamental American right of presumption of innocence with the police-state mentality of assumed guilt. Like many repressive governments, advocates of coerced abstinence say that we should not worry. Our children, friends, and relatives in jail cells for minor drug violations are not prisoners—they are simply patients undergoing the new therapy of coerced abstinence—a form of "tough love." But it is seldom the children, friends, or relatives of those advocates who are experiencing the most brutal punishments. These are reserved for the underclass unfortunates who are drawn into the illicit industry as the "mules" who deliver the illicit products to the consumers whose illicit demands create the illicit market to which the illicit industry is a response. It is disproportionately members of the lower class who are populating our prisons on a scale unequaled in this nation's past.

Other advocates of present drug policies argue that certain drugs are not bad because they are illegal; they are illegal because they are bad. History, however, indicates that a century ago the groups that successfully lobbied to criminalize drugs were equally motivated by erroneous impressions of who and why certain groups used specific chemical substances and what the results would be. With respect to its potentially harmful consequences, alcohol is a much graver public threat than many and perhaps most controlled substances, but we forsook criminalization of alcohol not only because it did not work but also because during Prohibition too many prosperous and upright citizens were exposed to violence, corrupt officials, and criminal punishment. Tobacco is probably more addictive than many illegal drugs and certainly more lethal. If behavioral science does not support a claim that the war on drugs is about preventing future criminal conduct, and if we permit the use of other drugs with equal or more severe social and medical costs, we cannot claim that the war on drugs is about preventing crime or saving lives. What, then, is it about? It seems that we are less willing to acknowledge that the present war is not working in part because those feeling the lash of the law are seen as the undeserving poor and minorities who might as well be in prison.

V. Conclusion

Our nation's drug policy has squandered hundreds of billions of dollars, locked up millions of Americans, destroyed countless families and neighborhoods, created immeasurable violence and corruption, and played havoc with foreign policy, all under the contention that things would be even worse without present policies. Unfortunately, this contention does not survive even superficial analysis. Instead of hard evidence, moral reflex reactions and embedded stereotypes seem to drive the drug policy of the United States with harsh consequences for those at the lower rungs of our society. Indeed, when one looks closely, the only real explanation for our ever-expanding, yet doomed, national drug policy appears to be a jihad—a holy war that must be fought to protect the lower classes from immoral drugs regardless of the resulting human costs.

NOTES

1. Statement by President Richard Nixon, after announcing the establishment of the super agency, The Drug Enforcement Agency, White House, 1973. *See* EVA BERTRAM ET AL., DRUG WAR POLITICS: THE PRICE OF DENIAL 108 (1996).

2. Informing America's Policy on Illegal Drugs: What We Don't Know Keeps Hurting Us 1 (CHARLES F. MANSKI ET AL., NATIONAL RESEARCH COUNCIL, 2001).

3. U.S. CENSUS BUREAU (1972); U.S. DEP'T COMMERCE (1972).

4. *See* Leonard E. Birdsong, *Drug Decriminalization and Felony Disenfranchisement: The New Civil Rights Causes*, 2 BARRY L. REV. 73, 85 (2001).

5. BUREAU OF JUSTICE STATISTICS, *Prisoners in 2003*, 1, 9 (Nov. 2004), *available at* http://www.ojp.usdoj.gov/bjs/pub/pdf/p03.pdf (noting at yearend 2003, the United States had incarcerated 2,212,475 persons, of whom 33.5 percent were white, 45.7 percent were black, and 17.6 percent were Hispanic); BUREAU OF JUSTICE STATISTICS, *Education and Correctional Populations* 1, 12 (Apr. 15, 2003), *available at* http://www.ojp.usdoj.gov/bjs/pub/pdf/ecp.pdf (noting that 41 percent of inmates and 31 percent of probationers had not completed high school compared to 18 percent of the general population, and 11.6 percent of inmates were homeless and a majority were not working at the time of their arrest).

6. 370 U.S. 660 (1962).

7. Harrison Act, ch.1, 38 Stat. 785 (1914).

8. DAVID MUSTO, THE AMERICAN DISEASE: ORIGINS OF NARCOTICS CONTROL 286 (1999) [hereinafter MUSTO 1].

9. DAVID MUSTO, THE AMERICAN DISEASE: ORIGINS OF NARCOTICS CONTROL 6 (1987) [hereinafter MUSTO 2].

10. MUSTO 1, *supra* note 8.

11. The same constitutional misgivings led Congress to label the 1937 law prohibiting marijuana the Marijuana Tax Act. MUSTO 2, *supra* note 9.

12. *See* United States v. Jin Fuey Moy, 241 U.S. 394 (1915).

13. Reform Mayor William Strong who appointed Roosevelt police commissioner was defeated in the next election by a Tammany Hall nominee, largely as a result of Roosevelt's crusade to close saloons on Sundays. JAMES F. RICHARDSON, THE NEW YORK POLICE: COLONIAL TIMES TO 1901, at 259–67 (1970).

14. *Id.*

15. *Id.*

16. MUSTO 1, *supra* note 8; *see also* COMMON SENSE FOR DRUG POLICY, DRUG WAR FACTS (Douglas A. McVay ed., 4th ed. 2004); BUREAU OF JUSTICE STATISTICS, *Additional Correction Facts at a Glance, available at* http://www.ojp.usdoj.gov/bjs/gcorpop.htm (May 28, 2004).

17. MUSTO 2, *supra* note 9, at 257–58.

18. When questioned about prior drug use, President George W. Bush didn't deny such use. He simply stated that he did foolish things when he was young. Not only did Bill Clinton use illegal marijuana (even if he never inhaled), his brother also used drugs. In 1994, candidate Clinton asserted that the criminal justice system saved his brother's life. His brother served eighteen months for conspiracy and cocaine trafficking.

19. JOSEPH GUSFIELD, THE SYMBOLIC CRUSADE: STATUS, POLITICS, AND THE AMERICAN TEMPERANCE MOVEMENT (1986).

20. I.e., crimes considered in aid of themselves, in the sense of being against the laws of nature and God as opposed to an act made criminal only by means of legislative enactment.

21. FEDERAL BUREAU OF INVESTIGATION, *Crime in the United States 2003*, UNIFORM CRIME REPORTS, *available at* http://www.fbi.gov/ucr/03cius.htm (Mar. 28, 2005); *see also* DRUG WAR FACTS, *supra* note 16, at 26–30.

22. FEDERAL BUREAU OF INVESTIGATION, *supra* note 20, at 270.

23. DRUG WAR FACTS, *supra* note 16, at 26–30.

24. Dan Forbes, *Prime Time Propaganda*, salon.com, Jan. 13, 2000.

25. Confidential United States Drug Enforcement Report (May 1989) (unpublished report on file with author).

26. DRUG WAR FACTS, *supra* note 16, at 22.

27. *Id.* at 86–90.

28. *Id.* at 34–41.

29. UNITED NATIONS OFFICE ON DRUGS AND CRIME, GLOBAL ILLICIT DRUG TRENDS 15, 22 (2003).

30. AUGUST VOLLMER, THE POLICE AND MODERN SOCIETY (1936).

31. *See* Stephen P. Duke & Albert C. Gross, America's Longest War: Rethinking Our Tragic Crusade against Drugs 27–28 (1994) (citing Ethan Nadelmann on criminalizing tobacco) (emphasis added).

About the Contributors

MARGARET A. BERGER is the Suzanne J. and Norman Miles Professor of Law at Brooklyn Law School. She teaches evidence, civil procedure, and courses on science and the law. The co-author of *Weinstein's Evidence*, she has authored chapters in the Federal Judicial Center's Reference Manuals on Scientific Evidence, and has served as the Reporter to the Advisory Committee on the Federal Rules of Evidence.

M. GREGG BLOCHE is a Professor of Law at Georgetown University Law Center, a Visiting Fellow at The Brookings Institution, an Adjunct Professor at the Bloomberg School of Public Health at Johns Hopkins University, and Co-Director of the Georgetown-Johns Hopkins Joint Program in Law and Public Health. He has written extensively and frequently on U.S. and international health law and policy.

DAVID L. CALLIES is the Benjamin A. Kudo Professor of Law at the William S. Richardson School of Law, University of Hawaii (Manoa). He recently authored *Taking Land: Compulsory Purchase and Regulation in Asian-Pacific Countries* and is co-author of *The Quiet Revolution in Land Use Control; The Taking Issue; Cases and Materials on Land Use*; and *Property Law and the Public Interest.*

PAUL D. CARRINGTON is Professor of Law at Duke University.

PAUL Y. K. CASTLE is an assistant District Attorney in Onslow County, North Carolina. He received his Ph.D. from the University of Chicago in 2001 and his J.D. from Duke University in 2004. He is a member of the New York and North Carolina Bars.

LANCE COMPA is a Senior Lecturer at Cornell University's School of Industrial and Labor Relations, where he teaches U.S. and international labor law. He also serves as counsel to trade unions and human rights organizations involved in international labor rights complaints and cases. He has conducted workers' rights investigations and reports in Cambodia, Chile, the Dominican Republic, Guatemala, Haiti, Mexico, and Sri Lanka.

JAMES D. COX is the Brainerd Currie Professor of Law at Duke Law School where he specializes in corporate and securities law. In addition to his texts *Financial Information, Accounting and the Law; Cox and Hazen on Corporations*; and *Securities Regulations Cases and Materials* (with Hillman & Langevoort), Professor Cox has published extensively in the areas of market regulation and corporate governance as well as having testified before the U.S. House and Senate on insider trading and market reform issues.

PAULA A. FRANZESE is the Peter W. Rodino Professor of Law at Seton Hall University. Her scholarly writing examines privatization, exclusionary zoning, and affordable housing, among other things. She is co-author of *Property Law and the Public Interest* and has also published in the areas of commercial and contracts law and legal ethics.

MARC GALANTER is the John and Rylla Bosshard Professor Emeritus of Law and South Asian Studies at the University of Wisconsin-Madison and Centennial Professor at the London School of Economics and Political Science. A leading figure in the empirical study of the legal system, he is an outspoken critic of misrepresentations of the American civil justice system and of the inadequate knowledge base that makes the system so vulnerable to misguided attacks. His latest book, a study of contemporary American anti-lawyerism, is *Lowering the Bar: Lawyer Jokes and Legal Culture*.

JULIUS G. GETMAN holds the Earl E. Sheffield Regents Chair at the University of Texas-Austin School of Law. A preeminent scholar in the field of labor law, he has pioneered empirical studies and continues to do extensive field work. He is author or co-author of several texts, including *The Betrayal of Local 14: Paperworkers, Politics and Permanent Replacements* and *In the Company of Scholars: The Struggle for the Soul of Higher Education*.

LAWRENCE O. GOSTIN is Professor and Associate Dean for Research and Academic Programs at Georgetown University Law Center; Professor of Public Health at the Johns Hopkins University; and Director of the Center for Law & the Public's Health at Johns Hopkins and Georgetown Universities. He is Adjunct Professor of Public Health (Faculty of Medical Sciences) and Research Fellow (Centre for Socio-Legal Studies) at Oxford University.

JOEL F. HANDLER is Richard C. Maxwell Professor of Law and Professor, School of Public Affairs, at UCLA. His scholarly writing focuses on poverty, social welfare reform, and the European conception of social citizenship. His latest publications include *Social Citizenship and Workfare in the United States and Western Europe: The Paradox of Inclusion* and *Hard Labor: Women and Work in the Post-Welfare Era.*

TRINA JONES is Professor of Law at Duke University.

THOMAS E. KAUPER is the Henry M. Butzel Professor of Law at the University of Michigan Law School. He has written extensively in the fields of property and antitrust. In recent years, his work has focused on international antitrust and competition policy of the European Union. An antitrust expert, Professor Kauper has served as deputy assistant attorney general in the Office of Legal Counsel and as assistant attorney general in charge of the Antitrust Division for the U.S. Department of Justice.

SANFORD LEVINSON is a member of the School of Law (where he holds the W. St. John Garwood and W. St. John Garwood Centennial Chair) and the Department of Government at the University of Texas, Austin. The co-editor of *Processes of Constitutional Decisionmaking,* he is also author of *Constitutional Faith* and *Wrestling With Diversity,* and the co-editor of *Constitutional Stupidities, Constitutional Tragedies.* He has taught courses on the Constitution and the welfare state at the University of Texas, Harvard, and Yale Law Schools.

JOHN LINEHAN graduated from Williams College and is a member of the class of 2006 at the University of Virginia School of Law. Upon graduation he will work as an associate in the Washington, D.C., office of LeBoeuf, Lamb, Greene & MacRae LLP.

JOSEPH D. MCNAMARA is a research fellow at the Hoover Institution, Stanford University. During his thirty-five in law enforcement, he served as chief of police for San Jose, California, and Kansas City, Missouri. The author of several books, he is widely recognized as an expert in criminal justice, police technology and management systems, crime prevention, and international drug control policies.

Burt Neuborne is the John Norton Pomeroy Professor of Law and Legal Director of the Brennan Center for Justice at NYU Law School. For thirty years, he has been one of the nation's foremost civil liberties lawyers, serving as National Legal Director of the ACLU, Special Counsel to the NOW Legal Defense and Education Fund, and as a member of the New York City Human Rights Commission. He has argued many Supreme Court cases, and litigated hundreds of important constitutional cases. Among his best known scholarly works is *Political and Civil Rights in the United States.*

Jeffrey O'Connell is the Samuel H. McCoy, II Professor of Law at the University of Virginia where he specializes in accident and insurance law. Professor O'Connell is the co-author of the principal work that proposed no-fault auto insurance and the author or co-author of twelve books dealing with accident law. His latest book, co-authored with Peter Bell, is entitled *Accidental Justice: The Dilemmas of Tort Law.*

Judith Resnik is the Arthur Liman Professor of Law at Yale Law School. She has chaired the Sections on Procedure, Federal Courts, and Women in Legal Education of the American Association of Law Schools, is the co-author (with Owen Fiss) of *Adjudication and Its Alternatives: An Introduction to Procedure* and is the author of *The Processes of the Law.* She is a member of the American Academy of Arts and Sciences and of the American Philosophical Society.

Richard L. Schmalbeck is Professor of Law at Duke University, and former Dean of the University of Illinois College of Law. He has served as an advisor to the Russian Federation in connection with its tax reform efforts. A prolific author, his recent scholarly work has focused on issues involving nonprofit organizations and the federal estate and gift taxes.

Danielle Sarah Seiden is Project Director at the UCLA Center for Community Health where she specializes in HIV and health issues affecting low-income populations.

Richard E. Speidel is the Beatrice Kuhn Professor of Law Emeritus at Northwestern University School of Law and former dean of Boston University School of Law. Professor Speidel's teaching and research interests are in the areas of basic contract law, commercial law (with emphasis upon the Uniform Commercial Code), international sales and arbitration. He is co-author of two major casebooks and a treatise on Federal Arbitration Law. His latest book is entitled *American Arbitration Law: A Critical Assessment.*

GERALD TORRES is the H.O. Head Centennial Professor in Real Property Law at the University of Texas-Austin and former president of the Association of American Law Schools. A leading figure in critical race theory, Torres is also an expert in agricultural and environmental law. His latest book, *The Miner's Canary: Enlisting Race, Resisting Power, Transforming Democracy* with Harvard law professor Lani Guinier, was described by *Publisher's Weekly* as "one of the most provocative and challenging books on race produced in years."

DAVID M. TRUBEK is Voss-Bascom Professor of Law and Senior Fellow of the Center for World Affairs and the Global Economy at the University of Wisconsin-Madison. From 1989–2001 he served as the UW-Madison's Dean of International Studies and Director of its International Institute. His works address numerous subjects including the role of law in economic development, social policy in the European Union, the role of the legal profession in society, law and social theory. and new forms of governance.

ELIZABETH WARREN is the Leo Gottlieb Professor of Law at Harvard University. Her latest book, *All Your Worth*, has been listed on the nonfiction best-seller lists for the *Wall Street Journal* and the *New York Times*. The Two-Income Trap: Why Middle-Class Parents Are Going Broke, a preceding book, has been quoted extensively in congressional debates and by presidential candidates. Professor Warren served as Chief Adviser to the National Bankruptcy Review Commission and as Vice-President of the American Law Institute.

LAWRENCE A. ZELENAK is the Pamela B. Gann Professor of Law at Duke University where he teaches income tax, corporate tax, a tax policy seminar, and torts. His publications include numerous articles on tax policy issues and a treatise on federal income taxation of individuals.

Index

SCHIPS. *See* State Children's Health Insurance Program (SCHIPS)

Schumpeter, Joseph, 39–40

Segregation: statutory claims, exclusion, 154–56; zoning and districting, 151–53

SEIU. *See* Service Employees International Union (SEIU)

Sen, Amartya, 320

Service Employees International Union (SEIU), 256

Servicemen's Readjustment Act, 1944, 343

Settlement: "confidential settlement agreements," 76–77; Dalkon Shield litigation, secret agreements among litigants, 85n83; definition, 64; examples of, 66; first use, 80n20

Shaw, George Bernard, 191

Shays' Rebellion, 1787, 2

Sherman Act, 1890, 6, 122–23; preservation of small firms, 124; violation as felony, 132

Shulman, Harry, 247; grievance/arbitration system of collective bargaining, 245–46

Simpson v. Union Oil Co., 127, 129, 134

Slemrod, Joel, 181

Small business: benefits from antitrust legislation, 122–23; benefits from mergers, 136–37; mergers protective of, 126–28; protective antitrust cases, 128–33; Sherman Act, 124

Smith, Adam, 3, 4, 6

Smith v. Central Soya, Inc., 304–5

Smoot-Hawley tariffs, 218

Social Accountability International (SAI), 234

Social Darwinism, 5, 13, 23, 341

Social Security, 400; history of tax receipts and benefits, 175–77; long-term solvency of, 175; Social Security Act, 1935, 364; Social Security Amendments, 1983, 176; taxes finance income tax cut, 177–78

Soros, George, 47

Southern Burlington County NAACP v. Township of Mount Laurel, 152–53

Spirit of Law, 1

Starling v. Valmac Industries, 302

State Children's Health Insurance Program (SCHIPS), 367

Statute of Frauds, 304

Steelworker trilogy, 255

Stewart, Potter, 22, 27–28, 32, 34

Strict products liability, 349

Strong, Theron G., 88

Sun Microsystems, 132

Sunstein, Cass, 22

Supplemental Security Income (SSI), 379

Supreme Court of the US, 11–12; political affiliations, 32–33; political party differences, 21–22; poor lawyering challenges, 72; predispute resolution clauses, 73–74; rights-seeking more difficult, 71; support of arbitration, 255–56

Swift v. Tyson, 389

Synar, Mike, 286

TANF. *See* Temporary Assistance for Needy Families (TANF)

Taxation: absolute dollars of tax cuts, 168–69; Bush tax cuts, pretax income, 180–82; Bush tax cuts, Treasury's analyses, 185n5; Bush tax cuts and middle class, 183–84; Earned Income Tax Credit (EITC), 373; federal income, revenue distribution, 7–8; funding public programs, 6–7; income tax theory, 181–82; middle class tax cuts, 164 illu; percentage increases in after-tax incomes, 166–68; percentage shares of pretax income, 1979 and 2001, 179 table; pretax income,